Noam Chomsky

World Orders Old and New

Pluto  Press

This edition published in the UK in 1997 by
Pluto Press, 345 Archway Road, London N6 5AA

Published by arrangement with the
American University in Cairo Press

ISBN 0 7453 1320 5

10 9 8 7 6 5 4

Printed in the European Union
by Antony Rowe, Chippenham, England

World Orders Old and New

CONTENTS

PREFACE

The material that follows is based on three lectures at the American University in Cairo in May 1993, considerably expanded and updated in ways that reflect, in part, the seminars, meetings, and very enlightening personal discussions that occupied a large part of that all-too-brief visit. There are many friends, new and old, whom I would like to thank for their kindness and thoughtful commentary. I will mention only one, Dr. Nelly Hanna, whose gracious hospitality and tireless assistance, apart from contributing immeasurably to the personal pleasure that my wife and I felt from a memorable experience, helped me to understand at least something about Egypt, past and present, in ways I could not have otherwise.

I would also like to thank a great many other friends around the world who are part of the informal networks that have developed over the years among people who exchange press reports, documents, monographic studies, and all sorts of other material outside of the standard channels, along with commentary and analysis. Being separate from and critical of established institutions carries costs and annoyances, but also joys and opportunities, not least the contacts that develop with people of a similar cast of mind and with similar interests and concerns, many of whom have to work under conditions of considerable adversity, a not infrequent concomitant of dissidence and intellectual independence. I have relied extensively here, as often before, on materials that I would never have been able to discover in other ways. I would like to list names at this point, but the people I have in mind know who they are, and others would hardly appreciate the nature and importance of these interactions among people who may have rarely if ever even met, but have found ways to cooperate in very constructive ways to escape institutional constraints.

1

MARCHING IN PLACE

The fall of the Berlin Wall in November 1989 can be taken as the symbolic end of an era in world affairs in which major events fell under the ominous shadow of the Cold War, with its constant threat of nuclear annihilation. That conventional picture is certainly not false, but it is nevertheless partial and misleading. By uncritically adopting it, we seriously misunderstand the recent past, and are not well-situated to comprehend what lies ahead.

1. The Cold War and Population Control

The conventional framework of interpretation has served very well the interests of those who held the reins. It provided an efficient mechanism of "population control," to borrow some of the jargon of counterinsurgency doctrine. Control of its domestic population is the major task of any state that is dominated by particular sectors of the domestic society and therefore functions primarily in their interest; that is, any "really existing state." The two superpowers of the Cold War era were at opposite extremes of the contemporary spectrum with regard to internal freedom and democracy, but the problem of population control was common to their domestic power structures: in the Soviet Union, the military–bureaucratic network established by Lenin and Trotsky as they took power in October 1917, moving quickly to crush all socialist and other popular tendencies; in the United States, the industrial–financial–commercial sector, concentrated and interlinked, highly class conscious, and increasingly transnational in the scope of its planning, management, and operations.

The Cold War confrontation provided easy formulas to justify criminal action abroad and entrenchment of privilege and state power at home. Without the annoying need for thought or credible evidence, apologists on both sides could explain reflexively that however regrettable, the acts were undertaken for reasons of "national security" in response to the threat of the cruel and menacing superpower enemy. An ancillary convention comes into play as policy shifts for tactical reasons, or invocation of the threat is no longer needed, or its absurdity becomes too manifest to conceal. At that stage, the fears that were whipped up are to be seen as exaggerated by understandable Cold War passions. Now we will "change course" and be more realistic—until the next episode requires that the record be replayed. The routine is familiar to the point of boredom through the Cold War years.

A useful corollary is that problems faced by the victims of our depredations—Vietnamese, Cubans, Nicaraguans, and a host of others—are their own fault, since whatever we may have done is now relegated to ancient and irrelevant history. A similar stance has been common more generally as older forms of colonialism are replaced by more efficient modes of subjugation.

As the Soviet Union disappeared from the scene, the doctrinal system adopted standard procedures without missing a beat. The entire record of the Cold War years is to be deposited in the archives, the slate washed clean of terror, aggression, economic warfare, and other crimes that have taken an awesome human toll. Whatever happened was the product of Cold War tensions, to be put behind us, teaching us no lessons about ourselves and offering no guide to the future towards which we grandly march with heads held high, observing with dismay the failure of our traditional victims to approach our lofty moral and material standards. Discussion of the moral obligation of humanitarian intervention—no trivial question—is rarely tainted by reflection about the American role in the world, its significance and import, its institutional roots. Few have urged that Iran undertake humanitarian intervention in Bosnia, as it offered to do. Why? Because of its record and the nature of its institutions. In the case of Iran—or any other power—inquiry into these questions is appropriate. But in our case, review of the historical record is nothing more than "sound-bites and invectives about Washington's historically evil foreign policy," international affairs specialist Thomas Weiss writes with derision, hence "easy to ignore." A perceptive comment, accurately discerning the most valued principles of the official culture.

Today "American motives are largely humanitarian," historian David Fromkin declares. The present danger is excess of benevolence; we might undertake yet another selfless mission of mercy, failing to understand that "there are limits to what outsiders can do" and that "the armies we dispatch to foreign soil for humanitarian reasons" may not be able "to save people from others or from themselves." The view is shared by elder statesman George Kennan, a leading critic of Cold War policies, who writes that it was a historic error for the United States to reject any effort to negotiate a peaceful settlement of conflicts with the Russians for forty years; one of the benefits of the end of the Cold War is that such issues may finally enter the arena of debate. Kennan too renews the traditional counsel that we restrict our foreign engagements, recognizing that "it is primarily by example, never by precept, that a country such as ours exerts the most useful influence beyond its border"; countries unlike ours may undertake the grubbier pursuits. We must also bear in mind "that there are limits to what one sovereign country can do to help another," even the most virtuous. Others question that stance on the grounds that it is unfair to deprive suffering humanity of our attention, necessarily benevolent.[1]

The mechanisms of control naturally differ in a totalitarian state and a state capitalist democracy, but there have been striking features in common throughout the Cold War era. When the Russians sent tanks to East Berlin, Budapest, or Prague, or devastated Afghanistan, the population could be mobilized and clients abroad pacified by invocation of the threat of the evil empire, poised to strike; the same was true as state power imposed a brutal repressive apparatus while assuring the privilege and authority of the *Nomenklatura*, the armed forces and security services, and military industry. Similar devices were deployed for population control within the United States as it conducted its global programs of violence and subversion while maintaining the Pentagon-based state industrial policy that has been a prime factor in economic growth, and instituting the regime of "sacrifice and discipline" called for in National Security Council memorandum NSC 68, the major secret Cold War document (April 1950), which outlined "the necessity for just suppression," a crucial feature of "the democratic way," with "dissent among us" curbed while public resources are shifted to the needs of advanced industry.

The pattern persists with little change. One revealing example is the standard current interpretation of the campaign of slaughter, torture, and destruction that the United States organized and directed in Central America through the 1980s to demolish the popular organizations that were taking shape, in part under Church auspices. These threatened to create a base for functioning democracy, perhaps allowing the people of this miserable region, long in the grip of U.S. power, to gain some control over their lives; therefore, they had to be destroyed. This shameful episode of imperial violence is now routinely depicted as an illustration of our high ideals and our success in bringing democracy and respect for human rights to this primitive region. There were some excesses, it is conceded, but these are attributable to the Cold War tensions in which the region was embroiled—an absurdity, but one that has always been on the shelf, ready to be dusted off when needed.

It has been intriguing to observe the desperate search for some new enemy as the Russians were visibly fading through the 1980s: international terrorism, Hispanic narcotraffickers, Islamic fundamentalism, or Third World "instability" and depravity generally. The project was conducted with its usual delicacy: thus the category of "international terrorism" is cleansed of any reference to the contributions of the United States and its clients, which break all records but remain unmentionable in media and respectable scholarship; the drug war frenzy evaded the leading role of the CIA in creating and maintaining the post–World War II drug racket as well as the state role in allowing U.S. banks and corporations to profit handsomely from the sale of lethal narcotics; and so on down the list.[2]

The basic insight was well expressed by a nineteenth-century critic of the compulsory education designed to convert independent farmers to docile wage laborers, to "educate them to keep them from our throats," as Ralph Waldo Emerson parodied elite fears of a politicized majority: "Them as read newspapers knows too much 'bout other folks's sins en not 'nough 'bout thar own," he said. That about sums up what thousands of pages of detailed documentation and analysis have shown.[3]

The Cold War has had a certain functional utility for state and doctrinal managers, offering ritual patterns of apologetics for any horror or injustice. The serviceability of the conventional picture for dominant elements offers some reason for caution about its accuracy. The historical record reveals that such skepticism is warranted. I will indicate why I think this is the case, filling in some background later: for world order in general in the next chapter, for the Middle East in particular in the final one.

2. New World Orders

With the Cold War at an end, there were calls for a New World Order. These came in several varieties. The earliest was published by the nongovernmental South Commission, chaired by Julius Nyerere and consisting of leading Third World economists, government planners, religious leaders, and others. In a 1990 study,[4] the Commission reviewed the recent record of North–South relations culminating in the catastrophe of capitalism that swept through traditional colonial domains in the 1980s, apart from the Japanese sphere in East Asia, where states are powerful enough to control not only labor, as is the norm, but also capital, so that economies were somewhat insulated from the ravages of the market. To mention one aspect, capital flight from Latin America approximated the crushing debt, not a problem in East Asia, where the hemorrhage was stanched by tight controls.

The South Commission observes that there were some gestures toward Third World concerns in the 1970s, "undoubtedly spurred" by concern over "the newly found assertiveness of the South after the rise in oil prices in 1973." As this problem abated and the terms of trade resumed their long-term shift in favor of the industrial societies, the core industrial powers lost interest and turned to "a new form of neo-colonialism," monopolizing control over the world economy, undermining the more democratic elements of the United Nations, and in general proceeding to institutionalize "the South's second-class status"—the natural course of events, given the relations of power and the cynicism with which it is exercised.

Reviewing the miserable state of the traditional Western domains, the Commission called for a "new world order" that will respond to "the South's plea for justice, equity, and democracy in the global society," though its analysis offers little basis for hope.

The prospects for this call are revealed by the attention accorded to it, or to the report generally, which also passed silently into oblivion. The West is guided by a different vision, one outlined forthrightly by Winston Churchill as an earlier New World Order was being constructed after World War II:

The government of the world must be entrusted to satisfied nations, who wished nothing more for themselves than what they had. If the world-government were in the hands of hungry nations, there would always be danger. But none of us had any reason to seek for anything more. The peace would be kept by peoples who lived in their own way and were not ambitious. Our power placed us above the rest. We were like rich men dwelling at peace within their habitations.[5]

To rule is the right and duty of the rich men dwelling in deserved peace.

It is only necessary to add two footnotes. First, the rich men are far from lacking ambition; there are always new ways to enrich oneself and dominate others, and the economic system virtually requires that they be pursued, or the laggard falls out of the game. Second, the fantasy that *nations* are the actors in the international arena is the standard doctrinal camouflage for the fact that within the rich nations, as within the hungry ones, there are radical differences in privilege and power. Removing the remaining veil of delusion from Churchill's prescription, we derive the guidelines of world order: the rich men of the rich societies are to rule the world, competing among themselves for a greater share of wealth and power and mercilessly suppressing those who stand in their way, assisted by the rich men of the hungry nations who do their bidding. The others serve, and suffer.

These are truisms. As described over two hundred years ago by Adam Smith, the often-misrepresented hero of contemporary Western self-congratulation, the rich men follow "the vile maxim of the masters of mankind": "All for ourselves, and nothing for other people." They naturally use state power to achieve their ends; in his day, the "merchants and manufacturers" were "the principal architects" of policy, which they designed to assure that their interests would be "most peculiarly attended to," however "grievous" the impact on others, including the general population of their own societies. If we do not adopt Smith's method of "class analysis," our vision will be blurred and distorted. Any discussion of world affairs that treats nations as actors is at best misleading, at worst pure mystification, unless it recognizes the crucial Smithian footnotes.

As in any complex system, there are further nuances and secondary effects, but in reality, these are the basic themes of world order. There is no little merit in the description of world order, old and new, as "codified international piracy."[6]

America's loyal subsidiary in the project of keeping the hungry nations under control is less encumbered by the need for prettifying the message than Washington and its domestic chorus. Britain can appeal to an imperial tradition of refreshing candor, unlike the United States, which has preferred to don the garb of saintliness as it proceeds to crush anyone in its path, a stance that is called "Wilsonian idealism" in honor of one of the great exponents of violent military intervention and imperial repression, whose ambassador to London complained that the British had little use for his mission to correct "the moral shortcomings of foreign nations."[7]

Britain has always "insisted on reserving the right to bomb niggers," as the distinguished statesman Lloyd George put the matter after Britain had made sure that the 1932 disarmament treaty would place no barrier on aerial bombardment of civilians, unwilling to relinquish its major device for controlling the Middle East. The basic thinking had been articulated by Winston Churchill. As Secretary of State at the War Office in 1919, he was approached by the RAF Middle East command in Cairo for permission to use chemical weapons "against recalcitrant Arabs as experiment." Churchill authorized the experiment, dismissing qualms as "unreasonable": "I do not understand this squeamishness about the use of gas," he responded with annoyance. "I am strongly in favour of using poisoned gas against uncivilised tribes. . . . It is not necessary to use only the most deadly gasses; gasses can be used which cause great inconvenience and would spread a lively terror and yet would leave no serious permanent effects on most of those affected." Chemical weapons were merely "the application of Western science to modern warfare," Churchill explained. "We cannot in any circumstances acquiesce in the non-utilisation of any weapons which are available to procure a speedy termination of the disorder which prevails on the frontier." Poison gas had already been used by British forces in North Russia against the Bolsheviks, with great success according to the British command. The "uncivilised tribes" who needed a dose of "lively terror" at the time were mainly Kurds and Afghans, but air power was used quite effectively to save British lives, following a model pioneered by Woodrow Wilson's Marines as they slaughtered the niggers in Haiti.[8]

The British style flourished again as racist frenzy swept the West during the Gulf conflict of 1990–91. John Keegan, a prominent British military historian and journalist, outlined the common view succinctly: "The British are used to over 200 years of expeditionary forces going overseas, fighting the Africans, the Chinese, the Indians, the Arabs. It's just something the British take for granted," and the war in the Gulf "rings very, very familiar imperial bells with the British." Britain is therefore well-placed to undertake the Churchillian mission, which the editor of the *Sunday Telegraph*, Peregrine Worsthorne, termed the "new job" for "the post–Cold War world": "to help build and sustain a world order stable enough to allow the advanced economies of the world to function without constant interruption and threat from the Third World," a task that will require "instant intervention from the advanced nations" and perhaps "pre-emptive action." Britain is "no match for Germany and Japan when it comes to wealth creation; or even for France and Italy. But when it comes to shouldering world responsibilities we are more than a match"—world responsibilities being understood in the Churchillian sense. Though in social and economic decline, Britain is "well qualified, motivated, and likely to have a high military profile as the mercenary of the international community," the military correspondent of the London *Independent* comments.[9]

Worsthorne's "new job" is in fact a venerable one, another indication that "the post–Cold War world" is to be much like what came before.

During the same months, the Western business press proposed a similar role for the United States, which, having cornered the world "security market," should run a global protection racket, Mafia-style, selling "protection" to other wealthy powers who will pay a "war premium." Paid for its services by German-led continental Europe and Japan and relying on the flow of capital from Gulf oil production, which it will dominate, the United States can maintain "our control over the world economic system" as "willing mercenaries," a method employed during the Gulf war with much success. International economist Fred Bergsten notes that "'Collective leadership' in the Gulf war meant that the United States led and the United States collected—overfinancing its marginal military costs and thus turning an economic profit on the conflict"—not to speak of juicy contracts for reconstructing what was destroyed, huge weapons sales, and other forms of tribute for the victors.[10]

Shortly after the South Commission called for a "new world order" based on justice, equity and democracy, George Bush appropriated the phrase as a rhetorical cover for his war in the Gulf. As bombs were raining on Baghdad, Basra, and miserable conscripts hiding in holes in the sands of southern Iraq, the president announced that the United States would lead "a new world order—where diverse nations are drawn together in common cause, to achieve the universal aspirations of mankind: peace and security, freedom and the rule of law." We are entering an "era full of promise," Secretary of State James Baker proudly announced, "one of those rare transforming moments in world history."

The message was elaborated by Thomas Friedman, chief diplomatic correspondent of the *New York Times*. The principle guiding President Bush in the Gulf war, Friedman explained, "was that unless international boundaries between sovereign nation states are respected, the alternative is chaos"—thinking, perhaps, of Panama, Lebanon, Nicaragua, Grenada . . . . But the basic issue, Friedman continued, is far deeper: "America's victory in the cold war was . . . a victory for a set of political and economic principles: democracy and the free market." At last, the world is coming to understand that "the free market is the wave of the future—a future for which America is both the gatekeeper and the model."[11]

And so on endlessly in the ideological institutions—the media, scholarship, the intellectual community generally—in a chorus of self-adulation scarcely troubled by the odd discordant note far at the periphery that suggests a look at the actual U.S. record with regard to functioning democracy and free market discipline.

It is George Bush's call for a "new world order" that resounded, not the plaintive plea of the South, unreported and unheard. The reaction to the two near-simultaneous calls for a New World Order reflects, of course, the power relations. The timing of the two calls is fortuitous, coming at the 500th anniversary of the voyages that set in motion the European conquest of the world, establishing Churchill's rich men in their well-appointed habitations while bringing "dreadful misfortunes" to the victims of "the savage injustice of the Europeans," in the words of Adam Smith at an earlier stage of the global conquest.

We can appreciate the nature of these "dreadful misfortunes" by looking at the earliest victims, Haiti and Bengal, described by the European conquerors as prosperous, richly endowed, and densely populated, later a source of enormous wealth for their French and British despoilers, now the very symbols of misery and despair. Historical reality is further underscored by a look at the one country of the South that was able to resist colonization, Japan, the South's sole representative in the rich men's club, with some of its former colonies in tow, all having flatly rejected the prescriptions for "development" dictated by Western power. We learn still more by looking at "the first colony of the modern world," Ireland, deindustrialized (much like other colonies, notably India) and radically depopulated,[12] in part through the rigid application of sacred "laws of political economy" which forbade meaningful assistance or even termination of food exports from Ireland during the devastating famine of the 1840s, with effects that linger until today in the country whose "economic performance has been the least impressive in western Europe, perhaps in all Europe, in the twentieth century."[13] The lessons that were already clear to Adam Smith are much more dramatically obvious today, to those who choose to see.

The European conquest is commonly described in more neutral terms by those who set the rules: thus we refer euphemistically to developed and developing societies, or the North–South divide. Though the full picture is complex, in its essentials the divide is real enough. It has deepened in recent years, quite sharply in the 1980s. I will come back in the next chapter to some of the mechanisms of global management in the modern era, and their effects in rich and hungry nations alike.

3. A Test Case: Iraq and the West

Since those who proclaimed the advent of a new era with such pride chose Western policies towards Iraq as the prime illustration of their principles and intentions, it would only be proper to observe how these evolved. George Bush's "new world order," if its meaning was not clear at once, certainly left no mysteries in the immediate aftermath of the Gulf war—or more accurately, the Gulf slaughter; the term "war" hardly applies to a confrontation in which one side massacres the other from a safe distance, meanwhile wrecking the civilian society. That phase having ended, the victors stood by silently while Saddam crushed the Shiite and Kurdish uprisings right under the eyes of Stormin' Norman Schwartzkopf, whose forces even refused to allow rebelling Iraqi generals access to captured equipment. In the words of David Howell, Chairman of the U.K. House of Commons Foreign Affairs Committee, allied policy in effect "said to Saddam, 'It is all right now, you are free to commit any atrocities you like.'" Saddam's new slaughters pained our delicate sensibilities, government and media assured us, but they were necessary to ensure "stability," a magic word that applies to whatever meets the demands of the rulers.[14]

Having helped to implement the stability of the graveyard, Washington turned to the next task: economic strangulation. The reasons were outlined by the *Times* chief diplomatic correspondent. The population of Iraq was to be held hostage to induce the military to overthrow Saddam, Friedman explained. If Iraqis suffered sufficient pain, the Bush administration reasoned, some general might take power, "and then Washington would have the best of all worlds: an iron-fisted Iraqi junta without Saddam Hussein," a return to the happy days when Saddam's "iron fist . . . held Iraq together, much to the satisfaction of the American allies Turkey and Saudi Arabia"—and, of course, their superpower patron.[15]

The reality of the New World Order was exhibited with dazzling clarity while the applause was still resonating.

The news was hardly a surprise in the South, which did not take part in the triumphalism of the day. In a typical reaction, the *Times of India* had observed a few days after the New World Order was grandly proclaimed that the West seeks a "regional Yalta where the powerful nations agree among themselves to a share of Arab spoils"; the conduct of the Western powers "has revealed the seamiest sides of Western civilisation: its unrestricted appetite for dominance, its morbid fascination for hi-tech military might, its insensitivity to 'alien' cultures, its appalling jingoism. . . ." A leading Third World monthly in Malaysia condemned "the most cowardly war ever fought on this planet." The foreign editor of Brazil's major daily wrote that "What is being practiced in the Gulf is pure barbarism—ironically, committed in the name of civilization. Bush is as responsible as Saddam. . . . Both, with their inflexibility, consider only the cold logic of geopolitical interests [and] show an absolute scorn for human life." As the Iraqi tyrant crushed the popular rebellions in March 1991, a leading figure in the Iraqi democratic opposition, London-based banker Ahmad Chalabi, observed that the United States was "waiting for Saddam to butcher the insurgents in the hope that he can be overthrown later by a suitable officer," an attitude rooted in the U.S. policy of "supporting dictatorships to maintain stability." The outcome would be "the worst of all possible worlds" for the Iraqi people, whose tragedy is "awesome"; and "the best of all worlds" for Washington, as Thomas Friedman was soon to explain, if only Saddam's iron-fisted rule can persist under a different and less embarrassing name.[16]

Even before, the contours of Bush's New World Order had been clear enough. Saddam's invasion of Kuwait evoked a sudden and unexplained departure from standard operating procedure: The U.S.–U.K. alliance determined that Iraq's crime of aggression must not stand, unlike numerous others of the recent past; and furthermore, it must be countered by force without exploration of a negotiated settlement, in violation of international law and the UN Charter. As conceded at once, diplomatic options appeared to be available, but they were flatly rejected as not acceptable to the state that monopolizes the means of violence and intends to establish firmly its dominant role.

On August 22, 1990, three weeks after Iraq's conquest of Kuwait, the *Times*'s Thomas Friedman laid out the reasons for Bush's "hard line." Washington intended to block the "diplomatic track," Friedman explained, for fear that negotiations might "defuse the crisis" at the cost of "a few token gains in Kuwait" for the Iraqi dictator (perhaps "a Kuwaiti island or minor border adjustments," matters long under dispute). The Iraqi withdrawal offers that so troubled Washington, considered "serious" and "negotiable" by an administration Middle East specialist, were reported a week later in the suburban New York journal *Newsday*—apparently the only journal in the United States or U.K. to report the essential facts then or later, though hints elsewhere showed that they were well known. The *Times* then noted in the small print that it had received the same information, but had suppressed it. The story quickly disappeared, along with later opportunities for "defusing the crisis" by peaceful means. The Bush administration made it clear that there would be no negotiations, and that closed the matter. The issue was not discussed in Congress, and was barred from the media with the most marginal of exceptions. Britain seems to have attained even darker ignorance.[17]

Discussion of the prospects for economic sanctions, in contrast, was tolerated—though not the fact that the sanctions might have worked already, as the unmentionable withdrawal proposals suggested. Debate over this matter was harmless. Who could know, after all, what the effect of sanctions would be, and in conditions of uncertainty, the judgment of the authorities would prevail. The "diplomatic track" was a different matter, however. Pursuing that was too dangerous, given Washington's fears that it might lead to Iraqi withdrawal, undermining the opportunity to smash a defenseless country to bits and teach a few useful lessons about obedience.

The impressive exercise of doctrinal control was of considerable significance. Up to the onset of Bush's bombing in mid-January 1991, polls revealed that by 2–1, the American population favored a framework for peaceful settlement that was close to Iraqi proposals leaked by Bush administration officials but kept out of the press (apart from *Newsday* and occasional snippets elsewhere). Had respondents known that such proposals were on the table, regarded by U.S. officials as realistic, and rejected by the administration without consideration, the figures would have been far higher, and it is likely that Washington would have been compelled to pursue the diplomatic options—with what success, no one knows, though ideologists are happy to give the answers that power demands. The significance of these facts with regard to the state of American democracy is evident, but must also be suppressed, and is.

It is the task of responsible scholarship to keep such matters remote from public awareness. That responsibility is indeed faced. Thus, in a highly praised academic study regarded as the standard current work of scholarship on the Gulf conflict, Lawrence Freedman and Efraim Karsh open by praising "the scope and originality of our analysis" which uses "evidence from *all* available sources," as distinct from mere journalism, unable to attain such heights. They then proceed to ignore even the most obvious sources on pre-war diplomatic interactions, which they grossly misrepresent in their scanty comments, along with much else.[18] Reviewers solemnly observe that the authors demonstrate the futility of diplomacy, an easy task when relevant evidence is systematically suppressed.

Under intense U.S. pressure and threats, the UN Security Council went along with Washington's designs, finally agreeing to wash its hands of the matter and leave it to U.S.–U.K. power, in violation of the Charter but in recognition that the procedures laid down there cannot be followed in the face of U.S. intransigence. The government of Kuwait helped out by spending hundreds of millions of dollars to buy Security Council votes, according to Kuwaiti investigators looking into some $500 million missing from Kuwait Investment Office funds. With the UN now restored to obedience to Washington, as in its earliest years, it was praised effusively for the "wondrous sea change" that silenced "most of its detractors" and freed President Bush to create a "new world order to resolve conflicts by multilateral diplomacy and collective security" (*New York Times*). The standard explanation for this sudden conversion to good behavior was that the Soviet Union had collapsed and would therefore no longer obstruct Washington's efforts to implement the noble ideals of the founders. Journalists, statesmen, and scholars vied to see who could more outrageously distort the actual record of obstruction of UN initiatives on peace and human rights. Buried too far down the memory hole for any eye to see was the fact that the United States had been far in the lead in vetoing Security Council resolutions on a wide range of such issues, with the U.K. a strong second and France a distant third, ever since the UN fell out of U.S. control with decolonization and the growing independence of other states; the record in the General Assembly, which was quite similar, has also been consigned to oblivion, where the essential facts are destined to remain.[19]

As the bombs fell, the American population was called upon to admire "the stark and vivid definition of principle . . . baked into [George Bush] during his years at Andover and Yale, that honor and duty compels you to punch the bully in the face"—the words of the White House reporter who, a few days earlier, had released a leaked Bush administration Policy Review on "third world threats," which concluded that "in cases where the U.S. confronts much weaker enemies"—the only ones it makes sense to fight—"our challenge will be not simply to defeat them, but to defeat them decisively and rapidly"; any other course would be "embarrassing" and might "undercut political support," recognized to be thin.[20]

The response to Bush's forceful reiteration of the principle that you punch the bully in the face, once you are sure that he is securely bound and beaten to a pulp, was surely watched with interest by specialists in population control. The second national newspaper joined in, applauding the "spiritual and intellectual" triumph in the Gulf: "Martial values that had fallen into disrepute were revitalized," and "Presidential authority, under assault since Vietnam, was strengthened" (E.J. Dionne, *Washington Post*). At the outer limits of American liberalism, the *Boston Globe*, with barely a gesture towards the dangers of overexuberance, hailed the "victory for the psyche" and the new "sense of nationhood and projected power" under the leadership of a man who is "one tough son of a bitch," a man with "the guts to risk all for a cause" and a "burning sense of duty," who showed "the depth and steely core of his convictions" and his faith that "we are a select people, with a righteous mission in this earth," the latest in a line of "noble-minded missionaries" going back to his hero Teddy Roosevelt—who, we may recall, was going to "show those Dagos that they will have to behave decently" and to teach proper lessons to the "wild and ignorant people" standing in the way of "the dominant world races." *Globe* Washington correspondent Thomas Oliphant lauded "the magnitude of Bush's triumph" over a much weaker enemy, ridiculing the "uninformed garbage" of those who carp in dark corners. "Bush's leadership has transformed the Vietnam Syndrome into a Gulf Syndrome, where 'Out Now!' is a slogan directed at aggressors, not at us," he proclaimed with pride, reflexively adopting the standard doctrine that the United States was the injured party in Vietnam, defending itself from the Vietnamese aggressors. We now raise high "the worthy and demanding standard that aggression must be opposed, in exceptional cases by force," Oliphant continued—though, oddly, we are not to march on Jakarta, Tel Aviv, Damascus, Ankara, Washington, and a long series of other capitals.[21]

The exultant display of fascist values is worthy of notice along with the self-righteous moralism, a traditional feature of the intellectual culture.

There is a good deal more to learn from the response to Bush's resort to force. Those who acclaimed the ringing messages about the wondrous "era full of promise" had to craft the historical record skillfully, excising crucial facts. One was that the call for a New World Order dedicated to "peace and security, freedom and the rule of law" was delivered by the only head of state to stand condemned by the World Court for the "unlawful use of force," though of course the Court's condemnation of the Reagan–Bush terrorist war against Nicaragua was dismissed with contempt by Washington, the media, and intellectual opinion generally; the judgment merely discredited the Court, respectable commentators explained. Another crucial fact was that the "noble-minded missionary" had opened the post–Cold War era in December 1989 by invading Panama (Operation Just Cause), well aware when he announced the New World Order "that removing the mantle of United States protection would quickly result in a civilian or military overthrow of Endara and his supporters" (Latin America specialist Stephen Ropp)—that is, the puppet regime of bankers, businessmen, and narcotraffickers installed by Bush's invasion. Also to be ignored was the U.S. veto of two Security Council resolutions condemning its aggression (helped by Britain, to be sure), along with the General Assembly resolution that denounced the invasion as a "flagrant violation of international law and of the independence, sovereignty and territorial integrity of states" and called for the withdrawal of the "U.S. armed invasion forces from Panama." Also expunged from the record was the March 30, 1990 resolution of the Group of Eight (the Latin American democracies) expelling Panama, which had been suspended under Noriega, because "the process of democratic legitimation in Panama requires popular consideration without foreign interference, that guarantees the full right of the people to freely choose their governments," obviously impossible under a puppet regime maintained by foreign force. Gone also was the fact that estimates of the civilian toll of the invasions of Panama and Kuwait were comparable prior to the international reaction, deflected by U.S. power in the case of Panama.[22]

In the same category are the inquiries of the Organization of American States (OAS) and the Inter-American Commission on Human Rights (IACHR) into the human and material cost of the invasion and U.S. responsibility for deaths, injuries, and property damage, with claims of over $1 billion, and thousands reported killed. Panamanian reactions continue to be "easy to ignore," even four years after liberation. In its annual report on human rights, January 1994, Panama's governmental Human Rights Commission charged that the right to self-determination and sovereignty of the Panamanian people continues to be violated by the "state of occupation by a foreign army," reviewing U.S. army, air force, and DEA operations in Panama, including a DEA agent's assault on a Panamanian journalist and attacks on Panamanian citizens by U.S. military personnel. In its accompanying report, the nongovernmental Human Rights Commission added that democracy has meant nothing more than formal voting while government policies "do not attend to the necessities of the most impoverished," whose numbers have significantly increased. Per capita income is now below 1985 levels with huge disparities. Half the population lives in "poverty" (understood to mean half the income required to obtain "basic necessities") and a third in "extreme poverty" (below half the income of the "poverty" level), according to the Church and the State Social Emergency Fund. Also irrelevant.[23]

The cheering section not only proved equal to these tasks, but also lived up to its obligation not to comprehend the significance of another crucial fact: Bush's greatest fear when Iraq invaded Kuwait was that Saddam would mimic his achievement in Operation Just Cause. According to the account of Washington planning by investigative reporter Bob Woodward of the *Washington Post*, regarded as "generally convincing" by U.S. government Middle East specialist William Quandt, President Bush feared that the Saudis would "bug out at the last minute and accept a puppet regime in Kuwait" after Iraqi withdrawal. His advisers expected that Iraq would withdraw, leaving behind "lots of Iraqi special forces in civilian clothes," if not armed forces as the United States did in Panama, while taking over two uninhabited mudflats that had been assigned to Kuwait in the British imperial settlement to block Iraq's access to the sea (Gen. Norman Schwartzkopf). Chief of Staff Gen.

Colin Powell warned that the status quo would be changed under Iraqi influence, even after withdrawal, again as in Panama. Freedman and Karsh, who labor to present the U.S.–U.K. effort in the most favorable possible light, conclude that in this "textbook case of aggression,"

> Saddam apparently intended neither officially to annex the tiny emirate nor to maintain a permanent military presence there. Instead, he sought to establish hegemony over Kuwait, ensuring its complete financial, political and strategic subservience to his wishes,

much as intended by the United States in Panama, and achieved. Saddam's scheme "turned sour," they continue, because of the international reaction; to translate to doctrinally unacceptable truth, because the United States and Britain did not follow their usual practice of vetoing or otherwise nullifying the international reaction to such "textbook cases of aggression" as U.S.–South Vietnam, Turkey–Cyprus, Indonesia–East Timor, Israel–Lebanon, U.S.–Panama, and many others. Freedman and Karsh do not seem to realize that even their own conclusion suffices to undercut completely the central argument of their book, demonstrating that the "cynics" they berate for failing to appreciate the nobility of their heroes were right on target.[24]

With a bit more historical depth one might note that Saddam's intentions, as Freedman and Karsh describe them (along with U.S. planners), were rather similar to what Britain instituted in Kuwait in order to ward off the nationalist threat in 1958: a dependency under British control. To understand these facts, however, it would be necessary to look at the relevant documentary record, which Freedman and Karsh entirely ignore, along with virtually every other commentator on the Gulf conflict.[25]

Reactions to the U.S.–U.K. insistence on force in the Gulf mirrored traditional colonial relations fairly closely, a fact that provides some further insight into the realities of the New World Order. But the condemnation of the U.S.–U.K. war in much of the South was scarcely noticed, except as a potential problem: Would the dictatorships be able to subdue their populations, as all right-thinking democrats hoped, preventing them from disrupting the crusade? Little was reported of what these backward people were saying. The West much prefers the occasional voice from the Third World, or the Third World at home, which recognizes that the path to prestige and influence is to assure the rich men who rule that they are not at fault, however badly they might have behaved in the distant past; it is social and cultural inadequacies of the traditional servants that brought them to their sorry state. In contrast, authentic dissident voices in the Third World are unwelcome. A striking example is the treatment of the Iraqi democratic opposition before, during, and directly after the Gulf war: its authentic representatives, however conservative and respectable, were barred from any contact with Washington and were almost completely shut out of the U.S. media, apart from the margins. They were saying quite the wrong things: pleading for democracy before the invasion of Kuwait while Washington and its allies were tending to the needs of Saddam Hussein and their own pocketbooks; for pursuit of peaceful means while the United States and Britain moved to restrict the conflict to the arena of violence after Saddam broke the rules in August 1990; and for support for the anti-Saddam resistance in March 1991, while Washington returned to its preference for Saddam's "iron fist" in the interests of "stability."[26]

Another feature of the New World Order illustrated in those grim months is the racism and hypocrisy with which it is suffused. Saddam's attack on the Kurds was extensively covered, evoking a public reaction that forced Washington to take some reluctant steps to protect the victims, with their Aryan features and origins. His even more destructive attack on Shiite Arabs in the South evoked little coverage or concern. Meanwhile, ongoing Turkish atrocities against the Kurds virtually escaped notice in the U.S. media, as continues to be the case.[27]

The sincerity of the concern for the Kurds is easily assessed by a look at what happened when public pressures dissipated. The Kurdish areas are subject to the sanctions against Iraq and to Iraqi embargo in addition. The West refuses to provide the piddling sums required to satisfy the basic needs of the Kurds. "Kurdish and Western specialists estimate about $50 million would be needed to buy back a sufficient portion of the [Kurdish] wheat crop to protect the poorest Kurds and prevent Baghdad from undercutting the northern Iraqi economy," the *Washington Post* reports, but donors have come up with only $6.8 million, a pittance. Returning home from a "fruitless two-month trip trying to raise funds in the United States, Europe and Saudi Arabia," Kurdish Democratic Party leader Massoud Barzani said the alternatives facing his people were to "become refugees again in Iran and Turkey," or "we surrender to Saddam Hussein." Meanwhile "in southern Iraq, where conditions are most acute, the UN no longer maintains a permanent presence," the executive director of Middle East Watch reports, and a UN mission in March 1993 "did not even ask permission to visit the marshes" where the Shiite population is under attack. The UN Department of Humanitarian Affairs prepared a half-billion dollar relief and rehabilitation program for Kurds, Shiites, and poverty-stricken Sunnis in central Iraq. UN members pledged a pathetic $50 million, the Clinton administration offering $15 million, "money left over from contributions to a previous U.N. program in northern Iraq."[28]

The policy of holding the Iraqi population hostage requires efficient economic warfare, a practice in which Washington has much experience, including embargoes against Cuba, Nicaragua, and Vietnam in recent years to punish them for insufferable disobedience and to ensure that others learn what such behavior entails. The embargo against Iraq has left Saddam's power unaffected while causing many more civilian casualties than the bombardment itself. A study conducted by leading U.S. and foreign specialists estimated "that an excess of more than 46,900 children died between January and August 1991," far more since, a slaughter that ranks high on the contemporary list.

UNICEF's representative in Iraq, Thomas Ekvall, reported that by 1993 infant mortality had tripled to 92 per thousand while nearly one-quarter of babies were severely underweight at birth, up from 5 percent in 1990; he added that sanctions "have caused tens of thousands of deaths among young children and are plunging the population into ever-worse poverty." UNICEF's relief program is "threatened by an acute lack of money," having received only "7 percent of an appeal launched in April for $86 million." His report was scarcely noted, much like the conclusion of the later UNICEF study *The Progress of Nations* that "Iraqi children, at the rate of 143 per 1,000, were more likely to die than children in almost any country outside of Africa" (AP). British Labour MP Tam Dalyell and Middle East correspondent Tim Llewellyn, returning from Iraq in May 1993, reported that the excess of children's deaths was "well over 100,000" by that time according to the (Kurdish) Iraqi Minister of Health. UNICEF confirmed the figures and analysis given by the minister, including a sharp increase in malnutrition, dangerously low birth rates, and child deaths from vaccine-preventable disease and contaminated water supplies; the spread of malaria and other diseases that had long been eradicated; collapse of hospitals that are forbidden to import pediatric beds or chemicals vital for surgery on grounds that the materials could be used for weapons. In pediatric hospitals, they saw babies dying of severe malnutrition and lack of medicine; and like others, found that support for Saddam was growing among people who now perceive that the global rulers are intent on punishing *them*, not their criminal leader. The accuracy of the perception is confirmed by consistent U.S. policies elsewhere against those who have dared to stand up to the master, as victims around the world can attest.[29]

Meanwhile the United States continues to bomb Iraq at its pleasure. Bush's final gesture on leaving office in January 1993 was to order forty-five Tomahawk cruise missiles to be fired at an industrial complex near Baghdad; thirty-seven hit the target, one struck the Rashid Hotel, killing two people. Five months into his term of office, Bill Clinton demonstrated that he too is capable of ordering the Pentagon to strike defenseless targets, winning much applause for his manliness and courage, and demonstrating once again that his "Mandate for Change" (the slogan he borrowed from Eisenhower) meant "Business as Usual," contrary to illusions that were widespread in Europe and parts of the Third World. The incident is worth a closer look; it tells us still more about the New World Order.

On June 26, 1993, President Clinton ordered a missile attack on Iraq.[30] Twenty-three Tomahawk cruise missiles were fired at an intelligence headquarters in downtown Baghdad. Seven missed the target, striking a residential area. Eight civilians were killed and a dozen wounded, Nora Boustany reported from Baghdad. Among the dead were the well-known artist Layla al-Attar and a man found with his baby son in his arms. It is understood that a missile attack will inevitably have technical failures, but its "main advantage," Defense Secretary Les Aspin explained, is that "it does not put U.S.

pilots at risk" as more accurate bombing would do—only Iraqi civilians, who are expendable.

Clinton was greatly cheered by the results, the press reported. "I feel quite good about what transpired and I think the American people should feel good about it," the deeply religious president said on his way to church the next day. His pleasure was shared by congressional doves, who found the missile attack to be "appropriate, reasonable and necessary"; "we've got to show these people that we're not sitting targets for terrorism" (Representatives Barney Frank and Joseph Moakley, leading Massachusetts liberals).[31]

The attack was announced as retaliation for an alleged Iraqi attempt to assassinate ex-President Bush in April on a visit to Kuwait, where the accused were on trial under dubious circumstances as the missiles were launched. In public, Washington claimed to have "certain proof" of Iraqi guilt, but it was quietly conceded that this was false: "Administration officials, speaking anonymously," informed the press "that the judgment of Iraq's guilt was based on circumstantial evidence and analysis rather than ironclad intelligence," a *New York Times* editorial observed. The fact, considered trivial, was barely noted and quickly forgotten.[32]

At the UN Security Council, U.S. ambassador Madeleine Albright defended the resort to force with an appeal to Article 51 of the UN Charter. Article 51 authorizes the use of force in self-defense against "armed attack," until the Security Council takes action. Under international law, such self-defense is authorized when its necessity is "instant, overwhelming, and leaving no choice of means and no moment for deliberation, and must be limited by that necessity and kept clearly within it." To invoke Article 51 in bombing Baghdad two months after an alleged attempt to assassinate a former president scarcely rises to the level of absurdity, a matter of little concern to commentators.[33]

The *Washington Post* assured the nation's elites that the facts of this case "plainly fit" Article 51. "Any President has a duty to use military force to protect the nation's interests," the *New York Times* added, while expressing some skepticism. "Diplomatically, this was the proper rationale to invoke," the editors of the liberal *Boston Globe* declared: "Clinton's reference to the UN charter conveyed an American desire to respect international law." Others offered still more creative interpretations of Article 51, "which permits states to respond militarily if they are threatened by a hostile power," the *Christian Science Monitor* reported. Article 51 entitles a state to use force "in self-defence against threats to one's nationals," British foreign secretary Douglas Hurd instructed Parliament, supporting Clinton's "justified and proportionate exercise of the right of self-defence." There would be a "dangerous state of paralysis" in the world, Hurd continued, if the United States were required to gain Security Council approval before launching missiles against an enemy that might, or might not, have ordered a failed attempt to kill an ex-president two months earlier.

No one, however, seems to have reached quite the heights scaled by Washington in defending its invasion of Panama, when UN ambassador Thomas Pickering informed the Security Council that Article 51 "provides for the use of armed force to defend a country, to *defend our interests*" (my emphasis), and the Justice Department added that the same provision of the Charter entitles the United States to invade Panama to prevent its "territory from being used as a base for smuggling drugs into the United States."[34]

The force of this intriguing legal doctrine is clarified, perhaps, by the outcome a few years later, as the State Department acknowledged that "aside from the United States itself, newly democratic Panama is the most active center for cocaine 'money laundering' in the Western Hemisphere," a fact played down by Washington, "some law enforcement authorities and other critics argue," because it "wants to promote the longevity of Panama's democratic leaders" (*Washington Post*)—that is, the leaders protected from overthrow by "the mantle of United States protection," and presiding over a "democracy" that is an irrelevant formality for the impoverished majority, the Human Rights Commission alleges. "Drugs and their rewards are more visible today than in General Noriega's time," the *Economist* reports, including hard drugs. A senior employee of the Panama Branch of Merrill Lynch was one of those caught in a DEA operation as they were laundering Colombian cocaine cash through Panama's large financial industry, the one real economic success story of the "occupation by a foreign army." "All they were doing is what almost every bank in Panama does," a local investigative reporter commented. All exactly as predicted when the troops landed to restore the mainly white oligarchy to power and ensure U.S. control over the strategically important region and its financial institutions.[35]

Clinton's appeal to international law was widely endorsed by intellectual opinion and by the more obedient U.S. clients, notably Britain and Russia, though in Russia (still not quite civilized) the government's abject kowtowing was quickly condemned by the press and parliament. In Britain, reactions varied. The *Guardian* condemned the bombing, ridiculing the performance of "the ever-loyal British ambassador Sir David Hannay," who gave the only "ringing endorsement" at the UN. The London *Times*, in contrast, praised Clinton's "resolute action," noting that "challenges in the international arena" must "be met by a vigorous response, if necessary by force of arms": "One of the greatest achievements of the 1980s, the era of Ronald Reagan and Margaret Thatcher, was to signal that the West was not only unprepared to appease its enemies but would also actively defend its interests." Just whose interests were defended by the huge atrocities that these stalwarts organized or supported in Central America, Southeast Asia, Africa, and the Middle East, we are not told.[36]

The London *Times* editors also evaded the question of how others are entitled to react to the aggression, assassination attempts, and other atrocities in which their heroes have engaged over the years. That only makes sense; the rich rulers have rights denied to their subjects, including the right to murder and torture, and to mock international law and conventions. While some questioned the appeal to Article 51,[37] they refrained from drawing the immediate conclusion: the attack was a criminal act that should be punished accordingly.

It is, incidentally, not difficult to imagine how the world would look if Washington's code of behavior were adopted generally: it would be a jungle, in which the powerful would work their will as they choose. It would, in short, be much like what we see as we look around us without the blinders of ideology and doctrine.

The *Washington Post* praised Clinton for "confronting foreign aggression" and relieving the fear that he might be less prone to violence than his predecessors. The bombing, the *Post* recognized with satisfaction, refuted the dangerous belief that "American foreign policy in the post–Cold War era was destined to be forever hogtied by the constraints of multilateralism"— that is, by international law and the UN Charter.

Many commentators saw the decision to attack Iraq as politically astute, gaining public support for the president at a difficult moment, as the population rallied 'round the flag—or more accurately, huddled beneath it— a standard reaction to apparent crisis. Viewing the same scene from a very different perspective, American TV correspondent Charles Glass, writing in London, asked "what is the connection between an Iraqi artist named Layla al-Attar, and Rickey Ray Rector, a black man executed in 1992 for murder in Arkansas?" The answer, he pointed out, is Bill Clinton's need to improve his ratings, in one case, by sending missiles to bomb Baghdad, in the other, by returning to Arkansas in the midst of his presidential campaign to supervise the execution of a mentally incapacitated prisoner, proving "that a Democrat could be tough on crime."[38]

Clinton's public relations specialists have their fingers on the nation's pulse. They know that in unprecedented numbers, people are disillusioned, skeptical, and troubled over the conditions of their lives, their apparent powerlessness, and the decline of democratic institutions, feelings intensified by a decade of Reaganism; it is hardly a surprise that Reagan ranks alongside of Nixon as the most unpopular living ex-president, particularly disliked by working people and "Reagan Democrats." The image-makers also know that the Clinton administration will not address the problems of ordinary people; any meaningful measures would infringe upon the prerogatives of its primary constituencies, and therefore are excluded. For the executives of a transnational corporation, professionals linked to the power structure, and other privileged sectors, it is important for the world to be properly disciplined, for advanced industry to be granted its huge public subsidies, and for the wealthy to be guaranteed security. It does not matter much if public education and health deteriorate, the useless population rots in slums and prisons, and the basis for a livable society erodes for the public at large. In adopting these basic guidelines for policy, the current administration is at one with its predecessors.

Under such conditions, the public must be frightened and diverted. The collapse of urban communities has consequences that really are frightening to people compelled to live with the consequences; in a depoliticized society, many will welcome the harsh whip of state power against those who threaten them, seeing no alternative. The same attitudes extend to foreign hordes. They were articulated by the populist president Lyndon Johnson when he warned that "we are outnumbered 15 to one" by hostile forces poised to "sweep over the United States and take what we have"; lacking the means to bomb them to dust in their lairs, we would be "easy prey to any yellow dwarf with a pocket knife."[39] Throughout the period when he was exhibited to the public, the pathetic figure playing cowboy appealed to the same sense of imminent doom if we let down our guard, whimpering about Sandinistas marching on Texas, monstrous air bases in Grenada, and other such grim threats to our existence.

Cold War propaganda served the purpose of intimidation for many years, "scaring Hell out of the American people" in a style that was "clearer than truth," as the influential Senator Arthur Vandenberg and his mentor Dean Acheson advised in the late 1940s. Inundated by this deluge, much of the population lives in dread of foreign devils about to descend upon them and steal what little they still have. Through the 1980s, the United States became an object of no little derision abroad as the tourist industry periodically collapsed because Americans, frightened by images of crazed Arabs, were afraid to venture to Europe, where they would be far safer than in any American city. During the Gulf conflict, the terror was palpable; one could find wealthy towns a hundred miles from nowhere that were fortifying themselves in fear of Arab terrorists, if not Saddam himself. Meanwhile, a flood of propaganda about our unique generosity and the ungratefulness of the wretches who benefit from it has led to a cultural condition in which almost half the population believes that foreign aid is the largest element of the federal budget and another third select welfare as the chief culprit, also far overestimating the proportion that goes to Blacks and to child support; less than a quarter give the correct answer, military spending, and surely few are aware that these expenditures are in large part welfare for the rich, much like the minuscule "aid" program that is one of the most miserly in the developed world.[40]

As we have seen, doctrinal managers leaped into the fray as soon as President Bush determined to resort to force in response to Saddam's invasion of Kuwait. Clinton strategists, anxious to save a sinking presidency from total shipwreck, anticipated similar favors, and were not disappointed.

Some recognized that Clinton could have ordered a still more savage bombardment of Baghdad without incurring any loss of lives that matter. But that would not have been in Washington's interests. The president "did not want to risk serious civilian casualties," Thomas Friedman observed. "A strike with more civilian casualties would have probably resulted not in widespread support for Washington, but rather sympathy for Iraq," and would therefore have been unwise.[41]

Despite this powerful argument against mass murder, not everyone was pleased with the president's restraint. *New York Times* columnist William Safire condemned the administration for administering "a pitiful wristslap" instead of a full-scale attack on "Saddam's war machine and economic base—setting back all hopes of recovery for years." His scorn was shared by the *New Republic*, a leading voice of American liberalism. Its editors were, however, pleased by the "silence of the Arab world," which thus signaled its approval for Clinton's decisive action.[42]

As the editors knew, the bombing was criticized throughout the Arab world, even by Washington's allies, and was condemned by the League of Arab States as an act of aggression. An editorial in the Bahraini daily *Akhbar al-Khalij* observed that "Arab land has become such fair game for America that Clinton did not even bother to search for a reasonably convincing pretext with which to justify the latest aggression," confident of support in the UN Security Council, which "has become little more than an appendage of the U.S. State Department"; "What is really happening is that America is humiliating the Arab people whenever it has a chance." "To cut a long story short, this attack on Iraq was a clear case of an international thug hitting a regional one on the principle that others should butt out," a reporter in Bahrain added. At the other end of the Arab world, the official press in Morocco accused Clinton of exploiting "the new world order in order to enslave the countries and people of the world" and using the Security Council as "an organ of American foreign policy." As for the family dictatorships of the Gulf, insofar as they were "silent," it was to distance themselves from an act that caused great bitterness in the Arab world.[43]

Though quite false, the editors' claim becomes intelligible when we recall the doctrinal norms, which they illustrated further in reminding their readers that President Bush had "organized the opinion of the world against Saddam" as he launched the attack against Iraq in January 1991. This conventional formula too is grossly false—if "the world" is taken to include its people. But it is correct if we take "the world" to consist of its rich white faces and obedient Third World clients. Similarly, if we understand "the Arab world" to include only Arabs who satisfy the criteria of Western elites, the claim that "the Arab world" approves of Clinton's missiles is accurate enough, indeed tautologous.

The alleged plot against Bush was "loathsome and cowardly," President Clinton declared. The missile attack was "essential to protect our sovereignty" and "to affirm the expectation of civilized behavior among nations." Others agreed that the "plot to kill a former president" is "an outrageous crime" (*Washington Post*), "an act of war" (*New York Times*). William Safire spelled out the argument further: it is "an act of war ... when one head of state tries to murder another. If clear evidence had shown that Fidel Castro ordered the killing of President Kennedy, President Johnson would surely have used military force to depose the regime in Havana."[44]

The rhetorical device selected is instructive. Of course, Safire knows full well that his hypothetical example reverses the actual historical record. He and his readers are aware of the repeated attempts of the Kennedy administration to assassinate Fidel Castro, the last of them set in motion on the very day of Kennedy's assassination. But a truly refined imperial arrogance permits the bland inversion of the facts, with confidence that colleagues and the educated community generally will not "notice" that according to the preaching of Western moralists, U.S. attempts to assassinate Castro were "loathsome and cowardly acts of war" which entitled Castro to use military force to depose the regime in Washington, had that been possible, and surely justified bombs in Washington in retaliation for Kennedy's "outrageous crime."

The fact that a respected columnist is capable of drawing the analogy to Castro and Kennedy in this manner is remarkable enough. But it scarcely hints at the corruption of the intellectual community. Throughout this entire farce, the major media and journals of opinion were successfully defended from crucial facts that must have occurred at once to any literate person: Washington holds the world record for attempts to assassinate foreign leaders, including Castro (at least eight plots involving the CIA from 1960 through 1965, the Senate's Church Committee reported) and Patrice Lumumba, and played a leading role in the killing of Salvador Allende and of U.S. ally Ngo Dinh Diem after a coup set in motion by John F. Kennedy, and applauded by Kennedy a few days after the assassination in a secret cable to his Saigon ambassador, who was instrumental in executing it. In a free and independent press, this would have been the lead story. It was, however, avoided with exceptions so rare as to be virtually undetectable, though it should be noted that in letters to the press, many people were able to recognize that 2 + 2 = 4, like Orwell's Winston Smith before he too was broken.

It may be worth recalling the justifications that were offered for the attempts to assassinate Castro when the Church Committee investigated these programs in 1975. Kennedy's CIA director John McCone testified that Castro was a man who would

> seize every opportunity before a microphone or television to berate and criticize the United States in the most violent and unfair and incredible terms. Here was a man that was doing his utmost to use every channel of communication of every Latin American country to win them away from any of the principles that we stood for and drive them into Communism. Here was a man that turned over the sacred soil of Cuba in 1962 to the Soviets to plant nuclear warhead shortrange missiles

—in defense against an expected U.S. invasion of Cuba (a plausible expectation from the Cuban and Soviet perspective, as Defense Secretary Robert McNamara later acknowledged), and well after the onset of CIA-run terrorist attacks on Cuba including assassination attempts.[45] In the face of such unspeakable crimes, it is understandable that Washington should attempt to assassinate the perpetrator; and that thirty years later, we are entitled to recall the Kennedy–Castro interchange only as offering a hypothetical justification for bombing Baghdad after an alleged attempt to assassinate a former president.

A no less revealing feature of media commentary on Clinton's criminal attack was the frequent reference to Reagan's air strike against Libya in 1986, killing dozens of Libyan civilians. Thus Thomas Friedman noted that "in the raid on Libya, Colonel Qaddafi was personally targeted, members of his family were killed, and he narrowly escaped being blown apart in his tent." Conclusion? The attempted assassination of Qaddafi is a worthy precedent for Clinton's missile attack against Baghdad.[46]

At this point, we enter a world that is truly surreal, defying comment, though its norms are clear enough: assassinations, terrorism, torture, and aggression are crimes that must be harshly punished when the targets are people who matter; they are not even worth mentioning, or are laudable acts of self-defense, if perpetrated by the chief Mafia don himself. So self-evident are these truths that close to 100 percent of reporting and commentary on Clinton's attack upheld them, even citing U.S. attempts to assassinate foreign leaders as justification for the U.S. attack on Iraq! The rulers of any totalitarian state would be impressed.

Outlining Washington's reasoning, Thomas Friedman explained why Clinton did not target Saddam Hussein personally: "It has always been American policy that the iron-fisted Mr. Hussein plays a useful role in holding Iraq together," and, officials say privately, "the United States is better off with a unified Iraq than with seeing it broken into Kurdish, Shiite and Sunni Muslim states, which could destabilize" the region.[47] That has been true enough, from the days when Saddam was a great friend of the United States and Britain, who joined their allies in lavishing aid upon him while he gassed Kurds and tortured dissidents. The essential reasoning stayed in place as the U.S.–U.K. military operations ended and Saddam turned to slaughtering Shiites and Kurds with the heroes of the Gulf looking on in silence, while Washington hoped to attain "the best of all worlds: an iron-fisted Iraqi junta without Saddam Hussein," settling finally for second-best: Saddam's "iron fist" (Friedman).

The Clinton administration's tactical choices were in part determined by the consideration noted by the Secretary of Defense: Why put the lives of American soldiers at risk merely to reduce civilian casualties? But the operative principle is far more general: human life has value insofar as it contributes to the wealth and power of the privileged. It is the interests of the rich men who run the world that determine the basic contours of policy.

The principle is well illustrated by the treatment of Saddam Hussein, Noriega, and numerous other tyrants: fine fellows as long as they serve our interests, vermin to be exterminated if they get in our way. The guiding moral doctrines entitle the United States to bomb the invader of Kuwait and starve his subjects, but huge slaughters in the course of Indonesia's invasion and annexation of East Timor, dwarfing Saddam Hussein's crimes in Kuwait, are of no concern. These crimes do not obligate or entitle the United States and Britain to bomb Jakarta, or even to refrain from providing decisive military and diplomatic support for its aggression and mass murder, joined by the other powers that see opportunities for profit. During the worst years of the Indonesian aggression, the media observed a proper silence or transmitted official lies. Today, the Anglo–American guardians of virtue, and their associates, are happily robbing East Timor's oil jointly with the Indonesian conquerors; the tale unfolds in silence, though one imagines that someone might have noticed had Libya joined with Iraq to exploit Kuwait's oil after Saddam's conquest. A decade before Indonesia's Western-backed invasion and annexation of East Timor, its current leader Suharto, hailed as a "moderate" who is "at heart benign" by Western opinion, launched the greatest massacre since the Holocaust. Hundreds of thousands of people, mostly landless peasants, were slaughtered in a few months. This "boiling bloodbath," as *Time* magazine called it, was reported quite graphically, with great enthusiasm and euphoria. The *New York Times* saw the events as "a gleam of light in Asia." Scholars offered them as justification for the U.S. invasion of Vietnam, which encouraged the Indonesian generals to cleanse their land in the approved style. This incredible reaction evoked no comment at the time, and is unmentionable in retrospect.[48]

Similarly, mass murder in the Guatemalan highlands and in Bosnia cannot be impeded, and may indeed be abetted (as in Guatemala), if the interests of the world rulers so determine. The rules of engagement in Bosnia are highly restrictive; in Somalia, in contrast, UN (in effect, U.S.) forces are authorized to carry out massive retaliation, with many civilian casualties.[49] The distinction is clear: retaliation would be costly to the West in Bosnia, while Somalis are weak enough to be fair game. For the same reasons, U.S. ground troops are allowed in Somalia, but not in Bosnia. Terrible atrocities in Haiti could have been stopped with a few gestures, but the United States and its partners have not been eager to restore to power a democratically elected representative of the poor, President Jean-Bertrand Aristide, whose efforts to help the vast majority of the population were condemned as "divisive" acts of "class warfare" by government and media, as distinct from the usual pattern of brutal exploitation by the kleptocracy, which elicit little comment as long as the rabble are subdued. Washington made clear that the elected president would be permitted to return after the military coup that overthrew him only on the condition that effective power is placed in the hands of a "moderate" representing the business sector, with the popular movements that swept him into office devastated and marginalized.

The operative principle is that actions are to be guided by self-interest. The basic question is "What is in it for us?" as the *New York Times* described the conclusions of a Clinton White House panel on intervention, highlighting these words. No longer will we be guided by altruism, the Clinton adminis- tration determined, as in the days when we turned large parts of the world into graveyards and deserts, bringing starvation and despair to Central America, Southeast Asia, and numerous other targets of our benevolence. Now the sole guiding principle is our own self-interest, in this new more humane era of liberal democracy—where the phrase "our own self-interest," as always, must be reinterpreted in terms of the crucial Smithian footnotes to the Churchillian doctrine.

Abiding by that principle (as it has, pretenses aside), the United States can send ground troops in massive force to Somalia well after the famine had receded and good photo opportunities were guaranteed, expecting little short-term resistance from teenagers with rifles. But not to Bosnia, where the slaughter is approaching genocide; or to Angola, where it appears to be even worse but there is no need to react or even to go beyond an occasional report, since Western interests are not at risk and the primary agent, Jonas Savimbi, is a long-time U.S. client extolled as a "freedom fighter" by leading political figures, even declared to be "one of the few authentic heroes of our time" by Jeane Kirkpatrick after his forces had boasted of shooting down civilian airliners with hundreds killed, along with numerous other atrocities, while murdering and destroying on a truly heroic scale with U.S. and South African support. Best to leave all of this in the dark corners, along with the ongoing atrocities committed in Afghanistan by another CIA favorite, the fanatic Islamic fundamentalist Gulbuddin Hekmatyar.[50]

We can proceed, case by case, through a long and gruesome list. Of course, historical circumstances always vary somewhat even in closely parallel cases (say, East Timor and Kuwait), a fact that offers a window of opportunity for apologists whose task it is to produce a justification for whatever course the powerful may select. But comparative study quickly shows that the reasons offered for action or inaction, even if by accident they happen to be sound in some particular case, are rarely the operative ones. The latter are inexpressible, except sometimes by a cynic of the Churchillian variety.

Ideologists are right to uphold Washington's policy towards Iraq as a test case for the heralded New World Order. The first lesson it teaches is that the United States remains a violent and lawless state, a stance that is fully endorsed by its allies and clients, who understand that international law is a fraud to which the powerful appeal when they seek some veil, however transparent, for whatever they choose to do. A second lesson, equally familiar, is that such behavior can proceed with impunity in an intellectual culture that recognizes few limits in its services to power. We have to turn to Third World dictatorships to hear the truisms that are suppressed in civilized societies: the New World Order is "new" only in that it adapts traditional policies of domination and exploitation to somewhat changed contingencies; it is much admired by the West because it is recognized to be a device to keep "the countries and people of the world" in their proper place.

The bottles may be new; the wine, however, is of ancient vintage.

4. The Cold War Reconsidered

The present moment is a proper one to rethink the confrontations of East and West and of North and South, to ask how these divisions in global order are related, and to consider the likely consequences of the end of the Cold War and other changes of world order in recent years.

The conventional picture, once again, is that for most of the century, and certainly from 1945, the East–West conflict has set the basic framework for international affairs and domestic policies: military, economic, and ideological. In this conflict, Western actions were defensive only, a response to the criminal behavior of the enemy: its aggression, expansionism, terror, and subversion worldwide. Given this fundamental asymmetry, the West adopted a purely defensive posture: "deterrence" and "containment," or the more far-reaching strategy of "roll back" to eliminate the source of the aggression. There can be no question of "containing" the United States; to raise this issue would be senseless, and it therefore does not form part of the vast literature on containment. Similarly, the study of deterrence tends to skirt its most notable success: Soviet deterrence of a second American invasion of Cuba.

This picture of the world was drawn in stark lines by the Reaganites, but it is often forgotten that they broke no new ground. It would be hard to surpass the fanaticism of the primary Cold War document, NSC 68 of April 1950, written by Paul Nitze with Dean Acheson looking over his shoulder, and adopted by the liberal Truman administration. Its frenzied rhetoric is rarely quoted, perhaps considered something of an embarrassment, but it is well to attend to the mind-set of highly respected planners and policy intellectuals.[51]

The document has the tone of an unusually simple-minded fairy tale, contrasting ultimate evil (them) with absolute perfection (us). The "compulsion" of the "slave state" is to achieve "the complete subversion or forcible destruction of the machinery of government and structure of society" in every corner of the world that is not yet "subservient to and controlled from the Kremlin." Its "implacable purpose" is to "eliminate the challenge of freedom" everywhere, gaining "total power over all men" in the slave state itself and "absolute authority over the rest of the world." By its very nature, the slave state is "inescapably militant." Hence no accommodation or peaceful settlement is even thinkable. We must therefore act to "foster the seeds of destruction within the Soviet system" and "hasten [its] decay" by all means short of war (which is too dangerous for us). We must avoid diplomacy and negotiations except as a device to placate public opinion because any agreements "would reflect present realities and would therefore be unacceptable, if not disastrous, to the United States and the rest of the free world," though after the success of a "roll back" strategy we may "negotiate a settlement with the Soviet Union (or a successor state or states)."

The authors concede that the fiendish enemy is far weaker than its adversaries in every relevant respect. This disparity confers further advantages on the enemy: being so backward, it "can do more with less," at once midget and superman. Our situation is thus truly desperate.

Since "the Kremlin design for world domination" is a necessary property of the slave state, there is no need to provide evidence to establish any of the conclusions that had such an enormous impact within the United States and for the world. Nothing pertinent is offered in this lengthy analysis.[52]

The innate evil of the slave state is highlighted by comparison with the United States, a nation of almost unimaginable perfection. Its "fundamental purpose" is "to assure the integrity and vitality of our free society, which is founded upon the dignity and worth of the individual," and to safeguard these values throughout the world. Our free society is marked by "marvelous diversity," "deep tolerance," "lawfulness" (our cities being marvels of tranquillity, and white collar crime unknown), a commitment "to create and maintain an environment in which every individual has the opportunity to realize his creative powers." The perfect society "does not fear, it welcomes, diversity" and "derives its strength from its hospitality even to antipathetic ideas," as illustrated by the McCarthyite hysteria of the day, perhaps. The "system of values which animates our society" includes "the principles of freedom, tolerance, the importance of the individual and the supremacy of reason over will." "The essential tolerance of our world outlook, our generous and constructive impulses, and the absence of covetousness in our international relations are assets of potentially enormous influence," particularly among those who have been lucky enough to experience these qualities at first hand, as in Latin America, which has so benefited from "our long continuing endeavors to create and now develop the Inter-American system." Since these are necessary properties of the United States, just as ultimate evil is a necessary property of its enemy, there is no need to consider the factual record in proclaiming our perfection—a wise decision.

So it continues, in a secret internal document—which, in fact, captures rather well the quality of intellectual discourse in the public domain as well, though in fairness to Acheson, we should recall his awareness that it would be necessary "to bludgeon the mass mind of 'top government'" with the Communist threat in a manner "clearer than truth" in order to gain approval for the planned programs of rearmament and intervention.[53]

Little changes as we move on to the present. In the Spring 1993 issue of the sober scholarly journal *International Security*, the Eaton Professor of the Science of Government and Director of the Olin Institute of Strategic Studies at Harvard, Samuel Huntington, informs us that the United States must maintain its "international primacy" for the benefit of the world. The reason is that alone among nations, its "national identity is defined by a set of universal political and economic values," namely "liberty, democracy, equality, private property, and markets"; "the promotion of democracy, human rights, and markets are far more central to American policy than to the policy of any other country." Since this is a matter of *definition*, so the Science of Government teaches, evidence is again irrelevant. In evaluating Washington's promotion of human rights, for example, we may put aside the close correlation between U.S. aid (including military aid) and torture demonstrated in several studies, running right through the Carter years, an inquiry that would be pointless to undertake as George Shultz, Jeane Kirkpatrick, Elliott Abrams, and the rest of that merry crew took the reins.[54] Such considerations are the province of small minds, unable to appreciate Higher Truths.

More generally, it is simply an error of logic to compare the odes to our magnificence with the factual record. Those who find it hard to grasp this basic truth may turn for instruction to the tough-minded "realistic" school of the science of government. Its leading figure, Hans Morgenthau, discerned that the "transcendent purpose" of the United States is "the establishment of equality in freedom in America," and indeed throughout the world, since "the arena within which the United States must defend and promote its purpose has become world-wide." A competent scholar, and an unusually decent person and independent thinker by the standards of the elite culture, Morgenthau recognized that the historical record is radically inconsistent with the "transcendent purpose." But he hastened to remind us that facts are irrelevant to necessary truths: to adduce the facts is "to confound the abuse of reality with reality itself," recapitulating "the error of atheism, which denies the validity of religion on similar grounds." Reality is the unachieved "national purpose" revealed by "the evidence of history as our minds reflect it"; the actual historical record is merely the abuse of reality, an insignificant artifact.[55]

Standard doctrines are thus immune to evaluation and critique, as in the more extreme forms of religious fundamentalism. It is difficult to believe that such pronouncements are intended seriously. Perhaps they are not, as Acheson's cynical comments suggest. Similarly, Huntington had explained earlier that: "You may have to sell [intervention or other military action] in such a way as to create the misimpression that it is the Soviet Union that you are fighting. That is what the United States has done ever since the Truman Doctrine." By the same logic, "Gorbachev's public relations can be as much a threat to American interests in Europe as were Brezhnev's tanks," Huntington explained, offering yet another insight into the reality of the Cold War.[56]

The hysteria of NSC 68 scarcely abated during the Eisenhower–Dulles years, and was renewed as the next Democratic administration took office, drawing heavily from the liberal intelligentsia. Kennedy warned that we must be on guard against the "monolithic and ruthless conspiracy" that is dedicated to world conquest. His inner circle was selected to reflect these sentiments. Secretary of Defense Robert McNamara informed Congress in his confirmation hearings that:

> There is no true historical parallel to the drive of Soviet Communist imperialism to colonize the world. . . . Furthermore, there is a totality in Soviet aggression which can be matched only by turning to ancient history, when warring tribes sought not merely conquest but the total obliteration of the enemy. . . . Soviet communism seeks to wipe out the cherished traditions and institutions of the free world with the same fanaticism that once impelled

winning armies to burn villages and sow the fields with salt so they would not
again become productive. To this primitive concept of total obliteration, the
Communists have brought the resources of modern technology and science.
The combination is formidable. Twentieth century knowledge, when robbed
of any moral restraints, is the most dangerous force ever let loose in the world.
And the entire literature of Soviet communism can be searched without
turning up the faintest trace of moral restraint,

as he had doubtless learned from his immersion in that literature. This is "the
spirit in which I believe the education program of our Defense Establishment
should be conducted," McNamara testified.

Kennedy's second top adviser on security affairs, General Maxwell
Taylor, urged that the United States radically increase military spending.
"Without making a specific estimate," Taylor held, "one may be sure that the
total bill will exceed any peacetime budget in United States history."[57] Given
our necessary perfection and their innate evil, this seemed right to the wise
men of Camelot.

Kennedy's "action-intellectuals" proceeded with a huge military buildup,
justifying their program on the basis of a "missile gap" that they knew to be
fraudulent; to be more precise, real enough, but in favor of the United States,
by a large margin. This was the second major Cold War military buildup, the
first having been undertaken by the Truman administration in accord with
NSC 68, on the pretext that the Korean war, which broke out shortly after the
memorandum was presented, established its thesis about the "Kremlin
design for world domination," a deduction as implausible then as it remains
today, but valid by virtue of policy needs. The Reaganites preferred a
fabricated "window of vulnerability" as they implemented President Carter's
proposals for military expansion, discovering that the window had been
closed all along when the business community came to be concerned about
the consequences of their military Keynesian extravagances. Meanwhile
intellectuals across the political spectrum concocted tales of Russia marching from strength to strength, taking over such powerhouses as Mozambique
and Grenada while the Free World trembled in helpless impotence.[58] Needless to say, the collapse of these fantasies a few years later led to no self-
examination or reevaluation: on the contrary, it proved that the prophets of
imminent doom were absolutely right, their warnings having just fended off
catastrophe in the nick of time.

In 1980, the task of the moment was to provide reasons for a renewed
stimulus to the economy and a more aggressive international posture, which
in due course opened a new phase of U.S. international terrorism and
subversion. That is justification enough. Much the same was true of the other
two major cases of military build-up (1950, 1961).

Even a cursory review of the facts suggests that the conventional picture
of the Cold War is a rickety structure indeed. A closer look only strengthens
that conclusion. Let's consider a few questions that would be raised by a
reasonable person interested in understanding the nature of the East–West
conflict.

National Security

The first question has to do with the role of national security in policy formation. Of course, threats to security are constantly invoked, perhaps even believed (see note 58); that is close to a universal, for any state. Accordingly, appeal to security tells us little, particularly if we allow sufficient latitude to the notion "security." In some of the most careful and thorough contemporary scholarship, "national security" is construed so broadly as to include the assurance that in the indefinite future, no potential adversary (in the Cold War era, the USSR) will command the resources to threaten the United States; given that an independent course might lead to incorporation within the adversary's influence and power, neutralism too constitutes a genuine threat to "national security." The proposition that policy is guided by security concerns then becomes vacuous and invulnerable, in contrast to ideas, which, right or wrong, at least have some identifiable content, such as the thesis that policy is designed to ensure that U.S.-based corporations (which, uncontroversially, heavily influence policy formation) will be free to operate as they please in the international economy. And by similar logic, any other state has a right to control global society for reasons of "national security." We are left nowhere.[59]

The idea that security requires total world domination came all the more easily to Cold War planners because its basic elements were so familiar. Throughout American history, it has been a practice to invoke vast enemies about to overwhelm us. "The exaggeration of American vulnerability—in the most basic sense of the vulnerability of the North American homeland to direct attack from outside—has been a recurring feature of debates over American foreign and defense policy for at least a hundred years," historian John Thompson points out; and indeed can be traced well beyond. Naval construction in the 1880s was justified by "harrowing pictures of British, Chilean, Brazilian, and even Chinese warships shelling" American cities. The annexation of Hawaii was necessary to fend off British attacks against mainland ports, which "lie absolutely at the mercy of her cruisers" (Senator Henry Cabot Lodge). The Caribbean and the homeland itself were threatened by the German navy before World War I. Preparing the country for entry into World War II in October 1941, President Roosevelt described a "secret map made in Germany by Hitler's Government" outlining plans to bring "the whole continent under their domination"; the map was real enough, having been planted by British intelligence. And on, and on. Ronald Reagan's speechwriters were simply keeping step when they had him warn that the Sandinistas were just "two hours' flying time from our own borders" and "just two days' driving time from Harlingen, Texas." The demand for "preponderance" is as American as apple pie.[60]

The doctrinal framework that underlies the demand was also firmly in place long before the Cold War. The United States is, after all, uniquely magnificent. It was therefore a highly honorable enterprise to cleanse the continent of people "destined to extinction" and "as a race, not worth preserving"; "essentially inferior to the Anglo-Saxon race," they are "not an improvable breed" so that "their disappearance from the human family would be no great loss" (President John Quincy Adams, who much later was to recant, recognizing the policies he had implemented to be "among the heinous sins of this nation, for which I believe God will one day bring [it] to judgement," and hoping that his belated stand might somehow aid "that hapless race of native Americans, which we are exterminating with such merciless and perfidious cruelty"). The extermination was all the more just in the light of the legal doctrine, enunciated by President Monroe, that the inferior race must "of right" give way "to the more dense and compact form and greater force of civilized population," since "the earth was given to mankind to support the greatest number of which it is capable and no tribe or people have a right to withhold from the wants of others more than is necessary for their own support and comfort." Accordingly, "the rights of nature demand and nothing can prevent" the "rapid and gigantic" expansion of White settlement into Indian territory, with the just extermination that inevitably follows.

Such ideas, traced by early ideologues back to John Locke, have a contemporary resonance as well—always applied with delicate selectivity, to be sure.

The continent having been purified of the native scourge, the doctrines extended naturally to the entire world. The conquest of the West would provide the springboard for the millennial "emancipation of the world" by American "pecuniary and moral power," the influential New England cleric Lyman Beecher explained in 1835, adopting terms that would captivate a deeply religious culture, and that are reiterated only a shade more crudely by his secular successors, as in NSC 68 and much public discourse.[61]

During the Cold War, the threads were woven together in the demand for preponderance, which is our right and our need: our right by virtue of the nobility that inheres in us by definition, and our need given the imminent threat of destruction by fiendish enemies. The conventional cover term is "security."

With the Cold War over, the masks can be drawn aside at least slightly, and elementary truths, sometimes expressed in serious scholarship, can be publicly entertained. Among them is the fact that the appeal to security was largely fraudulent, the Cold War framework having been employed as a device to justify the suppression of independent nationalism—whether in Europe, Japan, or the Third World. "The USSR's demise has . . . forced the American foreign policy elite to be more candid in articulating the assumptions of American strategy," two foreign policy analysts observe in the lead article in *Foreign Policy*. We can no longer conceal the fact that "Underpinning U.S. world order strategy is the belief that America must maintain what is in essence a military protectorate in economically critical regions to ensure that America's vital trade and financial relations will not be disrupted by political upheaval"; this "economically determined strategy articulated by the foreign policy elite ironically (perhaps unwittingly) embraces a quasi-Marxist or, more correctly, a Leninist interpretation of American foreign relations," and also vindicates the much reviled "radical" analyses of William Appleman Williams "and other left-wing historians."[62]

We need only add the usual Smithian proviso: the trade and financial relations to be preserved are "vital" for the architects of policy and the powerful state and private interests they serve. They are often far from "vital" for the general population, for whom they may be very harmful. That is the case, for example, when the internationalization of production bequeaths them the status of the superfluous people of the Third World, a consequence that can readily be justified by the logic of "economic rationality," if no longer so easily by the familiar appeal to "security."

Understanding "security" in more reasonable terms, we may ask to what extent it has been a genuine factor in policy formation. Consider again the three major military build-ups (Truman, Kennedy, Reagan), on pretexts that ranged from weak to fabricated, suggesting that different motives were at work under a security cover. The suggestion is reinforced by the fact that actual security threats were not addressed. Thus by 1950, there was indeed a potential threat to U.S. security: ICBMs with advanced nuclear warheads. But policy-makers undertook no efforts to inhibit the development of weapons that might, eventually, endanger American security. The history of weapons development follows this pattern right to the end of the Cold War.[63]

Other aspects of policy formation reveal the same lack of concern for security. There was constant talk of the Soviet military threat, but it is important to recall just how it was conceived. The idea that the Russians might attack Western Europe was never taken very seriously, though Soviet military power, it was recognized, did pose a dual threat: it served to deter U.S. intervention in the Third World, and there was a danger that the USSR might react to the incorporation of its traditional enemies Germany and Japan within a military alliance run by its implacable foe in Washington, a genuine threat to its security, Western planners recognized. The formation of NATO appears to have been motivated less by an expectation that Stalin's forces might attack Western Europe than by fear of a neutralist European "third force," a "shortcut to suicide," Acheson held, on the premises already outlined. Preparing for the Washington meetings that led to the establishment of NATO—and in response, the Warsaw Pact—U.S. planners "became convinced that the Soviets might really be interested in striking a deal, unifying Germany, and ending the division of Europe," Melvyn Leffler writes in his comprehensive scholarly study. This was regarded not as an opportunity, but as a threat to the "primary national security goal": "to harness Germany's economic and military potential for the Atlantic community"—thus blocking the "suicide" of neutralism.[64]

Note that "national security" is used here not to refer to the security of the nation, which could only be harmed by instituting a bitter East–West conflict in Europe, but to economic and political goals of quite a different kind; and long-range, Leffler makes clear. Similarly the phrase "Atlantic community" does not refer to its people, but to the rich men who are to rule, again conventional usage. In fact, the strength and appeal of popular forces posed a problem of great concern to U.S. and British planners. These were among the factors that led them to prefer partition of Germany to unification and neutralism, which might have enhanced the power of European labor and democratic tendencies generally. Like the Americans, the British Foreign Office saw little likelihood of Soviet aggression, being concerned more over "economic and ideological infiltration" from the East, which it perceived as "something very like aggression"; political successes by the wrong people are commonly described as "aggression" in the internal record. In a united Germany, British planners warned, "the balance of advantage seems to lie with the Russians," who could exercise "the stronger pull," with an appeal to labor that was much feared at the time. Division of Germany was therefore to be preferred, with the Soviet Union excluded from any voice over the heartland of German industry in the wealthy Ruhr/Rhine industrial complex, and the labor movement weakened. The genuine security threat of the Cold War thus advanced another good-sized notch.

On similar grounds, the United States never considered Stalin's proposals for a unified and demilitarized Germany with free elections in 1952. Further Soviet initiatives in the mid-1950s were also rebuffed, in fear that they might be serious. The State Department, in an internal message of January 1956, warned of the need to tie "Germany organically into [the] Western Community so as to diminish [the] danger that over time a resurgent German nationalism might trade neutrality for reunification with [a] view to seizing [a] controlling position between East and West." "This was no mere fantasy conjured up by a fevered imagination," Geoffrey Warner comments in a review of newly declassified materials. "The Russians had intimated at the Geneva foreign ministers' conference that they might be prepared to concede free elections in Germany in exchange for neutrality," and secret negotiations between East and West Germany were being planned, perhaps were underway, by 1955. Still more significant, the Kennedy administration ignored Khrushchev's call for reciprocal moves after his radical cutbacks in Soviet military forces and armaments through 1961–63 (well-known to Washington, but dismissed). Gorbachev's far-reaching proposals for reduction of Cold War tensions were also largely ignored, even considered threatening.[65]

The basic reasons were those outlined by Churchill, with the missing footnote added: accommodation might have undermined the rule of the rich men of the rich nations, allowing unacceptable popular elements to gain influence over planning and policy. The suicide of neutralism might well contribute to such dangers, which were easily suppressed in the preferred context of Cold War confrontation. In that context, the United States was able for many years to impose order within the rich men's club as well, on the principle outlined by Henry Kissinger in the early 1970s: lesser members of the club are to pursue their "regional interests" within the "overall framework of order" managed by the United States, the only power with "global interests and responsibilities." One of the major current questions is how long Europe and Japan will accept that subordinate role.

The fact that security was not a prominent factor in policy formation has not gone unnoticed. In his standard scholarly study of containment, John Lewis Gaddis agrees with George Kennan's view—common among rational policymakers and analysts, including President Eisenhower and others— that "it is not Russian military power which is threatening us, it is Russian political power" (October 1947). From his extensive review of the record, Gaddis concludes further that "To a remarkable degree, containment has been the product, not so much of what the Russians have done, or of what has happened elsewhere in the world, but of internal forces operating within the United States. . . . What is surprising is the *primacy* that has been accorded economic considerations [namely, state economic management] in shaping strategies of containment, *to the exclusion of other considerations*" (his emphasis).[66] But like most others, Gaddis regards this consistent pattern as a surprising curiosity rather than an indication of policy; the discovery suggests nothing about the appropriateness of the framework of "deterrence" and "containment." What is "surprising," perhaps, is the difficulty of undertaking the kind of rational analysis that would be routine in other domains of inquiry, even in this one when we consider other states, particularly official enemies.

Gaddis's implicit recognition of Cold War realities tells only half the story: the domestic side. We have to add the "more candid [articulation of] the assumptions of American strategy" that the "foreign policy elite" can at last acknowledge, Cold War pretexts having eroded: the "Leninist" doctrine "underpinning U.S. world order strategy," which demands that "America must maintain what is in essence a military protectorate in economically critical regions to ensure that America's vital trade and financial relations will not be disrupted by political upheaval."

The conventional framework does become plausible if we interpret the concept of "national security" broadly enough, seeing it to be threatened if anything is out of control, on the assumptions outlined at the beginning of this subsection. It would follow, then, that U.S. "national security" is at risk if a speck in the Caribbean seeks an independent path, so that Grenada must be returned to the fold by violence—to become a "showcase for capitalism," the Reagan administration proudly announced as it poured in huge quantities of "aid" that left the wreckage "in terrible economic shape" apart from the influx of banks that have turned the "showcase" into "a fast-growing haven for money laundering, tax evasion and assorted financial fraud" (*Wall Street Journal*).[67] If we understand "security" to be threatened by any limitation on control over resources and markets, the conventional doctrines make perfect sense.

On the same assumptions, we can appreciate the justification for the Western invasion of Russia in 1918 offered by Gaddis in an influential retrospective study of the Cold War. The invasion was defensive, he concludes. It was undertaken "in response to a profound and potentially far-reaching intervention by the new Soviet government in the internal affairs, not just of the West, but of virtually every country in the world," namely, "the Revolution's challenge—which could hardly have been more categorical—to the very survival of the capitalist order." "The security of the United States" was "in danger" already in 1917, not just in 1950, and intervention was therefore entirely warranted in defense against the change of the social order in Russia and the announcement of revolutionary intentions.[68] The analysis is considered uncontentious, on the tacit assumptions already reviewed. By the same logic, "containment" and "deterrence" are cover terms for intervention and subversion by the United States and its allies.

A standard charge against the USSR was that its concept of "security" was so all-embracing that it entailed insecurity for everyone else—exactly the analysis of U.S. policy that we are invited to adopt by analysts of American policy today, in this case, recognizing its justice.

The conclusions are stark and clear. The conventional interpretation of the Cold War is plausible if we attribute to the United States a stance much like the image of "the Kremlin design for world domination" portrayed so luridly in NSC 68. Of course, Western commentators will be quick to point out the obvious distinction between the two cases: we are Good and they are Evil, and therefore it is only right and just that we should be in charge. Our essential goodness is unaffected by the disasters we have brought to large parts of the world, as we protected our "security." To cite the facts of history is to fall prey to "moral equivalence," or "political correctness," or "the error of atheism," or one of the other misdeeds concocted to guard against the sins of understanding and insight into the real world.

The Onset

The answer to the first question is that authentic security concerns were at most a minor factor in Cold War planning. A second natural question is: When did the conflict begin, and why? We have already seen one authoritative answer: the Cold War began when the Bolsheviks launched their aggressive "challenge . . . to the very survival of the capitalist order," compelling the West to assume the defensive stance it maintained from its 1918 invasion of Russia to the roll back strategy of NSC 68 and beyond. Gaddis's dating of the origins of the conflict is realistic, and shared by other serious historians.

Consider George Kennan, one of the leading architects of the post–World War II world, and a respected diplomatic historian as well, noted particularly for his scholarly work on Soviet–American relations. Here he traces the origins of the Cold War to the dissolution of the Constituent Assembly by the Bolsheviks in January 1918. This act created the breach with the West with "an element of finality," Kennan observes. British ambassador to Russia Sir George Buchanan was "deeply shocked," and advocated armed intervention to punish the crime. The Western invasion followed, and was taken quite seriously; as noted, Britain even used poison gas in 1919, no small matter shortly after World War I. Secretary of State Winston Churchill minuted that he "shd. v. much like the Bolsheviks to have it, if we can afford the disclosure" of this weapon; it was not only "recalcitrant Arabs" who merited such treatment, in his view. The idealistic Woodrow Wilson was particularly distraught by the dispersal of the Constituent Assembly, Kennan writes, a reaction that reflects the "strong attachment to constitutionality" of the American public, deeply offended by the sight of a government with no mandate beyond "the bayonets of the Red Guard."[69]

History was kind enough to construct a controlled experiment to test the sincerity of these elevated sentiments. A few months after the Bolsheviks dissolved the Constituent Assembly, outraging civilized opinion, Woodrow Wilson's army dissolved the National Assembly in occupied Haiti "by genuinely Marine Corps methods," in the words of Marine commander Major Smedley Butler. The reason was its refusal to ratify a constitution imposed by the invaders that gave U.S. corporations the right to buy up Haiti's lands. A Marine-run plebiscite remedied the problem: under Washington's guns, the U.S.-designed constitution was ratified by a 99.9 percent majority, with 5 percent of the population participating. Wilson's "strong attachment to constitutionality" was unmoved by the sight of a government with no mandate beyond "the bayonets of the Marine occupiers"; nor Kennan's.

Quite the contrary. To this day the events figure in the amusing reconstructions entitled "history" as an illustration of U.S. "humanitarian intervention," and its difficulties (for us). Thus "Haiti's tragic history should be a cautionary tale for those now eagerly pursuing Operation Restore Hope in Somalia," Robert Kaplan warns, recalling the difficulties we face as we seek "to heal the body politic of a land that lacks the basis of a modern political culture." *Times* political analyst Elaine Sciolino recalls that the Marines "kept order, collected taxes, arbitrated disputes, distributed food and medicine, and even censored criticism in the press and tried political offenders in military courts," the worst sin of the occupation. According to Harvard historian David Landes, the benevolent Marine occupation "provided the stability needed to make the political system work and to facilitate trade with the outside." Another noted scholar, Professor Hewson Ryan of the Fletcher School of Law and Diplomacy at Tufts University, is effusive in his praise for what the United States accomplished in "two centuries of well-intentioned involvement," beginning with U.S. support for France's violent and destructive attempt to repress the slave rebellion of 1791. "Few nations have been the object over such a sustained period of so much well-intentioned guidance and support," he writes—so that Haiti's current state is something of a mystery. Ryan is particularly impressed with Wilson's kind insistence on eliminating such "unprogressive" features of the constitutional system as the provisions against takeover of lands by foreigners, referring to his forceful dissolution of the National Assembly.[70]

Haitians have somewhat different memories of American solicitude. Grassroots organizations, priests in hiding, and others suffering bitterly from the violence of the security forces expressed marked opposition to the plan to dispatch five hundred UN police to the terrorized country in 1993, seeing them as a cover for a U.S. intervention that evokes bitter memories of the nineteen-year Marine occupation—a strange view held only by "radical leftists," in media terminology. Under the heading "unhealed sores," Haitian anthropologist Michel-Rolph Trouillot points out that "most observers agree that the achievements of the occupation were minor; they disagree only as to the amount of damage it inflicted," including the acceleration of Haiti's economic, military, and political centralization, its economic dependence and sharp class divisions, the vicious exploitation of the peasantry, the internal racial conflicts much intensified by the extreme racism of the occupying forces, and perhaps worst of all, the establishment of "an army to fight the people."[71] If ever noted, such reactions may be attributed to the backwardness and ignorance of Haitians, or the fact that "even a benevolent occupation creates resistance . . . among the beneficiaries" (Landes).

Gone from "history" along with the forceful dissolution of the National Assembly and imposition of the U.S.-dictated constitution is the restoration of virtual slavery, Marine massacres and terror, the establishment of a state terrorist force (the National Guard) that has kept its iron grip on the population ever since, and the takeover of Haiti by U.S. corporations, much as in the neighboring Dominican Republic, where Wilson's invading armies were only a shade less destructive.

Accordingly, Wilson is revered as a great moral teacher and the apostle of self-determination and freedom, and we may now consider returning to the heady days of Wilsonian idealism. The Bolsheviks, in contrast, had so violated our high ideals by dispersing the Constituent Assembly that they had to be overthrown by force.

The Cold War began in deceit and continued the same way, until the very end.

The Events of the Cold War

A third question that will be raised by anyone seeking to determine the nature of the Cold War is: What were the events that constituted it? Here we have to distinguish two phases: the period from the Bolshevik revolution to World War II, and the period of renewal of the conflict from the end of World War II to the final collapse of the Soviet Union. Consider first the Soviet side.

The first phase saw the quick demolition of incipient socialist tendencies, the institutionalization of a totalitarian state, and extraordinary atrocities, particularly under Stalin. Abroad, the USSR was not a major actor, though its leaders did what they could to undermine socialist and libertarian tendencies, their leading role in the demolition of Spanish libertarian social-ism being a prime example. No one considered the Soviet Union to be a *military* threat. Nevertheless, Western policies were much the same as those adopted as the second phase began.

The ideological facet of Western policy deserves at least brief mention. The Bolshevik takeover was recognized as an attack on socialism very quickly by a large part of the left, including leading left intellectuals, ranging from some of the most prominent intellectuals of the Marxist left (Anton Pannekoek, Rosa Luxemburg, and others) to such independent socialists as Bertrand Russell, and of course the libertarian (anarchist) left quite generally. It is not impossible that Lenin and Trotsky saw their actions in a similar light, regarding them, on orthodox Marxist grounds, as a "holding action" until the revolution took place in the advanced capitalist centers (Germany), at which point Russia would revert to a peripheral backwater. The inheritors of the Bolshevik counterrevolution described their regime as the epitome of democracy and socialism. The West naturally derided the pretense of democracy, but welcomed with enthusiasm the equally ridiculous claim to socialist ideals, seizing the opportunity to undermine challenges to the authoritarian institutions of state capitalism by associating socialism with Soviet anti-socialist tyranny. For various reasons, including its power and global dominance, Western propaganda set the general terms of discourse, even on the left. The early critique of the Bolshevik undermining of socialist and other popular initiatives of the pre-revolutionary period was quickly marginalized. For authentic socialists, the collapse of Soviet tyranny would have been a time of rejoicing, another barrier to socialism having been removed. The actual reaction was quite different: laments about the death of socialism, which makes about as much sense as describing what happened as the death of democracy. The reaction reveals not only the power of the Western propaganda system, but also the extent to which people who were committed anti-Stalinists, even anti-Leninists and anti-Marxists, in fact had a rather different relation to the Soviet counterrevolutionary tyranny than their more conscious commitments might have indicated, a topic that merits exploration in itself.

Soviet crimes were plainly not a factor in engendering Western hostility. As the historical record makes clear, the United States and its partners easily tolerate atrocious crimes or commit them directly if the interests of the rich men are served thereby. Atrocities become criminal when they interfere with these interests; otherwise they are of little moment. When Russia was needed to absorb the blows of Hitler's war machine, Stalin was the likable "Uncle Joe." In internal discussion with his close advisers, Roosevelt defended Stalin's plans for the Baltic states and Finland, and the shift of Poland's borders to the West. Churchill signed his notes to Stalin "Your friend and war-time comrade," while the British Embassy advised that in the light of shared British–Soviet interests and backgrounds, a closer alliance might result from the current "good start towards developing an atmosphere of greater confidence with our difficult ally," perhaps impeding American postwar designs that Britain regarded with some uneasiness. In Big Three meetings, Churchill praised Stalin as a "great man, whose fame has gone out not only over all Russia but the world," and spoke warmly of his relationship of "friendship and intimacy" with the bloodthirsty tyrant. "My hope," Churchill said, "is in the illustrious President of the United States and in Marshal Stalin, in whom we shall find the champions of peace, who after smiting the foe will lead us to carry on the task against poverty, confusion, chaos, and oppression." "Premier Stalin was a person of great power, in whom he had every confidence," Churchill told his cabinet in February 1945, after Yalta; and it was important that he should remain in charge. Churchill was particularly impressed with Stalin's support for Britain's brutal suppression of the Communist-led anti-fascist resistance in Greece.

Stalin's awesome crimes were also of no concern to President Truman. Truman liked and admired Stalin, whom he regarded as "honest" and "smart as hell"; his death would be a "real catastrophe," Truman felt. He remarked privately that he could "deal with" Stalin, as long as the United States got its way 85 percent of the time. What happened inside the USSR was not his concern. Other leading figures agreed.[72]

As with a host of other murderers and torturers, the unacceptable crime is disobedience. The same is true of priests who preach "the preferential option for the poor," secular nationalists in the Arab world, Islamic fundamentalists, democratic socialists, or independent elements of any variety. The crimes of enemies, real or manufactured, are useful for propaganda purposes; they have little impact on policy. On that matter, the record is overwhelming.

In its second phase, from 1945, major events of the Cold War on the Russian side were its repeated interventions in the East European satellites and the invasion of Afghanistan, the one Soviet act of aggression outside the traditional route through which Russia had been invaded and virtually destroyed three times in this century. Meanwhile the Soviet leadership sought targets of opportunity elsewhere, sometimes lending assistance to victims of American attack, sometimes supporting such tyrants and killers as the Argentine neo-Nazi generals and Mengistu of Ethiopia. Internal crimes abated; though remaining very serious they were scarcely at the level of typical American satellites, a commonplace in the Third World, where the norms of Western propriety do not hold.

Commenting in 1990 on the "velvet revolution" in Czechoslovakia, Guatemalan journalist Julio Godoy—who had fled his country a year earlier when his recently reopened newspaper was blown up by state terrorists—observed that Eastern Europeans are, "in a way, luckier than Central Americans":

> While the Moscow-imposed government in Prague would degrade and humiliate reformers, the Washington-made government in Guatemala would kill them. It still does, in a virtual genocide that has taken more than 150,000 victims . . . [in what Amnesty International calls] a "government program of political murder."

That, he suggested, is "the main explanation for the fearless character of the students' recent uprising in Prague: the Czechoslovak Army doesn't shoot to kill. . . . In Guatemala, not to mention El Salvador, random terror is used to keep unions and peasant associations from seeking their own way." There is an "important difference in the nature of the armies and of their foreign tutors." In the Soviet satellites, the armies were "apolitical and obedient to their national government," while in the U.S. client states, "the army *is* the power," doing what they have been trained to do for many decades by their foreign tutor. "One is tempted to believe that some people in the White House worship Aztec gods—with the offering of Central American blood." They have created and backed forces in El Salvador, Guatemala, and Nicaragua that "can easily compete against Nicolae Ceausescu's Securitate for the World Cruelty Prize."[73]

In respectable Western circles, such elementary truths would be considered outlandish and grotesque, let alone the conclusions that follow. Western norms require that we compare Eastern and Western Europe to demonstrate our virtue and their vileness, a childish absurdity, since the regions have not been alike for half a millennium. Elementary rationality would lead someone interested in alternative social and economic paths to compare societies that were more or less alike before the Cold War began, say Russia and Brazil, or Bulgaria and Guatemala; Brazil and Guatemala are particularly natural choices, as countries with considerable prospects (particularly Brazil) and under tight U.S. management for a very long period, even hailed as success stories of the American way. Such comparisons, if honestly undertaken, would elicit some self-reflection among decent people, but there is no danger of that: rationality is strictly *verboten* in this case too, because its consequences are completely unacceptable.[74]

Soviet abuses in the second (post–World War II) phase cannot seriously be offered as a motive for Western hostility. Again, we have to look elsewhere.

Let us now turn to events of the Cold War on the U.S. side during its two phases. Though not yet a dominant world power during the first phase, the United States did respond to the Bolshevik threat, which it interpreted then much as Gaddis does in retrospect.[75] "The fundamental obstacle" to recognition of the USSR, the chief of the Eastern European Division of the State Department held, "is the world revolutionary aims and practices of the rulers of that country." These "practices," of course, did not involve literal aggression; rather, interfering with Western designs, which is tantamount to aggression. The "aims and practices" reached to the core industrial societies themselves, providing the occasion for the Wilson administration to initiate its Red Scare, which successfully undermined democratic politics, unions, freedom of the press, and independent thought, while safeguarding business interests and their control over state power. The story was re-enacted after World War II, again under the pretext of the Kremlin conspiracy. In both cases, the repression was welcomed by the business community, the media, and liberal intellectuals rather generally, and did bring a period of quiescence and passivity, until the spell was broken by the Great Depression (in the first case) and the popular movements of the sixties (in the second).

As part of its policy of containment of the Soviet political threat, the United States lent vigorous support to Mussolini from the moment of his March on Rome in 1922, a "fine young revolution," as the American ambassador described the imposition of fascism. A decade later, President Roosevelt praised the "admirable Italian gentleman" who had demolished the parliamentary system and forcefully held the line against the labor movement, moderate socialists, and domestic Communists. Fascist atrocities were legitimate because they blocked the threat of a second Russia, the State Department explained. Hitler was supported as a moderate for the same reason. In 1937, the State Department saw fascism as the natural reaction of "the rich and middle classes, in self-defense" when the "dissatisfied masses, with the example of the Russian revolution before them, swing to the Left." Nazism and fascism elsewhere therefore "must succeed or the masses, this time reinforced by the disillusioned middle classes, will again turn to the left." At the same time Britain's special emissary to Germany, Lord Halifax, praised Hitler for blocking the spread of Communism, an achievement that brought England to "a much greater degree of understanding of all his work" than heretofore, as Halifax recorded his words to the German chancellor while he was conducting his reign of terror. The U.S. business world agreed. Fascist Italy was a great favorite of investors, and major U.S. corporations were heavily involved in Nazi war production, sometimes enriching themselves by joining in the plunder of Jewish assets under Hitler's Aryanization program. "U.S. investment in Germany accelerated rapidly after Hitler came to power," Christopher Simpson points out in a recent study, increasing "by some 48.5% between 1929 and 1940, while declining sharply everywhere else in continental Europe" and barely holding steady in Britain.[76]

In a recent review of British records, Lloyd Gardner concludes that "for the British, the immediate problem was still Russia," not Germany, during the period of the Stalin–Hitler pact (until June 1941). Deciding that war was necessary, high British officials "centered not on German efforts at partition [of Poland], which London had already dealt with as acceptable, but on the Nazi–Soviet pact, which was not acceptable."[77]

Support for fascism ended when it was recognized to be a real threat to Western interests. But the support was resumed very quickly. In Italy, American forces reinstated the traditional conservative order from 1943, including leading fascist collaborators, meanwhile dispersing the antifascist resistance, one aspect of the general program of the early postwar years to the same ends, worldwide. Subversion of Italian democracy was a major CIA project, at least into the 1970s, when the records run dry. In Greece, the same imperatives led to the first postwar counterinsurgency campaign, with enormous casualties and destruction.

The values guiding U.S. and British policy were revealed with particular clarity in northern Italy, which was under the control of the anti-Nazi resistance when Allied armies arrived, finding a functioning social order and economic base. British labor attaché W. H. Braine, who had the strong support of the British Labour Party, was particularly concerned over initiatives that workers had taken on their own. They had blocked dismissal of workers and, worst of all, established worker–management councils, selecting worker representatives after "arbitrary replacement" of business leaders, actions that must be reversed, Braine advised. He recognized that unemployment was the most serious problem, but "that is, however, Italy's own problem"; in contrast, restoration of the traditional order was the problem of the Allied forces. They pursued their priorities efficiently, safeguarding property, disarming the resistance, and bringing its Committee of National Liberation "to order," historian Federico Romero observes approvingly. The resistance, he writes, "useful though it was from a military point of view, had always inspired mistrust among the Allies, since it was a free political and social movement that was hard to control." It was becoming "a source of independent power and as such had to be changed." That accomplished, the military government would give special attention to "the education of the minds of the Italians towards a democratic way of life," the head of the Allied Control Commission, U.S. Admiral Ellery Stone, declared in a report that the State Department found "excellent."

Worker–management councils were particularly opposed by the Allied Military Government [AMG], "in accord with the views of the industrialists and the moderate political forces," Romero explains, using the term "moderate" in the conventional sense. The goal was to restore power to the hands of management, to overcome "ideological suggestions for restructuring the social order," to preserve the traditional "social hierarchy," and to prevent any popular challenge to "property ownership and hierarchy in industry" and any "anti-Fascist purge inspired by class-based criteria"; the last a consideration of considerable importance, in the light of the past history of the "moderates" who were to be restored to control. Once the government was firmly in the hands of the center-right, the unions split and marginalized, hierarchy in industry restored, and "order and discipline as well as full management control [returned] to the workplace," there was a welcome return to "normalcy," with "industrial relations founded on tripartite cooperation between government, industry, and unions"—in the proper measure. AMG power was thus able "to keep the working-class drive for political power in check, to rein in the most radical impulses of victorious antifascism, and to place the structure of industrial power under control, thus saving the prerogatives of the entrepreneurs."

Workers generally were a problem because they were "very influential" in the unions, Romero comments, thus undermining order. They had to be taught proper American-style apolitical unionism. The model was the AFL, in which a "small circle of union officials" were in charge of policy with nothing more than general approval at conventions, keeping "their close connections" with U.S. intelligence and the State Department, and focusing

on "eminently politico-strategic as opposed to merely trade union" operations. The problem posed by the Communists was that they enjoyed the
confidence of the population thanks to their "personal integrity" and "un-
equivocal anti-Fascist records," American labor attaché John Adams observed, and "the Communist Party is a true mass party whose principal aim
is the improvement of the material conditions of the workers." The popularity
of the party among workers was based on the fact that Communists alone
were "capable of offering an effective defense of their interests and the
prospect of improving their future social conditions" (Romero, paraphrasing
Adams). It therefore had to be undermined as well, along with the unions, in
the interests of "moderation" and "democracy." The United States made it
absolutely clear that aid would be denied and Italy would be left destitute and
helpless unless voters met their obligations, as they did under considerable
duress, establishing democracy. More forceful measures were planned if
those employed did not suffice to achieve the required outcome of "the
democratic process."[78]

Other U.S. operations in the years that followed included the overthrow
of the conservative parliamentary regime in Iran in 1953, restoring the Shah
and his brutal rule; the destruction of Guatemala's ten-year democratic
interlude, placing in power a collection of mass murderers who would have
won nods of approval from Himmler and Goering, with atrocities peaking in
the 1980s, always with the backing or direct participation of the United States
and its client states; support for France's effort to reconquer its former
colonies in Indochina, then the establishment of a Latin American–style
terror state in South Vietnam in violation of the 1954 Geneva accords, then
a murderous attack on South Vietnam under Kennedy when the state
terrorists could not control their own population, leading to a major war in
which millions were slaughtered and three countries devastated; the establishment and support for neo-Nazi National Security States in Latin America
from the early 1960s; the slaughter and destruction in Central America in the
1980s; and many similar exploits too numerous to mention.

Reviewing the events of the Cold War, we find, to a good first approxi-
mation, a picture like the following. At home, the Bolsheviks at once
established a totalitarian military–bureaucratic dictatorship, which reached
incredible levels of atrocities in the 1930s. Abroad, they helped suppress
socialism and freedom in the first phase of the Cold War, and in the second
phase repressed their satellites, often brutally, invaded Afghanistan, and
acted elsewhere in the normal cynical great power style. As for the United
States, in the first phase it employed the "Bolshevik threat" to beat back a
threat to business power at home and abroad. In the second phase, at home
the United States established a military-based industrial system, further
entrenching corporate power while weakening labor and other popular
elements; abroad, it carried out large-scale subversion, terror, and outright
aggression in the Third World while helping to shape the industrial societies
in the interests of the traditional masters, laying the basis for a world system

dominated by transnational corporations and finance. The East–West conflict is peripheral to the crucial events of the Cold War era, though by no means missing. It provided both powers with methods of population control, and each was able to interfere with the designs of the other by supporting targets of attack and by the deterrent effect of a powerful military. These features were by no means comparable: the global reach and violence of the United States far exceeded that of the second superpower; internal repression within the USSR was vastly beyond anything within the United States itself, though in the second phase, not at the level of U.S. satellites and clients; and the USSR may have exercised a greater deterrent effect on the ambitions of its rival, though here the lack of evidence from Soviet archives leaves important gaps of understanding.

Again, if the events of the Cold War constitute the Cold War, or even a large part of it, the conventional picture is very far from the mark.

Before and After

Consider a last question that evidently bears on the nature of the Cold War: What changes did it bring to policy formation? How did the events of the Cold War differ from those that preceded and followed? For the USSR, the question cannot seriously be raised, since the society changed so radically in 1917 and again as the Cold War ended. But for the United States, it is meaningful and informative.

Just before the Bolshevik takeover, Woodrow Wilson invaded Mexico, Haiti, and the Dominican Republic, with a lasting impact in the last two cases, particularly dreadful in Haiti. One reason was the extreme racism of the Wilson administration and its military forces, bad enough in the Dominican Republic, but an utter disgrace in Haiti, where it was undisguised. A high State Department official explained to Wilson's Secretary of State Robert Lansing that

> It is well to distinguish at once between the Dominicans and the Haitians. The former, while in many ways not advanced far enough for the highest type of self-government, yet have a preponderance of white blood and culture. The Haitians on the other hand are negro for the most part, and, barring a very few highly educated politicians, are almost in a state of savagery and complete ignorance.

Accordingly, Haiti requires "as complete a rule . . . as possible" by the American occupiers "for a long period of time," while lesser controls will suffice in the Dominican Republic.[79] Lansing quite agreed. His own view was that "the African race are devoid of any capacity for political organization and lack genius for government. Unquestionably there is an inherent tendency to revert to savagery and to cast aside the shackles of civilization which are irksome to their physical nature," a fact "which makes the negro problem practically unsolvable" in the United States as well. Lansing was, in fact, more catholic in his contempt for the human species, selected elements apart, as we see directly.

In Nicaragua, safely under Marine occupation, Wilson imposed a treaty that granted the United States perpetual rights to construct a canal, the purpose being to forestall any competitor to the Panama Canal. The treaty was an utter fraud, as recognized even by former Secretary of State Elihu Root, who noted that the government of a country under foreign military occupation has no legitimacy, surely no right "to make a treaty so serious for Nicaragua, granting us perpetual rights in that country." Costa Rica and El Salvador charged that the treaty infringed on their rights, a plea that was upheld by the Central American Court of Justice that had been established at U.S. initiative in 1907. The Wilson administration dealt with the problem by effectively destroying the Court; few noted the parallel when the United States dismissed the World Court condemnation of its attack on Nicaragua in 1986. A few years later, Wilson recognized a completely fraudulent election in Nicaragua and "acquiesced in a counterfeit reelection in Cuba in 1916–17," Latin Americanist Paul Drake observes, again in 1921, and in Honduras in 1919.[80]

It should not be thought that such actions were inconsistent with the high-minded principles of self-determination that Wilson preached. As Wilson made clear, the principles that are reverently entitled "Wilsonian idealism" did not apply to people "at a low stage of civilization," who must be given "friendly protection, guidance, and assistance" by the colonial powers that had tended to their needs in past years. Wilson's Fourteen Points held that in questions of sovereignty, "the interests of the populations concerned must have equal weight with the equitable claims of the government whose title is to be determined," the colonial ruler. Posturing aside, Wilson scarcely departed from the Churchillian doctrine.[81]

In short, the essential guidelines of U.S. policy did not change when the Bolsheviks took power, at once instituting the East–West conflict with "an element of finality." Adjustments were largely tactical, if we agree to use that mild phrase for the enthusiastic support for European fascism and dictatorship elsewhere (notably Venezuela, with its enormous oil resources).

The Cold War came to a definitive end with the fall of the Berlin wall in November 1989. George Bush celebrated the occasion by invading Panama, wasting no time in announcing that nothing would change. The U.S.–U.K. reaction to the second act of post–Cold War aggression, Iraq's invasion of Kuwait, merely reinforced this conclusion, as have subsequent events.

There was also no delay in demonstrating that the contempt for democracy that has long been a leading feature of U.S. policy and intellectual culture would persist without change. A typical example as the Cold War was fading was the 1984 election in Panama, stolen with fraud and violence by the murderous gangster Manuel Noriega, then still a U.S. friend and ally. The achievement was hailed by the Reagan administration, which had secretly funded the designated winner, to whom it sent a congratulatory message seven hours before his "election" had been certified. Secretary of State George Shultz flew down to legitimate the fraud, praising the election as "initiating the process of democracy" and challenging the Sandinistas to match Panama's high standards. Noriega's intervention successfully barred the victory of Arnulfo Arias, regarded by the State Department as an "undesirable ultranationalist," while the selected victor, a former student of Shultz's, was a well-behaved client, known ever since as "fraudito" in Panama.

In 1989, Noriega stole another election with less violence, this time eliciting a show of wrath from Washington and the media. In the interim, Noriega had shown improper signs of independence, offending the master by lack of sufficient enthusiasm for Washington's terrorist war against Nicaragua and in other ways. He had thus joined "that special fraternity of international villains, men like Qaddafi, Idi Amin, and the Ayatollah Khomeini, whom Americans just love to hate," the prominent TV commentator Ted Koppel orated. Koppel's colleague at ABC, anchorman Peter Jennings, denounced Noriega as "one of the more odious creatures with whom the United States has had a relationship." CBS's Dan Rather placed him "at the top of the list of the world's drug thieves and scums"—again, an insight missed in 1984. Others followed suit. When the odious creature was put on trial in the United States, having been kidnapped by the U.S. troops who invaded and occupied Panama, the charges against him were almost entirely from the period when he was a U.S. favorite, a fact that gained little notice. By the doctrine of "change of course," *now* we demand virtuous behavior on the part of Panamanian leaders. Briefly. Attention quickly declined as the poverty level rapidly increased, basic services collapsed, the U.S. puppet government lost what limited popularity it had, and human rights violations rose along with drug trafficking, which "may have doubled" since the invasion while money laundering has "flourished," the General Accounting Office of Congress reported, while the doctrinal managers averted their gaze.[82]

As the Berlin wall fell in November 1989, elections were held in Honduras, which had been converted into a base for U.S. terror in the region. The two candidates represented large landowners and wealthy industrialists. Their political programs were virtually identical; neither challenged the military, the effective rulers, under U.S. control. The campaign was confined to insults and entertainment. Human rights abuses by the security forces escalated before the election, though not to the level of El Salvador and Guatemala. Starvation and misery were rampant, having increased to a shocking level during the "decade of democracy" thanks largely to the neoliberal agroexport programs touted by U.S. advisers, and unprecedented U.S. "aid" that caused an unprecedented human catastrophe, as now conceded even in journals that were passionately calling on the United States to restore errant Nicaragua to the "Central American mode" of the U.S. terror states.[83] Also rising nicely were capital flight, profits for foreign investors, and the debt burden.

Accordingly, the elections were "an inspiring example of the democratic promise that today is spreading throughout the Americas," President Bush declared, no less inspiring than the one in Panama in 1984, or those in El Salvador in 1982 and 1984, with opposition leaders safely murdered and civil society demolished by U.S.-run terrorists (called "security forces").

In the same month, November 1989, the electoral campaign opened in Nicaragua. Its 1984 elections do not exist in U.S. commentary. The United States could not control them, so they are banned outright from the doctrinal system. Only those well outside the reigning intellectual culture are aware of the positive reports of numerous Western observers, including a hostile official Dutch government delegation so tolerant of U.S.-backed atrocities that they saw no problem in the exclusion of the "left" from El Salvador's elections by terror and mass murder, European parliamentary delegations, the professional association of Latin American scholars, the leading figure of Central American democracy, José Figueres, and many others, critical of the Sandinistas but in accord that the elections were well-run and fair, remarkably so for a country under attack by a superpower. Also under a ban is the fact that the 1990 elections had long been scheduled; loyalty to the state requires that they were held only because of U.S. pressures, which were therefore justified, so this doctrine too is adopted without question.

As the campaign opened in November 1989, the White House and Congress at once made it clear that the terror and economic warfare would continue unless the U.S. candidate was elected. In the United States—indeed, the West generally—none of this was considered an interference with "the democratic process." The U.S. candidate was duly elected in February 1990. In Latin America, the outcome was generally interpreted as a victory for George Bush, even by those who celebrated it. In the United States, in contrast, it was hailed as a "Victory for U.S. Fair Play," with "Americans United in Joy" in the style of Albania and North Korea, as *New York Times* headlines proudly proclaimed. At the dissident extreme, *Times* columnist Anthony Lewis was overjoyed at the success of Washington's noble "experiment in peace and democracy," which gave "fresh testimony to the power of Jefferson's idea: government with the consent of the governed. . . . To say so seems romantic, but then we live in a romantic age." The victory showed how the United States has "served as an inspiration for the triumph of democracy in our time," the editors of the liberal *New Republic* exulted. Even critical scholarship agrees that "the most free and fair national election in that country's history" is one of the triumphs of the Reagan era, a period "when U.S. efforts to promote Latin American democracy were particularly notable" (Abraham Lowenthal).

The *Times*'s Kim Il Sung rendition is accurate: the media and respectable intellectual opinion were indeed "United in Joy" in hailing the success in subverting democracy, fully aware of how the grand victory was achieved. Thus, *Time* magazine rejoiced over the latest of the "happy series of democratic surprises" as "democracy burst forth" in Nicaragua, outlining the methods of "U.S. Fair Play" with admirable frankness: to "wreck the economy and prosecute a long and deadly proxy war until the exhausted natives overthrow the unwanted government themselves," with a cost to us that is "minimal," leaving the victim "with wrecked bridges, sabotaged power stations, and ruined farms," and providing Washington's candidate with "a winning issue," ending the "impoverishment of the people of Nicaragua."[84]

Indeed, "we live in a romantic age," when electoral victories can be won by such pure Jeffersonian means.

For untutored folk who may sense some residual problems here, there are ready answers. Reviewing a study of U.S. policy towards Latin America by Robert Pastor, *New York Times* Central America and Washington correspondent Clifford Krauss remarks derisively that "he automatically takes exception to the Reagan administration's Central America policy, particularly in Nicaragua, but he fails to make a persuasive case that the Sandinistas would have competed in fair elections had they been free of military pressure." Two points merit notice. First, like a mere 100 percent of his colleagues in the Free Press and respectable intellectual culture, Krauss excludes from history the 1984 elections in Nicaragua; they did not take place, by the doctrine of presidential infallibility. But more interesting is his easy acceptance of the doctrine that we have the right to use our power in arbitrary ways to achieve our ends, and what we achieve by violence and strangulation is "fair"—not an innovation to be sure; there are distinguished predecessors, whom we need not name.

Krauss's doctrine is considered uncontroversial. Thus, from democratic socialist left to far right, the major criticism of the U.S. attack on South Vietnam and its neighbors (invariably called "the defense of South Vietnam") was that it failed; opinion then divides on whether U.S. goals could have been attained at reasonable cost, and whether we consider only cost to us, or also to them (the ultraliberal view). There was little reaction when the U.S. military command stated that its terrorist forces invading Nicaragua were directed to avoid military forces and hit "soft targets." When the State Department confirmed U.S. support for attacks on agricultural cooperatives, arousing protest from Americas Watch, Michael Kinsley, who represents the dovish left in mainstream commentary and television debate, cautioned against thoughtless condemnation of Washington's official policy. Such international terrorist operations cause "vast civilian suffering," he agreed, but they may nevertheless be "sensible," even "perfectly legitimate," if they "undermine morale and confidence in the government" that the United States seeks to overthrow. Terror is to be evaluated by sober "cost–benefit analysis," which seeks to determine whether "the amount of blood and misery that will be poured in" yields "democracy," in the special sense of U.S. political culture. Like aggression, terror must satisfy the pragmatic criterion of efficacy, nothing more. The same criterion continues to extend automatically to client states, as we shall see.

At the other end of the political spectrum, the doctrine is interpreted by Nestor Sanchez, a high Pentagon official under Reagan, who was "plainly impatient . . . with renewed interest in the Salvadoran war," the press reported, when the UN Truth Commission produced evidence of U.S. government complicity in terrible massacres. "We won," Sanchez said. "Why do we have to beat a dead horse? You go into a prize fight and the winner knocks out the contender, and then you question the blow? That's stupid."[85]

The spectrum of opinion extends all the way from those who hold that anything goes if you win, to the soft-hearted souls who feel that rivers of "blood and misery" are meritorious only if something like Honduras rises to the surface: "democracy." The ethical standards of the New World Order, and the meaning of "democracy" within it, are revealed again with great clarity.

The Nicaragua story, to which we return in the next chapter, took the familiar next step in 1994. On March 15, U.S. Assistant Secretary of State Alexander Watson announced that "with the conflicts of the past behind us, the Clinton administration accepts the Sandinistas as a legitimate political force in Nicaragua with all the rights and obligations of any party in a democracy supposing that it uses only peaceful and legitimate methods," as we did through the 1980s, setting the stage for a "fair election," by U.S. standards. The brief Reuters report noted that "the United States financed the Contra rebels against the Soviet-backed Sandinista government." Translating from Newspeak, Washington followed standard procedure, doing everything it could to compel Nicaragua to abandon its efforts to maintain a nonaligned stand and balanced trade and to turn to the Russians as a last resort, so that Washington's attack could be construed as part of the Cold War conflict raging in our backyard, now to be dispatched to the category of irrelevance for understanding ourselves, or what the future holds. Here we see, clearly delineated, the real significance of the Cold War for policy.[86]

Elsewhere in the region, the democratic revolution proceeded on course. In November 1993, Hondurans went to the polls again, for the fourth time since 1980. They voted against the neoliberal structural adjustment programs and the "economic miracle" they are to bring with them. But as widely recognized, the gesture is empty; the rich and powerful will permit nothing else. "The voters have no real options for improving their living standards which worsen every day," Mexico's major newspaper *Excelsior* reported— familiar with "economic miracles" in its own country. Three-fourths of those who went to the polls "live in misery and are disenchanted with formal democracy." Hondurans' purchasing power is lower than in the 1970s, and the rule of the Generals is more firmly established. There are other beneficiaries as well, the Honduran College of Economists points out: "a group of privileged exporters and local investors linked to financial capital and multinational corporations who have multiplied their capital" in a country where "growing economic polarization is generating ever more evident contrasts, between the rich who do not hide the ostentation of their moral misery and the ever more miserable poor." "At least one of every two dollars coming to Honduras has left in the last three years [1991–93] to pay the interest on more than $3 billion foreign debt," *Excelsior* continues. Debt service now represents 40 percent of exports; and though almost 20 percent of the debt was forgiven, it has increased by almost 10 percent since 1990.[87]

In March 1994, the "democracy promotion" project reached El Salvador. The elections conducted in the 1980s to legitimize the U.S.-backed terror state were hailed at the time as impressive steps towards democracy ("demonstration elections," as Edward Herman accurately called them). But with the policy imperatives of those days gone, the pretense has been quietly shelved. It is the 1994 elections that are to represent the triumph of the Washington-inspired democratic revolution.

The elections were indeed an innovation in that at least the forms were maintained, pretty much. "Tens of thousands of voters who had electoral cards were unable to vote because they did not appear on electoral lists," the *Financial Times* reported, "while some 74,000 people, a high number of which were from areas believed to be sympathetic to the FMLN [opposition], were excluded because they did not have birth certificates." FMLN leaders alleged that more than 300,000 voters were excluded in such ways, charging "massive" fraud. The left coalition presidential candidate Rubén Zamora estimated "conservatively" that over 10 percent of voters were barred. Central America correspondent David Dye estimated that the government "managed to avoid getting mandatory voting cards into the hands of 340,000 voters and denied them outright to 80,000 others (many of whom live in zones formerly controlled by the guerrillas)," and "disproportionately FMLN supporters." There was also "a suspect voting list containing the names of many dead Salvadorans." The coordinator of the Vigilance Board that was supposed to oversee the vote count, Felix Ulloa, said that "after fighting against impunity in the judiciary and armed forces, we have run up against electoral impunity as well."

The UN mission downplayed the problems, but independent observers were not convinced. "I used to give them the benefit of the doubt," the official British observer commented, "but it comes to the point when you have to say it is bad faith," referring to the "bad administration" of the election by the governing Arena party, which received almost half the votes cast, and the UN mission reaction.[88]

But the irregularities, whatever they may have been, do not change the fact that the elections broke new ground at a formal level. There was no blatant fraud or massive terror; rather, minor fraud against the background of the successful use of terror and repression, with a narrow aspect that received some attention, and a broader and more significant one that did not.

The fate of the church radio station is a symbolic illustration of the progress that has been made. Just before the 1980 assassination of Archbishop Oscar Romero on orders of Arena founder and hero Roberto D'Aubuisson, the station was twice bombed off the air after the archbishop had delivered homilies criticizing the government. But fourteen years later, when officials were infuriated with Archbishop Arturo Rivera Damas's homily criticizing Arena and its founder for their involvement in terror, the radio station was not blown up to silence the homily that was to be delivered the next Sunday, right before the election. Rather, just as the mass started, the state-owned telephone company cut the lines that would have allowed the homily to be broadcast as it is every week, opening the line again after it was completed.[89]

In the 1994 elections, the United States supported Arena, the party of the death squads, a fact understood throughout though denied for propaganda reasons. Partial declassification of documents, mostly from the early 1980s, has revealed that much. It also illustrates once again the main reason why documents are classified in the first place: not for security reasons, as alleged, but to undermine American democracy by protecting state power from popular scrutiny. In February 1985 the CIA reported that "behind ARENA's legitimate exterior lies a terrorist network led by D'Aubuisson and funded by wealthy Salvadoran expatriates residing in Guatemala and the United States," using "both active-duty and retired military personnel in their campaigns"; "death squads in the armed forces operate out of both urban military headquarters and rural outposts." The CIA noted "the broad sponsorship for rightwing terrorism by ARENA," providing ample evidence of relationships with the security forces, including high-level officers. The main death squad, the "Secret Anti-Communist Army," was described in a "Selective Study on Death Squads" of the CIA and State Department as the "paramilitary organization" of Arena, led by the Constituent Assembly security chief and drawing most of its members from the National Police and other security forces. "Membership in ARENA's death squad varies between 10 and 20 individuals, composed of members of the military, the National Police, the Treasury Police and selected civilians," targeting primarily "their principal competitors for political power," the "revolutionary left and members of the Christian Democratic Party." The Reagan Administration consistently denied the detailed facts known to it, attributing death squad activity to rightwing extremists with no high-level government or military involvement or institutional responsibility.

The military and police themselves, of course, were the major terrorist forces, carrying out the great mass of the atrocities against the civilian population, funded directly from Washington, which was also responsible for their training and direction. The released documents reveal Arena involvement in terror as recently as 1990, including the vice president and its 1994 presidential candidate.[90]

As the 1994 elections approached, there was a "resurgence in death squad–style murders and death threats," Americas Watch observed, concluding that "no issue represents a greater threat to the peace process than the rise in political murders of leaders and grassroots activists" of the FMLN, assassinations that "became more frequent, brazen, and selective in the fall of 1993." These "injected a level of fear, almost impossible to measure, into the campaign," enhanced by government cover-ups and refusal to investigate, part of a pattern of violation of the peace treaty, to which we return. The government's own human rights office and the UN Observer Mission reported the "grave deterioration in citizen security" made worse by "organized violence in the political arena." This proceeds against the backdrop of an "astronomical rise of crime in post-war El Salvador," Americas Watch reports, and "reliable" evidence that the army and National Police are involved in organized crime.[91]

The major political opposition, Rubén Zamora's left coalition, not only lacked resources for the campaign that was virtually monopolized by Arena, but was "unable to convince supporters or sympathizers to appear in campaign ads because they fear retaliation from the right" (*New York Times*). Terror continued at a level sufficient to give substance to such fears. Among those who took the threat seriously was José María Mendez, named El Salvador's "Lawyer of the Century" by three prestigious legal associations. He fled the country shortly after, threatened with death unless he convinced the vice-presidential candidate of the left coalition to resign.

Foreign observers were struck by the lack of popular interest in the "elections of the century." "Salvadorans Ambivalent Toward Historic Poll," a headline in the *Christian Science Monitor* read, reporting fear and apathy, and concern that war will return unless Arena wins. The 45 percent abstention rate was about the same as ten years earlier, at the peak of the violence (not to speak of Salvadorans who fled abroad). An analyst quoted by the *New York Times* (political scientist Héctor Dada) attributed the low participation "to a deliberate disenfranchisement of voters and a sense of apathy among the electorate." As for those who voted, another analyst, Luis Cardenal, observed that "the electorate voted more than anything for tranquillity, for security." "The war-weary populace bought the ruling party's party line, which equated ARENA with security and the left with instability and violence," *Christian Science Monitor* reporter David Clark Scott added. That is plausible enough. Any other outcome could be expected to lead to revival of the large-scale terror and atrocities.[92]

These assessments bear on the broader aspects of the successful use of violence. Before the election, church and popular sources attributed the "climate of apathy" to the fact that "hunger and poverty reign among a population whose demands have received no attention, which makes the electoral climate difficult."[93] In the 1970s, popular organizations were proliferating, in part under church auspices, seeking to articulate these demands in the political arena and to work to overcome hunger, poverty, and harsh oppression. It was that popular awakening that elicited the response of the state terror apparatus and its superpower sponsor, committed as always to a form of "democracy promotion" that bars the threat of democracy—by extreme violence, if necessary, as in this case. Here as elsewhere, the programs of the terrorist superpower were highly successful, leading to the "climate of apathy," the search for security above all else, and the general conditions in which "free elections" become tolerable.

The lesson of the election, Héctor Dada observed, "was that without a [strong] civil society, you cannot have free, democratic elections. These elections laid bare the real problem. You have to build democratic structures in order to guarantee elections."[94] That is both accurate and well understood by the powerful. It is the basic reason why formal democratic procedures are restricted, where possible, to situations in which civil society has either been demolished by violence or sufficiently intimidated and undermined to ensure an approved outcome, with no "free political and social movements" that are "hard to control," as in Italy after liberation, and elsewhere over and over again. The pattern is common up to the level of virtual invariance, and remains obscure only to those who are dedicated to remaining in ignorance themselves, and inducing blindness in others.

A January 1994 conference of Jesuits and lay associates in San Salvador considered both the narrow and the broad aspects of the state terrorist project. Its summary report concludes that "it is important to explore to what degree terror continues to act, cloaked by the mask of common crime. Also to be explored is what weight the culture of terror has had in domesticating the expectations of the majority vis-a-vis alternatives different to those of the powerful, in a context in which many of the revolutionaries of yesterday act today with values similar to the long powerful."[95]

The latter issue, the broader one, is of particular significance. The great achievement of the massive terror operations of the past years organized by Washington and its local associates has been to destroy hope. The observation generalizes to much of the Third World and also to the growing masses of superfluous people at home, as the Third World model of sharply two-tiered societies is increasingly internationalized, a matter to which we return. These are major themes of the "New World Order" being constructed by the privileged sectors of global society, with U.S. state and private power in the lead.

A rational observer can easily comprehend the meaning of the "broad bipartisan agreement in Washington today that fostering democracy in Latin America—and elsewhere, for that matter—is a legitimate and significant goal of the U.S. policy and that the United States can be effective in pursuing that aim" (Abraham Lowenthal, expressing a near-uniform consensus). Praise for this stance is untroubled by the frank recognition that democratic advances have been uncorrelated (even negatively correlated) with U.S. influence, and that in recent years, the United States has continued "to adopt prodemocracy policies as a means of relieving pressure for more radical change, but inevitably sought only limited, top-down forms of democratic change that did not risk upsetting the traditional structures of power with which the United States has long been allied" (former Reagan State Department official Thomas Carothers, surveying Reaganite policies). Any qualms can again be deflected by the doctrine of "change of course." Carothers describes the goal of these "democracy assistance projects" (in which he was directly involved while serving in Reagan's State Department) as to maintain "the basic order of . . . quite undemocratic societies" and to avoid "populist-based change" that might upset "established economic and political orders" and open "a leftist direction." He observes that where democratic change occurred—primarily in the southern cone, where U.S. influence was least—Washington opposed it while later taking credit for it, and that where U.S. influence was preponderant, it sought the kind of "democracy" that he accurately describes. He regards the "U.S. impulse to promote democracy" as "sincere" but generally ineffective, and often limited to rhetoric. The policies were flawed, he holds (though in an oddly systematic way), and were failures. An alternative interpretation is that the policies succeeded in their actual aims, which is why they are acclaimed in the culture of respectability, and why they fall into a pattern that is close to exceptionless.[96]

A highly instructive illustration of persistent U.S. policy is one that is rarely discussed: Colombia, which has taken first place in the competition for leading terrorist state in Latin America—and, to the surprise of no one familiar with "sound-bites and invectives about Washington's historically evil foreign policy," has become the leading recipient of U.S. military aid, accompanied by much praise for its stellar accomplishments. Here the Cold War connection is close to zero—as, in reality, it was in the other cases as well. The example merits close attention.

Latin Americanist John Martz writes that "Colombia now enjoys one of the healthiest and most flourishing economies in Latin America. And in political terms its democratic structures, notwithstanding inevitable flaws, are among the most solid on the continent," a model of "well-established political stability." The Clinton administration is particularly impressed by outgoing President César Gaviria, whom it successfully promoted as Secretary General of the Organization of American States because, as the U.S. representative to the OAS explained, "he has been very forward looking in building democratic institutions in a country where it was sometimes dangerous to do so," also "forward looking . . . on economic reform in Colombia and on economic integration in the hemisphere," code words that are readily interpreted.[97] That it has been dangerous to build democratic institutions in Colombia is true enough, thanks in no small measure to President Gaviria, his predecessors, and their supporters in Washington.

The "inevitable flaws" are reviewed in some detail—once again—in 1993–94 publications of the major human rights monitors, Americas Watch and Amnesty International.[98] They find "appalling levels of violence," the worst in the hemisphere. Since 1986, more than twenty thousand people have been killed for political reasons, most of them by the Colombian military and police and the paramilitary forces that are closely linked to them; for example, the private army of rancher, emerald dealer, and reputed drug dealer Victor Carranza, considered to be the largest in the country, dedicated primarily to the destruction of the leftwing political opposition Patriotic Union (UP), in alliance with police and military officers. The department in which Carranza operates (Meta) is one of the most heavily militarized, with some thirty-five thousand troops and thousands of police. Nevertheless, paramilitary forces and hired killers operate freely, carrying out massacres and political assassinations. An official government inquiry in the early 1980s found that over a third of the members of paramilitary groups engaged in political killings and other terror in Colombia were active-duty military officers; the pattern continues, including the usual alliances with private power and criminal sectors.

More than fifteen hundred leaders, members, and supporters of UP have been assassinated since the party was established in 1985. This "systematic elimination of the leadership" of UP is "the most dramatic expression of political intolerance in recent years," AI observes—one of the "inevitable flaws" that make it "dangerous to build democratic institutions," if not quite the danger that the Clinton administration sought to identify. Other "dangers" were illustrated at the March 1994 elections, largely bought by the powerful Cali cocaine cartel, critics allege, noting the history of vote-buying in this "stable democracy," the vast amounts of money spent by the cartel, and the low turnout.[99]

The pretext for terror operations is the war against guerrillas and narcotraffickers, the former a very partial truth, the latter "a myth," AI concludes in agreement with other investigators; the myth was concocted in large measure to replace the "Communist threat" as the Cold War was fading along with the propaganda system based on it. In reality, the official security forces and their paramilitary associates work hand in glove with the drug lords, organized crime, landowners, and other private interests in a country where avenues of social action have long been closed, and are to be kept that way by intimidation and terror. The government's own Commission to Overcome Violence concluded that "the criminalization of social protest" is one of the "principal factors which permit and encourage violations of human rights" by the military and police authorities and their paramilitary collaborators.

The problems have become much worse in the past ten years, particularly during President Gaviria's term, when "violence reached unprecedented levels," the Washington Office on Latin America (WOLA) reports, with the National Police taking over as the leading official killers. Nineteen ninety-two was the most violent year in Colombia since the 1950s, when hundreds of thousands were killed; 1993 proved to be still worse.[100] Atrocities run the gamut familiar in the spheres of U.S. influence and support: death squads, "disappearance," torture, rape, massacre of civilian populations under the doctrine of "collective responsibility," and aerial bombardment. Elite counterinsurgency and mobile brigades are among the worst offenders. Targets include community leaders, human rights and health workers, union activists, students, members of religious youth organizations, and young people in shanty towns, but primarily peasants. Merely to give one example, from August 1992 to August 1993, 217 union activists were murdered, "a point that demonstrates the strong intolerance on the part of the State of union activity," the Andean Commission of Jurists comments.[101] The official concept of "terrorism" has been extended to virtually anyone opposing government policies, the human rights reports observe.

One project of the security forces and their allies is "social cleansing"—that is, murder of vagrants and unemployed, street children, prostitutes, homosexuals, and other undesirables. The Ministry of Defense formulated the official attitude toward the matter in response to a compensation claim: "There is no case for the payment of any compensation by the nation, particularly for an individual who was neither useful nor productive, either to society or to his family."

The security forces also murder suspects, another practice to which we return that is familiar in U.S. domains, and accepted as routine. The plague of murder for sale of organs, rampant through the domains of U.S. influence, has also not spared Colombia, where undesirables are killed so that their corpses "can be chopped up and sold on the black market for body parts" (AI), though it is not known whether the practice extends to kidnapping of children for this purpose, as elsewhere in the region (see pp. 134, 137 and references cited).

The Colombian model is that of El Salvador and Guatemala, the Human Rights groups observe. The doctrines instilled by U.S. advisers and trainers can be traced back directly to the Nazis, as Michael McClintock documented in an important study that has been ignored. Colombia has also enjoyed the assistance of British, German, and Israeli mercenaries who train assassins and perform other services for the narco–military–landlord combine in their war against peasants and social activism. There seems to have been no attempt to investigate the report of Colombian intelligence that North Americans have also been engaged in these operations.[102]

Other similarities to Washington's Salvador–Guatemala model abound. Consider, for example, the case of Major Luis Felipe Becerra, charged with responsibility for an army massacre by a civilian judge, who fled the country under death threats days after issuing the arrest warrant (her father was then murdered). But the warrants were not served, because Major Becerra was in the United States undergoing a training course for promotion to Lieutenant-Colonel. Returning after his promotion, Lt.-Col. Becerra was appointed to head the army's press and public relations department, despite a recommendation by the Procurator Delegate to the Armed Forces that he be dismissed for his part in the peasant massacre. In April 1993, charges against him were dropped. In October, he was again implicated in a massacre of unarmed civilians. Under the pretext of a battle against guerrillas, troops under his command executed thirteen people in a rural area; the victims were unarmed, the women were raped and tortured, according to residents of the area.[103]

But impunity prevails, as is regularly the case. The story is that of Central America, Haiti, Brazil, indeed wherever the Monroe Doctrine extends, along with the Philippines, Iran under the Shah, and other countries that have some properties in common, though the doctrinal requirement is that we not notice the curious fact, or entertain the thesis it might suggest.

A detailed 1992 investigation by European and Latin American church and human rights organizations concludes that "state terrorism in Colombia is a reality: it has its institutions, its doctrine, its structures, its legal arrangements, its means and instruments, its victims, and above all its responsible authorities." Its goal is "systematic elimination of opposition, criminalization of large sectors of the population, massive resort to political assassination and disappearance, general use of torture, extreme powers for the security forces, exceptional legislation, etc. ...."[104] The modern version has its roots in the security doctrines pioneered by the Kennedy administration, which established them officially in a 1962 decision of truly historic importance, which shifted the mission of the Latin American military from "hemispheric defense" to "internal security": the war against the "internal enemy," understood in practice to be those who challenge the traditional order of domination and control.

The doctrines were expounded in U.S. manuals of counterinsurgency and low intensity conflict, and developed further by local security authorities who benefited from training and direction by U.S. advisers and experts, new technologies of repression, and improved structures and methodologies to maintain "stability" and obedience. The result is a highly efficient apparatus of official terror, designed for "total war" by state power "in the political, economic, and social arenas," as the Colombian minister of defense articulated the standard doctrine in 1989. While officially the targets were guerrilla organizations, a high military official explained in 1987 that these were of minor importance: "the real danger" is "what the insurgents have called the political and psychological war," the war "to control the popular elements" and "to manipulate the masses." The "subversives" hope to influence unions, universities, media, and so on. Therefore, the European–Latin American *State Terror* inquiry observes, the "internal enemy" of the state terrorist apparatus extends to "labor organizations, popular movements, indigenous organizations, opposition political parties, peasant movements, intellectual sectors, religious currents, youth and student groups, neighborhood organizations," and so on, all legitimate targets for destruction because they must be secured against undesirable influences. "Every individual who in one or another manner supports the goals of the enemy must be considered a traitor and treated in that manner," a 1963 military manual prescribed, as the Kennedy initiatives were moving into high gear.

The ideology of the war against "subversives" undertaken by the U.S.-backed state terrorists merits comparison with the thinking developed in the leading Cold War document, NSC 68, with regard to the superpower itself (see p. 3). NSC 68 warns that we must overcome such weaknesses in our society as "the excesses of a permanently open mind," "the excess of tolerance," and "dissent among us." We must "distinguish between the necessity for tolerance and the necessity for just suppression," the latter a crucial feature of "the democratic way." It is particularly important to insulate our "labor unions, civic enterprises, schools, churches, and all media for influencing opinion" from the "evil work" of the Kremlin, which seeks to subvert them and "make them sources of confusion in our economy, our culture and our body politic." Lavishly funded "conservative" foundations are busily at work on the same project today. In the United States, of course, we do not call out the death squads to preserve democracy by "just suppression." Third World client states are more free in their choice of methods to excise the cancer.

The war against the "internal enemy" in Colombia escalated in the 1980s as the Reaganites updated the Kennedy doctrines, moving from "legal" repression to "systematic employment of political assassination and disappearance, later massacres" (*State Terror*). Atrocities escalated. A new judicial regime in 1988 "allowed maximal criminalization of the political and social opposition" in order to implement what was officially called "total war against the internal enemy." The use of paramilitary auxiliaries for terror, explicitly authorized in military manuals, also took new and more comprehensive forms; and alliances with industrialists, ranchers and landowners, and later narcotraffickers were more firmly entrenched. The 1980s saw "the consolidation of state terror in Colombia," the inquiry concludes.

In its December 1993 study, Americas Watch observes that "most of the material used by and training provided the Colombian army and police come from the United States," mainly counterinsurgency equipment and training. A study of the "drug war" by the U.S. General Accounting Office in August 1993 concluded that U.S. military officials have not "fully implemented end-use monitoring procedures to ensure that Colombia's military is using aid primarily for counter-narcotic purposes," an oversight with limited import, considering what falls under the rubric of "counter-narcotic purposes." Washington's own interpretation of such purposes was nicely illustrated in early 1989 when Colombia asked it to install a radar system to monitor flights from the south, the source of most of the cocaine for the drug merchants. The U.S. government fulfilled the request—in a sense; it installed a radar system on San Andrés island in the Caribbean, five hundred miles from mainland Colombia and as far removed as possible on Colombian territory from the drug routes, but well-located for the intensive surveillance of Nicaragua that was a critical component of the terrorist war, then peaking as Washington sought to conclude its demolition of the "peace process" of the Central American presidents (as it did, another fact unlikely to enter history). A Costa Rican request for radar assistance in the drug war ended up the same way.[105]

From 1984 through 1992, 6,844 Colombian soldiers were trained under the U.S. International Military Education and Training Program, over two thousand from 1990 to 1992, as atrocities were mounting. The Colombian program is the largest in the hemisphere, three times that of El Salvador. U.S. advisors are helping build military bases, officially to "increase the battle-fronts against the guerrillas and narcotrafficking operations." Washington is also supporting the "public order" courts that operate under conditions that severely undermine civil rights and due process.

In July 1989, the State Department submitted a report entitled "Justification for Determination to Authorize Export–Import Act Guarantees and Insurance for Sales of Military Equipment to Colombia for Antinarcotics Purposes," the official cover story. The report states: "Colombia has a democratic form of government and does not exhibit a consistent pattern of gross violations of internationally recognized human rights." Three months later, the UN Special Rapporteur on Summary Executions, Amos Wako, returned from a visit to Colombia with severe warnings about the extreme violence of the paramilitary forces in coordination with drug lords and government security forces: "There are currently over 140 paramilitary groups operating in Colombia today [which are] trained and financed by drug traffickers and possibly a few landowners. They operate very closely with elements in the armed forces and the police. Most of the killings and massacres carried out by the paramilitary groups occur in areas which are heavily militarized [where] they are able to move easily . . . and commit murders with impunity. In some cases, the military or police either turn a blind eye to what is being done by paramilitary groups or give support by offering safe conduct passes to members of the paramilitary or by impeding investigation." His mandate did not extend to the direct terror of the security forces, which far outweighs the depredations of its informal allies.

A few months before the State Department praise for Colombia's humane democracy, a church-sponsored development and research organization published a report documenting atrocities in the first part of 1988, including over three thousand politically motivated killings, 273 in "social cleansing" campaigns.[106] Excluding those killed in combat, political killings averaged eight a day, with seven murdered in their homes or in the street and one "disappeared." "The vast majority of those who have disappeared in recent years," WOLA added, "are grassroots organizers, peasant or union leaders, leftist politicians, human rights workers and other activists," over fifteen hundred by the time of the State Department endorsement. Perhaps the State Department had in mind the 1988 mayoral campaigns, in which twenty-nine of the eighty-seven mayoral candidates of the UP were assassinated along with over a hundred of its candidates for municipal councilor. The Central Organization of Workers, a coalition of trade unions formed in 1986, had by then lost over 230 members, most of them found dead after brutal torture.

Recall also that in 1988, the more advanced forms of "maximal criminalization of the political and social opposition" were instituted for "total war against the internal enemy," as the regime of state terror consolidated. By the time the State Department report appeared, the methods of control it found praiseworthy were being still more systematically implemented. From 1988 through early 1992, 9,500 people were assassinated for political reasons along with 830 disappearances and 313 massacres (between 1988 and 1990) of peasants and poor people.[107]

The primary victims of atrocities were, as usual, the poor, mainly peasants. In one southern department, grassroots organizations testified in

February 1988 that a "campaign of total annihilation and scorched earth, Vietnam-style," was being conducted by the military forces "in a most criminal manner, with assassinations of men, women, elderly and children. Homes and crops are burned, obligating the peasants to leave their lands." The State Department had a plethora of evidence of this sort before it when it cleared Colombia of human rights violations. Its own official Human Rights reports, however, attributed virtually all violence to the guerrillas and narcotraffickers, so that the United States was "justified" in providing the mass murderers and torturers with military equipment.

That, of course, was the "bad old days" of 1989, when the Cold War was still raging. Moving to the present, matters become worse, for reasons explained by President Gaviria in May 1992. When questioned about atrocities by the military in the Colombian press, he responded that "the battle against the guerrillas must be waged on unequal terms. The defense of human rights, of democratic principles, of the separation of powers, could prove to be an obstacle for the counterinsurgency struggle."[108]

During the Bush years, the U.S. Embassy "did not make a single public statement urging the government to curb political or military abuses," WOLA observes, while U.S. support for the military and police increased.[109] When the Clinton administration took over in January 1993, it called for a change in policy: more active U.S. participation in the terror. For fiscal year 1994, the administration requested that military financing and training funds be *increased* by over 12 percent, reaching about half of proposed military aid for all of Latin America. Congressional budget cuts for the Pentagon interfered with these plans, so the Administration "intends to use emergency drawdown authority to bolster the Colombia account," Americas Watch reports.

The Human Rights organizations (Amnesty International, Human Rights Watch) are committed to international conventions on human rights. Thus AI reports open by stating that the organization "works to promote all the human rights enshrined in the Universal Declaration of Human Rights and other international standards." In practice, however, the commitment is skewed in accord with Western standards, which are significantly different. The United States, in particular, rejects the universality of the Universal Declaration, while condemning the "cultural relativism" of the backward peoples who fall short of our exalted standards. The United States has always flatly rejected the sections of the Universal Declaration dealing with social and economic rights, and also consistently disregards, ignores, and violates much of the remainder of the Declaration—even putting aside its massive involvement in terror, torture, and other abuses.[110]

The Human Rights Groups say little about social and economic rights, generally adopting the highly biased Western perspective on these matters. In the case of Colombia, we have to go beyond these (in themselves, very valuable) reports to discover the roots of the extraordinary violence. They are not obscure. The president of the Colombian Permanent Committee for

Human Rights, former minister of foreign affairs Alfredo Vásquez Carrizosa, writes that it is "poverty and insufficient land reform" that "have made Colombia one of the most tragic countries of Latin America," and are the source of the violence, including the mass killings of the 1940s and early 1950s, which took hundreds of thousands of lives. Land reform was legislated in 1961, but "has practically been a myth," unimplemented because landowners "have had the power to stop it" in this admirable democracy with its constitutional regime, which Vásquez Carrizosa dismisses as a "facade," granting rights that have no relation to reality. The violence has been caused "by the dual structure of a prosperous minority and an impoverished, excluded majority, with great differences in wealth, income, and access to political participation."

And as elsewhere in Latin America, "violence has been exacerbated by external factors," primarily the initiatives of the Kennedy Administration, which "took great pains to transform our regular armies into counterinsurgency brigades, accepting the new strategy of the death squads," ushering in "what is known in Latin America as the National Security Doctrine, . . . not defense against an external enemy, but a way to make the military establishment the masters of the game . . . [with] the right to combat the internal enemy, as set forth in the Brazilian doctrine, the Argentine doctrine, the Uruguayan doctrine, and the Colombian doctrine: it is the right to fight and to exterminate social workers, trade unionists, men and women who are not supportive of the establishment, and who are assumed to be communist extremists."[111]

It is in this precise sense that the Cold War guided our policies in the subject domains. The results are an income distribution that is "dramatically skewed," WOLA observes, another striking feature of the domains of longstanding U.S. influence, from which we are to draw no conclusions. The top 3 percent of Colombia's landed elite own over 70 percent of arable land, while 57 percent of the poorest farmers subsist on under 3 percent. Forty percent of Colombians live in "absolute poverty," unable to satisfy basic subsistence needs, according to a 1986 report of the National Administration Bureau of Statistics, while 18 percent live in "absolute misery," unable to meet nutritional needs. The Colombian Institute of Family Welfare estimates that four and a half million children under fourteen are hungry: that is, one of every two children, in this triumph of capitalism, a country of enormous resources and potential, lauded as "one of the healthiest and most flourishing economies in Latin America" (Martz).[112]

The "stable democracy" does exist, but as what Jenny Pearce calls "democracy without the people," the majority of whom are excluded from the political system monopolized by elites, more so as political space has been "rapidly closing by the mid-1980s." For Colombian elites, the international funding agencies, and foreign investors, "democracy" functions. But it is not intended for the public generally, who are "marginalized economically and politically." "The state has reserved for the majority the 'state of siege' and all the exceptional repressive legislation and procedures that can guarantee order where other mechanisms fail," Pearce continues, increasingly in recent years. That is democracy in exactly the sense of regular practice—and even doctrine, if we attend closely.

Given the range of consensus, it is not surprising that nothing changed as the Clinton administration took over. It faced at once two cases of severe threat to democracy, critical ones because U.S. influence is decisive: Angola and Haiti.

In Angola, U.S.-backed "freedom fighter" Jonas Savimbi lost a UN-monitored election, at once resorting to violence, exacting a horrendous toll. While finally joining the rest of the world in recognizing the elected government, the United States did nothing. "Chester Crocker, the principal United States specialist on African affairs and architect of U.S. diplomacy ["constructive engagement"] in southern Africa, has called for . . . the holding of a second presidential election." The atrocities, apparently surpassing Bosnia, are scarcely reported, and no curiosity is aroused by the armaments available to this long-term client of the United States and South Africa.[113]

In Haiti, the democratically elected president is acceptable only if he abandons his popular mandate, catering to the interests of the "moderates" in the business world, those sometimes called "civil society" in the nation's press. Meanwhile, the U.S.-trained military thugs conduct their reign of terror, "ruthlessly suppressing Haiti's once diverse and vibrant civil society," Americas Watch reports, referring to the "remarkably advanced" array of popular organizations that gave the large majority of the population a "considerable voice in local affairs" and even in national politics—the wrong kind of democracy, which must be demolished. Though "Washington's capacity to curb attacks on civil society was tremendous," Americas Watch continues, "this power was largely unexercised by the Bush administration," which "sought to convey an image of normalcy" while forcefully returning refugees fleeing the terror.

During the presidential campaign, Clinton bitterly condemned Bush's inhuman policies. On taking over in January 1993, he made them harsher still, tightening a blockade to prevent refugees from fleeing Haiti, a gross violation of international law, comparable—were it imaginable—to Libya barring air traffic from the United States. During the June 1993 Vienna conference on human rights, amidst much Western posturing about the sanctity of the Universal Declaration of Human Rights, the Clinton administration demonstrated its reverence for its explicit provisions on right of asylum (Article 14) by intercepting a sailboat with eighty-seven Haitians crowded aboard, returning them to the prison of terror and torture in which they are locked; they were fleeing poverty, not political persecution, the administration determined—by ESP. That practice continued while terror raged unabated, ensuring that even if Aristide is permitted to return, "he would have difficulty transforming his personal popularity into the organized support needed to exert civilian authority," Americas Watch observes, quoting priests and others who fear that the destruction of the popular social organizations that "gave people hope" has undermined the great promise of Haiti's first democratic experiment.[114]

To much acclaim, Washington finally succeeded in achieving the desired outcome—no great surprise. Under severe pressure, in July President Aristide accepted the U.S.–UN terms for settlement, which were to allow him to return four months later in a "compromise" with the gangsters who overthrew him and have been robbing and terrorizing at will since. Aristide agreed to dismiss his Prime Minister in favor of a businessman from the traditional mulatto elite who is "known to be opposed to the populist policies during Aristide's seven months in power," the press announced with relief, noting that he is "generally well regarded by the business community," "respected by many businessmen who supported the coup that ousted the President," and seen as "a reassuring choice" by coup-supporters. A very diligent media addict might discover a July 26 report of UN/OAS observers who said they were "very concerned that there is no perceptible lessening of human rights violations," as the state terrorists continued their rampage. An August 11 update, also barely noted, reported an increase in "arbitrary executions and suspicious deaths" in the weeks following the UN-brokered accord, over one a day in the Port-au-Prince area alone; "the mission said that many of the victims were members of popular organizations and neighborhood associations and that some of the killers were police."[115]

Atrocities in the subsequent weeks mounted high enough to gain notice, but no action. As the press reported "terrifying stories" of terror, murder, and threats to exterminate all members of the popular organizations, the Clinton administration announced that the UN Mission, including U.S. elements, "will rely on the Haitian military and police to maintain order," that is, on "those groups that have been held largely responsible for the politically motivated killings in the first place": the mission "will have no mandate to stop Haitian soldiers and paramilitary elements from committing atrocities." "It is not a peacekeeping role," Secretary of Defense Aspin explained. "We are doing something other than peacekeeping here." Meanwhile, following the course it has pursued throughout, the press reported concerns of U.S. officials that *President Aristide* "isn't moving strongly to restore democratic rights" (*Wall Street Journal*). "Even as the situation has grown worse, foreign diplomats have increasingly blamed Father Aristide for what they say is his failure to take constructive initiatives," Howard French wrote, using the standard device to disguise propaganda as reporting.

The meaning of the term "constructive initiatives" was spelled out more fully as Washington proceeded to undermine Aristide in subsequent weeks, pressuring him to "broaden the government" to include conservative business sectors and the military, in the interests of "democracy." One will search in vain for a proposal that some government be "broadened" to include popular elements, even if they constitute an overwhelming majority. The main thrust of policy had been indicated by Secretary of State Warren Christopher during his confirmation hearings, in a ringing endorsement of democracy. Christopher "stopped short of calling for [Aristide's] reinstatement as President," Elaine Sciolino reported. "'There is no question in my mind that because of the election, he has to be part of the solution to this,' Mr. Christopher said. 'I don't have a precise system worked out in my mind as to how he would be part of the solution, but certainly he cannot be ignored in the matter.'"[116]

After the military coup that overthrew Aristide, the OAS instituted an embargo, which the Bush administration reluctantly joined, while making clear to its allies and clients that it was not to be taken seriously. The official reasons were explained a year later by Howard French: "Washington's deep-seated ambivalence about a leftward-tilting nationalist whose style diplomats say has sometimes been disquietingly erratic" precludes any meaningful support for sanctions against the military rulers. "Despite much blood on the army's hands, United States diplomats consider it a vital counterweight to Father Aristide, whose class-struggle rhetoric . . . threatened or antagonized traditional power centers at home and abroad." Aristide's "call for punishment of the military leadership" that had slaughtered and tortured thousands of people "reinforced a view of him as an inflexible and vindictive crusader," and heightened Washington's "antipathy" towards the "clumsy" and "erratic" extremist who has aroused great "anger" in Washington because of "his tendency toward ingratitude."[117]

The "vital counterweight" is therefore to hold total power while the "leftward tilting nationalist" remains in exile, awaiting the "eventual return" that Bill Clinton promised on the eve of his inauguration. Meanwhile, the "traditional power centers" in Haiti and the United States will carry on with class struggle as usual, employing such terror as may be needed in order for plunder to proceed unhampered. And as the London *Financial Times* added at the same time, Washington was proving oddly ineffective in detecting the "lucrative use of the country in the transshipment of narcotics" by which "the military is funding its oil and other necessary imports," financing the necessary terror and rapacity—though U.S. forces seem able to find every fishing boat carrying miserable refugees. Nor had Washington figured out a way to freeze the assets of "civil society" or to hinder their shopping trips to Miami and New York, or to induce its Dominican clients to monitor the border to impede the flow of goods that takes care of the wants of "civil society" while the embargo remains "at best, sieve-like."[118]

These late-1992 observations understate the facts. Washington continues to provide Haitian military leaders with intelligence on narcotics trafficking—which they will naturally use to expedite their activities and tighten their grip on power. It is not easy to intercept narcotraffickers, the press explains, because "Haiti has no radar," and evidently the U.S. Navy and Air Force cannot find a way to remedy this deficiency. The military and police command are U.S.-trained, and doubtless retain their contacts with U.S. military and intelligence. According to church sources, officers of the Haitian military were seen at the U.S. Army base in Fort Benning, Georgia, home of the notorious School of the Americas, as recently as October 1993.[119]

On February 4, 1992, the Bush Administration lifted the embargo for assembly plants, "under heavy pressure from American businesses with interests in Haiti," the *Washington Post* reported. The editors judged the decision wise: the embargo was a "fundamental political miscalculation" that "has caused great suffering, but not among the gunmen. Since it hasn't served its purpose, it is good that it is being relaxed"—not tightened so as to serve its professed purpose, as those who endure the "great suffering" were pleading. A few months later, it was noted in the small print that Washington "is apparently continuing to relax controls on goods going to Port-au-Prince from the United States," allowing export of seeds, fertilizers, and pesticides. For January–October 1992, U.S. trade with Haiti came to $265 million, according to the Department of Commerce, apparently unreported here in the mainstream.[120]

The *New York Times* also gave a positive cast to the undermining of the embargo, reported under the headline "U.S. Plans to Sharpen Focus of Its Sanctions Against Haiti." "The Bush Administration said today that it would modify its embargo against Haiti's military Government to punish anti-democratic forces and ease the plight of workers who lost jobs because of the ban on trade," Barbara Crossette reported. The State Department was "fine tuning" its economic sanctions, the "latest move" in administration efforts to find "more effective ways to hasten the collapse of what the Administration calls an illegal Government in Haiti."[121] We are to understand that the "fine tuning" is designed to punish the "illegal Government" that applauds it and to benefit the workers who strenuously oppose it (not to speak of U.S. investors, unmentioned). Orwell would have been impressed, once again.

As Clinton took over, the embargo became still more porous. The Dominican border was wide open. Meanwhile, U.S. companies continued to be exempted from the embargo—so as to ease its effects on the population, the administration announced with a straight face; only exemptions for U.S. firms have this curious feature. There were many heartfelt laments about the suffering of poor Haitians under the embargo, but one had to turn to the underground press in Haiti, the alternative media here, or an occasional letter to learn that the major peasant organization (MPP), church coalitions, labor organizations, and the National Federation of Haitian Students continued to call for a real embargo.[122] Curiously, those most distressed by the impact of the embargo on the Haitian poor were often among the most forceful advocates of a still harsher embargo on Cuba, notably liberal Democrat Robert Torricelli, author of the stepped-up embargo that the Bush adminis-tration accepted under pressure from the Clintonites. Evidently, hunger causes no pain to Cuban children. The oddity passed unnoticed.

As did the impact of Clinton's tinkering with the embargo on Haiti. "U.S. imports from Haiti rose by more than half last year [1993]," the *Financial Times* reported, "thanks in part to an exemption granted by the U.S. Treasury for imports of goods assembled in Haiti from U.S. parts." U.S. exports to Haiti also rose in 1993. Exports from Haiti to the United States included food (fruits and nuts, citrus fruit or melons) from the starving country, which increased by 3,500 percent from January–July 1992 to January–July 1993, on Clinton's watch, while officials and commentators soberly explained that the pain they felt for hungry Haitians kept them from joining the call for a functioning embargo. "The Clinton administration still formally declares its support for Mr Aristide, but scarcely disguises its wish for a leader more accommodating to the military," the *Financial Times* reported, while "European diplomats in Washington are scathing in their comments on what they see as the United States's abdication of leadership over Haiti."[123]

By March 1994, Washington had succeeded in blocking efforts to impose a meaningful embargo or to punish the killers or their supporters. Its own plan "would leave the military largely in place," AP reported, though it "does not state a date for Father Aristide's return to Haiti and does not guarantee him a role in a proposed 'national unity' government that would include his enemies." The circle closes. Aristide's rejection of the plan merely demonstrated anew his "intransigence" and "meager" democratic credentials.[124]

At the far right, the Haitian Chamber of Commerce could scarcely contain its delight as it debated measures to join army leaders in establishing a "new, broadly based government" with at most symbolic participation of the elected president, "with the assumption that nobody, including the Administration in Washington, wants Aristide back," a participant in the debate commented. A senior U.S. official quoted by the *Wall Street Journal* insisted that the United States was not backing away from Aristide, while noting that Washington "had never called for" his "immediate return" but rather "always preferred to have Haiti first build a functioning government" without him, after which he *might* return, though the Clinton administration's current proposals "could possibly lead to a situation in which Mr. Aristide doesn't return" at all. Secretary of State Christopher reiterated that President Aristide "continues to be a major factor in the policy" the administration is crafting, with an unknown role. Meanwhile, officials made it clear that any such role will be contingent on Aristide's agreement to extend the government to traditional power sectors while excluding the population ("broadening his political base") and to accept a merely symbolic presence. If only he can overcome his intransigence, we can proceed towards "democracy," meanwhile basking in glory as "the gatekeeper and the model" for a wondrous future.[125]

Lawrence Pezzullo, the government's special adviser for Haiti, testified before Congress in March 1994 about the plan that the administration was supporting, having presented it as the outcome of deliberations among a broad group of Haitian legislators brought to Washington to seek a democratic settlement. The Clinton administration backed the plan with enthusiasm as the optimal solution, representing Haitian democrats, and harshly condemned Aristide for his intransigence in rejecting this forthcoming proposal—which had nothing to say about the return of the elected president to Haiti and the removal of the worst of the state terrorists from power. Under questioning, Pezzullo conceded that the plan had in fact been concocted in the offices of the State Department, which selected the "Haitian negotiators" who were to ratify it in Washington. Included among them were right-wing extremists with close military ties, notably Frantz-Robert Mondé, a former member of Duvalier's terrorist Tontons Macoute and a close associate of police chief Lt.-Col. Joseph Michel François, the most brutal and powerful of the Haitian state terrorists (incidentally, another beneficiary of U.S. training). "In other words, the operation was a hoax," Larry Birns, director of the Council on Hemispheric Affairs, observed, yet another effort to ensure that democracy is "promoted" in Haiti in the familiar way—without any "populist-based change" that might upset "established economic and political orders" and open "a leftist direction" (Carothers).[126]

In Haiti too, the threat that the rabble might enter the public arena has been reduced, perhaps overcome, yet another sign of the wondrous prospects now that the Great Satan has been defeated.

There is a particle of truth in the flood of self-adulation about "the yearning to see American-style democracy duplicated throughout the world [that] has been a persistent theme in American foreign policy."[127] The rulers are more willing than before to tolerate formal electoral procedures, recognizing that the economic catastrophe of the eighties and the disciplinary effects of Western-run market forces, selectively applied, have narrowed political options considerably, so that the democratic threat is attenuated. That aside, little has changed with regard to our "yearning for democracy." Democracy is a grand thing in our "romantic age," but only when it does "not risk upsetting the traditional structures of power with which the United States has long been allied."

Other developments underscore the same conclusion: post–Cold War policies continue with no change, apart from tactical modification. Take Cuba, subjected to U.S. terror and economic warfare from shortly after Castro took power in January 1959.[128] By October, planes based in Florida were carrying out strafing and bombing attacks against Cuban territory. In December, CIA subversion was stepped up, including supply of arms to guerrilla bands and sabotage of sugar mills and other economic targets. In March 1960, the Eisenhower administration formally adopted a plan to overthrow Castro in favor of a regime "more devoted to the true interests of the Cuban people and more acceptable to the U.S.," which will determine "the true interests of the Cuban people," not the Cuban people, who, as Washington knew from its own investigations, were optimistic about the future and strongly supported Castro. Recognizing this unfortunate fact, the secret plan emphasized that Castro must be removed "in such a manner as to avoid any appearance of U.S. intervention." After the failure of their invasion, the Kennedy liberals mounted their remarkable terrorist operations against Cuba. The campaign was canceled by Lyndon Johnson, renewed by

Richard Nixon. Meanwhile the crushing embargo was maintained, ensuring that Cuba would be driven into the hands of the Russians.

Throughout, the pretext was the Soviet threat. Its credibility is easily assessed. When the decision to overthrow Castro was taken in March 1960, Washington was fully aware that the Russian role was nil. And with the Russians gone from the scene, U.S. strangulation of Cuba was tightened further. During the 1992 presidential campaign, Bush extended the blockade, under pressure from Clinton, who called for harsher measures against Cuba. Protests from the European Community and Latin America were ignored. The press happily records the collapse of Cuban society and the suffering of its people, attributed primarily to the evils of Communism, not what the United States has done. Routinely, articles on Cuba's travail make slight mention of any U.S. role, often none at all, a display of moral cowardice that would be extraordinary, were it not such a commonplace.

To a rational observer, once again, the conclusion is clear: the Cold War provided pretexts, not reasons. It is only reinforced by a look at earlier history. The United States has opposed Cuban independence since its earliest days. Thomas Jefferson advised President Monroe not to go to war for Cuba, "but the first war on other accounts will give it to us, or the Island will give itself to us, when able to do so." Monroe's Secretary of State John Quincy Adams, the intellectual author of the doctrine of Manifest Destiny, described Cuba as "an object of transcendent importance to the commercial and political interests of our Union." He joined many others in urging support for Spanish sovereignty until Cuba would fall into U.S. hands by "the laws of political ... gravitation," a "ripe fruit" for harvest. That happened by the end of the century, as the British deterrent declined, allowing Washington to take over the island under the pretense of defending its independence, turning it into a U.S. plantation and a haven for wealthy Americans and criminal mobs. The collapse of that regime in 1959 evoked the response just reviewed.

The Cold War, to be sure, had some impact on policy. Soviet power deterred outright U.S. aggression, and its support managed to keep Cuba alive despite U.S. terror and economic warfare. But the Cold War only changed the framework in which long-standing policies were executed. Many other examples illustrate the same fact, as reviewed in detail elsewhere.

The crucial point is that basic policies that had long been justified in Cold War terms not only persist after its end, but are often even intensified. The pattern is systematic, including the Middle East, to which we return.

The Cold War framework had both positive and negative aspects for U.S. power. On the positive side, it offered efficient mechanisms of population control; before the Bolshevik takeover, the population had to be mobilized in fear of the Huns, the British, and other devils, foreign and indigenous. On the negative side, the Cold War created some space for nonalignment and neutralism, to the dismay of the world rulers, who had no choice but to accommodate to these realities. The Cold War conflict also impeded U.S.

intervention and domination in well-known ways. As already noted, similar considerations held for the lesser superpower, now departed.

These features of the Cold War quickly came to the fore as it ended. The invasion of Panama was so routine as to be a mere footnote to history, but it broke the pattern in two respects. First, new pretexts were required; the demon Noriega and Hispanic narcotraffickers were conjured up to replace the Soviet menace. Second, as Reagan's Latin American specialist Elliott Abrams observed, the United States could now act without concern about a possible Soviet response. The same factors were operative as the United States moved to undercut the fear that Saddam Hussein might try to follow Bush's Panama model in Kuwait. Again, the Soviet menace had to be replaced, this time, by a new Hitler poised to conquer the world. His enormous crimes, overlooked when the United States and Britain found him a worthy ally, could now be invoked to whip up war fever. And, as many commentators pointed out, the United States and Britain could now safely place half a million troops in the desert and use force as they chose, confident that there would be no reaction.

Recognition of Cold War realities was implicit in analyses of U.S. options as it faded away. At the year's end, the *New York Times* regularly runs think-pieces on major issues. The December 1988 contribution on the Cold War was written by Dimitri Simes, senior associate at the Carnegie Endowment for International Peace. He observed that with the Russians out of the way, it should be possible "to liberate American foreign policy from the straight-jacket imposed by superpower hostility."[129] Washington will be "liberated" in three ways. First, it can shift NATO costs to European competitors. Second, it can end "the manipulation of America by third world nations," taking a harsher line on debt and "unwarranted third world demands for assistance." But most important, the "apparent decline in the Soviet threat . . . makes military power more useful as a United States foreign policy instrument . . . against those who contemplate challenging important American interests." Washington's hands will be "untied" if concerns over "Soviet counteraction" decline, permitting it "greater reliance on military force in a crisis." Simes cites the 1973 oil embargo, when leading scholars called for the United States to take over the oil fields (to "internationalize" them, as Walter Laqueur phrased the idea), but Washington could not because its hands were "tied." And "the Sandinistas and their Cuban sponsors" will be "a little nervous" that Gorbachev may not react, Simes added, "if America finally lost patience with their mischief."

In plain English, U.S. violence, terror, robbery, and exploitation will be able to proceed without the annoying impediments portrayed as the Kremlin's "global designs" in the official culture.

The end of the Cold War also required new devices to justify the Pentagon system. Each year, the White House sends a report to Congress explaining that the military threat we face requires huge expenditures—which, incidentally, sustain high technology industry at home and "just suppression" abroad. The first post–Cold War edition was in March 1990. The bottom line remained the same: we face terrible threats, and cannot relax our guard. But the argument yielding the conclusion was revised. U.S. military power must focus on the Third World, the report concluded, the prime target being the Middle East, where the "threats to our interests . . . could not be laid at the Kremlin's door"; the facts can at last be acknowledged after decades of deception, the Soviet pretext having lost its efficacy. We must develop additional forward basing, counterinsurgency, and low-intensity conflict capacities. And in light of "the growing technological sophistication of Third World conflicts," the United States must strengthen its "defense industrial base"—a euphemism for electronics and aerospace, metallurgy, and advanced industry generally—with state subsidy and incentives "to invest in new facilities and equipment as well as in research and development."[130]

In short, business as usual, apart from the modalities of population control and military strategy: in the former domain, a shift towards reality in identifying the enemy, in the latter, tactical changes.

These factors have many consequences. One has to do with government intervention in the domestic economy. A standard pretense is that other countries have "industrial policy," but the United States, true to the ideals of free market capitalism, eschews such heresies. Reality has been quite different from the earliest days of the Republic, but during the Cold War U.S. industrial policy could be hidden behind the veil of "security," the public subsidy to high tech industry masked as "defense spending." With the Soviet Union gone, that is a harder pose to maintain, a matter to which we return.

Another consequence is the change in military strategy. It had been understood across the political spectrum that the United States must maintain an intimidating military posture to carry out its global policies of intervention and subversion without fear of retaliation. Strategic nuclear weapons "provide a nuclear guarantee for our interests in many parts of the world, and make it possible for us to defend these interests by diplomacy or the use of theater military forces," Eugene Rostow observed just before joining the Reagan administration: they provide a "shield" that allows us to pursue our "global interests" by "conventional means or theater forces." At the same time, Carter's Secretary of Defense Harold Brown informed Congress that with our strategic nuclear forces in place, "our other forces become meaningful instruments of military and political control." The thinking goes back to the early postwar years.[131]

With the disappearance of the Soviet deterrent, these motives for strategic nuclear forces are less compelling. Presenting "the first outline of the [Clinton] Administration's foreign policy vision," National Security Adviser Anthony Lake focused on the fact "that in a world in which the United States no longer has to worry daily about a Soviet nuclear threat, where and how it intervenes abroad is increasingly a matter of choice"; Thomas Friedman's paraphrase, reporting the new Clinton doctrine under the headline "U.S. Vision of Foreign Policy Reversed," implying a dramatic policy change. That is the "essence" of the new doctrine, Friedman emphasized, a doctrine that clearly and explicitly reflects the understanding that the "nuclear threat" was the Soviet deterrent to U.S. intervention. Now that the "threat" is gone, intervention can be freely undertaken, as observed five years earlier by the foreign policy expert of the Carnegie Endowment for International Peace.

Turning from paraphrase to text, Lake's actual wording, highlighted by the *Times*, opens with this statement: "Throughout the cold war, we contained a global threat to market democracies: now we should seek to enlarge their reach." We now move from "containment" to "enlargement." Commentators were properly impressed by this enlightened "vision."

A rational person interested in what the Soviet leaders intended to do during the Cold War years would ask what they *did* do, particularly in the regions most fully under their control. A rational person interested in the intentions of U.S. leaders would, naturally, ask the very same question, Latin America being the most obvious test case. We are to understand, then, that when the Kennedy administration prepared the overthrow of the parliamentary government of Brazil, installing a regime of neo-Nazi killers and torturers, it was "containing the global threat to market democracies." That was surely the claim: Kennedy's ambassador Lincoln Gordon, who helped lay the basis for the coup and then moved to a high position in the State Department, lauded the generals for their "democratic rebellion," "a great victory for free world," which was undertaken "to preserve and not destroy Brazil's democracy." This democratic revolution was "the single most decisive victory of freedom in the mid–twentieth century," which prevented a "total loss to West of all South American Republics" and should "create a greatly improved climate for private investments"—the last comment offering at least a glimpse into the real world. We return to the aftermath.

The story was the same in Guatemala, Chile, and elsewhere: the "global threat" was nonexistent, as conceded, though there were many "Communists" in the technical sense of American usage, to which we return—those who seek independent development oriented to the needs of the domestic population, not foreign investors. The pattern is highly consistent, yet no one even asks the question that all would raise, and answer with proper contempt, if a Soviet leader were to have made the comparable claim. The fact that even the most trivial question cannot be raised, even contemplated, is no small tribute to the educational system and intellectual culture of the free world. Those who can bring themselves to ask it will have no difficulty in understanding the new and more benign doctrine of "enlargement."

To this bright vision of a grander future we need only add the conclusions of the White House panel on intervention, reported the following day, which announced the end of the era of altruism. Henceforth intervention will be where and how U.S. power chooses, the guiding consideration being: "What is in it for us?" The Clinton doctrine thus defines a new and more humane era of liberal democracy, receiving much applause for its virtue. To be sure, the "vision" is cloaked in appropriate rhetoric about "enlargement of the world's free community of market democracies," the standard accompaniment whatever is being implemented, hence meaningless—carrying no information, in the technical sense.[132]

Under the "revised vision," military spending is not expected to decline significantly. Clinton's budget is above the Cold War average in real dollars, and projections remain so, indeed rising by 1997. "Thus, not one major weapon has been terminated in the first Clinton budget," the Center for Defense Information (CDI) observes, including billions for the F–22 fighter, the B–2 bomber, the Trident II missile, and other huge military projects. There is, however, a shift of emphasis from large-scale nuclear weapons and ground forces to "strategic mobility and military power projection" in the Third World, so Clinton's Defense Department explained when announcing the new military budget in March 1993. Defense Secretary Aspin later outlined a "two-war scenario" which, military analyst David Evans points out, "is virtually guaranteed to generate enormous pressure to keep the defense budget closer to $300 billion than to $234 billion in the Pentagon's fiscal 1998 projection, as measured in 1994 dollars," an increase over the Bush years. The plans are based on such contingencies as a simultaneous Iraqi conquest of Saudi Arabian oil fields, with forces far greater than they deployed in Kuwait or now possess, and North Korean invasion of South Korea.

We must be prepared to counter "rogue leaders set on regional domination" who are developing advanced weapons capacities or planning "large-scale aggression," Secretary Aspin announced. Threats are posed not only by "major regional powers with interests antithetical to our own, but also by the potential for smaller, often internal, conflicts based on ethnic or religious animosities, state-sponsored terrorism, and subversion of friendly governments." All such potential problems must be countered by U.S. military force worldwide. "First, we must *keep our forces ready to fight*," to face "the challenges posed by the new dangers in operations like Just Cause (Panama), Desert Storm (Iraq), and Restore Hope (Somalia)." Who knows when we will again have to act rapidly to impose a corrupt puppet regime as in Operation Just Cause, to block some tyrant attempting to emulate our actions, or to exploit some occasion for a "paid political advertisement" on behalf of plans for an intervention force, as Chairman of the Joint Chiefs Colin Powell described Operation Restore Hope, "a public relations bonanza at just the right time" and "more a symbolic show for the world's television cameras than any serious effort to get a steady stream of food moving," as the press remarked in some rare moments of candor. For such reasons, we must remain "the only nation in the world which maintains large, costly armed forces solely for intervention in the affairs of foreign nations," close to $200 billion annually (CDI). With the Russians gone, Aspin explained, that is "what really determines the size of the defense budget now"—as it always did, if "defense" is properly understood, explaining why military budgets do not materially change with the end of the Cold War. "We are leaders because nature and history have laid that obligation on us," General Powell observed, repeating the ritual phrases inculcated from childhood, and reflexively reproduced on proper occasions by the educated classes.

While the plans of Clinton strategists are unlikely to be approved in the current economic climate, they reflect the thinking among military planners.[133]

Nuclear weapons are not to be discarded, but their mission is changing. They are no longer needed to provide a "shield" for global intervention; rather, to deal with "rogue nations." One of Dick Cheney's parting shots as Defense Secretary was a report to Congress entitled "Defense Strategy for the 1990s," which called for "new non-strategic nuclear weapons," military analyst William Arkin reports, a program continued by the incoming Clinton administration in line with the thinking of "a new, post–Gulf War constituency—nuclear zealots intent on developing a new generation of small nuclear weapons designed for waging wars in the Third World." Recall that the old strategic weapons had a similar function, providing a "nuclear umbrella" for the free use of conventional forces against "much weaker enemies."

A 1992 study of the Los Alamos nuclear weapons laboratory called for "very low-yield nuclear weapons" that "could be very effective and credible counters against future Third World nuclear threats," with the capacity to "destroy company-sized units" and underground command bunkers, and to "neutralize mobs." A 1991 study headed by the current (1993) chief of the U.S. Strategic Command, Gen. Lee Butler, and including senior officials of the Clinton administration, called for retaining nuclear weapons as an insurance policy against possible "Russian imperialism," along with plans for a "nuclear expeditionary force" aimed "primarily at China or other Third World targets," with weapon delivery by short-range aircraft, the B–2 stealth bomber (intended to replace the B–52s), Tomahawk missiles, or submarines. According to U.S. analysts, Russia is pursuing similar plans, indeed placing greater reliance on nuclear deterrence than during the Cold War. For Russia, China remains a prime concern, while the United States is focusing on "Iraqi style force," nuclear experts say. Both the United States and Russia "are discussing the idea of hitting rogue Third World countries that might try to develop their own nuclear weapons," the press reports, noting that their lists "are almost identical: North Korea is followed closely by such countries as Iran, Iraq, India and Pakistan."[134]

There is one consistent omission from the list of proliferators, namely, the one country that long ago developed a significant nuclear force "in secret"— that is, without acknowledgment, though the facts have been common knowledge for years. As documented elsewhere, evasion of Israel's nuclear programs and their intent has been remarkable, notably in the *New York Times*, the Newspaper of Record. The evasion continues, sometimes taking curious forms indeed. Thus a *Times* report by Clyde Haberman, headlined

"Israel Again Seeks A Deal With an Outcast," discusses Israel's efforts to persuade North Korea not to provide nuclear-capable missiles with a range of six hundred miles to Iran, another "rogue state." Haberman does recognize that there is a double standard at work: namely, against Israel. True, Israel has been in contact with states engaged in nuclear proliferation, the only charge against it in this context, but the reason is that it has "felt itself a victim of double standards and blatant hypocrisy," so that its deviation from righteousness is understandable.[135]

There is no inconsistency in the systematic omission of the most obvious example from the concerns over proliferation. As an instrument of U.S. power, Israel inherits from its patron immunity from analysis or criticism. For similar reasons, Saudi Arabia is no part of the Islamic fundamentalist wave that is to replace the Great Satan of the past. Nor were the CIA's clients in Afghanistan, until they began to aim their bombs in the wrong direction.

5. North–South/East–West

Without proceeding, it is clear enough that the conventional picture of the Cold War, while highly functional for power interests in East and West, does not withstand scrutiny, and never has. Too much is omitted, too many problems left unresolved, among them, those just reviewed: the limited role of authentic security concerns, the reasons for the outbreak of the East–West conflict, the events that constitute the Cold War, and the persistence of earlier policy right through the Cold War era and beyond, with little more than doctrinal and tactical change—indeed, intensification of policies that had been attributed to the Cold War.

We can gain a more realistic understanding of the Cold War by adopting a longer-range perspective, viewing it as a particular phase in the five hundred–year European conquest of the world—the history of aggression, subversion, terror, and domination now termed the "North–South confrontation." There have, of course, been changes of decisive importance through this period, one of the most noteworthy being the great expansion of the domain of freedom and social justice within the rich societies, largely a result of popular struggles. Another crucial change was brought by the Second World War: for the first time a single state had such overwhelming wealth and power that its planners could realistically design and execute a global vision. But major themes persist, including the Churchillian vision, amended with the crucial footnotes.

These persistent themes yield the essential contours of the North–South confrontation. The basic reasoning is spelled out with particular lucidity in U.S. planning documents, and illustrated in practice with much consistency. It has to be understood in the broader context of global planning, to which we return in the next chapter; but even in abstraction from this framework, the logic of the North–South confrontation is clear enough, and it sheds much light on the Cold War conflict.[136]

Firstly, independent nationalism ("ultranationalism," "economic nationalism," "radical nationalism") is unacceptable, whatever its political coloration. The "function" of the Third World is to provide services for the rich, offering cheap labor, resources, markets, opportunities for investment and (lately) export of pollution, along with other amenities (havens for drug money laundering and other unregulated financial operations, tourism, and so on).

Secondly, "ultranationalism" that appears successful in terms that might be meaningful for poor people elsewhere is a still more heinous crime; the culprit is then termed a "virus" that may spread "infection" elsewhere, a "rotten apple" that might "spoil the barrel," like Arbenz's Guatemala, Allende's Chile, Sandinista Nicaragua, and a host of others. However it may be garbed in lurid tales of dominoes falling, the constant fear is the demonstration effect of a successful independent course.

The real issues are occasionally expressed with some clarity, as when Henry Kissinger warned that the "contagious example" of Allende's Chile might "infect" not only Latin America but also southern Europe—not in fear that Chilean hordes were about to descend upon Rome, but that Chilean successes might send to Italian voters the message that democratic social reform was a possible option and contribute to the rise of social democracy and Eurocommunism that was greatly feared by Washington and Moscow alike. The more vulgar propaganda exercises also commonly illustrate the interplay of real interest and doctrinal cover. A recent example is the State Department's Operation Truth, which, among other successes, concocted a Nicaraguan "Revolution without Borders" that was used to persuade Congress to provide $100 million in funding for Washington's proxy army attacking Nicaragua a few days after the World Court had called upon the United States to end its "unlawful use of force," and that helped for years to keep articulate opinion in line, unified in the demand that Nicaragua be returned to "the Central American mode" by terror or in some other way.[137] The hoax was based on a speech by Nicaraguan leader Tomás Borge in which he explained that we cannot "export our revolution" but can only "export our example" while "the people themselves . . . must make their revolutions"; in this sense, the Nicaraguan revolution "transcends national boundaries." In the hands of State Department propagandists, these remarks were instantly converted into a threat to conquer the hemisphere, before which we must cringe in fear.

The fraud was exposed at once, but to no avail: the hysterical charges continued to be trumpeted by political leaders and the media, considered too useful to be put aside merely on grounds of truth. The doctrine was a Sandinista *Mein Kampf*, George Shultz thundered, while also voicing the real fears disguised by Operation Truth: if the Sandinistas "succeed in consolidating their power," then "*all* the countries in Latin America, who *all* face serious internal economic problems, will see radical forces emboldened to exploit these problems." To deter what Oxfam once called "the threat of a good example," it is necessary to destroy the virus and inoculate the surrounding regions by terror, as in Southeast Asia, the southern cone of Latin America, and elsewhere repeatedly in the Third World, a course that must be pursued until the lessons are firmly implanted by the Godfather.[138]

One can therefore appreciate the "Unity in Joy" over the means by which "democracy burst forth" in Nicaragua. Not only can we revel in our "inspiring" achievements in "this romantic age," but we can even gain and impart useful lessons. Investigative reporter Robert Parry quotes one of the architects of the economic war against Nicaragua, Roger Robinson of Reagan's NSC, who told him in 1985, as the embargo was imposed, that "downgrading Nicaragua's economy could help in bringing a better day for that country." Robinson then joined the joyful chorus in 1990, observing that the outcome of the elections "will serve as a positive, instructive example of the role that carefully crafted economic and financial sanctions can play in the 1990s and the twenty-first century"—not to speak of the efficacy of terror, stilling the doubts of leading doves who feared that it might not be cost-effective.[139]

Whether from choice or the need to survive American hostility, the "ultranationalists" commonly found themselves relying on Soviet support, in which case they became tentacles of the evil empire, subversives and aggressors, Communists subject to attack in self-defense. The basic thinking, completely bipartisan in character, was explained by one of the leading doves of the Kennedy administration, Director of State Department Intelligence Roger Hilsman. Writing approvingly of the CIA overthrow of the governments of Iran (Mossadegh) and Guatemala (Arbenz), he observed that if the Communists remain "antagonistic" and use subversion, then we have a right "to protect and defend ourselves"—by overthrowing parliamentary regimes and imposing murderous terror states. Hilsman had played a leading role in the defense of South Vietnam from what John F. Kennedy called "the assault from the inside"—that is, the aggression by South Vietnamese peasants against the United States and its client regime, imposed and maintained by U.S. force because, as Washington fully recognized, it could not possibly withstand internal political competition.

The attitudes can be traced back to England's earliest conquest, when Edward I explained to his subjects in 1282 that "it would be more fitting and suitable at this time to burden himself and the inhabitants of his kingdom with the cost of wholly overthrowing the malice of the Welsh rather than to face in the future, as in the present, the afflictions of the conflict which they have caused." The malice of their servants has always afflicted the righteous, requiring stern measures in self-defense.[140]

The global rulers have never taken such misbehavior lightly. Metternich and the czar were deeply concerned over the threat to civilized values posed by the republican doctrines preached in the liberated colonies across the sea. As the upstarts had gained power, they wasted no time in adopting the same attitudes. When Haiti revolted against its French rulers in 1791, the United States at once joined the violent repression undertaken by the imperial powers, and when the slave revolt nevertheless succeeded, the U.S. reaction was harsh, uniquely so, in part because of concern that the "virus"—the idea that slaves could liberate themselves from White rule—might spread to native shores. The invasion of Florida in 1818 was in part motivated by the bad example set by "mingled hordes of lawless Indians and negroes" (John Quincy Adams), seeking freedom from tyrants and conquerors. Fear of freed slaves and even a possible "union of whites and Indians" was a factor in the annexation of Texas. And so on, to the present.

Even the tiniest deviation arouses great trepidations. Eisenhower's blockade of Guatemala was imposed for the "self-defense and self-preservation" of the United States, no less; "a strike situation" in Honduras that might "have had inspiration and support from the Guatemalan side of the Honduran border" is the only evidence cited in the secret planning record to justify this desperate anxiety. Similarly the Reaganites instituted a national emergency to defend the country from the "unusual and extraordinary threat" to its existence posed by Nicaragua under the Sandinistas.[141]

The vision is totalitarian: nothing may get out of control. The doctrine has achieved near-total compliance as well. At the dovish extreme, Robert Pastor, Carter's Latin American adviser and a respected scholar, writes that "the United States did not want to control Nicaragua or the other nations in the region, but it also did not want to allow developments to get out of control. It wanted Nicaraguans to act independently, *except* when doing so would affect U.S. interests adversely" (his emphasis). We want everyone to be free—free to act as we determine. Such sentiments arouse no comment, being considered unremarkable to enlightened opinion. They also find their place quite naturally within the new consensus among Cold War historians discussed earlier.[142]

The Cold War itself can be understood in no small measure in similar terms: as a phase of the North–South confrontation, so unusual in scale that it took on a life of its own, but grounded in the familiar logic.

Eastern Europe was the original "Third World," diverging from the West even before the Columbian era along a fault line running through Germany, the West beginning to develop, the East becoming its service area. By the early twentieth century, much of the region was a quasi-colonial dependency of the West. The Bolshevik takeover was immediately recognized to be "ultranationalist," hence unacceptable. Furthermore, it was a "virus," with considerable appeal elsewhere in the Third World. The Western invasion of the Soviet Union in response to "the Revolution's challenge . . . to the very survival of the capitalist order" (Gaddis) thus falls into place in a far broader framework, as do the subsequent policies of "containment" and "roll back" after the invasion failed to restore the old order.

Still more ominously, the Bolshevik virus reached to the home countries themselves. Secretary of State Lansing warned that if the Bolshevik disease were to spread, it would leave the "ignorant and incapable mass of humanity dominant in the earth"; the Bolsheviks were appealing "to the proletariat of all countries, to the ignorant and mentally deficient, who by their numbers are urged to become masters, . . . a very real danger in view of the process of social unrest throughout the world." Wilson was particularly concerned that "the American negro [soldiers] returning from abroad" might be infected by soldiers' and workers' councils in Germany. In Britain, a commission on industrial unrest established by Lloyd George in 1917 found that "hostility to Capitalism has become part of the political creed of the majority" of the miners in Wales. "There was no place outside of Russia where the [February] Revolution has caused greater joy than . . . Merthyr Tydfil," a Welsh miners' journal wrote, impressed particularly by the councils of workers and soldiers that developed before the Bolshevik takeover destroyed them. Like Wilson and Lansing, Lloyd George's commission took a "grave view as to the situation that is likely to develop immediately after" the war.[143]

The home front too, therefore, had to be defended from "the Revolution's challenge" and the afflictions it caused the rulers. Government violence and some remarkable feats of government and business propaganda took care of the problem. The "defense" was mounted throughout the capitalist world, taking a variety of forms, including the "admirable" achievements of fascism.

As the second phase of the Cold War opened, the challenge seemed more dangerous than ever. Having defeated Hitler, the "rotten apple" had grown to include Eastern Europe, undermining Western access to traditional resources. Its ability "to spoil the barrel" had also increased. Throughout the developed world, conservative ruling elites had been discredited by their association with fascism. The worker- and peasant-based anti-fascist resistance, often with a radical democratic thrust, had a great deal of prestige and popular outreach. The familiar measures were adopted without delay, all in defense of freedom and democracy.

Indigenous forces that threatened traditional structures of power were often linked to local Communists, with varying relations to the Soviet Union, later China. Many others, including committed anti-Communists, saw the Soviet model of development as worth emulating. The United States viewed these developments with grave concern. Now a global power, it extended worldwide the doctrines applied in its traditional regional sphere of influence: democracy and social reform are acceptable "as a means of relieving pressure for more radical change," but only if they keep to the "top-down forms of democratic change" that leave U.S. clients in power. These considerations impelled the crusade to restore the traditional order throughout Europe and Asia, undermining the anti-fascist resistance.

In July 1945, a major study of the State and War Departments warned of "a rising tide all over the world wherein the common man aspires to higher and wider horizons." We cannot be sure, they warned, that Russia "has not flirted with the thought" of associating with these dangerous currents; Russia "has not yet proven that she is entirely without expansionist ambitions" of this kind. We must, therefore, take no chances. The USSR must be ringed with military bases and not even granted a share of control of its only access to warm water at the Dardanelles. Planners feared that these plans might seem "illogical." But they dismissed the objection as superficial: it was a "logical illogicality," given the purity of Anglo–American motives and the danger that the Kremlin might foster the aspirations of the common man, the "economic and ideological infiltration" from the East that the British Foreign Office saw as the primary threat of Kremlin "aggression."

The problem was not easy to resolve. In June 1956, Secretary of State John Foster Dulles told German chancellor Konrad Adenauer that "the economic danger from the Soviet Union was perhaps greater than the military danger." The USSR was "transforming itself rapidly . . . into a modern and efficient industrial state," while Western Europe was still stagnating. A State Department report at the same time warned that "for the less developed countries of Asia, the USSR's economic achievement is a highly relevant one. That the USSR was able to industrialize rapidly, and as they see it from scratch is, despite any misgivings about the Communist system, an encouraging fact to these nations." In 1961, British prime minister Harold Macmillan warned President Kennedy that the Russians "have a buoyant economy and will soon outmatch Capitalist society in the race for material wealth." In the same years, China was coming to be feared as a model of development that would be attractive in the Third World, as was North Vietnam, later Cuba and others.

The virulence of the infection spreading from Russia and China was enhanced by the unfair advantages of indigenous Communists, who are able to "appeal directly to the masses," President Eisenhower complained. Secretary of State Dulles deplored the Communist "ability to get control of mass movements," "something we have no capacity to duplicate." "The poor people are the ones they appeal to and they have always wanted to plunder the rich"—the great problem of world history. Somehow, we find it hard to peddle our line, that the rich should plunder the poor, a public relations problem that no one has yet been clever enough to resolve.[144]

As Eisenhower put the matter ruefully in a staff discussion on problems in the Arab world, "the problem is that we have a campaign of hatred against us, not by the governments but by the people," who are "on Nasser's side." As for Nasser, he was "an extremely dangerous fanatic," John Foster Dulles concluded in August 1956, because of his stubborn insistence on a neutralist course—though even Nasser wasn't as bad as Khrushchev, "more like Hitler than any Russian leader we have previously seen," Dulles informed the National Security Council a year later.[145]

Eisenhower's concerns were expressed on July 15, 1958, as ten thousand Marines were wading ashore in Beirut after a coup in Iraq that broke the Anglo–American monopoly over Middle East oil and caused consternation in London and Washington, leading to a British decision "ruthlessly to intervene" if the nationalist rot spread to Kuwait by any means, endorsed by the United States, which took the same stance towards the vastly richer regions it controlled. The problems that troubled Eisenhower arose again in 1990–91. From Morocco to Indonesia, popular opposition to the U.S.–U.K. war ranged from substantial to overwhelming; in Arab states with any kind of "democratic opening" it could scarcely be contained. The hostility of the U.S.–U.K. leadership to democracy in the Arab world (as elsewhere, when it cannot be controlled) is quite understandable.[146]

The Soviet "rotten apple" was, of course, incomparably more dangerous than such lesser threats as Nicaragua or Guatemala, if only because, as under the czar, Russia was a major military force. Nonetheless, a substantial element in the Cold War conflict was the North–South confrontation, writ very, very large.

These realities are underscored by analyses of growth and development. Measuring Eastern European GDP per capita as a percentage of the OECD countries at several points in time, the World Bank notes continuing decline until World War I, then a sharp increase to 1950, declining slightly by 1973 and more by 1989. A 1990 World Bank report concludes that "the Soviet Union and the People's Republic of China have until recently been among the most prominent examples of relatively successful countries that deliberately turned from the global economy," relying on their "vast size" to make "inward-looking development more feasible than it would be for most countries," though "they eventually decided to shift policies and take a more active part in the global economy." From 1989, the economies of Eastern Europe went into free fall under the World Bank–IMF regimen, with industrial output and real wages deteriorating radically while the new rich enjoyed great prosperity and foreign investors gained new opportunities for enrichment, on the familiar Third World model of an "active part in the global economy."[147]

The Soviet Union reached the peak of its power by the late 1950s, always far behind the West. By the mid-1960s, the Soviet economy was in trouble, with notable decline in standard quality of life indicators. A huge military expansion sparked by the Cuban missile crisis of 1962, which revealed extreme Soviet vulnerability, leveled off by the late 1970s. The economy was then stagnating and the society coming apart at the seams. By the 1980s, the system collapsed, and the core countries, always far richer and more powerful, "won the Cold War." Much of the former Soviet empire can now be restored to its Third World status.

The Cold War is not simply the story of Chile, Guatemala, and a host of others, but there are compelling and instructive similarities, apart from scale.

From this perspective, we find ready answers to the four questions about the Cold War raised earlier (sec. 4). First, authentic security concerns were distinctly secondary, though not so ludicrous as in the case of much weaker Third World countries, where they were also invoked without shame. It is also not surprising that "strategies of containment" were motivated primarily by domestic economic considerations, as Gaddis found, though always cloaked with security pretexts—which may have been believed, a matter of little moment; it is a truism, familiar from daily experience, that beliefs are easily constructed to disguise interest, then firmly held, so that rational analysis will seek the sources of systematic beliefs, something we understand well in dealing with topics other than domestic power. Second, it makes sense to date the conflict from the first "challenge" in 1917–18, as in the case of lesser "ultranationalist rotten apples." The duplicity of the posturing is a familiar accompaniment of intervention in the Third World. Third, the constituent events of the Cold War fall into place without comment. And fourth, there is no reason to be surprised at the persistence of basic lines of policy before, during, and after the Cold War.

Disguises aside, the conclusions are clear. The primary enemy remains the Third World, which must be kept under control. One huge segment of the Third World that had escaped from its service role was militarily powerful, as it had been for centuries, sufficiently so as to pose a serious deterrent to the task of world control—the "obligation" that "nature and history" have "laid on us." It was also a "rotten apple," offering what U.S. planners regarded as an appealing alternative to others, even at home. Its murderous leaders were fine fellows, as long as they allow us a free hand; but they seemed insufficiently prepared to concede that right. Their very existence also offered options for "neutralism," in Europe and the Third World, interfering with the requirement of total control for the indefinite future ("preponderance"). With the deviants returned to the fold and the deterrent removed, the "shield" required for intervention and subversion is no longer needed. We may now intervene "by choice," asking "What is in it for us?" We also cast aside doctrines that have lost their utility for population control, conceding that the "threats to our interest could not be laid at the Kremlin's door," except insofar as the "Kremlin conspiracy" interfered with our commitment to keep a "military protectorate" over "economically critical regions" to guarantee the rights and needs of U.S. investors. It is not, however, that hypocrisy can end; rather, it will have to take new forms.

With the virus destroyed, we turn to the next stage, admiring our virtue while constructing new "showcases for capitalism and democracy," as proclaimed in 1954 for Guatemala, 1983 for Grenada, and regularly elsewhere when order is restored. When the "showcase" becomes something a bit different, the facts can be stored away in dusty cabinets, or if noticed, attributed to the irremediable defects of those we tried to rescue. All familiar. The current triumphalism in the North among the privileged and powerful, though hardly the general populations, and the despair throughout much of the South suggest something about just what has been going on under the guise of the Cold War, just who the victors and the vanquished are, and what principles have triumphed.

The matter merits a little thought. Wars are rarely simple affairs, pitting one antagonist (say, nation state) against another. There are always multiple dimensions, and the Smithian proviso is invariably relevant: the interests of the architects of policy commonly differ from those of the general population, much as in the case of Adam Smith's England, the least undemocratic state of his day. A look at who is celebrating after a conflict and benefits from it, and who is left in distress and suffering, often tells us something about the true victors and defeated, and indeed what the conflict was about. By that criterion, the victors of World War II included the financial and manufacturing interests that were mobilized in support of the fascist regimes and were largely reconstituted and restored to power by the official victors; the losers of World War II included leading elements of the anti-fascist resistance worldwide, ranging from radical democratic to Communist in orientation, and violently demolished or displaced and marginalized by the official victors. Not the conventional picture, but an accurate one, and one that does not lack relevance to an assessment of what was at stake. In the case of the Cold War, the outcome is celebrated by privileged elites in the state capitalist industrial world and some of their associates in the service areas, and by substantial parts of the ruling sectors of the East who have now joined forces with them. It is not being widely celebrated by the population of the East, much as they appreciate the end of the tyranny. For most of the Third World, it simply deepens the catastrophe of their lives. And for the mass of the population of the West, the major effect of the end of the Cold War is to provide new ways to undermine what the business press calls the "luxurious" life styles of "pampered" Western workers. The actual consequences have something to tell us about realities that look rather different after they have passed through the distorting prisms of power and authority.

In the post–Cold War period, the South can anticipate a worsening of oppression for the large majority while some sectors may be enriched, notably those linked to the masters of the global economy. The United States and its clients can resort more freely to violence, the deterrent having disappeared, but may not do so for other reasons. Changes in the domestic culture since the 1960s have raised the political costs of intervention, as recognized in the Bush administration planning document cited earlier (p. 11); and the evolution of the international economy offers more cost-effective techniques of domination and control, or simply marginalization. As for Eastern Europe, parts (e.g., the Czech Republic) should be able to rejoin the advanced economies, while much of the region reverts to its traditional Third World status, helped in that direction by the structural adjustment policies that typically create an economy subordinated to the needs of foreign investors and a two-tiered society, with islands of great privilege in a sea of misery, sometimes called "economic miracles" if investors benefit sufficiently. As long predicted, much of the ex-*Nomenklatura* is taking a prominent place among the new elites, having shifted allegiance from Soviet state power to international business and financial interests. These developments offer promising new weapons against the general population in the West as well, a matter to which we return.

2

THE POLITICAL–
ECONOMIC ORDER

In the last chapter, I discussed some continuities that extend through many centuries, notably those related to Europe's conquest of the world, a crusade now led by one of the European-settled colonies and including the one major Third World country never colonized, along with a few smaller ones that were also able to chart their own course, avoiding the neoliberal model that has helped keep the South in its service role.[1]

Through this long era there have been many significant changes, some already discussed. One crucial change was brought by the Second World War: for the first time a single state had such overwhelming wealth and power that its planners could realistically design and execute a global vision. As the war ended, the United States held about half of the world's wealth and was its greatest military power, enjoying unprecedented security; it had no enemies nearby, dominated both oceans as well as the richest and most developed regions across the seas, and controlled the world's major reserves of energy and other critical resources. The United States had long been the world's leading industrial power. The war severely harmed all others, while in the United States, uniquely immune from the war's devastation, production boomed, nearly quadrupling in scale.

From the early stages of World War II, U.S. planners recognized that they would be in a position to organize much of the world. Naturally, they intended to exploit these opportunities. From 1939 through 1945, extensive studies on the postwar world were conducted by the Council on Foreign Relations, which brings together internationally oriented corporate and financial circles, and top-level State Department planners. They designed what they called a "Grand Area," an integrated world economy that would satisfy the needs of the American economy and provide it with "the 'elbow room' . . . needed in order to survive without major readjustments"—that is, without modification of the domestic distribution of power, wealth, ownership, and control. The planners sought "national security," but in the expansive sense discussed earlier, which has little to do with the security of the nation.

It was at first assumed that Germany (though not Japan) would survive as a major power center. The Grand Area, then, was to be a non-German bloc, which was to incorporate at a minimum the Western hemisphere, the Far East, and the former British empire, to be dismantled along with other regional systems and incorporated under U.S. control. Meanwhile the United States extended its own regional systems in Latin America and the Pacific, excluding traditional colonial rulers. As it became clear that Germany would be defeated, Grand Area planning was modified to include the German bloc as well. A fly in the ointment was the Soviet Union, later China, to be dealt with by "containment" or preferably "roll back," in the framework discussed earlier.

The structure of the Grand Area was thought through with some care, later developed in government planning studies as events took their course. Highest on the list for global planners were the rich industrial societies. In the context of their needs, the traditional colonial domains were assigned their specific roles. An omnipresent issue was the challenge of the Communist states, which had seemingly escaped from their Third World status; this was the core problem of the Cold War, overcome with the reintegration of the Soviet empire and China into the global economy as largely subordinate sectors. Always in the background was the future of the United States itself. Its society was to be reshaped in a particular way, one that would, it was hoped, become a model for the industrial world. This last topic merits a close look for what it reveals about the dominant social forces and their thinking. We begin with this (sec. 1), then turning to the global context (sec. 3) after a historical interlude (sec. 2), concluding with a look at contemporary developments and where they might lead.

1. Securing the Home Front

The Enemy Within

The problems at home were in part social and ideological, in part economic. The Great Depression of the 1930s had brought forth a serious challenge to business domination, a great shock; the prevailing assumption had been that the threat of labor organizing and popular democracy had been buried forever. After some preliminary warnings, the Wagner Act of 1935 accorded rights to workers that had been won half a century earlier in England and elsewhere. That victory for working people and for democracy sent a chill through the business community. The National Association of Manufacturers (NAM) warned of the "hazard facing industrialists" in "the newly realized political power of the masses." That must be reversed, and "their thinking . . . directed " to more proper channels, or " we are definitely heading for adversity," the NAM warned.

A corporate counteroffensive was quickly launched, sometimes using the traditional recourse to state violence, but coming to rely more on thought

control: "scientific methods of strike-breaking" and "human relations";
campaigns to mobilize the public against "outsiders" preaching "communism and anarchy" and seeking to disrupt the communities of sober working-
men and farmers, housewives tending to their families, hard-working executives toiling day and night to serve the people—"Americanism," in which all
share alike in joy and harmony. The project built upon earlier propaganda
successes of the Public Relations (PR) industry, an American innovation,
which had beaten back a wave of anti-business sentiment in the early years
of the century and helped establish business domination after World War I,
conclusively it had been thought.

The latter achievement was aided by the experiences of the first government propaganda agency, Woodrow Wilson's Creel Commission, which had
helped to convert a pacifist country into jingoist warmongers when Wilson
decided to go to war. The propaganda successes greatly impressed the
American business world and others, among them Adolf Hitler, who attributed Germany's defeat to its ineptitude on the propaganda front in comparison with the Anglo–Americans. Wilson himself was described as "the great
generalissimo on the propaganda front" by Harold Lasswell, one of the
leading figures of modern political science, who began his career with
inquiries into propaganda and its uses in the West. Like other serious
investigators, he recognized that propaganda was of greater importance in
more free and democratic societies, where the public cannot be kept in line
by the whip. Keeping to prevailing norms, he advocated the more sophisticated use of this "new technique of control" of the general public, who are
a threat to order because of the "ignorance and superstition [of] . . . the
masses." As he explained in the *Encyclopaedia of the Social Sciences*, we
should not succumb to "democratic dogmatisms about men being the best
judges of their own interests." They are not; the best judges are the elites—
the rich men of Churchill's "rich nations"—who must be ensured the means
to impose their will, for the common good.

Like other leading intellectuals, and surely the business world, Lasswell
shared Secretary of State Lansing's fear of the "ignorant and incapable mass
of humanity," and the danger of allowing them to become "dominant in the
earth," or even influential, as Lansing (mistakenly) believed the Bolsheviks
intended. Articulating these concerns, the leading progressive intellectual
Walter Lippmann, the dean of American journalism and a noted democratic
theorist and commentator on public affairs, advised that "the public must be
put in its place" so that the "responsible men" may "live free of the trampling
and the roar of a bewildered herd." In a democracy, Lippmann held, these
"ignorant and meddlesome outsiders" do have a "function": to be "interested
spectators of action," but not "participants," lending their weight periodically to some member of the leadership class (elections), then returning to
their private concerns.

Lippmann represents the more progressive fringe of opinion. At the
reactionary end, we find those mislabeled "conservatives" in contemporary

ideology, who reject even the spectator role. Hence the attractiveness to Reaganite statist reactionaries of clandestine terror operations designed to leave the domestic population ignorant, along with censorship, agitprop on a novel scale, and other measures to ensure that a powerful and interventionist state will not be troubled by the rabble.

As Bakunin presciently observed over a century ago, this conception was common to the two major tendencies among the rising "new class" of intellectuals: those who would become the "Red bureaucracy," instituting "the worst of all despotic governments"; and those who see the path to privilege and authority in service to state–corporate power. In the West, the "responsible men" are guided by an intuitive understanding of a maxim formulated by David Hume as one of the First Principles of Government: to ensure that "the many are governed by the few" and to guarantee "the implicit submission with which men resign their own sentiments and passions to those of their rulers," the governors must control thought; "'Tis therefore, on opinion only that government is founded; and this maxim extends to the most despotic and most military governments, as well as to the most free and most popular"—in reality, far more to "the most free and most popular," for obvious reasons.[2]

Bakunin's analysis brings to mind much earlier reflections by Thomas Jefferson; rather generally, interesting connections can be drawn from classical liberal thought to the libertarian socialists of later years, who often saw themselves as its natural inheritors, the leading anarchosyndicalist Rudolf Rocker for one.[3] In his last years, Jefferson had serious concerns about the fate of the democratic experiment. He distinguished between "aristocrats and democrats." The aristocrats are "those who fear and distrust the people, and wish to draw all powers from them into the hands of the higher classes." The democrats, in contrast, "identify with the people, have confidence in them, cherish and consider them as the honest & safe, altho' not the most wise depository of the public interest." The aristocrats were the advocates of the rising capitalist state, which Jefferson regarded with much disdain because of the obvious contradiction between democracy and capitalism (whether in the state-guided Western model, or some other), particularly as new corporate structures—the "banking institutions and moneyed incorporations" of whom he had warned—were granted increasing powers, mainly by judicial decision. The modern progressive intellectuals who seek to "put the public in its place" and are free of "democratic dogmatisms" about the capacity of the "ignorant and meddlesome outsiders" to enter the political arena are Jefferson's "aristocrats," democratic only by comparison with the remainder of the operative spectrum. Jefferson's worst fears were more than realized as the spectrum of opinion settled into its modern version, accommodating to power and its exercise.

It is not, of course, that the democratic ideal collapsed entirely; rather, it was marginalized, though it remained alive in popular movements and was articulated by some intellectuals, most prominent among them, perhaps,

America's leading twentieth-century philosopher, John Dewey. Dewey recognized in his later years that "politics is the shadow cast on society by big business," and as long as this is so, "the attenuation of the shadow will not change the substance." Reforms are of limited utility; democracy requires that the source of the shadow be removed, not only because of its domination of the political arena, but because the very institutions of private power undermine democracy and freedom. Dewey was explicit about the anti-democratic power he had in mind: "Power today resides in control of the means of production, exchange, publicity, transportation and communication. Whoever owns them rules the life of the country," even if democratic forms remain: "business for private profit through private control of banking, land, industry, reinforced by command of the press, press agents and other means of publicity and propaganda"—that is the system of actual power, the source of coercion and control, and until it is unraveled we cannot talk seriously about democracy and freedom. In a free and democratic society, workers should be "the masters of their own industrial fate," not tools rented by employers, a position that traces back to leading ideas of classical liberalism articulated by Wilhelm von Humboldt and Adam Smith, among others. It is "illiberal and immoral" to train children to work, "not freely and intelligently, but for the sake of the work earned," in which case their activity is "not free because not freely participated in." Hence industry must be changed "from a feudalistic to a democratic social order," based on workers' control and federal organization in the style of G.D.H. Cole's guild socialism and much anarchist and left-Marxist thought. As for production, its "ultimate aim" is not production of goods but "the production of free human beings associated with one another on terms of equality," a conception inconsistent with modern industrialism in its state capitalist or state socialist varieties, and again with roots in classical liberal ideals.[4]

Dewey also had no illusions about the hidden premise that lies behind the self-serving rhetoric about "responsible men," "wise men," "best minds," "aristocracy of intellect and character,"[5] and so on. Lippmann, for example, did not ask why he was one of the "responsible men" but not Eugene Debs, who, far from joining that august company, was serving a ten-year jail sentence. The answers are not hard to find, even if unspoken.

With the narrowing of the doctrinal system over the years, fundamental libertarian principles now sound exotic and extreme, perhaps even "anti-American." It is well to remember, then, that they are "as American as apple pie," with origins in traditional thinking that is ritually lauded though distorted and forgotten. This is an important feature of the deterioration of democracy in the current period, at the intellectual as at the institutional level.

Business propaganda makes its distinctive contributions to these processes. Consider an essay by Michael Joyce, president of the Bradley Foundation, one of the rightwing foundations dedicated to narrowing the ideological spectrum, particularly in schools and colleges, still further to the right. Joyce begins with rhetoric drawn from the libertarian left, condemning the narrow sense of citizenship that restricts it to the "episodic, infrequent, albeit boring, duty" of voting, after which the citizen "is supposed to get out of the way, and let the experts take over." He advocates a richer concept of citizenship, participation in civil society, outside "the political sphere." Here "citizenly activity . . . occurs *not* episodically or infrequently, as with voting, but regularly and constantly": in the marketplace, holding a job, earning a living, family life, churches, fraternal and sororal lodges, PTA meetings, and other such "tasks" of "decent citizens."

As the uplifting tale unfolds, the "political sphere" disappears from view, left to forces unknown and unseen—or almost. Joyce does warn against "arrogant, paternalistic social scientists, therapists, professionals and bureaucrats, who claim exclusive right to minister to the hurts inflicted by hostile social forces," forming the "*bloated, corrupt, centralized bureaucracies*" of the "nanny state"; "corrupt intellectual and cultural elites in the universities, the media, and elsewhere," who denigrate "traditional mediating structures" as "benighted" and "reactionary"; "professional elites" who "call for more government programs—and more bureaucratic experts and professionals to minister to the hurts allegedly inflicted on hapless victims by industrialism, racism, sexism, and so on—in the course taking away yet more authority from citizens and civil institutions."

The citizen, then, must return to the wholesome task of looking for a job and going to church, while the "nanny state" is rid of the therapists and social scientists who now run the world, and left in the hands of—some absent force. Entirely missing from the picture are the actual centers of concentrated wealth and power, the people and institutions that determine what happens in the social and economic order and largely dominate the state, either by direct participation or imposition of narrow constraints on political choice, converting governmental authority into a powerful and interventionist "nanny state" that cares for their needs with much solicitude. In brief, the PR operation is more or less the analog of an account of Soviet Russia that overlooks the Kremlin, the military, and the Communist Party. In a totalitarian state, it would be impossible to carry off the farce; here it is quite easy, an interesting fact, which reveals the efficiency of business-run thought control, to which vast resources and thought have been dedicated for many years. Liberal Democrats play rather similar games, a matter to which we return.[6]

In the more free societies, state controls are rarely exercised directly. "The sinister fact about literary censorship in England," George Orwell wrote, "is that it is largely voluntary. Unpopular ideas can be silenced, and inconvenient facts kept dark, without any need for any official ban." The desired outcome is attained in part by the "general tacit agreement that 'it wouldn't do' to mention that particular fact," in part as a simple consequence of centralization of the press in the hands of "wealthy men who have every motive to be dishonest on certain important topics." As a result, "Anyone who challenges the prevailing orthodoxy finds himself silenced with surprising effectiveness." A decade earlier, John Dewey had observed that critique of "specific abuses" of "our un-free press" is of limited value: "The only really fundamental approach to the problem is to inquire concerning the necessary effect of the present economic system upon the whole system of publicity; upon the judgment of what news is, upon the selection and elimination of matter that is published, upon the treatment of news in both editorial and news columns." We should ask "how far genuine intellectual freedom and social responsibility are possible on any large scale under the existing economic regime." Not very far, he judged.[7]

The leading student of business propaganda, Australian social scientist Alex Carey, argues persuasively that "the 20th century has been characterized by three developments of great political importance: the growth of democracy, the growth of corporate power, and the growth of corporate propaganda as a means of protecting corporate power against democracy." The corporate counteroffensive of the late 1930s is one of several striking illustrations that he presents for this thesis.

The means for controlling the "public mind" were much extended by the newly available technology of radio, quickly taken over by the corporate sector in the United States, unlike the other advanced countries, which were less under business domination for a variety of historical reasons. The war put the project of reversing the democratic thrust of the 1930s on hold, but it was taken up forcefully as the war ended. Huge PR campaigns employed the media, cinema, and other devices to identify "free enterprise"—meaning state-subsidized private power with no infringement on managerial prerogatives—as "the American way," threatened by dangerous subversives. The technique of whipping up fear and hatred of "foreigners," "communists," "anarchists," and other miserable creatures was, of course, long familiar, virtually second nature to propagandists in a political culture with unusual Manichaean strains from its earliest days, one that is capable of the ranting of NSC 68, or the concept "un-American." Apart from the former Soviet Union, where "anti-Sovietism" was the highest crime, there are few intellectual communities that could treat with respect ludicrous and deceitful works on "Anti-Americanism," raging about departures from adequate servility to the Holy State. A book on "anti-Italianism" would only elicit ridicule in Milan or Rome, as in any society with a functioning democratic culture.[8]

Recognizing these peculiarities of American political culture, the U.S. Chamber of Commerce distributed more than a million copies of its pamphlet "Communist Infiltration in the United States" immediately after the war, along with another entitled "Communists Within the Government." In April 1947, the Advertising Council announced a $100 million campaign to use all media to "sell" the American economic system—as they conceived it—to the American people; the program was officially described as a "major project of educating the American people about the economic facts of life." Corporations "started extensive programs to indoctrinate employees," the leading business journal *Fortune* reported, subjecting their captive audiences to "Courses in Economic Education" and testing them for commitment to the "free enterprise" system—that is, "Americanism." A survey conducted by the American Management Association (AMA) found that many corporate leaders regarded "propaganda" and "economic education" as synonymous, holding that "we want our people to think right." The AMA reported that Communism, socialism, and particular political parties and unions "are often common targets of such campaigns," which "some employers view . . . as a sort of 'battle of loyalties' with the unions"—a rather unequal battle, given the resources available, including the corporate media, which continue to offer the services free of charge in ways to which we return.[9]

Others leaped into the fray as well. As is well known, the United States is unique among industrial societies in lacking comprehensive health insurance. Truman's efforts to bring the country into the modern world were bitterly attacked by the American Medical Association as "the first step" towards "the kind of regimentation that led to totalitarianism in Germany and the downfall of that nation." The Association's journal denounced "medical soviets" and the "gauleiters" who would run them and warned that advocates of national health care and insurance were inciting a socialist revolution. Its advertising firm launched the biggest campaign in American history to defeat proposed legislation, making up fake quotes from Lenin, appealing to Protestant clergymen on grounds that Christianity is threatened by politicians undermining "the sanctity of life," and distributing 54 million pieces of propaganda targeting various groups. The slogan of the national PR campaign was "The Voluntary Way is the American Way." Its basic theme was: "American medicine has become the blazing focal point in a fundamental struggle which may determine whether America remains free or whether we are to become a socialist state." The heresy was soundly thrashed.

With the costs of the highly inefficient and bureaucratized capitalist health care program becoming a serious burden for business, the issue of health care entered the government–media agenda in the 1990s—which is why we now find articles in the mainstream press ridiculing the propaganda campaigns of earlier years. The Clinton administration sought health reforms, but keeping strictly to two essential conditions: 1) the outcome must be radically regressive, unlike tax- or even wage-based programs; and 2) large insurance companies must remain in control, adding substantially to the costs of health care with their huge advertising expenditures, high executive salaries, and profits, along with the costs of their intricate bureaucratic mechanisms to micromanage to ensure minimal health care and the elaborate governmental regulatory apparatus necessary to keep the intricate system based on private profit functioning with at least some regard for public needs—"managed competition." The code phrase used to disguise these obstacles to a far more equitable and efficient government-run plan is that the latter is "politically impossible." The considerable popular support for some variety of national health care is therefore irrelevant.

Media coverage keeps well within the bounds set by state–corporate power. Thus a front-page *New York Times* article on public concern for health care reform mentions in passing, near the end, that 59 percent of respondents favor a model "that Mr. Clinton has rejected; a Canadian-style system of national health insurance paid for with tax money." The figure is remarkably high, given near-unanimous government–media dismissal of this option, which is off the agenda. The *Boston Globe* presented a "user's guide" to the baffled public, identifying and trying to clarify the issues that are under discussion. These are the six "guiding stars" presented by President Clinton— excluding, of course, the two unmentionables. The reporters quote experts who object to the "bewildering" complexity of the proposals in comparison to "the simpler government-run system" used elsewhere, but point out that this is not relevant: "It is hard to avoid complexity if one starts from the premise, as both Clinton supporters and his critics do, that a simpler government-funded health system is not an option." Since supporters and critics agree that we must have "managed care," no category remains to include those who disagree (including, it seems, the majority of the popula- tion, not to speak of grass-roots organizations, members of Congress, medical specialists, etc.)—except, perhaps, "anti-American."

The week before, the same journal gave extensive front-page coverage to a national survey it conducted with the Harvard School of Public Health that measured public reactions to three options: managed care, individual private care, and Medicare, the nationalized system for the elderly. The article compares reactions to the first two options, finding little significant differ- ence ("good news for the White House"). Data are cited demonstrating that Medicare wins handily on quality of care, ease of use, and most other measures, as it does on administrative costs and other factors not considered. And indeed, the reader who reaches paragraph 26 will find that "one striking finding is that elderly Medicare subscribers were the most satisfied of all insured Americans on virtually every measure of medical care and insurance system quality," a result that "some interpret" as an argument in favor of national health insurance. But it is the highly regressive and inefficient options that cater to the corporate–financial world that remain on the agenda. Medicare is to be cut, which will at least have the advantage of making paragraph 26 unnecessary in later studies.[10]

Since the 1940s, when major opinion polls began asking people's attitudes toward a universal health program, "the majority or large pluralities have consistently supported it," Vicente Navarro observes, "even at a cost of paying higher taxes." In 1989–90, support for a tax-based national health plan was in the 60–70 percent range (69 percent in February 1992). The huge administrative costs and restricted coverage of U.S. health care do not result from some curious feature of American culture or popular desires, as constantly alleged by journalists and scholars, but from the structures of power and propaganda, notably the weakness of the labor movement and business control of the doctrinal institutions.[11]

Postwar propaganda campaigns registered many other outstanding successes, recorded with pleasure by business organizations. The Chamber of Commerce reported that its attack on alleged Communists in government "led to Truman's loyalty program"—"inadequate but still a loyalty program," thus going at least part of the way towards eliminating people who might be tempted to help the poor "plunder the rich," even if not yet far enough. Another example was the fate of the Office of Price Administration (OPA), which had kept commodities within the reach of the public during the war. A massive campaign by the NAM and the Chamber of Commerce reduced public support for OPA from 80 percent in February 1946 to 26 percent eight months later. President Truman was forced to terminate its operations in the face of what he described as a huge business campaign "to destroy the laws that were protecting the consumer against exploitation." By 1947, a State Department public relations officer was able to gloat that "smart public relations [has] paid off as it has before and will again." Public opinion "is not moving to the right, it has been moved—cleverly—to the right." "While the rest of the world has moved to the left, has admitted labor into government, has passed liberalized legislation, the United States has become anti–social change, anti–economic change, anti-labor."

A few years later, sociologist Daniel Bell, then an editor of *Fortune* magazine, observed that "it has been industry's prime concern, in the post war years, to change the climate of opinion ushered in by . . . the depression. This 'free enterprise' campaign has two essential aims: to rewin the loyalty of the worker which now goes to the union and to halt creeping socialism," meaning the mildly reformist capitalism of the New Deal. The scale of business PR campaigns was "staggering," Bell noted. One significant effect was legislation that sharply restricted union activity, leading to the decline of unions that continues to the present. So thorough is the campaign that Labor Secretary Robert Reich, at the liberal fringe of the Clinton administration, tells us that "the jury is still out on whether the traditional union is necessary for the new workplace," what the press calls "the high performance work place of the future" that state–corporate authority is designing. "Unions are O.K. where they are. And where they are not"—which is almost everywhere by now—"it is not clear yet what sort of organization should represent workers," Commerce Secretary Ronald Brown, another "New Democrat," elaborates.

A parallel attack on independent thought, part of the "just suppression" that Truman's leading advisers called for in the Cold War context, succeeded once again in largely eliminating any open challenge to business domination. Much of the intellectual community and labor bureaucracy cooperated with enthusiasm. The campaign is often mislabeled "McCarthyism"; in reality, Senator McCarthy was a latecomer who exploited a climate of repression already established, causing serious damage before he was removed from the scene. These efforts restored the atmosphere of the 1920s, in large measure. Erosion of discipline under the impact of the popular ferment of the 1960s elicited renewed hysteria and even more dedicated efforts to establish doctrinal controls.

A congressional inquiry was informed that by 1978, American business was spending $1 billion a year on grassroots propaganda. These efforts were supplemented by what Carey calls "tree-tops propaganda," targeting educated sectors and seeking to eliminate any articulate threat to business domination. Methods ranged from endowed Professorships of Free Enterprise in universities to huge propaganda campaigns against the usual run of targets: taxes, regulation of business, welfare (for the poor), pointy-headed "bureaucrats" interfering with the creative entrepreneur, union corruption and violence, evil apologists for our enemies, and so on.[12]

The effects have been dramatic, as the "l-word" ("liberal") followed the "s-word" ("socialist") into obloquy and oblivion. The right-wing conquest of ideological institutions is of course not complete, a catastrophe to the totalitarian mentality, reflected in the extraordinary and often rather comical campaign raging in the United States and Britain to defend the ramparts from a takeover by "left fascists," omnipotent because they have still not been thoroughly rooted out. Indications that the labor movement has not been completely tamed arouse similar hysteria, illustrated in late 1993 in interesting ways, to which we return. That more advanced electoral democracies should exhibit such tendencies is entirely natural, for reasons already noted.

Functioning democracy is feared even more at home than abroad. Attempts of previously marginalized segments of the population to enter the political arena in the 1960s were condemned by frightened liberal elites as a "crisis of democracy." The resulting "ungovernability" can only be overcome by restoring popular sectors to passivity and obedience, the Trilateral Commission urged in its first major study, *The Crisis of Democracy*. The Commission, founded by David Rockefeller, brings together liberal internationalist elites from the United States, Europe, and Japan; Jimmy Carter was a member, and his administration was drawn almost entirely from the Commission. The American rapporteur, Professor Samuel Huntington of Harvard, looked back with some nostalgia to the golden age when "Truman had been able to govern the country with the cooperation of a relatively small number of Wall Street lawyers and bankers," so that democracy functioned smoothly, with no "crisis." Fear of the "ignorant and meddlesome outsiders" articulated by business leaders, government officials, and many leading intellectuals can be traced to the earliest modern democratic revolution in seventeenth-century England. It has not abated since.

Nor has the dedication to "historical engineering," to borrow the term invented by American historians as they enlisted in "Generalissimo Wilson's" ideological crusade. This phenomenon too provides much insight into Western political culture, and what we can anticipate as it designs a new order with fewer impediments on decision-makers. We might pause to look at a few typical cases of the enterprise of reshaping recent history to a form more suitable for domestic power.

Engineering Current History

One of the most revealing illustrations of the enterprise of historical engineering, its triumphs and limitations, is the interpretation of the Indochina wars from the earliest days through the retrospective reconstructions. U.S. involvement in Indochina was never popular, but by the late 1960s the effect on the public was becoming dramatic. One frightening aspect was the "Vietnam syndrome," a disease with such ominous symptoms as opposition to aggression, terror, and violence, and even sympathy for their victims. These "sickly inhibitions against the use of military force," as the symptoms were described by Reaganite intellectual Norman Podhoretz, were thought to have been cured by the glorious triumph over Grenada, when the United States was once again "standing tall," in the words of the president, after six thousand elite troops succeeded in overcoming the resistance of several dozen Cuban construction workers whom they had attacked and a few Grenadan militiamen, winning eight thousand medals of honor. But the malady proved resilient, a fact understood by planners (recall the leaked Bush planning document on defeating "much weaker enemies"). Bush and many commentators exulted that the Gulf conflict had finally eradicated the dread syndrome, wrongly again.

We might note in passing that the Grenada exploit was closely watched by top military commanders. General Schwartzkopf observed that the Cubans fought harder than expected in Grenada, teaching important lessons for the Gulf war. Here, the commanding General took no chances. The tactic adopted was to pulverize the Third World peasant army—hiding in the sand, immobile, and defenseless—after a flood of propaganda about its colossal artillery, sophisticated defenses, chemical weapons, and other exotic capacities, later conceded to be fakery. When the enemy was utterly demoralized, U.S. forces cut off escape, and the Air Force slaughtered those attempting to flee (including Asian workers and Kuwaiti hostages). Western military experts were amazed to discover that the United States, Britain, their NATO allies, and client states worldwide were actually able to overcome a minor Third World power which, even with substantial Western support, had been unable to withstand post-revolutionary Iran—isolated, lacking arms, its officer corps decimated. Laurence Freedman, head of the department of War Studies at Kings College of the University of London and co-author of a highly regarded book on the war, observed sagely that "The Gulf war certainly demonstrated that in a regular fight America and its allies remain the heavyweight champions. They can overwhelm all-comers, even those that have squandered vast resources on military assets . . . ," an astonishing accomplishment that may even surpass the Grenada triumph.[13]

U.S. intervention in Indochina received considerable attention from the early 1960s, when John F. Kennedy escalated from support for a Latin American–style terror state to outright aggression against South Vietnam. It has been a major project throughout to cast these events in the proper light. The achievements have been noteworthy. In over thirty years, one would be hard put to find a single phrase in the voluminous mainstream literature that even acknowledges the possibility that the U.S. attack was anything other than "the defense of South Vietnam"—unwise, the critics say. The totalitarian Soviet Union could not boast any such triumph after its invasion of Afghanistan.

Until the Tet offensive of January 1968 convinced the American business community that the affair was too costly, support for the war was overwhelming among articulate sectors, apart from growing qualms about the likelihood of success. The Tet offensive and the reaction of power centers to it instantly converted the intellectual community to "long-time opponents of the war," a fact previously unknown, also inspiring a remarkable rewriting of the earlier record that is immune to exposure and critical discussion. But the analytic stance scarcely changed.

At the outer limits of tolerable dissidence, the war came to be seen as an "error" based on misunderstanding and naiveté, yet another example of "our excess of righteousness and disinterested benevolence" (the leading Asia scholar John King Fairbank, presidential address, American Historical Society, December 1968). U.S. intervention began with "blundering efforts to do good," but "by 1969"—a year after corporate America had called for the enterprise to be liquidated—most people realized that it was "a disastrous mistake," that the United States "could not impose a solution except at a price too costly to itself" (*New York Times* dove Anthony Lewis). "We opposed the war because we believed . . . that 'Washington could "save" the people of South Vietnam and Cambodia from Communism only at a cost that made a mockery of the word "save,"'" the respected democratic socialist Irving Howe explained in his journal *Dissent* in 1979 (quoting Harvard international affairs specialist Stanley Hoffmann). These are characteristic reactions at the critical extreme.

As the conquest of history and ideology continues, more audacious moves can be contemplated. Thus, William Shawcross acknowledges that there were "careless White House policies, including the destruction of Cambodian villages"—referring to the purposeful attack on the peasant society that he himself had documented before ideological reconstruction had reached its current phase, a war initiated and maintained by Washington that devastated inner Cambodia, causing the flight of a million and a half refugees to Phnom Penh and leaving some 600,000 killed according to the CIA, with people dying in Phnom Penh alone at a rate of eight thousand a month as the U.S. client regime collapsed; not to speak of other "careless" policies in Laos and Vietnam. But, despite such U.S. oversights, Shawcross continues, "those of us who were opposed to the American effort in Indochina should be humbled by the scale of the suffering inflicted by the Communist victors—especially in Cambodia [where they were mobilized to a significant extent by the U.S. bombardment, as he knows] but in Vietnam and Laos as well."

And by similar reasoning, although there were "careless" Soviet actions in Afghanistan, nevertheless "those of us who opposed the Soviet attack," including Soviet dissidents, should be "humbled by the scale of the suffering inflicted by the Islamic fundamentalist victors." In this case, the Shawcross argument would be recognized to be absurd and grotesque, because Western intellectual culture is able to comprehend that someone might have a principled opposition to aggression and war crimes—when committed by an official enemy.

It is revealing that Shawcross now claims in print that he was so horrified by what the Khmer Rouge were doing from 1975 that "I decided to write a book about it. It became *Sideshow*"—which was, in fact, a book about *American* atrocities in Cambodia in the period *before* the Khmer Rouge takeover. His readers know that; he knows they know it. And they all know that it doesn't matter. What matters is to observe the "general tacit agreements" of the intellectual culture to which Orwell referred.[14]

The effect of the ideological warfare on the general public has been complex. Public opinion studies show that by 1990, the median estimate of Vietnamese casualties was 100,000, about 5 percent of the official figure; the discovery that Germans estimate Holocaust deaths at 300,000 might elicit some notice and concern, but this passes with no comment. Despite these shocking facts, over 70 percent of the public, unlike the articulate intellectuals, continue to regard the war as "fundamentally wrong and immoral," not a "mistake." Nevertheless, in one of the most stunning propaganda achievements of all of history, the doctrinal managers have succeeded in portraying Americans as the pathetic victims of the evil Vietnamese Communists, who, not satisfied with assaulting U.S. military forces defending Indochina from its people, now fail to open their country and archives totally to American investigators seeking remains of pilots maliciously shot down by the Vietnamese aggressors. "Hanoi knows today that we seek only answers without the threat of retribution for the past," President Bush proclaimed in October 1992. We can never forgive them for what they did to us, but we will magnanimously refrain from punishing them for their crimes and may even allow them to receive aid from abroad if only they confess their sins with proper humility and dedicate themselves to resolving the only moral issue that remains from a war that slaughtered millions of people and destroyed three countries.[15]

The uniformity of media subordination to these norms is astonishing. For a decade, the official justification for the project of "bleeding Vietnam" was alleged outrage over Vietnam's December 1978 invasion of Cambodia, an unspeakable crime of "the Prussians of Asia" (*New York Times*), who drove out Pol Pot (a Chinese client, hence indirectly a U.S. ally after Carter's "tilt towards China" earlier in the year) and terminated his slaughters after years of murderous Cambodian attacks on Vietnamese border regions. When the Prussians withdrew all forces, the propaganda system switched easily to the earlier pretext, the fate of missing Americans. Under pressure from the business community, concerned that it will be deprived of potential profits in Vietnam as rivals begin to ignore the U.S. embargo, Washington began to shift policy, perceiving "progress" in Vietnam's acknowledgment of its sins. Throughout, commentators in the press and elsewhere played their role with scarcely a slip. One can find an occasional word to the effect that Vietnamese suffered too, but close to 100 percent of commentary keeps to the doctrine that the United States is entitled to set ground rules for Vietnam's entry into the civilized world, maintaining an embargo and blocking funds from elsewhere until our tormentors cease their abuse. Only the rarest voice would disrupt the crusade by recalling the lack of concern over far greater numbers of missing soldiers from past wars, where nothing impedes in-depth inquiries; or by exploring the hideous U.S. record of atrocities against POWs in Vietnam, Korea, and the Pacific war—let alone by expressing shock over the abysmal moral depths of the entire exercise.

One wonders whether the Soviet propaganda system, had it survived, would have been capable of similar achievements. It is unlikely, even though it could have appealed to the fact that "no one knows for sure how many Soviet prisoners remain in Afghanistan or how many are held in prisons in Pakistan and Iran." Russia claims that three hundred soldiers are unaccounted for; "the Red Cross has the names of 18, three of whom they visit. They continue to try to find the remainder, but developments are slow," and of no interest to the powerful, who have nothing to gain by taking note of the problem, or even suggesting that their clients attend to it.[16]

A second illustration of the power of historical engineering, no less significant, is the version of U.S. accomplishments in the Reagan–Bush years being crafted as a contribution to contemporary triumphalism. Some examples have already been mentioned. Take one further case that brings out the essential themes and their import with particular clarity. The respected political commentator of the *Washington Post*, David Broder, reviewed the Republican record of the 1980s as the Clinton administration took over in January 1993. He found many faults, but conceded that even liberal critics must acknowledge their accomplishments: "from Afghanistan to El Salvador, the United States under the leadership of these Republicans effectively supported the people whose values and aspirations came closest to our own— and helped them prevail." And for that grand achievement of statesmanship and morality, even we liberals must praise them.[17]

Our "values and aspirations," then, are illustrated by those who hold power "from Afghanistan to El Salvador." That is, in fact, a reasonable thesis, just as a rational observer would judge Soviet "values and aspirations" by looking at the people they "helped prevail." Let's pursue the exercise briefly.

In Afghanistan, resistance forces liberated the capital city of Kabul in April 1992, "but this happy state of affairs lasted just one month," the Dutch daily *NRC Handelsblad* reports: "In May 1992, rockets landed in the densely packed bazaar of Kabul," initiating a reign of terror attributed largely to Gulbuddin Hekmatyar, who was able to shoot his way into the prime minister's office; the favorite of the United States and Pakistan, Hekmatyar demonstrated expertise in both terror and narcotrafficking while serving as our man in Afghanistan. In August 1992, steady rocketing by Hekmatyar's forces killed at least two thousand people, most of them civilians, and drove half a million people out of Kabul, Human Rights Watch reports. "By year's end," it adds, "international interest in the conflict had all but vanished and Afghanistan appeared to be on the brink of a humanitarian catastrophe," as Hekmatyar took the lead in terror, bombardment of civilian targets, cutting off the capital city's electricity and water, torture, and other atrocities "carried out with U.S.- and Saudi-financed weaponry." The ruling council meanwhile "announced its intention to enforce Islamic law throughout the country." As Broder was writing in praise of our agents in Afghanistan, they were bombarding the city with rockets and mortars, having already left it largely in ruins, the bazaar leveled, while surgeons from "Doctors without Borders" operate in the cellar of the hospital because "above ground, it is too dangerous." By summer 1993, the London *Economist* estimated that 30,000 people had been killed and 100,000 wounded in Kabul, where "electricity and running water are supplied for only a few hours a week, at the discretion of the prime minister, Gulbuddin Hekmatyar," while many Kabulis "reminisce about the good old days" under Communist terror, now surpassed. Across the border in Peshawar, Pakistan, the UN representative said that "almost all of the refugees arriving now are Kabulis, well-educated people who, during the communist government, stayed in Kabul but who are now fleeing because they are accused of being collaborators."[18]

Rocket and artillery shelling increased sharply in early 1994, driving another 150,000 people out of Kabul, with an estimated one thousand killed in eight weeks, about the same number as were killed in the past eight months in Sarajevo, Molly Moore reports. More than half the remaining population fled; the Red Cross estimates that Kabul's 1992 population of two million has shrunk to 700,000, of whom 300,000 are also refugees. Most refugees now are "urban, middle-class families with professional backgrounds." Tens of thousands are "living on barren plains strewn with land mines, without adequate food and in the midst of the Afghan winter." Many who remain in Kabul face starvation because "Hekmatyar's gunmen have stolen truckloads of wheat and other foods and have not allowed local merchants to bring produce and grains into the city."[19]

International interest "vanished" because the wrong people are doing the killing and destroying. This is not Pol Pot's Cambodia, where propaganda points could be scored and careers made by a show of anguish over atrocities; a *show* of anguish, as is readily demonstrated by a look at reactions to similar atrocities that could have been stopped, not merely lamented, had it not been for the silence and apologetics of those who agonize over enemy crimes. The situation was not different under Soviet totalitarianism, where the commissars also shed bitter and angry tears over the crimes of official enemies.

Turning to El Salvador, the upholders of our values and aspirations are the beneficiaries of the $6 billion in aid provided them by the U.S. government: the generals, business leaders, and their political party Arena, which held its convention just after receiving Broder's praise, dedicating itself anew to defending the memory of the founder, Roberto d'Aubuisson, one of Central America's great killers. Arena's candidate for the 1994 election, Armando Calderón Sol, declared that the party is united "more than ever to defend [d'Aubuisson's] memory," while the convention hall echoed with the Arena theme song, which pledges to make "El Salvador the tomb where the Reds will end up"—the term "Reds" being understood quite broadly, as events have shown. Shortly before, the exploits of d'Aubuisson and his followers had received some attention when the UN Truth Commission published its report on atrocities of the 1980s, attributing 85 percent of the horrendous record to the security forces trained, armed, and advised by the United States and another 10 percent to the death squads linked to them and to the wealthy business sector that the United States hopes to keep firmly in power.[20] The media meanwhile professed shock at the revelation of what they had chosen to suppress when it mattered. The Clinton administration responded by establishing a Commission to inquire into this grim history; its mandate is to improve procedures, nothing more, because "we don't want to refight the battles of the eighties. We're not a house-cleaning Administration." The Salvadoran government agreed, issuing an amnesty for the killers and torturers in gross violation of the peace accords that established the Truth Commission, which stated that the guilty must be punished, and rejecting the Truth Commission demand that the Supreme Court be dismantled in view of its record of complicity in atrocities.

The current U.S. favorites in El Salvador, and advocates of the Nestor Sanchez doctrine at home (see pp. 48–51), were not alone in condemning the Truth Commission report. It was also criticized by José María Tojeira, Jesuit provincial for Central America, who noted that the report ignored the role of the United States, which "bears responsibility for the violence along with the Salvadoran Armed Forces," from the late 1970s, "when US officials committed to the policies that caused the Salvadoran people such hardship." "Washington should now reexamine its foreign policy over the last decade with an eye toward launching an epoch of new relations with the Third World."[21]

We will wait a long time for that. Quite the contrary, respectable people now bask in self-praise over the victory of those who upheld their "values and aspirations" from Afghanistan to El Salvador.

It would be unfair to charge Broder and others with believing what they say. Rather, they doubtless genuinely believe that their own professed values—freedom, secularism, dignity of the individual, human rights, and so on—are upheld by the elements helped to power around the world by U.S. government actions. Self-righteousness comes naturally to those who are able to achieve their will by force. They may also rest confident that the doctrinal system will properly efface and sanitize the past, at least among educated sectors who are its agents and, arguably, its most naive victims.

Free Enterprise, Free Markets

Alongside the social and ideological problems confronting the "responsible men" as World War II ended there were serious economic issues. The Great Depression had eliminated any lingering belief that capitalism might be a viable system. New Deal measures had only limited impact in countering the depression, but massive wartime spending and state economic management proved an effective answer. Particularly impressed were the corporate executives who flocked to Washington to run the state-organized economy. After the war, pent-up consumer demand kept the economy afloat briefly, but by the late 1940s it was widely expected that the country was heading back to economic decline. Influential government–corporate circles took it for granted that state power must be called upon once again to rescue private enterprise.

Business leaders recognized that social spending could stimulate the economy, but much preferred the military Keynesian alternative—for reasons having to do with privilege and power, not "economic rationality." This approach was adopted at once, the Cold War serving as the justification. In 1948, with the economy sinking into recession, Truman's "cold-war spending" was regarded by the business press as a "magic formula for almost endless good times" (*Steel*). It was a way to "maintain a generally upward tone," *Business Week* commented, if only the Russians cooperated. In 1949, the editors noted with some relief that "so far, Stalin's 'peace feelers' have been brushed aside" by Washington, but remained concerned that his "peace offensive" might be serious, interfering with "the prospect of ever-rising military spending" and compelling a shift to social spending as an economic stimulus. The *Magazine of Wall Street* saw military spending as a way to "inject new strength into the entire economy," and a few years later, found it "obvious that foreign economies as well as our own are now mainly dependent on the scope of continued arms spending in this country," referring to the international military Keynesianism that finally succeeded in reconstructing state capitalist industrial societies abroad and laying the basis for the huge expansion of Transnational Corporations, mainly U.S.-based.

The Pentagon system was considered ideal for these purposes. It extends well beyond the military establishment, incorporating also the Department of Energy, which produces nuclear weapons, and the space agency NASA, converted by the Kennedy administration to a significant component of the state-directed public subsidy to advanced industry. These arrangements impose on the public a large burden of the costs of industry (research and development, R&D) and provide a guaranteed market for excess production, a useful cushion for management decisions. Furthermore, this form of industrial policy does not have the undesirable side-effects of social spending directed to human needs. Apart from unwelcome redistributive effects, the latter policies tend to interfere with managerial prerogatives; useful production may undercut private gain, while state-subsidized waste production (arms, Man-on-the-Moon extravaganzas, etc.) is a gift to the owner and manager, to whom any marketable spin-offs will be promptly delivered. Social spending may also arouse public interest and participation, thus enhancing the threat of democracy; the public cares about hospitals, roads, neighborhoods, and so on, but has no opinion about the choice of missiles and high-tech fighter planes. The defects of social spending do not taint the military Keynesian alternative. For such reasons, *Business Week* explained, "there's a tremendous social and economic difference between welfare pump-priming and military pump-priming," the latter being far preferable.

Military pump-priming was also well-adapted to the needs of advanced industry: computers and electronics generally, aviation, and a wide range of related technologies and enterprises. In recent years, Reagan's "Star Wars" (SDI) was sold to business executives on these grounds, and while it is now conceded that the system never had any military prospects, it is justified on the basis of the valuable by-products that might enrich private enterprise.[22]

The Pentagon system of course served other purposes. As global enforcer, the United States needs intervention forces and an intimidating posture to facilitate their use. Nevertheless, the economic role of the Pentagon system has always been central, a fact obliquely recognized by leading diplomatic historians (see p. 34) and well known to military planners. Army Plans Chief General James Gavin, in charge of Army R&D under Eisenhower, noted that "what appears to be intense interservice rivalry in most cases . . . is fundamentally industrial rivalry."[23] It was in part in recognition of these realities that NSC 68 called for "sacrifice and discipline," with social spending displaced in favor of an industrial base for the military—and incidentally, "private enterprise."

Post–World War II government–corporate planners had ample historical precedents as they sought to enhance the state role in the economy. From its origins, the United States had relied heavily on state intervention and protection for the development of industry and agriculture, from the textile industry in the early nineteenth century, through the steel industry at the end of the century, to computers, electronics, and biotechnology today. Furthermore, the same has been true of every other successful industrial society, a lesson of economic history that is of no slight importance for the South.

With the Cold War gone, new fears have been stimulated to sustain the Pentagon funnel for the public subsidy; recall the March 1990 White House submission to Congress (p. 70). One straightforward device is arms sales to the Third World. The Bush administration placed great emphasis on increasing these sales, particularly to the Middle East, while at the same time calling sternly for restraint in sales of arms to the region—by others. For the first time, the government took on an active role in gaining markets for military industry. The Gulf war was exploited to the full for these purposes. At the Paris Air Show in June 1991, the weapons that had so dramatically destroyed a defenseless Third World country were displayed with much pride, and hope. Corporations may hire halls to exhibit their wares; a great power can use cities and deserts, flourishing the carnage to no small effect. In 1990 and

1991, the Congressional Research Service reported, the United States was the largest arms supplier to the Third World; in 1992, the United States took 57 percent of the Third World arms market (compared with Russia's 9 percent). Saudi Arabia alone had $30 billion in outstanding contracts with U.S. arms suppliers in mid-1993, part of the huge arms buildup that has undermined the economy of this super-rich country, recycling oil wealth to the West, primarily the United States, not the people of the region.

The Clinton administration expanded the Reagan–Bush programs, to much industry applause. "The expected $28 billion to $30 billion in U.S. foreign military sales for this fiscal year is the biggest annual total ever," AP reported in August 1993, most of it ticketed for the Middle East. For the first time, the Secretary of Commerce was sent to the Paris Air Show and to potential Third World buyers (Malaysia, Saudi Arabia), "hawking American fighter planes," an aerospace industry analyst commented approvingly. Early industry concerns that Clinton might discourage arms proliferation proved as groundless as the fear that he might refrain from force; he is a "New Democrat," after all, free from the mushy liberal clichés of the past. Rhetoric and consultation about stemming the flow of arms proceed, but "the dirty little secret of the Big 5 talks on arms transfers," Lee Feinstein of the Arms Control Association in Washington comments, is that "the talks don't affect U.S. weapons sales."[24]

"Weapons Merchants Are Going Great Guns in Post–Cold War Era," a front-page *Wall Street Journal* story was headlined as Clinton entered his second year in office. "Since the end of the Cold War, even as Washington urges others to show restraint in the name of global security, the U.S. has become the world's pushiest arms merchant." This "selling spree" to the Middle East since "Mr. Bush set out to curb U.S. arms sales there" has been a major factor in this upsurge, no contradiction noted. Aggressive government efforts deserve much of the credit. "The total of weapons sales arranged through Washington [in 1993] topped $34 billion, an unprecedented level." "Such support elates the industry, of course," the *Journal* continues, quoting a Litton industries vice president who says: "Suddenly, we have a government that will actually help you in a transaction." The leading aircraft producer, Boeing, relied on military business for "most of its profits" in 1983, according to a company spokesman, and after a decline from 1989 to 1991, its defense and space division has had "a tremendous turnaround," a Seattle securities analyst observed. Boeing's now-dominant commercial business began as a military spinoff, and military technology continues to spur civilian production alongside the substantial revenues from military sales. Clinton's intervention to induce Saudi Arabia to buy $6 billion worth of U.S. jets, with financing provided by the Export–Import Bank, was a widely praised achievement. About 20 percent of Ex–Im Bank loans are used for aircraft purchases. One factor in engineering the Saudi deal was Washington's role as the kingdom's principal arms supplier, showing again how Pentagon spending can indirectly subsidize private power.

In such ways, the Clinton administration hopes to revitalize the aerospace industry, which produced an export surplus of over $45 billion in 1992, helping offset a merchandise trade deficit of $84.3 billion and also contributing to the $3 trillion global travel and tourism industry, possibly the world's largest industry and the source of major profits and a hefty favorable trade balance in services. Aircraft producers estimate $5.5 billion in after-tax profit for 1993, along with a further decline in aerospace employment, which has fallen by about one-third since its 1989 peak, in part because of shift of production abroad. As in the past, the Pentagon system plays a leading role, one reason why despite the end of the Cold War, "Bill Clinton will spend more on defense than Richard Nixon did two decades ago ($260 billion as against $230 billion in inflation-adjusted dollars), and the United States will spend more for national security than the rest of the world combined," with the military budget expected to increase in two years (national security specialist Lawrence Korb of the Brookings Institution). The terms "defense," "national security," etc., never wilt, no matter how much light pours on them.[25]

Though the Soviet pretext is gone, military spending is to remain a major stimulant to large sectors of the economy, including most of high technology. The "peace dividend" or "economic conversion" will be a mirage until some other mechanism is devised to allow the rich to feed at the public trough. Various rhetorical devices have been devised to obscure these realities: "security" is one; another is "jobs." Nothing is more inspiring than the fervent desire of corporation executives and political leaders to provide "jobs" and their dedicated labors to this end; the public virtually drowns in this display of compassion, while the same people devote themselves to removing jobs to high-repression, low-wage areas abroad, through corporate decision or government policy: a major function of the "aid" program, for example, is to enhance these services to private wealth.[26] While presiding over unprecedented job losses, George Bush waved the banner "Jobs, Jobs, Jobs" at every opportunity.

Commentators take all this seriously, or at least pretend to. There is, after all, no paradox. It is only necessary to understand that "jobs" is the Newspeak version of the unpronounceable term "profits." By accident, profits always seem to benefit from the policies undertaken in the name of "Jobs, Jobs, Jobs," while jobs disappear, another of those odd coincidences that must be kept from the public eye.

Clinton "New Democrats" are no less adept at the technique. A centerpiece of their inspirational literature was a popular book *Mandate for Change* published by the Clinton think tank, the Progressive Policy Institute. The first chapter is on "Enterprise Economics," which is to avoid the errors of old-fashioned liberalism, now dead, with its fallacious ideas about redistribution, entitlements and the like. The emphasis is now on "national investment," intended "to empower U.S. firms and workers." "Enterprise Economics focuses on the pivotal forces in the economic life of a free people: the enterprise of all workers and the enterprises where they produce the goods and services that comprise our national wealth." "Enterprise Economics has a single goal: To enable America's workers and firms to secure high-paying jobs, rising living standards, and higher profits." The word "profits" appears nowhere else: a concept too marginal to merit notice, profits are only for the benefit of "America's workers" and the impersonal "firms" that are somehow "theirs." Missing from the picture are bosses, executives, owners, financiers, and other such exotic categories—except that "wealthy investors" consumed too much in the bad Reagan years. There is occasional mention of "entrepreneurs"; they are the people who "create new businesses," and then, presumably, fade away, having assisted the workers and their firms. The picture is one of great concern for working people, their families, and their firms, all working together for the common good. Small wonder that unions seem unnecessary in the new harmonious workplace of the future with its communitarian values. This renewal of the standard themes of business propaganda usefully appropriates the label "progressive" so as to leave no space (apart from "anti-American") for traditional ideals of social justice and human rights, a significant element of the classical liberal thought to which homage is being cynically paid. The population who "emphatically . . . demanded a new direction for America" can rest assured that their voices have been heard, and can return to the spectator role as the "Mandate for Change" is enacted.

As Clintonite rhetoric was transformed to policy, its meaning was spelled out with no little clarity. We return to international economic policy. Domestic fiscal policies also clearly articulated the concerns for workers and their firms. Filing away his campaign promises to raise federal domestic investment, Clinton reduced such programs as a share of the economy (GDP), after four consecutive annual increases under President Bush that had partially reversed the Reaganite cuts that polarized the society further while harming prospects for the national economy—though not necessarily the narrow interests of the most privileged sectors. The decline under Clinton was sharpest in "human capital" investments (education and training programs); civilian R&D also fell while expenditures for physical capital remained steady. The facts received slight attention. Also largely off the agenda is the public charity for the wealthy through fiscal measures, which amount to hefty government welfare payments. Reviewing the scale of these devices, political scientist Christopher Howard points out that "one crucial fact remains: the middle- and upper-income classes are the main beneficiaries of the hidden welfare state." Thus "over 80% of the tax benefits for home mortgage interest, charitable contributions, and real estate taxes go to those earning more than $50,000," not to speak of "the large fraction of tax expenditures that subsidize corporate fringe benefits." To this one must, of course, add the Pentagon system, export promotion devices, direct "entitlement" subsidies to business of $51 billion a year along with over $53 billion in tax breaks to corporations (a sum that alone exceeds welfare programs to the poor by almost $30 billion), and other measures designed to provide taxpayer subsidies to the wealthy—to protect "jobs," in standard parlance.[27]

Despite the inefficiency of military-based industrial policy, the project has scored great successes. The computer industry is a prime example. In the 1950s, when computers were too clumsy and slow to be marketable, the cost of R&D and production was borne by the public, via the Pentagon system; in electronics generally, government funding covered 85 percent of all R&D in 1958. By the 1960s, computers could be sold for profit, and the public subsidy declined to about 50 percent. The public share increased again in the 1980s as the industry entered a new and costly phase. Similarly, the aeronautical industry, which spawned the enormously profitable tourism industry, has largely been a gift from taxpayer to corporations, via the Pentagon funnel, as were derivative technologies in metallurgy and electronics. Civilian aircraft constitute the leading U.S. export, running a net trade surplus of $17.8 billion in 1991, considerably more since. Furthermore, U.S. comparative advantage in the international economy increasingly lies in services, and "by far the largest export of U.S. services is travel and tourism, which accounts for a third of the service surplus," the *Wall Street Journal* reports; travel and tourism means aircraft. NASA offered new ways to milk the public for private gain, while also helping the Kennedy administration to arouse badly needed jingoist sentiments, at least until people tired of watching spacemen stumbling about the moon to no purpose.[28]

Government intervention in the economy in the service of private power takes many other forms. One of the most dramatic was the motorizing and suburbanization of America. This state–corporate campaign began with an illegal conspiracy by three major corporations, General Motors, Firestone Rubber, and Standard Oil of California, to purchase electric public transportation systems in forty-five cities, to be dismantled and replaced by buses; they were convicted of criminal conspiracy and fined a total of $5,000, doubtless causing them much agony. The federal government then took over, implementing plans by GM chairman Alfred Sloan. Infrastructure and central city capital stock were destroyed and relocated to suburban areas and huge sums devoted to interstate highways—under the usual pretext of "defense." Railroads were displaced in favor of government-financed motor and air transport. State and local governments played their part on the scene. By the mid-1960s, one out of six business enterprises was directly dependent on the motor vehicle industry. This vast government spending program provided another means to sustain the moribund system of private profit that had collapsed in the 1930s. It allayed Eisenhower's fears of "another Depression setting in after the Korean War," a U.S. Transportation Department official reported. One of the congressional architects of the highway program observed that "it put a nice solid floor across the whole economy in times of recession." The general impact on culture and society was immense, as on the economy itself. The public had little part in this massive social engineering project. It did not participate in the decisions, and consumer choice was a factor only within a narrowly structured framework of options designed by those who own and manage the society. The effect on American life and future generations can be debated; if there were benefits, they were incidental, not a serious element in planning, nor should anything else be expected in a state capitalist political economy with the public largely marginalized.[29]

The pharmaceutical industry and biotechnology today—the former enormously profitable, the latter expected to soar to even greater heights—also rely upon and demand public subsidy while instructing others on the virtues of "economic rationality." The same is true of agribusiness and services, in fact virtually every flourishing sector of the economy. All rely as well on state-aided market penetration abroad, by a variety of means ranging from violence to "aid."

Industrial Policy for the Nineties

With the decline of the Cold War, the traditional form of industrial strategy becomes more problematic. It is not surprising, then, that we now hear open discussion of the need for "industrial policy"—that is, new forms, no longer masked by the Pentagon system.

The old methods were running into difficulties for reasons beyond the loss of the standard pretext and the erosion of tolerance on the part of people suffering the effects of Reaganite spend-and-borrow abandon. The inefficiencies of the Pentagon system of industrial subsidy and planning were tolerable in the days of overwhelming U.S. economic dominance, less so as U.S.-based corporations face competitors who can design and produce directly for the commercial market, not awaiting possible spin-offs from high tech weapons or space shots. Furthermore, the cutting edge of industrial development is shifting to biology-based industry. Public subsidy and state protection for these enterprises cannot easily be hidden beneath a Pentagon cover. For such reasons alone, new forms of state intervention are required. In the 1992 electoral campaign, Clinton managers showed more awareness of these issues than their rivals, gaining support from sectors of the corporate world that recognized them to be more attuned to real world problems than Reaganite ideologues.

Not that Reaganites were reluctant to use state power to protect the wealthy from market forces. The primary mechanisms were the usual military Keynesian ones. A 1985 OECD study found that the Pentagon and Japan's state planning ministry MITI were distributing R&D funds much the same way, making similar guesses about new technologies. A major Pentagon funnel was SDI ("Star Wars"). The Reagan–Bush decade ended in fall 1992 with a well-publicized improvement in the economy, timed for the election and attributed in the business press to a sharp rise in military spending, much of it for computer purchases.

Largely through military expenditures, the Reagan administration had increased state share of GNP to over 35 percent in 1983, an increase of well over a third from a decade earlier. While almost all industrial societies have become more protectionist in past years, the Reaganites often led the pack, virtually doubling import restrictions to 23 percent, more than all postwar administrations combined. Then–Secretary of the Treasury James Baker "proudly proclaimed that Mr Ronald Reagan had 'granted more import relief to U.S. industry than any of his predecessors in more than half a century'" (Fred Bergsten, director of the Institute for International Economics in Washington). Bergsten adds that the Reagan administration specialized in the kind of "managed trade" that most "restricts trade and closes markets," voluntary export restraint agreements (VERs). This is "the most insidious form of protectionism," which "raises prices, reduces competition and reinforces cartel behaviour." The Clinton administration Economic Report to Congress (1994) cites a recent study that found that Reaganite protectionist measures reduced U.S. manufacturing imports by about one-fifth.

British MP Phillip Oppenheim, ridiculing Anglo–American posturing about "liberal market capitalism," notes that "a World Bank survey of non-tariff barriers showed that they covered 9 per cent of all goods in Japan—compared with 34 per cent in the United States—figures reinforced by David Henderson of the OECD, who stated that during the 1980s the United States had the worst record for devising new non-tariff barriers" (NTBs, basically, ways to strong-arm competitors). That conclusion is reiterated in a scholarly review by GATT secretariat economist Patrick Low, who concludes that NTBs cancel a good part of the effects of the tariff reductions that were "the most significant success story for postwar trade policy and multilateral trade diplomacy," citing estimates that restrictive effects of new Reaganite NTBs on U.S. trade were about three times those of new foreign NTBs. Oppenheim adds that OECD figures show U.S. state funding for non-military R&D to be about one-third of all civil research spending, as compared to 2 percent state funding in Japan. The Thatcher record is similar.[30]

The Reaganites also conducted the biggest nationalization in U.S. history (the Continental Illinois Bank bailout). A combination of deregulation and increased government insurance to reduce risk for investors inspired a binge of bad loans and corruption among Savings & Loan institutions, leaving the taxpayer with costs running to hundreds of billions of dollars. Similarly, the public is to bear the costs of bad debts incurred by commercial banks in the Third World. Susan George, who has tried to estimate these public costs, concludes that Japan "seems to be the only genuinely capitalist country in the OECD group," keeping to the capitalist principle that the taxpayer has no responsibility to pay for the mistakes of commercial banks. Those who proclaim the wonders of "free market capitalism" with most vigor understand that it is to be risk-free for the masters, as fully as can be achieved.[31]

That understanding is not confined to Western ideologues. After ten years of experimentation under the lash, the Pinochet free-market regimen collapsed causing "Chile's worst economic crisis in 50 years" (Chilean economist Patricio Meller), and the government had to intervene massively to bail out the sinking ship. The leading proponent of state intervention, economist David Felix notes, was "an institute which is a stronghold of Hayekian libertarianism and the major think tank of the Pinochetist wing of the Chilean elite," led by its president, Carlos Cáceres, who as Treasury Minister in 1983 "advised foreign banks that the Government was taking over responsibility for servicing their loans to private Chilean firms." Current odes to the Chilean "free market miracle" may occasionally take passing notice of the fact that the success of the new civilian government's economic program "has defied classical economic analysis," with "a huge tax increase to pay for new social programs" and sharp increase of the minimum wage (*Times* correspondent Nathaniel Nash), both efforts to come to terms with the disastrous effects of the Chicago school laissez-faire doctrine.[32]

Reagan "free marketeers" also enabled the steel industry to reconstruct by effectively barring imports and undermining unions to reduce labor costs. They left Washington with heavy new restrictions on European Community steel exports that the EC claims violate international trade rules; Washington's justification is alleged EC dumping, but the EC responds that total EC steel exports had fallen below the "voluntary quota" (the Reaganite NTB). Reaganite economic managers also sharply increased export-promotion by means of Export–Import bank credits in apparent "violation of the Gatt," Ex–Im Bank chairman John Macomber conceded.[33]

Responding to U.S. criticism of European Airbus subsidies, EC officials allege that U.S. civil aviation subsidies exceed EC subventions, including an effective subsidy of some $30 billion in indirect support from military spending. The EC's annual report on U.S. trade barriers in April 1993 cites tariffs of 20–50 percent on textiles, ceramics, glassware, and other products, "Buy American" legislation and local content requirements of 50–60 percent, and numerous other practices that contrast with "US rhetoric about free trade." About 10 percent of the two-thousand–page text of the North American Free Trade Agreement (NAFTA) involves intricate "rules of origin" requirements designed to keep foreign competitors out by ensuring a high percentage of value added in North America. One of the leading specialists on international trade, Columbia University economist Jagdish Bhagwati, observes that NAFTA is "dressed up as a great free trade move" though "it is evident that the main motivation is protectionist: Mexico becomes America's preferential market, with Japan and the EC at a disadvantage"; hence the "passionate support" for NAFTA as compared to GATT, where "any advantages America gains . . . are equally doled out to rivals." A leading advocate of trade regulation, Clyde Prestowitz, came to support NAFTA in part because its provisions favoring North American (effectively, U.S.) firms "will let us better compete with Asians."[34]

The Reagan administration conducted "what was effectively an 'industrial policy'" that rebuilt the U.S. computer chip industry by an agreement "essentially forced on Japan" to increase purchases of U.S. chips and by establishment of the government–industry consortium Sematech to improve manufacturing technology, the *Washington Post* reported, quoting Charles White, vice president for strategic planning at Motorola, the second-biggest U.S. chip maker, who said: "You can't underestimate the government's role." The Defense Advanced Research Projects Agency (DARPA) provided half the $1 billion costs of Sematech, with effects radiating to many branches of U.S. industry. Total DARPA spending was running at $1.5 billion annually by 1992, allegedly to spur development of "defense technologies"; in practice, the cutting edge of technology. Another DARPA project from the early 1980s was high-performance computing. "DARPA became a pivotal market force," *Science* magazine reports, "boosting massively parallel computing from the laboratory into a nascent industry," now to be extended through a multi-agency government supercomputing agency that will aim for speeds of a trillion operations per second, focusing more on "the crowded field of young supercomputer companies it had played a role in creating" than on university teams.[35]

Sematech represents "an important break with past trends in Defense Department R&D support," University of California economist Laura Tyson pointed out in an influential study of state-managed trade and development. Previous DOD support for the semiconductor industry had "concentrated on developing hardened chip technology capable of withstanding a direct nuclear hit," while competitors were organizing production directly for the commercial market. The break reflects the growing recognition that in a more competitive world, the United States can no longer afford the luxury of concealing industrial policy within the Pentagon system. "The semiconductor industry, *wherever it has developed*, has been an explicit target of industrial policy," Tyson observes, "whether in the guise of military policy as in the United States or in the guise of commercial policy elsewhere in the world."[36]

Despite such achievements, the Reagan–Bush faction of the business party remained hampered by ideological extremism, unable to face current problems of industrial strategy as directly as their political opponents, some elements of the corporate–financial world assume. Clintonite thinking on this issue is reflected in the choice of Laura Tyson as Chairperson of the Council of Economic Advisors. Tyson was a founder and co-director of the Berkeley Roundtable on the International Economy, a corporate-funded trade and technology research institute that advocates unconcealed state industrial policy. She has "longstanding relationships with Silicon Valley companies that stand to benefit from the policies she advocates," *Times* business correspondent Sylvia Nasar notes. In support of these policies, Roundtable co-director Michael Borrus cites a 1988 Department of Commerce study showing that "five of the top six fastest growing U.S. industries from 1972 to 1988 were sponsored or sustained, directly or indirectly, by federal investment," the only exception being lithographic services. "The winners" in earlier years, he writes, "computers, biotechnology, jet engines, and airframes—were each the by-product of public spending for national defense and public health." The record goes back to the earliest days; "defense" and "public health" are the familiar Newspeak disguises, on a par with "jobs."[37]

A 1992 study of the National Academy of Sciences and Engineering proposed a $5 billion quasi-governmental company "to channel federal money into private applied research"; that is, publicly funded research that will yield private profit. Another report, entitled *The Government Role in Civilian Technology: Building a New Alliance*, called for new efforts to extend "the close and longstanding" government–industry relationship that has "helped to establish the commercial biotechnology industry." It recommended a government-funded "Civilian Technology Corporation" to assist U.S. industry to commercialize technology by encouraging "cooperative R&D ventures in pre-commercial areas"; "pre-commercial," to ensure that profit is restricted to private wealth and power. The ventures will be "cooperative," with the public paying the costs up to the point of product development. At that point costs change to gains, and the public hands the enterprise over to private industry, the traditional pattern.

"America cannot continue to rely on trickle-down technology from the military," Clinton stated in a document issued by his campaign headquarters in September 1992 ("Technology: The Engine of Economic Growth"). The old game is ending. In the "new era" planned by the Clinton administration, *Times* science writer William Broad reports, "the Government's focus on making armaments will shift to fostering a host of new civilian technologies and industries"—just as in the "old era," but then behind the Pentagon mask. "President Clinton proposes to redirect $76 billion or so in annual Federal research spending so it spurs industrial innovation" in emerging technologies—which were largely funded through the Pentagon system (and the National Institute of Health) in the "old era." A minimum of $30 billion is to be taken from the Pentagon's research budget as a "peace dividend" over four years for these purposes, Broad writes, noting that "significantly, the initiative would spend the same amount of money as Star Wars, $30 billion, in half the time."

Also significantly, Clinton's advisers knew all along that Star Wars was "only tangentially related to national defense," that its prime function was to serve as "a path to competitiveness in advanced technologies," as the Reagan administration had explained in Congressional Hearings (Clinton's close associate Robert Reich, now Secretary of Labor, writing in 1985 in the *New York Times* under the heading "High Tech, a Subsidiary of Pentagon Inc."). As noted earlier, the function of Star Wars was made clear to the business world from the start, while the public was properly intimidated with different stories.

The *Wall Street Journal* reports a study by Battelle Memorial Institute showing that research spending will remain sluggish because of "a slowdown in weapons development." "Government spending over the past five years has swung toward space and energy programs, and away from weapons development," the principal author of the report said. That is, government spending (the public subsidy) shifted from one component of the Pentagon system to the others. In another initiative of the same sort, one of the few steep increases in the Federal budget—an 80 percent jump to almost $1 billion a year for Fiscal Year 1994 with another 50 percent leap planned two years later—is designed to convert the National Institute of Standards and Technology to research support and funding for high-tech industry, selecting and backing critical technologies; the Institute is now besieged by corporations seeking grants and aid.[38]

"We're now going to develop an economic strategy much in the way we developed a national security strategy to fight the cold war," Kent Hughes, president of Clinton's Council on Competitiveness, proclaimed. It is necessary only to bring out the striking continuities as old policies are adapted to new circumstances, and to reinterpret the "cold war" and "national security" as what they were.

And to recognize that while Reaganites forged new paths in violating market orthodoxy for the benefit of U.S.-based corporations, they did not go far enough to satisfy the business community. Recall, for example, their sharp increase in export-promotion by credits from the Export–Import Bank (a federal agency)—in apparent violation of GATT rules, as conceded. Clinton wasted little time in expanding these violations. While administration rhetoric on the marvels of "free trade" boomed on the front pages as part of the PR campaign to ram through an unpopular (and in fact, highly protectionist) version of a North American "free trade" agreement (NAFTA), the business sections reported a new National Export Strategy that is to go far beyond the "less coordinated efforts" of Reagan and Bush, with a planned expansion of GATT-violating Ex–Im Bank lending. The administration opposes the measures it is implementing, the press reports, because "they amount to government subsidies that distort international markets." But there is no contradiction. As explained by Ex–Im Bank president Kenneth Brody, "by creating such a program in the United States, the Clinton administration would have more influence in seeking international limits on such lending." The president also approved an independent program that would release $3 billion in loan guarantees to domestic and foreign buyers of U.S.-built ships—again, for the purpose of inducing others to end such practices, the *Wall Street Journal* explained.

The logic will be recognized instantly: war brings peace, crime brings law, arms production and sales bring arms reduction and nonproliferation, etc. In simple words, anything goes, as long as there is a good answer to the question: "What is in it for us?"—the guiding theme of the new Clinton Doctrine on intervention (see p. 24).

The simple truths were underscored by Clinton's Treasury Secretary Lloyd Bentsen: "I'm tired of a level playing field," he said. "We should tilt the playing field for U.S. businesses. We should have done it 20 years ago." In fact, "we" (meaning state power) have been doing it for almost two centuries, dramatically so in the past fifty years, even more under the Reaganites. But that is the wrong image to convey. As usual, the programs were described in the business press, known for its dedication to the needs of working people, as aimed at increasing "jobs," the word "profits" being noticeably missing, in accord with established Orwellian practice.[39]

The United States is, of course, not alone in such practices. The European Community, Japan, and the newly industrializing countries (NICs) have their own array of devices for promoting economic development in violation of market principles. Summarizing well-known phenomena, a 1992 OECD study concludes that "oligopolistic competition and strategic interaction among firms and governments rather than the invisible hand of market forces condition today's competitive advantage and international division of labor in high-technology industries,"[40] as in agriculture, pharmaceuticals, services, and major areas of economic activity generally. The vast majority of the world's population, subjected to market discipline and regaled with odes to its wonders, are not supposed to hear such words, and don't.

A related matter is the traditional business demand that the public, via government, pay the costs of the infrastructure required for private power and profit, everything from roads to education. By now, even such enthusiasts of Reagan's party for the rich as the *Wall Street Journal* are concerned by the consequences of the policies they advocated, such as the deterioration of the state college systems that supplied the needs of the corporate sector. "Public higher education—one the few areas where America still ranks supreme—is being pounded by state spending cuts," the *Journal* worriedly reports, echoing the concerns of businesses that "rely heavily on a steady stream of graduates" for skilled personnel and on applied research that they can take over. This is one of the long-predicted consequences of the cutback of federal services for all but the wealthy and powerful, which devastated states and local communities.[41]

Class war is not easy to fine tune.

Frivolous Reaganite policies left the country deeply in debt. Interest on the federal debt skyrocketed, now reaching the scale of the days when the costs of the World War had to be faced. Had the borrowing been used for productive investment or R&D, it could have been justified. But it was not. Rather, it was largely frittered away in luxury consumption, financial manipulations and swindles, and other Yuppie fun-and-games—much as in Thatcherite England, the other "revolution" greatly admired by the privileged. A National Science Foundation study at the peak of the mania estimated that R&D expenditures declined by 5 percent for companies involved in mergers and acquisitions compared to a 5 percent rise for others.[42] Meanwhile real wages declined, hunger and poverty rose rapidly, and the society began to take on a distinct Third World aspect. Given the debt, the kinds of "moderate increase in infrastructure spending" and other devices that Clinton advisers were willing to contemplate might not be feasible, even if they had not been quickly shot down by Congress.[43]

Contributing to these difficulties is the great success of the propaganda campaigns designed to create a political culture of opposition to taxation, regulation, and government spending—carefully honed to exempt the state intervention that keeps profits flowing and wealth concentrated. The impact on the general public is hard to judge. Anti-government sentiment is substantial and increasing. By May 1992, half the population called for a new party to replace Democrats and Republicans, and hatred of "bureaucrats" and "politicians" mounted to new heights. But such facts have to be seen against the background of skepticism about all institutions and professions, reaching unprecedented levels. In 1992, over 80 percent of the population felt that "the economic system is inherently unfair," as the president of a major polling organization summarized popular feelings. Changes in the economic system to overcome this "inherent unfairness," needless to say, are not on the policy agenda or in the arena of public discussion, except among "anti-Americans" who do not adequately display their love for "the American way" and their awe for the grandeur of its leaders.[44]

2. Some Lessons of History

As mentioned earlier, postwar planners relied on ample historical practice as they turned to state power to rescue the system of private profit, while waving the banner of free enterprise and markets as a weapon against the weak. More generally, successful industrial societies have consistently relied on departures from market orthodoxies, while condemning their victims to market discipline. Since the work of Alexander Gerschenkron, it has been widely understood that "late developers" have relied on various methods of state intervention and managed development.[45] The same was true of their predecessors. The contemporary significance of the issue makes it useful to recall briefly some of the earlier history.

"The fountain and origin of British foreign investments" and "the main foundations of England's foreign connections," John Maynard Keynes observed, was the piracy of the Elizabethan plunderers—terrorists, in contemporary lingo. By the mid-seventeenth century, a combination of military superiority, state monopolies, and government backing secured the commercial supremacy in the Mediterranean that "provided much of the foundation for the rise of English commercial power throughout the world during the following century," Robert Brenner concludes in a major study of the English revolution, while the same factors gave England a powerful Indian Ocean base for its later expansion in South Asia; the great achievement of the revolution was to raise government support for commercial development "almost to the level of a principle." State power displaced the commercially more advanced but militarily weaker Dutch in the North Atlantic, as it had enabled English Merchant Adventurers to drive out the powerful Hanse of German merchants along with Italian and Flemish rivals. The conquest of India brought huge profits to England in the eighteenth century, while the state expanded to unprecedented efficiency and scale, far beyond its continental rivals.[46]

The American colonies followed a similar course, graduating from piracy and terror in colonial days to large-scale state intervention in the economy after independence, and conquest of resources and markets. Taking up and far extending the Federalist program that they had opposed on grounds of popular democracy, Republicans (later Democrats) constructed a centralized developmental state committed to creation and entrenchment of domestic manufacture and commerce, subsidizing local production and barring cheaper British imports, constructing a legal basis for private corporate power, and in numerous other ways providing an escape from the stranglehold of comparative advantage. Their achievement was "loading the dice in favor of entrepreneurs while protecting their enterprises and gains from democratic interference," historian Charles Sellers observes in an insightful recent study.[47]

The Cotton Kingdom in the south, which fueled Britain's industrial development as well as that of its former colony, was hardly a tribute to the wonders of the market. It was based on slavery, having been established by massacre and expulsion of the natives in a vigorous exercise of state terror, savagery, chicanery, and treaty violation. As always, the exercise was cloaked with a show of great humanitarianism and attention to legal niceties, illustrated—to keep only to the more humane and civilized exponents—by the thoughts of Presidents Adams and Monroe, already cited (pp. 30–31). A major goal of the annexation of Texas was to gain a monopoly of (slave-produced) cotton, then the most important commodity in world trade, analogous to oil today. The achievement "places all other nations at our feet," President Tyler proclaimed. "I doubt whether Great Britain could avoid convulsions" if the United States were to block cotton exports to its despised rival. The newly acquired power should guarantee "the command of the trade of the world," President Polk's Secretary of Treasury informed Congress. It was not until it gained overwhelming dominance that the United States began to insist on the stern principles of "economic rationality," continuing to violate them as it chose.

Slavery too was justified on humanitarian grounds, not entirely without reason: owners of property tend to treat it more carefully than those who merely rent and can discard it without loss. "Under slavery, after all, the native is bought as an animal," a senior administrator in Portuguese Angola argued. "His owner prefers him to remain as fit as a horse or ox." But when "the native is not bought," only hired, and is "called a free man," then "his employer cares little if he sickens or dies . . . , because when he sickens or dies his employer will simply ask for another"—at least, if unions, workers' rights, job security ("inflexibility") and other irrational interferences with free markets can be overcome. The facts were well understood by American workers who derided the hypocrisy of bosses "professing to be abolitionists . . . and making slaves at home," imposing "wage slavery" that is in some ways even more onerous than chattel slavery. "The poor negro has a master, both in sickness and health," early union organizers commented, "while the poor white man is a slave as long as he is able to toil, and a pauper when he can toil no more." Workers organized "to abolish Wage Slavery before we meddle with Chattel Slavery," and after the Civil War, bitterly complained that those who fought for freedom for the slaves were now subjected to a form of wage slavery that was hardly less abominable, as the industrial revolution based on "free labor" rapidly expanded. Whites and Blacks alike served other purposes. Modern gynecological surgery, for example, was developed by respected medical researchers who were free to torture helpless Irish indigent women as well as slaves in their experimental work; Mengele might have been impressed.[48]

Britain's stand on economic liberalism was similar. Only in the mid-nineteenth century, when it had become powerful enough to overcome any competition, did England embrace free trade, deploring the departures from virtue and rationality of others seeking industrial development. The doctrines were abandoned when Japan proved to be too formidable a competitor in the 1920s; the imperial preference system Britain imposed in 1932 was an important factor contributing to the Pacific war. Countries under colonial rule were "deindustrialized," essentially by force. England's longest-held colony, Ireland, is an example, particularly interesting in comparison with similar countries in Europe that were free from imperial power, therefore able to develop.[49] Another example is India. Bengal, the first part of India to be conquered, "was destabilized and impoverished by a disastrous experiment in sponsored government," John Keay observes in his history of the East India company. The conqueror, Robert Clive, described the textile center of Dacca in 1757 as "extensive, populous, and rich as the city of London"; by 1840 its population had fallen from 150,000 to thirty thousand, Sir Charles Trevelyan testified before the House of Lords, "and the jungle and malaria are fast encroaching. . . . Dacca, the Manchester of India, has fallen from a very flourishing town to a very poor and small town." It is now the capital of Bangladesh.

At the time of the English takeover, India was comparable to England in industrial development. The conqueror industrialized while Indian industry was destroyed by British regulations and interference. British observers, though liberal in orientation, recognized the need for such measures. Had they not been undertaken, Horace Wilson wrote in his *History of British India* in 1826, "the mills of Paisley and Manchester would have been stopped in their outset, and could scarcely have been again set in motion, even by the power of steam. They were created by the sacrifice of Indian manufacturers."

Contemporaries graphically described the vicious "oppression and monopolies" of the British conquerors as they robbed and destroyed Bengal's agricultural wealth and advanced textiles, strewing the land with corpses as they converted wealth to misery, turning "dearth into a famine," often ploughing up "a rich field of rice or other grain . . . in order to make room for a plantation of poppies" if company officials "foresaw that extraordinary profit was likely to be made by opium" (Adam Smith). Britain's Permanent

Settlement of 1793 extended the "experiment" beyond Bengal. Land was privatized, yielding wealth to local clients and the British rulers while "the settlement fashioned with great care and deliberation has to our painful knowledge subjected almost the whole of the lower classes to most grievous oppression," a British enquiry commission concluded in 1832. The director of the East India Company conceded that "the misery hardly finds a parallel in the history of commerce. The bones of the cotton-weavers are bleaching the plains of India."

The experiments of the IMF and World Bank designed by contemporary theorists are not without precedent.

The experiment in India was not a total failure, however. "If security was wanting against extensive popular tumult or revolution," the Governor-General of India, Lord Bentinck, observed, "I should say that the 'Permanent Settlement,' though a failure in many other respects and in most important essentials, has this great advantage, at least, of having created a vast body of rich landed proprietors deeply interested in the continuance of the British Dominion and having complete command over the mass of the people," whose growing misery is therefore less of a problem than it might have been. The lesson has been applied by the masters throughout their Third World domains and in Eastern Europe today; it has obvious analogues at home.

By the nineteenth century, India was financing more than two-fifths of Britain's trade deficit, providing a market for British manufactures as well as troops for its colonial conquests and the opium that was the staple of its trade with China, compelled by British arms to import lethal narcotics. As local industry declined, Bengal was converted to export agriculture, first indigo, then jute, producing over half the world's crop by 1900 though not a single mill for processing was ever built there under British rule. Manufacturing industries which had been comparable to its own at the time of the conquest, as British government analysts later conceded, not only failed to develop, but were largely eliminated, as India sank into rural misery.

After contributing massively to Britain's wealth and power for centuries, India finally gained independence—destitute, overwhelmingly agrarian, with a population that was "abysmally poor" suffering from mortality rates that were "among the world's highest" (Dennis Merrill). The liberation finally "broke the pre-independence stagnation," Ramesh Thakur observes. "India's economy grew three times as fast in the 1950s and 1960s as during the British raj, and faster than the rate of British growth during its comparable stage of development in the eighteenth and nineteenth century."[50] But unlike Britain, India sought to enter a world already dominated by far more powerful rivals, no easy task. We will pick up this story later.

In an enlightening study of modern Egypt, Afaf Lutfi Al-Sayyid Marsot argues that its history illustrates much the same pattern. Muhammad Ali's attempts to develop cotton textiles in the 1830s, she observes, "came at a time of similar expansion in England, where the industrial revolution had arisen on the basis of that one commodity" behind high protectionist walls, the norm ever since. The French consul had warned in 1817 that "the silk factories that are being established in Egypt will deal a deadly blow to those of Italy, and even ours." Foreign officials and merchants were no less concerned about cotton-based industry, though some sneered at "this absurd project wanting to turn to manufacturing a nation whose major interests lie in agriculture"; Egypt's agricultural wealth had been the prime target of Napoleon's invasion in 1798. The British consul urged that Egypt "would gain very much by destroying [factories] and importing all manufactures from Europe."

Britain needed markets, and was not about to tolerate Egyptian competition. Britain also "did not want a new independent state in the Mediterranean, one that was militarily and economically powerful and therefore able to check her advances in that area and in the Persian Gulf," Marsot adds. "No ideas therefore of fairness towards Mehemet [Ali] ought to stand in the way of such great and paramount interests" of Britain, foreign minister Palmerston declared, expressing his "hate" for the "ignorant barbarian" who dared to seek an independent course, dismissing "his boasted civilization of Egypt as the arrantest humbug" while deploying Britain's fleet and financial power to terminate Egypt's quest for independence and economic development.

Adopting the familiar stance, Britain demanded that Egypt abandon its efforts to protect infant industry, as Britain itself had done, and adopt the gospel of free trade that would keep it locked into dependency as a source of (agricultural) raw materials. British power undermined what seemed to be a promising base for industrial development in Egypt, imposing the destructive free trade regimen.

Deprived of the ability to nurture industry, and of the control of external markets that was another crucial feature of European industrial development, Muhammad Ali's efforts failed. "Industrialization was doomed to fail in Egypt," Marsot writes, "not through the shortcomings of the Egyptians, but because of external European pressures which used Ottoman legal control over Egypt to kill off any potential rivalry to their own industrial ventures." Britain's stranglehold extended beyond textiles. "Egyptian shipyards could have continued to flourish, as did those of Greece, had the Egyptians been allowed to keep their freedom to manoeuvre on an open market, and had been allowed to keep the commercial links that were encouraged in Greece but removed from Egypt." The treaty imposed by Britain in 1838 "operated in the same fashion among the rest of the Arab territories of the area, and rendered their artisan production equally non-competitive." The collapse of Muhammad Ali's efforts to develop sufficient military forces left the country "at the mercy of mercenaries and foreign troops." His public works projects imposed a severe burden on the peasantry, but "the disruptions occasioned by these public works, which at least directly benefited the population at large, were nothing compared to the disruptions that affected the fallah when the Suez Canal was built." In this great project "hailed by Europe as a marvel of technology," the Egyptian worker was "shamelessly exploited by his government and by the French builders of the canal," leaving 100,000 dead, yielding enormous wealth for Europe while it "led to a costly debt which took [Egypt] over three decades to pay off, and to the inevitable occupation of the country"—consequences not "bemoaned" by the many European critics of Muhammad Ali, she comments.[51]

Pursuit of what Adam Smith called the "vile maxim of the masters of mankind" has followed much the same course over and over again in the two centuries since the conquest of Bengal, always suffused with self-righteousness, inspired by the holy doctrines of a version of economic theory that is immune to abundant—one might perhaps argue, consistent—empirical refutation, and that has the miraculous quality of invariably benefiting the masters, who are also the paymasters, a suggestive fact that is rarely explored.[52] The tale of misery is filed away in a dusty corner when the standard consequences arise yet again. New "experiments" are designed that yield the same results: disaster for the experimental animals, who are given no more say than fruit flies in a genetics experiment, but impressive success for those who conduct the experiments.

The imperial record is, of course, not entirely uniform. A highly apologetic Stanford University symposium comparing Soviet and American dependencies recognizes that while "Latin-Americans claim mainly economic exploitation," "Soviet exploitation of Eastern Europe is principally political and security-oriented." One result is that Eastern Europe had a higher standard of living than the USSR, in part the result of a huge Soviet subsidy to its satellites, amounting to $80 billion in the decade of the 1970s, according to U.S. government sources. "Soviet dominion was in fact that unique historical perversity, an empire in which the center bled *itself* for the sake of its colonies, or rather, for the sake of tranquility in those colonies," Lawrence Weschler observes.[53]

Japan followed a different course. Discussing the economic growth of South Korea and Taiwan, Bruce Cumings observes that unlike the West, Japan brought industry to the labor and raw materials rather than vice versa, leading to industrial development under state–corporate guidance. Under colonial rule, both Taiwan and Korea may have had higher rates of GDP growth than Japan, and by the end of the 1930s, Robert Wade observes, Taiwan was the biggest trader in the region. Japan's colonial policies were brutal, but they laid a basis for economic development. The Chinese nationalist forces that conquered Taiwan after being expelled from the mainland "benefited enormously from their inheritance of Japanese state monopolies," Alice Amsden writes, "and the whole interventionist approach taken by the Japanese to the development of an occupied territory was not lost to the Guomindang" as it took control. Taiwan's remarkable postwar growth largely resumed the rapid growth under Japanese colonialism, which had doubled per capita income in the dominant agricultural sector (despite a population increase of 43 percent) in a half-century of Japanese rule. Industry expanded in the 1930s to include chemical and metallurgical sectors along with infrastructure development that "proved highly beneficial in postwar years." As in the Soviet satellite case, "the welfare of Taiwanese peasants in the first half of the twentieth century may have exceeded that of Japanese peasants," Amsden adds, noting that the population also became "relatively well educated" as a foundation was built for postwar economic development. This proceeded under "state management of almost every conceivable economic activity," relying on import substitution in a protected home market, a "deluge of U.S. aid" in the 1950s and 1960s, the "critical role" of "flows of foreign direct investment" in later years, and harsh suppression of labor.[54]

In the usual imperial style, Japanese authorities were much impressed with their accomplishments, and intended to extend the benefits elsewhere as their armies conquered Manchuria in the 1930s—to create an "earthly paradise" in independent Manchukuo after they had rescued its population from "Chinese bandits," they proclaimed. Their vicious counterinsurgency operations prefigured U.S. operations in South Vietnam, as did the rhetorical accompaniment. The major difference is that as world ruler, the United States has been able to reshape the facts and historical memories. No one speaks of Japanese (or Soviet) "altruism," or "noble causes," or "carelessness" in their "defensive efforts." Immune from critical comment, the world ruler can grind the victims of its criminal atrocities under foot because they do not sufficiently confess their sin of resistance against the foreign aggressor that destroyed their country and society, while the sober opinion that blandly reports this dismal scene bewails the inability of Japan to own up to its crimes in Asia. In the very issue of the *New York Times* that reports George Bush's lament about Vietnam's continuing failure to concede its criminal attacks against us and satisfy our historically unprecedented demands, the adjacent front-page column reports the visit of the Japanese Emperor to China, where he failed to "unambiguously" accept the blame "for [Japan's] wartime aggression," revealing again the deep flaw in the Japanese character that so sorely puzzles American commentators.[55] It is virtually inconceivable that a respectable American intellectual would comment on this juxtaposition, probably even perceive that something might be amiss. Such are the perquisites of unchallenged power.

The Japanese right-wing, however, does not hesitate to bring forth the comparative record. The countries that were once under Japanese rule are "success stories" while the U.S.-ruled Philippines are an economic disaster, a leading figure in the (then) governing Liberal Democratic Party observed correctly, while the Philippine "showcase of democracy" is largely an empty form under landlord rule.[56]

Europe's global conquest also took varying forms. There are differences between direct conquest and the indirect controls of "neocolonialism," "informal empire," "free trade imperialism," or the IMF. But major features are common throughout the complex record. The patterns imposed centuries ago, and often since, will be readily recognized by those subjected to contemporary neoliberal fundamentalism.

Analysis of the recurrent patterns should not be confused with a version of "dependency theory" that seeks to demonstrate the inevitability of "development of underdevelopment." Historical conditions are too varied and complex for anything that might plausibly be called "a theory" to apply uniformly: under special conditions, world rulers saw it in their interest to permit, even sometimes to assist, forms of "economic nationalism" and public investment to which they were in principle opposed. And though concentrated power reaches considerable heights, it is far from total. Again, the world is too complex for that. What remains uniform is an array of truisms: pursuit of the "vile maxim"; design of policy for the benefit of its "principal architects" however others may suffer; the Churchillian maxims, amended to eliminate residual doctrinal camouflage; and the tales of benevolence, altruism, naiveté, and so on, spun by the "responsible men" to clear their own consciences, pacify the public, and prepare the ground for the next "experiment."

3. "The Government of the World"

The first order of business for global planners in 1945 was the reconstruction of the rich industrial societies. Early thoughts of converting Germany into an agrarian nation were quickly abandoned, as were promises of reparations for its devastation of Eastern Europe. Germany and Japan were recognized to be the "great workshops," which would have to be at the core of the industrial world that was to be reconstituted within the overarching framework of U.S. power.

Several interrelated problems had to be addressed: the prestige of the anti-fascist resistance that was slated for demolition in favor of traditional rulers, who were discredited by their ties to fascism; the influence of the "rotten apple" looming in the East; and the specter of a neutralist third force, social democratic in character, that might seek an independent role. The worst geopolitical nightmare was a more or less unified Eurasia out of U.S. control, a vastly larger counterpart to the fears of European unity that guided the island nation of Britain in earlier centuries.

An immediate concern was the "dollar gap" that kept industrial powers from purchasing U.S. manufactures and agricultural surplus. To overcome it was a critical necessity, Dean Acheson and other leading planners felt; lacking such markets, the U.S. economy would sink back into depression or face state intervention of the kind that would interfere with corporate prerogatives rather than enhancing them. Furthermore, wartime profits had left the masters of the U.S. economy with great reserves of capital they sought to invest, primarily in the rich countries of the West. For these reasons alone, reconstruction of the industrial world along lines suitable to U.S. power was the leading item on the global agenda.

A variety of measures were adopted to undermine the anti-fascist resistance and the labor movement, restore the traditional conservative order, and promote economic growth along lines that would benefit U.S. exporters and investors. A large-scale aid program was attempted from the late 1940s, with limited results. The shift to international military Keynesianism proved more satisfactory. The huge rearmament programs and the Korean war gave a powerful stimulus to the European and Japanese economies. Later the Vietnam war further enriched Europe while helping to raise Japan to a major industrial power and sparking the "takeoff" of the East Asian NICs—by that time, imposing costs that the United States found unacceptable.

The traditional service areas found their natural places within this general scheme, their importance enhanced by the loss of Western control over traditional agricultural and energy resources of Eastern Europe. Each region was assigned its status and "function" by planners. The United States would take charge of the Western hemisphere, driving out French and British competitors. The Monroe Doctrine was effectively extended to the Middle East, where Washington's British client was expected to provide assistance. Africa was to be "exploited" for the reconstruction of Europe, while Southeast Asia would "fulfill its major function as a source of raw materials for Japan and Western Europe" (George Kennan and his State Department Policy Planning Staff, 1948–49). The United States would purchase raw materials from the former colonies, thus reconstructing triangular trade patterns whereby the industrial societies purchase U.S. manufacturing exports by earning dollars from raw materials exports by their traditional colonies. By this reasoning, sophisticated and carefully articulated, former colonies could be granted nominal self-government, but often little more.[57]

For the former colonies, the principles of global planning entailed that "ultranationalist" tendencies must be suppressed. U.S. interests were seen to be threatened by "radical and nationalistic regimes" that are responsive to popular pressures for "immediate improvement in the low living standards of the masses" and development for domestic needs. The reasons are clear: such tendencies conflict with the need for "a political and economic climate conducive to private investment," with adequate repatriation of profits (NSC 5432/1, 1954), and the need for "protection of our raw materials" (Kennan). In a comprehensive secret policy review in 1948, Kennan cautioned that "we should cease to talk about vague and . . . unreal objectives such as human rights, the raising of the living standards, and democratization"; we must "deal in straight power concepts," not "hampered by idealistic slogans" about "altruism and world-benefaction," if we are to maintain the "position of disparity" that separates our enormous wealth from the poverty of others.

The profoundly anti-democratic thrust of U.S. policy in the Third World, with the recurrent resort to terror to marginalize or destroy popular organization, follows at once from the principled opposition to "economic nationalism," commonly an outgrowth of popular pressures. Quite independently of the Cold War, these have been salient features of policy. There is every reason to expect them to persist.

As discussed earlier, the heresy of independent nationalism with the wrong priorities—"the masses" rather than foreign investors—becomes an even more serious threat to the "national security" of the United States if "stability" is threatened by the feared demonstration effect of successful independent development. This reasoning too is sometimes spelled out clearly in internal documents. As Washington prepared to reverse Guatemala's brief experiment with democracy in 1954, a State Department official warned that Guatemala "has become an increasing threat to the stability of Honduras and El Salvador. Its agrarian reform is a powerful propaganda weapon; its broad social program of aiding the workers and peasants in a victorious struggle against the upper classes and large foreign enterprises has a strong appeal to the populations of Central American neighbors where similar conditions prevail." "Stability" means security for "the upper classes and large foreign enterprises," what is commonly termed "the national interest."

In postwar planning, the destiny of the South remained much as before, now within a general framework of liberal internationalism, modified as needed in the interests of U.S. investors and associates elsewhere. The conflict between U.S. policy and independent Third World development was deeply rooted in the structure of the world system. The persistent resort to violence and economic warfare is a natural concomitant of these fundamental principles.

The principles are expressed and pursued with particular clarity in regard to Latin America, where they were largely free of complicating factors. In the early postwar period, the United States was powerful enough to achieve a policy goal that can be traced to the early days of the Republic: displacing imperial rivals and realizing the goals of the Monroe Doctrine. Its meaning was explained by Secretary of State Lansing with an argument that President Wilson found "unanswerable," though it would be "impolitic," he felt, to state it openly: "The United States considers its own interests. The integrity of other American nations is an incident, not an end"—much like the interests of the "bewildered herd" at home. "Latin America's role in the new world order" of the post–World War II era, historian Stephen Rabe observes, was "to sell its raw materials" and "to absorb surplus U.S. capital." In the formulation of the senior historian of the CIA, Gerald Haines, Washington's goal was "to eliminate all foreign competition" from Latin America so as "to maintain the area as an important market for U.S. surplus industrial production and private investments, to exploit its vast reserves of raw materials, and to keep international communism out"; intelligence could find no evidence that it was trying to "get in," even if this were a possibility, but we have to bear in mind the tacit understanding that "communism" includes all of those devils who incite the poor to "plunder the rich," in Dulles's phrase.[58]

Latin Americans had rather different goals. They advocated what a State Department officer described as "the philosophy of the New Nationalism [that] embraces policies designed to bring about a broader distribution of wealth and to raise the standard of living of the masses." Another State Department adviser commented that "economic nationalism is the common denominator of the new aspirations for industrialization. Latin Americans are convinced that the first beneficiaries of the development of a country's resources should be the people of that country." These mistaken priorities ran directly counter to Washington's plans. The issue came to a head at a February 1945 hemispheric conference, where the United States put forth its "Economic Charter of the Americas," which called for an end to economic nationalism "in all its forms." The first beneficiaries of a country's resources must be U.S. investors and their local associates, not "the people of that country."

Given the power relations, Washington's position prevailed. One result is that instead of the "broader distribution of wealth" sought by Latin Americans, "the region has the most unequal income distribution in the world," the World Bank reported in September 1993, predicting "chaos" unless governments "act aggressively against poverty," which is truly appalling in its depths and scale.[59]

In Latin America, the Truman and Eisenhower administrations opposed "excessive industrial development" that infringes on U.S. interests. Latin American countries were to complement the U.S. economy, not compete with it; in short, no independent development guided by domestic needs. The same was true elsewhere, except that broader interests of the industrial countries arose as well, the United States having "assumed, out of self-interest, responsibility for the welfare of the world capitalist system," as Haines puts it.

For Asia, a 1949 NSC study called for a policy of "reciprocal exchange and mutual advantage." "General industrialization in individual countries could be achieved only at a high cost as a result of sacrificing production in fields of comparative advantage." Accordingly, the United States must find ways of "exerting economic pressures" on countries that do not accept their role as suppliers of "strategic commodities and other basic materials," the germ of later policies of economic warfare, Bruce Cumings observes. Prospects for independent development were seen to be slight, as well as unwelcome: "none of [the Asian countries] alone has adequate resources as a base for general industrialization," the NSC study determined, though India, China, and Japan may "approximate that condition." Japan's prospects were regarded as quite limited: it might produce "knick-knacks" and other products for the underdeveloped world, a U.S. survey mission concluded in 1950, but little more. Though doubtless infused by racism, such conclusions were not entirely unrealistic before the Korean war revived Japan's stagnating economy.

In Asia, it was necessary to depart from the guiding principles to counter the appeal of Communist "rotten apples," to which countries in the U.S. sphere might otherwise "accommodate," not a serious problem in the Western Hemisphere, despite much hysteria over the slightest infringement on U.S. control.

Africa, as noted, was left for Europe to "exploit." We turn to the Middle East in the next chapter.

Aid programs quite generally followed the same priorities. Marshall Plan aid for European reconstruction was guided by planning imperatives already mentioned. Few dollars actually left American shores; in large part, the aid program was a taxpayer subsidy to U.S. exporters and investors, from which Europe gained economically though with conditions on its domestic societies and their place in the international order: a subordinate role for labor within, and the subordinate role in the global arena later reviewed succinctly by Kissinger (pp. 33–34). More than 10 percent of Marshall Plan aid was spent on imports of oil; over half the oil supplied to recipient countries was financed by such payments, part of a more general program of shifting Europe to an oil-based economy. These policies served to undermine coal mining unions, considered politically unreliable, and to extend U.S. control, given U.S. domination of available oil resources. World Bank loans were directed to European reconstruction, with great benefits to American corporations. From 1946 to 1953, 77 percent of such loans went to buy American goods and services, with a quid pro quo: "Bank policy sought to stimulate, directly or indirectly, private investment and private enterprise."[60] U.S. taxpayers provided the funds, while U.S. corporations benefited doubly: from exports, and from improved investment opportunities. Possible trickle-down effects were, as always, "an incident, not an end."

Like the Marshall Plan, the Food for Peace program (PL 480) is commonly described as "one of the greatest humanitarian acts ever performed by one nation for the needy of other nations" (Ronald Reagan). In reality, PL 480 has served the purposes for which it was designed: providing a public subsidy for U.S. agribusiness; advancing U.S. policy goals by inducing people to "become dependent on us for food" (Senator Hubert Humphrey, one of the leading figures of American liberalism and an architect of the program in the interest of his Minnesota farming constituency); undermining food production for domestic needs and thus helping to convert Third World countries to agroexport, with accompanying benefits for the powerful U.S. transnational food industry and producers of fertilizers and chemicals; contributing to counterinsurgency operations through the military use of local currency counterpart funds; and financing "the creation of a global military network to prop up Western and Third World capitalist governments" by requiring that counterpart funds be used for rearmament (William Borden), thus also providing an indirect subsidy to U.S. military producers. The United States employs such "export subsidies (universally considered an 'unfair' trading practice) to preserve its huge Japanese market," among other cases (Borden). The effect on Third World agriculture and survival has often been devastating.[61]

The counterrevolutionary aims of the aid policies were outlined in a confidential 1958 State Department report entitled "Moderating the African–Asian Revolution": "We do not want to prevent change in the less developed areas, but neither can we accept the prospect of its evolving along lines which could throw Asia and Africa open to the unrestrained play of revolutionary enthusiasm and national ambition. We want to help new governments to attain their reasonable goals"—"reasonable" as we determine. As in Latin America and the Middle East, they can be free—as long as the masters do not "lose control."[62] The immediate concern in this case was the "economic nationalism" that might be inspired by the Chinese model. Kennedy's Alliance for Progress had similar motives, the culprit in this case being Cuba.

All of this could easily be framed within Cold War propaganda, on the assumptions already discussed: "national security" requires that no adversary (specifically the USSR) pose a potential threat, however remote, so that "preponderance" is a necessity; independent development is a prelude to incorporation within the Evil Empire ("the suicide of neutralism"). Having mastered these simple ideas, ideological managers could attribute every lapse from purity—which is to say, policy initiatives generally—to the unfortunate necessities of the Cold War, a most convenient scheme, which has to be modified today by the discovery of new Satans: "rogue states," "Islamic fundamentalism," the "growing technological sophistication" of the Third World, and so on.

While neoliberalism was the order of the day for the South, departures were allowed, sometimes encouraged, when the "rotten apple" effect threatened. By the 1950s, it was feared that underdeveloped countries, already susceptible to the Soviet virus, might see a model in China, which seemingly "had hit upon a formula for rapid development that might prove attractive throughout Asia, the Near East, and Africa."[63] Such concerns led to occasional willingness to support Third World independent development and even departures from reliance on private enterprise, contrary to general U.S. policy. Aid to Taiwan and South Korea as they undertook their programs of state-coordinated industrial development reflected such considerations. U.S. policy toward India is an instructive example: its international and domestic policies were despised, but it was given limited support as a counterweight to China.

Like other colonies, India sought to enter the modern world after freeing itself from foreign rule—in India's case, to return to the course of industrialization and modernization that Britain had blocked, indeed reversed; the same was true of Egypt, to which we turn later. In the Eisenhower years and briefly beyond, the United States offered some aid to India, though with considerable reluctance because of its neutralism and effort to pursue independent development along classic state-protected lines. Reviewing recently declassified records, Dennis Merrill finds little concern for India's needs. By 1950, American officials recognized that India faced terrible famine, in which some ten to thirteen million might perish, it was anticipated. But the Truman administration had no interest in providing wheat from the abundant surpluses the government had purchased as part of the public subsidy to large-scale U.S. agriculture. Some officials favored aid, because of benefits for the United States; food to save millions of people from imminent starvation might counter "Communist subversion" and prevent the rise to power of a government that "would be decidedly worse from our point of view" than the much-disliked Nehru (George McGhee). After the Korean war broke out, Dean Acheson offered India aid provided that India shows that it "understands the depths of the danger we now face" by joining the anti-Communist crusade; in contrast, we had no obligation to "understand the depths of the danger India then faced." Five months after India requested aid, it was granted a loan, repayable in strategic materials.

"No reliable statistics exist on how many additional famine-related deaths occurred during this period," Merrill comments, adding that "During 1950 and 1951, as millions of Indians struggled each day to survive on as little as nine ounces of foodgrains, American policy makers sought to work India's distress to America's advantage" in its Cold War policies and search for strategic materials.

Nothing changed in later years. The government and the press called for aid not to help India, but because "what happens in India will have a tremendous impact on the decisions made in other countries in Asia, in the Near East, in Africa and even in the Americas" (Vice President Richard Nixon). India will be "the main test for Western-aided economic development in Asia," *Business Week* commented. Senator John F. Kennedy called for aid to help India win the race against China, which was pursuing a "planning effort being put under consideration all over the world." We cannot live "surrounded by a sea of enemies," President Eisenhower said: to protect "our own interests and our own system," we must try to understand the Third World's "deep hunger" for improved living standards, even if its development patterns depart somewhat from the "free enterprise" model we seek to impose on others. In January 1963, President Kennedy reiterated this reasoning, urging Congress to look over "very carefully" the consequences for us if countries "turn communist just because we did not give a certain amount of aid"; we must "put aid on the basis it will best serve our interests."[64]

The main way in which aid can "serve our interests" is as an indirect public subsidy for U.S.-based corporations, a fact well understood by business leaders. In the case of India, representatives of the Business Council for International Understanding—a properly Orwellian title—testified before Congress in February 1966 on their problems and achievements. India would "probably prefer to import technicians and knowhow rather than foreign corporations," they noted, but "Such is not possible; therefore India accepts foreign capital as a necessary evil." The groundwork for India's submission was laid by foreign aid, which "has forced a modification of India's approach to private foreign capital [to] a more accommodating attitude."

As an example, they cite negotiations to double the fertilizer capacity that is "desperately needed in India." The U.S. consortium "insisted that to get the proper kind of control majority ownership was in fact needed," but India balked. India soon conceded, abandoning its objection that "the American

Government and the World Bank would like to arrogate to themselves the right to lay down the framework in which our economy must function," the *New York Times* reported approvingly, under the heading "Drift from Socialism to Pragmatism." India granted easy terms to private foreign investors under "steady pressure" from the United States and the World Bank, having little choice, because they controlled "by far the largest part of the foreign exchange needed to finance India's development and keep the wheels of industry turning." The American companies that India was compelled to admit on U.S. terms insisted upon importing all equipment and machinery despite India's admitted capacity to meet such requirements, and on importing liquid ammonia, a basic raw material, rather than using abundantly available indigenous naphtha, which, if developed, might increase India's independence. Indians expressed "near exasperation," the U.S. press reported, saying that "we have done everything we can to attract foreign capital for fertilizer plants, but the American and the other Western private companies know we are over a barrel, so they demand stringent terms which we just cannot meet" while Washington "doggedly insists that deals be made in the private sector with private enterprise."[65]

Great power aid programs continue to be motivated primarily by the interests of the donors. "The developing countries themselves bear the major burden for development," Carter's Secretary of State Cyrus Vance explained in March 1979, not those who had left them in their present condition. American aid should be designed to bring them "more fully into the world trading system" with "new codes and tariff reductions in multilateral trade negotiations"; it aims at a "common understanding of the responsibilities of both governments and corporations to create a better environment for international investment and the flow of technology."[66]

For India, the Soviet Union offered other options, whatever one may think of them. By the 1980s that phase was over and India too succumbed to the global catastrophe of capitalism, subjecting itself to the IMF regimen. The effects are reviewed by University of Ottawa development economist Michel Chossudovsky in a leading Indian economic journal. India "had a fair degree of autonomy in relation to the British colonial government," he points out, while "under the IMF–World Bank tutelage, the union minister of finance reports directly to [World Bank headquarters] in Washington DC, bypassing the parliament and the democratic process." Government budget proposals are "repetitive and redundant," repeating agreements signed with the World Bank. The Indian press has remarked that American styles and spelling have come to replace the British usage of Indian bureaucrats in key government documents, which come directly from offices in Washington. Central government ministries are staffed with former IMF and World Bank employees, part of the "parallel government" established in India by "the Washington-based international bureaucracy." Without the impediment of democratic processes, the rulers from afar can proceed with "crushing the rural and urban poor" and enriching the rich, in the familiar fashion. As in Latin America under the Alliance for Progress and since, much of the rural population is declining into chronic starvation and food consumption is dropping while food exports boom—much to the pleasure of Tata Exports, if not to peasants subjected to "economic genocide." Farmers are being driven to bankruptcy and real earnings of workers are falling. Deaths from starvation in relatively prosperous rural areas were reported as the New Economic Policy was phased in, now given still starker form under the guidance of the international bureaucracy. Most social sector expenditure has been reduced in current budgets, even more rapidly than other expenditures, a policy that "augurs terribly for the children of the poor in Indian society," two Indian economists conclude after reviewing the effects of structural adjustment programs in a wide range of countries of the South.

There are beneficiaries, including Indian elites and foreign investors and consumers. The diamond industry is an example. Seven out of ten diamonds sold in the West are cut in India, with super-cheap labor, now being driven down to still greater depths of misery. But there is a bright side: "We pass some of the benefits to our overseas customers," a major diamond exporter observes. Workers and their families may starve to death in the New World Order of economic rationality, but diamond necklaces are cheaper in elegant New York shops, thanks to the miracle of the market.[67]

The self-serving goals of "aid" became still more transparent as the West was "liberated" from the need to counter Soviet blandishments. In 1991, three-quarters of Britain's bilateral aid commitments were tied to British goods and services, and of the aid committed through multilateral agencies, each pound is expected to generate 1.4 pounds spent the same way. Others follow the same path. It is a commonplace that the "main motive" of aid "has not been to end poverty but to serve the self-interest of the giver, by winning useful friends, supporting strategic aims, or promoting the donor's exports" (*Economist*). This "carelessness," as the *Economist* calls the regular practice, leads to the "bizarre" result that "the richest 40% of the developing world's population still gets more than twice as much aid per head as the poorest 40%," most of it going to "countries that spend most on guns and soldiers, rather than health and education." About "half of all aid is still tied to the purchase of goods and service from the donor country," a practice that "costs developing countries some 15–20% of the value of the aid because they pay higher import prices"—"folly," the journal terms it, as it would be, were the goals anything beyond self-interest.[68]

Exceptions would be hard to find. States are not moral agents, as Kennan and others understood very well. Admiration for their "altruism" and "generosity" is the province of the commissar, like the call for reimposition of colonial benevolence by the "civilized world," which must return to its "mission to go out to these desperate places and govern" the backward peoples it had cared for with such tender solicitude, then cruelly abandoning them to their fate under the impact of "liberal opinion" and the "moral defensive" the foolish liberal sentimentalists imposed on the traditional benefactors.[69] The call for reinstitution of the benefits of slavery is still waiting in the wings.

4. The Balance Sheet

For Churchill's rich and satisfied nations, which rule by right, the results of postwar planning and policy were generally satisfactory, even spectacular. U.S. investors reaped enormous gains with the growth of the domestic economy and rapid expansion of overseas investment. The Marshall Plan "set the stage for large amounts of private U.S. direct investment in Europe," Reagan's Commerce Department observed in 1984, laying the groundwork for the Transnational Corporations (TNCs) that increasingly dominate the world economy. TNCs were "the economic expression" of the "political framework" established by postwar planners, *Business Week* observed in 1975, lamenting the apparent decline of the golden age of state intervention in which "American business prospered and expanded on overseas orders, . . . fueled initially by the dollars of the Marshall Plan" and protected from "negative developments" by "the umbrella of American power."

Even with hindsight, it is hard to think of measures that postwar planners could have taken that would have been more advantageous for U.S. private and state power. Talk of U.S. "errors" in building up eventual competitors, or complaints about the ingrates who fail to "return the favors" by catering to current U.S. needs,[70] could be taken seriously if accompanied by some indication of how the interests represented by the global planners could have been better served.

The Traditional Victims

The effects on the Third World were about as one might expect, becoming still more harsh in recent years. The UN Human Development Program (UNDP) reported that the gap between the rich and poor nations doubled from 1960 through 1989. These results are attributable in large part to the dual policies pursued by the rich rulers: "free market" principles are imposed on the poor via the structural adjustment programs dictated by the IMF and World Bank, acting "as bill-collecting agencies for the creditor countries," Susan George aptly comments; meanwhile the powerful countries protect their own firms from the ravages of the market, at considerable cost to the Third World.

The World Bank reports that protectionist measures of the industrial countries reduce national income in the South by about twice the amount of official aid—much of it serving strategic ends, the rest largely a form of export promotion, hence directed mainly to the richer sectors of the "developing countries," less needy, but better consumers. In the 1980s, twenty of twenty-four OECD countries increased protectionism, Reaganites often leading the crusade against the principles of economic liberalism. In Latin

America, the real minimum wage declined sharply from 1985 through 1992 under the impact of neoliberal structural adjustment programs, while the number of poor rose almost 50 percent between 1986 and 1990—"economic miracles," in technical terminology, because real GDP rose (in parallel with external debt) while the wealthy and foreign investors were enriched. IMF studies show "a strong and consistent pattern of reduction of labor share of income" under the impact of its "stabilization programs" in Latin America, Manuel Pastor observes. Latin American foreign debt grew by over $45 billion from December 1991 to June 1993, to reach a total of $463 billion, a German Press Agency study of seventeen Latin American countries revealed, among other disheartening statistics; all of this in the course of a much-acclaimed recovery with grand prospects—for some.

Reviewing World Bank data on the seventy-six countries of the Third World and Eastern Europe that were exposed to structural adjustment programs through the 1980s, Rehman Sobhan shows that a large majority suffered significant decline in important development indices—growth in fixed investment (productive capacity), in exports, and in the economy generally—as compared with "the bad old days of the 1960s and 70s when government controls and market distortions were supposed to be crippling economic performance." Even on inflation, specifically targeted by the international bureaucracy, the effects were inconclusive. The few "success stories" are dubious, aid-driven or based on exports of primary products; Chile, the most heralded example, relies on copper for more than 30 percent of export revenues and agroexport for most of the rest, and thus is highly subject to "terms of trade shock" resulting from policies of the rich powers. The Philippines, more under U.S. influence than the rest of Asia, had the largest exposure to structural adjustment reforms in Asia. Following the rules rigorously, it fell into protracted recession, the collapse highlighted by its location in the growth center of the world economy. Furthermore, the long-term costs of privatization, which often means selling off profitable and socially important enterprise for short-term gain, have yet to be felt, a number of economists have warned. The record of the economic management imposed by the "ideologically-driven regimes" of the United States, Britain, and a few other rich countries, and the international financial institutions that "tend to follow each shift in the political wind in the US quite closely," is hardly inspiring, Sobhan concludes.

Resource transfers from South to North amount to "a much understated $418 billion" from 1982 to 1990, Susan George estimates, the equivalent in today's dollars of some "six Marshall Plans for the rich through debt service alone." In the same years, the debt burden increased 61 percent, 110 percent for the "least developed" countries. Meanwhile, commercial banks are protected by transfer of their bad debts to the public sector, ensuring that the poor will pay an inordinate burden of the costs in both the lender and the debtor countries. In 1991, debtor nations paid out $24 billion more in interest payments than they received from all new loans and aid. Even the IMF and

World Bank "are now net recipients of resources from the developing countries," the South Commission observes.

Included among the "developing countries" that fund the wealthy are those of sub-Saharan Africa, where starvation and misery are rampant thanks in no small measure to the much-admired U.S. policy of "constructive engagement," which helped South Africa cause 1.5 million killed and over $60 billion in damage in the neighboring countries in that period while maintaining its illegal hold on Namibia. To these figures we may add the half million children who die every year as a direct result of the debt repayment on which the rich insist, UNICEF reports, and the eleven million children who die each year from easily treatable diseases, a "silent genocide," WHO director-general Hiroshi Nakajima observes, "a preventable tragedy because the developed world has the resources and technology to end common diseases worldwide" but lacks "the will to help the developing countries"— a euphemism for the countries colonized and controlled by the West.[71]

We would not hesitate to describe these policies as genocidal if they were implemented by some official enemy.

The effects on children are particularly dramatic. The most vulnerable members of society, their well-being "is indicative of the state of a society," Madhura Swaminathan and V.K. Ramachandran point out. Horrible abuse of children in Western domains has long been a shocking scandal, occasionally reported as a human interest story—about *them*, not *us*; atrocities in Soviet domains, in contrast, were traced to the source of power. Countries that adopted structural adjustment reforms from the early 1980s have a particularly dismal record. A 1992 UNICEF study, reviewed by Swaminathan and Ramachandran, "makes one point emphatically: in the 1980s, structural adjustment programmes and the prolonged recession that followed them did great harm to the welfare of children." Sharp reversal of progress in infant mortality, nutrition, education, and other indices correlated closely with onset of these programs, which also increased such "abhorrent features of contemporary capitalist society" as child labor and child prostitution. One striking exception was Chile, where popular pressures placed certain limits on the U.S.-backed dictatorship and the market reforms it imposed by violence, so that public intervention continued even under the regime of Pinochet and the Chicago boys.[72]

In Latin America, only one country showed an "unambiguous decline in the infant mortality rate" in the 1980s, Swaminathan and Ramachandran report: Cuba, a deviation now being corrected while Western moralists gloat over this further triumph of their ideals. A second example in the early 1980s was Nicaragua, "now challenging Haiti for the unwanted distinction of being the most destitute country in the Western hemisphere," the experienced Latin America correspondent Hugh O'Shaughnessy reports, reviewing the success of the leading U.S. foreign policy initiative of the 1980s. Infant mortality, which had been declining rapidly, is now "the highest in the continent and, according to the UN, a quarter of Nicaraguan children are malnourished" while diseases that had been controlled under Sandinista health reforms "are rampant." Women run soup kitchens on street corners "in order to save tens of thousands of youngsters from starvation," while "retinues of tiny, hungry children wait at every set of traffic lights, eager to wipe your car or simply begging," or turn to prostitution and theft. The finance minister "boasts that Nicaragua has the lowest inflation in the western hemisphere—never mind that its four million people are starving." Sandinista "health, nutrition, literacy and agrarian programs have been scrapped by a government pressed by the International Monetary Fund and Washington to privatise and cut public spending." The right is not satisfied: "It wants to destroy the Sandinistas, even if that means war," and it "knows it has the support of the US government." It therefore refuses to join peace talks planned by Central American foreign ministers and OAS officials "who came on a mission of mediation" but "left in despair" after the rejection by Washington's clients. Despite its success in driving misery to Haitian levels under rigorous application of the rules of economic rationality, Washington is not satisfied. "'The United States has a visceral need to annihilate the Sandinistas once and for all,' said one foreign affairs expert."[73]

The privatization and cuts in public spending demanded by the international bureaucracy have further effects on Nicaragua's economy, or what remains of it. "The private bankers and big business interests associated with them enjoy the protection of the state banking system, taking advantage of the high interest rates to engage in speculative activities," a group of Nicaraguan economists observe, estimating that $60 million left the country through new private banks in 1992 alone; "while the economy's liquidity—measured in money—has fallen 14%, the resources in the hands of the private banks grew 28% in the first half of 1993, provoking the current shortage of money in circulation that is affecting the population so seriously." Investment is virtually nonexistent. Meanwhile the U.S. Senate, having funded a murderous terrorist war against Nicaragua, now demands proof from its government that *Nicaragua* is not engaged in international terrorism as a condition for receiving a trickle of aid—a tiny fraction of the reparations to which Nicaragua was entitled under the World Court decision, which itself dealt with only a tiny fraction of U.S. crimes. Not content with these depths of moral cowardice, the Senate demands further that the FBI be admitted to Nicaragua to investigate its alleged involvement in international terrorism, with worse yet to come, as we shall see directly. No real surprise, in a world in which Washington's bombing of Libya in an attempt to assassinate Qaddafi is offered as a worthy precedent for the bombing of Baghdad in retaliation for an alleged plot to assassinate ex-President Bush, and Vietnam is condemned to still further suffering because it has not yet groveled to the satisfaction of its torturers.

Despite their victory, U.S. policy makers are not satisfied. Nicaragua's people must suffer more to atone for the crimes they have committed against us. In October 1993, the IMF and World Bank, virtually U.S.-run, presented new demands of unusual severity. Unlike many others, Nicaragua will receive no relief from its crushing debt. It must eliminate credits from the Industry and Commerce Bank (BANIC), one of the remaining state banks, and privatize enterprises and government operations such as postal services, energy, and water, to ensure that poor people really feel the pain—unable to give their children water to drink, for example, if they cannot pay, thanks to over 60 percent unemployment. It must cut public expenditures by $60 million, eliminating much of what remains of health and welfare services—a figure that was perhaps selected for its symbolic value; as noted, that is the sum shipped out the previous year by the already privatized banks.

Privatization ensures that banks follow sound economic principles, playing the New York stock market rather than giving credits to poor farmers, and thus using resources more efficiently. With credits unavailable, the 1993 bean harvest was lost despite a good rainy season, a catastrophe for the population. In the main cotton-producing areas, not an acre was sown in 1993 because of lack of credits—though the most powerful producers, including the minister of agriculture and cattle-ranching and the president of the High Council of Private Enterprise, Ramíro Gurdián, received over $40 million in loans last year, *Barricada Internacional* reports. Central America specialist Douglas Porpora writes that 70 percent of what limited credits there are go to "a small number of large export producers," in accord with standard U.S. policies of enriching the wealthy sectors involved in agroexport. Farmers had been driven out of these regions by Somoza, who had taken over the land for cotton export, part of the "economic miracle" hailed in the United States, as the economy grew while the population starved under the most admired neoliberal principles. After years of intense pesticide use, much of the soil has lost its fertility. Banana exports and other agricultural production have also collapsed, and sugar mills, including those which had become profitable under government control, are being shut down, apparently in a campaign by the former owners, now restored, to destroy the unions and reverse the gains in workers' rights of the past years.

On Nicaragua's Atlantic coast, 100,000 people were starving in late 1993, church sources report, receiving aid only from Europe and Canada. Most are Miskito Indians. Nothing was more inspiring than the laments about the Miskitos after a few dozen were killed and many forcibly moved by the Sandinistas in the course of the U.S. terrorist war, a "campaign of virtual genocide" (Reagan), the most "massive" human rights violation in Central America (Jeane Kirkpatrick), far outweighing the slaughter, torture, and mutilation of tens of thousands of people by the neo-Nazi gangsters they were directing and arming, and lauding as stellar democrats, at the very same time. What has happened to the laments, now that tens of thousands are starving?

The answer is simplicity itself. Human rights have purely instrumental value in the political culture; they provide a useful tool for propaganda, nothing more. Ten years ago the Miskitos were "worthy victims," in Edward Herman's useful terminology, their suffering attributable to official enemies;

now they have joined the vast category of "unworthy victims" whose far worse suffering can be added to our splendid account. What more need be said?

It is only fair to add that the wonders of the free market have opened up alternatives, not only for rich landowners, speculators, corporations, and other privileged sectors, but even for the starving children who press their faces against car windows at street corners at night, pleading for a few cents to survive. Describing the miserable plight of Managua's street children, David Werner, the author of *Where There is No Doctor* and other books on health and society, writes that "marketing shoe cement to children has become a lucrative business," and imports from multinational suppliers are rising nicely as "shopkeepers in depressed communities do a thriving business with weekly refills of the children's little bottles" for glue-sniffing, said to "take away hunger." The miracle of the market is again at work, though Nicaraguans still have much to learn.

Some of the distance yet to be traveled was revealed in a Canadian Broadcasting Company documentary, *The Body Parts Business*, "a gruesome litany of depredation," reporting murder of children and the poor to extract organs, "eyeballs being removed from living skulls by medical pirates armed only with coffee spoons," and other such entrepreneurial achievements. Such practices, long reported in Latin America and perhaps now spreading to Russia, have recently been acknowledged by one of the most prized U.S. creations, the government that upholds "our values and aspirations" in El Salvador, where the procurator for the defense of children reported that the "big trade in children in El Salvador" involves not only kidnapping for export, but also their use "for pornographic videos, for organ transplants, for adoption and for prostitution." Hardly a secret, Hugh O'Shaughnessy observes, recalling an operation of the Salvadoran army in June 1982 near the River Lempa, where the U.S.-trained troops "had a very successful day's baby-hunting," loading their helicopters with fifty babies whose "parents have never seen them since." O'Shaughnessy's report on "Takeaway babies farmed to order" appeared in the London *Observer* the same day that the *New York Times* featured Anthony Lake's uplifting and admired remarks on "enlargement" of our traditional mission of mercy and benevolence (p. 71).[74]

In passing, we should note that trade in body parts does not pass entirely without censure. President Clinton approved a National Security Council recommendation to impose limited sanctions against Taiwanese exports to punish Taiwan "for its alleged failure to crack down adequately on trafficking in rhino horns and tiger parts," the *Wall Street Journal* reported under the heading: "U.S. Will Punish Taiwan for Trade In Animal Parts." Taiwan complained that it was "unfairly targeted to appease environmentalists and their backers in Congress." It was "singled out" unfairly; China and South Korea have just as bad a record of trafficking in body parts, the Taiwanese complained. But "there are easier, more realizable goals there," the director of an environmentalist group explained. As for Brazil, El Salvador, Mexico, Guatemala, and other countries engaged in the body parts trade, no questions have been raised.[75]

American liberals, who called for restoration of "regional standards" and return of Nicaragua to the "Central American mode" right through the U.S.-run atrocities of the 1980s, and who lauded the "Victory of U.S. Fair Play" when "the exhausted natives" finally threw in the towel, unable to withstand further torture, should be delighted by their achievements in this "romantic age."

Again, we can observe the appurtenances of power and its conventional attributes: the ability of the powerful to set the terms of discussion, and the fury elicited by any challenge to their right to rule. As we have seen, these privileges determine who is victim and who is oppressor, the true victims being regularly transmuted into savage tormentors of their innocent torturers. Thus the Vietnamese must make amends for their crimes against *us*, and Nicaragua must prove to *us* that it is not engaged in terror. The record is replete with complaints about the poor who seek to plunder the rich (Dulles); the Cuban leader whom we must assassinate because he would "berate and criticize the United States in the most violent and unfair and incredible terms" (McCone); the Palestinians who conduct "terrorist acts against the State of Israel" (the Intifada, in official U.S. government terminology) when they do not silently bend their heads after decades of "sheer accumulation of endless humiliations and casually committed brutalities," the "crucial factor" eliciting resistance (Israeli journalist Danny Rubinstein, who has covered the occupation with great distinction for years); and generally, the terrorists and villains who rise up to attack us—when they can momentarily escape the boot that rests on their necks.

Nicaragua is a particularly revealing case. Torturing Nicaragua is a ritual going back to 1854, when the U.S. Navy destroyed a coastal town to avenge an alleged insult to U.S. officials and the millionaire Cornelius Vanderbilt. As is well-known, international law is taken to establish rights by virtue of regular practice. It has therefore long been our established right to torture Nicaragua, a right exercised without a second thought through the final savagery of our client Somoza, who slaughtered tens of thousands with our aid and approval (disguised with much deceit) when the desperate population finally arose. The refusal of the new government to genuflect in the proper manner aroused sheer frenzy. One congressman described "the lust that members [of Congress] feel to strike out against Communism" in Nicaragua. Opinion divided between those who called for brutal terror to punish the crime of disobedience, and those who felt that terror might not be "cost-effective" so that we should find other means to "isolate" the "reprehensible" government in Managua and "leave it to fester in its own juices" (Senate dove Alan Cranston). The "visceral need to annihilate the Sandinistas" is nothing new.

Nicaragua's efforts to pursue the peaceful means required by international law aroused particular fury. Senior U.S. government officials demanded that an invitation to Daniel Ortega to visit Los Angeles be withdrawn "to punish Mr. Ortega and the Sandinistas for accepting the Contadora peace proposal," the *Times* reported without comment, referring to peace efforts that the U.S. government was able to undermine. The World Court condemnation of the United States evoked further tantrums. Washington's threats finally compelled Nicaragua to withdraw the claims for reparations awarded by the Court, after a U.S.–Nicaragua agreement "aimed at enhancing economic, commercial and technical development to the maximum extent possible," Nicaragua's agent informed the Court. The withdrawal of just claims having been achieved by force, Washington moved to abrogate the agreement, suspending its trickle of aid with demands of increasing depravity and gall. In September 1993, the Senate voted 94–4 to ban any aid if Nicaragua fails to return or give adequate compensation (as determined by Washington) for properties of U.S. citizens seized when Somoza fell—assets of U.S. participants in the crushing of the beasts of burden by the tyrant who had long been a U.S. favorite. Nothing will satisfy the lust to punish the transgressors, even their reduction to Haitian standards. Nor will the United States rest until the military is under Washington's control, a crucial element of U.S. policy towards Latin America for fifty years, or until the world comes to understand what virtually limitless power will achieve if offended in any way.[76]

A third Latin American country with traditionally high standards for child welfare and other social indices was compelled by U.S. pressure to cut health and other social spending and to privatize services, with the inevitable consequence of sharpening inequalities and harming the weak: Costa Rica. The founder of Costa Rican democracy, José Figueres, bitterly condemned Washington's "effort to undo Costa Rica's social institutions, to turn our whole economy over to the businesspeople, and to do away with our social insurance" and national institutions, "turning them over to the local oligarchy or to U.S. or European companies." In vain.[77]

It is noteworthy that while the United States was lending decisive support to state terrorists who met approved "regional standards" by slaughtering and torturing tens of thousands of hapless victims, these three countries were singled out for U.S. attack: in the case of Cuba and Nicaragua, by war, terror, and economic strangulation; in the case of Costa Rica, by subversion and pressures for "liberalization" that became almost manic in intensity, in part connected with the war against Nicaragua, in part simply from hostility to an island of social democracy in Washington's "backyard" horror chamber.

The pattern is so systematic that it is hard to miss, almost as striking as the correlation between U.S. aid and torture. It is "missed," however. The United States did not target these specific countries because it prefers to see children die, any more than its aid programs are motivated by a love of torture and mutilation. Rather, the pervasive patterns are incidental corollaries of a fundamental commitment: the antagonism to independent development that interferes with the climate for business operations and with the "function" of Third World countries in the global economy.

Study of particular cases yields considerable insight into guiding principles. Few examples are more revealing than Brazil.[78] A country with extraordinary natural advantages, the potential "Colossus of the South" had long been regarded by U.S. observers as "a mighty realm of limitless potentialities"; "no territory in the world is better worth exploitation than Brazil's," the *Wall Street Journal* rhapsodized in 1924.

The United States took over in 1945, removing traditional European rivals and converting the Colossus into a "testing area for modern scientific methods of industrial development," Gerald Haines observes in his highly regarded monographic study. Under close U.S. guidance, Brazil followed approved neoliberal doctrine, though with periodic departures to head off consequences that were catastrophic for the rich, not only the population generally. From the 1960s the United States lent vigorous support to a military dictatorship for which the groundwork was laid by the Kennedy administration. Our neo-Nazi clients were able to impose economic orthodoxy more rigorously, popular opposition having been quelled by ample doses of torture and "disappearance." They constructed an "economic miracle" that was greatly admired, despite some reservations about the sadistic violence by which it was instituted. Brazil became "the Latin American darling of the international business community," *Business Latin America* reported in 1972, much as Mussolini and Hitler had been in earlier years. The chairman of the U.S. Federal Reserve, Arthur Burns, praised the "miraculous" work of the ruling torturers and their neoliberal technocrats, who scrupulously applied the economic doctrines of the "Chicago boys." When these experts were called in by another collection of fascist killers in Chile a year later, they held up Brazil "as the exemplar of a glowing future under economic liberalism," David Felix recalls.

True, the "miracle" had a few flaws. Over 90 percent of the population lived under conditions of increasing misery, for many, comparable to Central Africa. In rural areas with ample fertile land—in the hands of landowners protected by the security forces and devoted to agroexport in the approved manner—medical researchers describe a "new species," pygmies, with 40 percent the brain size of humans, the result of protracted starvation. Cities compete for world championships in child slavery and murder of street children by security forces. University of São Paulo professor of theology Father Barruel informed the UN that "75% of the corpses [of murdered children] reveal internal mutilation and the majority have their eyes removed," allegedly for an international organ transplant racket. The luckier ones survive, sniffing glue to relieve hunger. The litany of horrors is endless.

Writing in 1989, Haines agreed with the judgment of the business community. He described the results of more than four decades of U.S. dominance and tutelage as "a real American success story"; "America's Brazilian policies were enormously successful," bringing about "impressive economic growth based solidly on capitalism." This triumph of capitalist democracy stands in dramatic contrast to the failures of Communism, though admittedly the comparison is unfair—to the Communists, who had nothing remotely like the favorable conditions of this "testing area" for capitalism, with its huge resources, no foreign enemies, free access to international capital and aid, and benevolent U.S. guidance for half a century.

The success is real. U.S. investments and profits boomed, the tiny elite is doing wonderfully, and macroeconomic statistics are favorable: an "economic miracle" in the technical sense. Until 1989, Brazil's growth far surpassed that of much-lauded Chile, now the star pupil, Brazil having suffered total collapse, thus automatically shifting from a triumph of market democracy to an illustration of the failures of statism if not Marxism. With only 60 percent of Chile's per capita GDP in 1970, Brazil advanced to about the Chilean level by 1980, retaining that position through 1988.[79] If during these wonderful years the conditions of Eastern Europe were beyond the wildest dreams of most of the population, that's the way the cookie crumbles. We will wait a long time before such minor details as these, readily duplicated over much of the world, break through the chorus of self-adulation celebrating the triumph of capitalism over its adversaries.

The crushing Third World debt results primarily from the collapse of commodity prices in the early 1980s combined with monetarist financial policies in the West. Economist Melvin Burke points out that "high interest rates [in the United States] and capital flight, not failed development policies or public enterprises, were responsible for the Mexican crisis of the 1980s," while "in many ways, U.S. prosperity was gained at the expense of the third world, . . . including capital flight from Mexico and other debtor countries in Latin America," now more deeply indebted than ever. The loans, granted to our favorite dictators and oligarchs so that they could purchase luxury goods and export capital to the West, are now the burden of the poor, who had nothing to do with them, and the taxpayer at home.

Having "reached the astronomic level of $1.35 trillion" and "still growing year by year," Third World debt has "huge ramifications," Britain's shadow minister for overseas development, Michael Meacher, observes. The debt, along "with the concomitant option of debt relief, is now a major device for securing compliance" to Western demands. "What is abundantly clear," the South Commission observes, "is that the North has used the plight of developing countries to strengthen its dominance and its influence over the development paths of the South," forcing the weak "to reshape their economic policies to make them compatible with the North's design."

The West demands strict payment, however extraordinary the human toll, but there are "instructive exceptions," Meacher notes: Poland was granted a $15 billion write-off "in order to facilitate its transition from a communist to a capitalist economy"—in which Western investors look forward to ample rewards; and Egypt was relieved of $11 billion "in order to buy its support for the alliance against Saddam Hussein in the Gulf War." But in sub-Saharan Africa, children are to die by the hundreds of thousands each year to ensure compliance with the noble principles of economic liberalism. "The moral is clear," Meacher concludes: "debt forgiveness is determined not by pressures to relieve world poverty, but by meeting the contingent political interests of the dominant western nations"—more precisely, the economic and strategic interests of their ruling elements. Exactly as the senior associate of the Carnegie Endowment for International Peace advised in 1988, with the Soviet Union gone the United States can tighten its grip on the undeserving poor.[80]

Only the willfully blind can fail to see the mechanisms at work.

The Home Countries

What is really happening is brought out by a closer analysis of the UNDP figures on the rapidly growing gap between rich and poor. Canadian political economist Ian Robinson notes that the scale of the gap "is even more striking if, instead of looking at the income of rich and poor *nations*, we look at that of rich and poor *people*." In 1960, the GNP ratio between the countries with the richest 20 percent of the world's population and those with the poorest 20 percent was 30:1; by 1989, it had reached 60:1. But the same UNDP figures reveal that "the ratio of the incomes of the richest and poorest 20 percent [*of people*] was about 140:1," not merely 60:1. Its data show that "more than half of the inequality between the richest and the poorest 20 percent of the world's people . . . is a function not of income inequalities *among nations*, but of income inequalities *within* nations," Robinson observes. To cite a comparable example, the U.S. government National Center of Health Statistics found that "the degree of inequality in mortality rates," one telling index of inequality, more than doubled from 1960 to 1986, a "class gap" that is "widening."[81]

In short, we must not overlook the crucial footnote to the Churchillian maxim: the "class analysis" of policy on which Adam Smith insisted, commonly evaded by his successors, with the natural expectation that "our" policies may prove quite harmful to us, while highly beneficial to those who design and implement them. We might also note that "inequality" has an antiseptic sound, more soothing than what it means: starving children, broken families, criminal violence, and all the social pathology that arises from the end of hope.

These changes within nations extend across all "three worlds": the state capitalist industrial powers, the "developing countries" of the South, and the former Communist states, now largely returning to their Third World origins. In all cases, the effects are attributable in no small measure to the selective application of neoliberal economic dogmas: fetters for the weak and poor, cast aside by the rich and powerful when the consequences are not to their liking.

Within the rich nations, this selective application provides a kind of microcosm of the international scene. With corporate profits under pressure, governments have cut back on social spending while maintaining or even extending the welfare state for the rich. The processes are clearly illustrated in the United States, Britain, Australia, and New Zealand, which "danced with the dogmas" imposed on the weak (though only to a limited extent, being powerful enough to violate the rules), and suffered accordingly; I borrow the phrase of British conservative MP Ian Gilmour in his incisive critique of the "Thatcher revolution."[82] But others are not far behind, for structural reasons inherent in the New World Order.

In Reaganite America, a combination of military Keynesian excesses designed to profit the rich and fiscal policies with the same goal quickly turned the country from the world's leading creditor to its leading debtor. Under a trillion dollars when Reagan took office, the debt more than doubled to $2.1 trillion by 1986 after regressive tax cuts and increased Pentagon spending, reaching over $4.4 trillion when Reagan–Bush handed their legacy over to their successors. Senator Daniel Patrick Moynihan, chairman of the Senate Finance Committee and one of the Senate's most knowledgeable fiscal specialists, concludes that the "strategic deficits" of the Reagan years were driven by a "hidden agenda": raising a barrier against eventual social spending and other government initiatives not acceptable to corporate America. Federal cutbacks imposed intolerable burdens on states and municipalities, with deleterious social consequences on a broad scale. The problems were much exacerbated by the highly successful PR campaigns organized by the business community to "get government off our backs" and cut taxes, while ensuring that their needs were amply satisfied by a powerful and interventionist state. Corporate and household debt also grew rapidly.

Regressive fiscal policies led to luxury consumption and financial shenanigans while investment relative to GNP declined to the lowest level among the seven leading industrial powers (G–7); even that low level relied increasingly on capital imports. Huge trade deficits resulted. Real per capita GDP declined from the Carter years, personal savings fell, infrastructure spending fell to half the rate of the 1960s though government spending did not decline. Inflation was the one area of improved statistical performance, largely because of the fall in the price of oil. Borrowing maintained a superficial prosperity for many, though it could not be long maintained except for the richest sectors, who did indeed benefit.

Labor economists Lawrence Mishel and Jared Bernstein found "more than 17 million workers, representing 13.2 percent of the labor force, . . . unemployed or underemployed in July [1992]," a rise of eight million during the Bush years, as the effects of Reaganite designs sank in. Furthermore, some three-quarters of the rise in unemployment is permanent loss of jobs. The stagnation of real wages for over a decade changed to sharp decline in the Reagan years. By 1987, the decline extended to the college-educated who soon after faced job loss; these effects are probably traceable in large part to the course of the Pentagon budget, as government funding of military-related (high tech) industry leveled off in 1985–86, then reducing to closer to the Cold War average. Real wages declined for the lower 60 percent of American males, rising (not to speak of other income) for the top 20 percent. MIT economist Rudiger Dornbusch points out that of the gain in per capita income in Reagan–Bush years, "70% accrued to the top 1% of income earners, while the bottom lost absolutely," so that "for most Americans, it is no longer true that the young generation can count on being economically ahead of its parents," a significant turning point in the history of industrial society. Mid-1992 polls found that 75 percent of the population do not expect life to improve for the next generation.

The Reagan years accelerated processes already underway. Income inequality had declined until 1968, then rose steadily, surpassing the figures for the Great Depression by 1986. In these two decades, average income of the bottom fifth of American families declined about 18 percent while it increased about 8 percent for the richest fifth, Ian Robinson points out, tendencies that continue since. Through these years, "the U.S., of all industrialized nations, experienced the greatest growth of inequality, combined with the greatest earnings declines of lower paid workers," economic journalist Richard Rothstein reports. An OECD study found increasing inequality in most of the richer countries through the 1980s, the most extreme increase being in Thatcherite Britain, the second in the United States, which opened the decade with the most unequal distribution of the lot and kept that prize by the end. The U.S. record was particularly bad for more vulnerable sectors: the elderly, children, and single-mother families (most of them in the paid labor force, the United States ranking third highest in that category, contrary to floods of right-wing propaganda). The 1993 UNICEF study *The Progress of Nations* found that American and British children are considerably worse off than in 1970. Among industrialized countries, the proportion of American children below the poverty line is now twice that of the next worst performer, Britain, and about four times that of most others, with a 21 percent increase from 1970, mainly the result of cutbacks in government services, UNICEF director James Grant comments.

"The major institutional factor that affected the U.S. wage structure is the decline of unions," U.S. Labor Department chief economist Lawrence Katz concludes. One of the great successes of the Reagan years was to step up the attack on unions, opening the way to firing of workers for supporting unionization, strike breaking by hiring of "permanent replacements," and other devices that have undermined a leading force for democratization and social justice. The results are highly encouraging to privileged sectors. A front-page story in the *Wall Street Journal* reports "a welcome development of transcendent importance": "the increasingly competitive cost of U.S. labor," thanks to the harsh attack on labor through a combination of state power and improved opportunities to shift production abroad. U.S. labor costs per unit output fell 1.5 percent in 1992, while costs increased in Japan and Europe, as well as Taiwan and South Korea. In 1985, hourly pay in the United States was higher than the other G–7 countries. By 1992, it had fallen to below its wealthy competitors, apart from Britain, where Thatcher had done even better in punishing working people. Hourly wages were 60 percent higher in Germany that in the United States, 20 percent higher in Italy. The United States has not yet reached South Korea and Taiwan, but progress is being made.

With urban society in crisis, the jail population zoomed to by far the highest level in the industrial world, surpassing Russia and South Africa. Poverty reached new heights in deteriorating cities and rural areas, while infrastructure collapsed. Homelessness became a national disgrace. In the last half of the 1980s, hunger grew by 50 percent, to some thirty million people. By early 1991, even before the effects of recession of the Bush years, researchers found that twelve million children in the world's richest country, with unparalleled advantages, lack sufficient food to nourish the body and maintain growth and development. In Boston, a wealthy city and one of the world's leading medical centers, the City Hospital, which caters to the general population, was forced to set up a malnutrition clinic for children, resorting to triage because of limited facilities, particularly in the winter, when parents have to make the agonizing choice between heat and food.[83]

In October 1993, the Census Bureau reported that "the ranks of poor Americans swelled 1.2 million to 36.9 million last year, while the wallets of the richest got fatter," the *Wall Street Journal* reported. Median family incomes were 13 percent below the 1989 level, and poverty levels were the same as "in the depths of the fierce early-1980s recession," before the heralded "boom years." Analysts expect the long-term trend of poverty rates "to continue to be upward," with "eroding wages, shrinking state assistance for the poor, and an increase in single-parent families" as social bonds erode. "The income inequalities that accelerated in the early 1980s continued into 1992, with the top fifth of American households increasing their already disproportionate share of income" to 47 percent of the total. "The rich clearly did get richer," an author of the Census Bureau stated, while incomes of the bottom fifth of families held steady at $7,328, barely a subsistence level. A 1994 Commerce Department study found that the percentage of full-time workers receiving poverty-level wages had risen by half during the Reagan years, from 12 percent in 1979 to 18 percent by 1992 ($13,000 per year). The net worth of American households fell 12 percent from 1988 to 1991, the Census Bureau reported, having risen little during the "boom years of the 1980s," and fallen for many. Child poverty increased by 47 percent from 1973 to 1992, reaching 20 percent of all children, an increase from 12 million to 14 million since the last count a year earlier. The poverty level is defined as an annual income of $11,186 for a family of three. "They learn hopelessness very quickly," the director of the Tufts University study said, realizing "that they cannot affect their environment. In a hopeless situation, people do things they would not otherwise consider," including violent crime, an epidemic to be controlled by draconian punishments, not attention to the causes, prevailing doctrine holds.[84]

During the first two years of the economic recovery from 1991, wages continued to fall for both blue-collar and white-collar workers, with continued growth of the gap between them. Only above the 90th percentile have wages risen over 1989. Furthermore, after twenty-eight months of recovery, unemployment had not fallen, something new in the postwar era. There is also an increase in part-time and temporary employment, not by choice but because of improvement in the "flexibility" of the labor market, a very good thing for economic health, according to received doctrine; "flexibility" is a technical term meaning that when you go to bed at night, you don't know whether you have a job the next morning. In 1992, almost 28 percent of the jobs created were temporary, with another 26 percent in government, primarily at the state and local level. In 1993, 15 percent of new jobs were temporary, leaving 24.4 million part-time and temporary workers, 22 percent of the work force, the highest level ever. The country's biggest private employer is Manpower, the largest of the temp agencies, with 600,000 people on its payroll, 200,000 more than General Motors.

As the recovery progressed, job creation increased. The month of March 1994 exceeded all expectations, eliciting an enthusiastic front-page story in the *New York Times* (as elsewhere) on the good news, the largest gain in six years. Only in the final paragraph of the continuation page inside do we find ambiguous figures meaning, as the *Financial Times* expressed it, that "in fact, in March 349,000 of the 456,000 new jobs were part time. Manufacturing employment only rose by 12,000."[85]

In England, the Thatcher government quickly created the worst crisis for manufacturing industry since the industrial revolution, destroying almost one-third of the manufacturing plant within a few years by blind pursuit of Friedmanite and laissez-faire doctrines that were falsified at every turn. The results were a "miserable performance" for the economy, Gilmour observes, with growth rate declining and poverty rapidly increasing as Thatcherite ideologues played "Good Samaritan only to the better off." London began to take on the appearance of "a third-world capital." These developments took place despite a huge shot-in-the-arm for the economy provided by North Sea oil and the sharp decline in prices of Third World exports, Gilmour adds. Economist Wynne Godley observes that the Thatcher period is characterized by slower growth, lessened ability to compete in world markets, sharp increase in government and household debt and unemployment, "hysterical ups and downs" in a startlingly unstable economy, along with loss of manufacturing capacity.

A quarter of the population, including 30 percent of children under sixteen, live on less than half the average income, "the nearest thing to an official poverty line," the press reported in July 1993, a sharp increase from 1979 under Thatcherite discipline, which led to a cut of 14 percent in income of the poorest families. Inequality soared, surpassing even Reaganite America in the increase in inequality though not yet reaching American heights (the order of inequality among the rich countries in 1984–87, the last period for which firm data are available, is: United States, Australia, Israel, United Kingdom, Canada . . .). The British Commission on Social Justice reports that income inequality is higher than it has been for over a hundred years. During the Thatcher decade, the income share of the bottom half of the population fell from one-third of all income to one-fourth, with a three-fold increase in the number of children living in low-income households. Regular reports fill in the details. The government plans to make squatting a criminal offense, eliminating the margin for survival provided by abandoned buildings and underground tube stations. Increasing numbers of people are losing water, as the private industry disconnects households unable to pay bills, a form of "germ warfare," microbiologist John Pirt comments. The shape of the intended future is coming more clearly into view.[86]

"The wealth gap, a growing feature of the 1980s, will go on widening for the next five years at least," the market research organization Mintel reports, noting the "increasing demand for luxury goods and services, while . . . a growing proportion of households only have sufficient income for staple products and necessities"—an observation with "important implications for business markets." The share of total income of the top 20 percent of households grew from 35 percent in 1979 to 40 percent in 1992, while the share of the bottom 20 percent fell from 10 percent to 5 percent, the study reports, the gap increasing more rapidly in the past few years as Thatcherite policies settled more firmly in place. The charitable organization Action for Children, founded in 1869 with the queen as patron, concludes in a recent study that "the gap between rich and poor is as wide today as it was in Victorian times," and in some ways worse. A million and a half families cannot afford to provide their children with "the diet fed to a similar child living in a Bethnal Green Workhouse in 1876," a "sad reflection on British society." European Commission (EC) figures show that Britain has proportionately more children living in poverty than any European country apart from Portugal and Ireland, and the proportion is rising faster than any country in Europe. The EC reports further that Britain during the 1980s became one of the poorest countries in Europe, falling behind Italy and some regions of Spain. A year earlier, Britain was sent to "Europe's poorhouse," the *Financial Times* observed, "technically poor enough to apply for extra European Community cash" along with Spain, Ireland, Portugal and Greece.[87]

As in Reaganite America, there is a veneer of prosperity resulting in large part from borrowing and shift of resources to the more wealthy, amidst social and economic decay. And in some circles, the results are welcome indeed. "Finally, the Payoff from Thatcher's Revolution," a headline reads in *Business Week*, which reports enthusiastically that "Britain's surprising resurgence holds some lessons for the Continent," particularly "declining labor costs," now a third less than the Western European average; lower corporate taxes; and greater "labor flexibility," as in the United States. "Credit goes largely to Margaret Thatcher, whose reforms are now bearing fruit." This "new labor market has proven a potent lure to outsiders," who are happy to use Thatcher's achievements to boost profits and to drive their own workforce down to similar levels. "When [workers] see jobs disappearing, it has a salutary effect on people's attitudes," a British manufacturing director observes in the *Wall Street Journal*, also impressed with the "payoff from Thatcher's revolution," which is leaving Britain "with a low-paid, low-skill work force." Jobs are being created thanks to the improved conditions of exploitation and the salutary attitudes they bring, but "virtually all the net new jobs have been part-time; most of them go to women and pay less than full-time jobs," and "the number of full-time British employees with weekly pay below the Council of Europe's 'decency threshold' is up to 37% from 28.3% in 1979," thanks to the new "labor flexibility" and the weakening of unions and workers' rights.[88]

Australia danced with the same dogmas, in this case under a Labour government. The result was a "dismal tale of economic failure," conservative Robert Manne points out in the business press, reviewing the "disaster." "The era after de-regulation was akin to large-scale experimentation in a chemical laboratory where previously unmixed elements were combined," one leading political analyst observed. The consequences were much as in the United States and Britain, and more cruelly, Third World countries that are far more vulnerable: massive transfer of wealth from poor to rich, unemployment, attack on labor, decline of productive investment, growth in family and child poverty, increased foreign ownership, and an actual reduction in national income. "Following their role models in the United States and United Kingdom, Australia's plutocracy embarked on an orgy of greed and avarice on a scale never before seen in the country," political scientist Scott Burchill comments.[89]

The experience should "have, at the very least, planted the seeds of doubt," Manne comments. In all three societies the doubts were allayed by what MIT economist Paul Krugman describes as a "combination of mendacity and sheer incompetence," referring specifically to attempts to suppress the truth "by the *Wall Street Journal*, the U.S. Treasury Department, and a number of supposed economic experts," a record that demonstrates "the extent of the moral and intellectual decline of American conservatism."[90]

New Zealand danced with the dogmas of market monetarism with even greater vigor and enthusiasm, carrying out "the most comprehensive economic reform programme undertaken by any OECD country in recent decades," OECD economists Isabelle Joumard and Helmut Reisen observe, concluding that the experiment was a near-total failure. The official recipe was instituted in 1984. Comparing the period 1977–84 with 1984–89, the OECD economists find a sharp decline in the contribution of the tradable sector (manufacture, mining, agriculture) to GDP, and in share of OECD manufactured exports. The reforms caused severe structural damage; without them, manufactured export would have been about 20 percent higher, they calculate.

New Zealand economist Tom Hazeldine, a specialist in international trade, carries the review of the "coup" by "market radicals" to 1993. Registered unemployment, almost nonexistent before, reached 14.5 percent, the highest level in the OECD after Spain. A huge debt ($11 billion) was quickly created. There was almost no economic growth, and the slight growth of productivity resulted mainly from labor-shedding. While business starts increased, business failures increased even faster, so that the rate of *successful* business formation declined, thanks to the magic of the market. Government expenditures sharply increased, from 30 percent of GDP to 49 percent; social democracy had a much smaller state presence and "was a lot cheaper—and better—with everyone in a job," Hazeldine comments. Markets not only make huge errors, but are also very expensive to run. "The share of GDP taken up by the 'market-making' industries—financial and business services—nearly doubled, from just over 5% to just under 10%," Hazeldine reports, while "employment in the 'market-minding' sectors—police, the law, insurance, security guards—has also risen disproportionately." No compensating gains can be detected, apart from the usual benefits to the rich at home and abroad.

Hazeldine departs from professional rigor to make a related point, of perhaps even greater long-term significance. Under the market monetarist experiments, "the things that count in life" sharply deteriorated along with its narrower economic conditions: "love and friendship; work and play; security and autonomy," the "empathy" and "feeling of obligation" and sympathy "binding New Zealanders together" in a livable society. The grand experiment had "appalling results" across the board, Hazeldine concludes. The same consequences are dramatically evident in the United States and Britain, and are a natural concomitant to exaltation of market values.[91]

Earlier experience, briefly reviewed in section 2, would have led one to expect nothing different. The post–World War II era simply extends the story. Each of the successful industrial societies pursued some mixture of state capitalist development programs, adapted to the needs of domestic power. Japan, rejecting standard neoclassical economic counsel, designed a form of industrial policy that assigned a predominant role to the state, creating a system that is "rather similar to the organization of the industrial bureaucracy in socialist countries and seems to have no direct counterpart in the other advanced Western countries," Tokyo University economist Ryutaro Komiya points out in his introduction to a study of Japan's postwar economic policies by a group of prominent Japanese economists. They review a variety of measures adopted to increase "production, investment, research and development, modernization or restructuring" in some industries while decreasing them in others, modifying market-determined allocation of resources and level of economic activity. "The 'ideology' of industrial policy during this [early postwar] period was not based on neoclassical economics or Keynesian thinking, but was rather neomercantilist in lineage," another contributor observes, and "also was distinctly influenced by Marxism." One eminent conservative Japan scholar describes Japan as "the only communist nation that works" (Chalmers Johnson). Heavy protection, subsidies and tax concessions, financial controls, and a variety of other devices were employed to overcome market deficiencies, in violation of doctrines of comparative advantage and international specialization that would have delayed or undermined Japan's industrial progress. Market mechanisms were gradually introduced by the state bureaucracy and industrial–financial conglomerates as prospects for commercial success increased. The radical defiance of orthodox economic precepts set the stage for the Japanese miracle, the economists conclude.

The NICs in Japan's periphery resumed the economic development that was underway under Japanese colonialism, adopting a similar model. There are numerous other examples illustrating "the positive association between state intervention and the acceleration of economic growth that is now generally accepted to prevail in cases of Third World capitalist development" (Alice Amsden), as, indeed, for the major industrial societies throughout their histories.[92]

Given its own historical experience, and its somewhat intermediate position in the neocolonial order, it is not surprising that Japan has vigorously criticized the structural adjustment programs of the World Bank and IMF. An official Japanese government critique reviews the reasons why reliance on comparative advantage, liberalization and market mechanisms, privatization, "efficiency" without concern for "fairness and social justice," long-discredited "trickle-down" assumptions, and other contemporary shibboleths reflects a "lack of vision" that is "truly lamentable." The critique passed without notice.[93]

As throughout history, such experiments with laissez-faire dogma are not failures for the designers, however others may fare. They are, furthermore, undertaken without support from the general public. The West likes to pretend that "democratically elected governments" in the South are eagerly following the recommendations of their advisers from the rich countries, but even the briefest acquaintance with recent history and social realities suffices to dismiss this cynical pretense.

Though Third World opinion is typically more attributed than sampled, those who look will find that it is less than euphoric about "the wave of the future." The South Commission report cited earlier is one example, ignored, like other discordant notes. Latin American bishops also labor in obscurity because of their faulty priorities. In December 1992, they held their Fourth General Conference in Santo Domingo, attended by the pope. The agenda was carefully managed by the Vatican, in fear that the bishops might pursue the path opened at the historic conferences of Medellín and Puebla in which they adopted "the preferential option for the poor," setting off the murderous Reagan–Bush terrorist campaigns to destroy this heresy, which threatened to help poor people take some control over their lives and address the brutal heritage of exploitation and misery in Washington's "backyard." Despite Vatican controls, the bishops warned against "the predominant neoliberal policy" of Bush's New World Order, which has sometimes caused democratic life to deteriorate and condemned the vast majority to even greater suffering. They also called for "promoting the social participation of the state [as] an urgently important line of pastoral work." The terrible poverty of the region "did not come about by itself," the Bolivian Conference of Bishops added, "but is the product of the current free market system, which lacks any controls, and the economic adjustments that are part of neoliberal policies that do not take into account the social dimension." The Bolivian bishops have the advantage of highly relevant first-hand experience, to which we return.[94]

The voices of the bishops too were unheard, not disturbing Western triumphalism.

Even in the democratic societies of the West, public opinion is a marginal factor at best. In Australia, "the key decisions [on neoliberal reforms] were undertaken without any public consultation and with little or no knowledge of their impact on Australian society and polity," Scott Burchill observes. Throughout the Reagan years, the U.S. public generally favored New Deal–style measures, far preferring social to military spending, even favoring new taxes if used for socially constructive ends. The case of health reform, mentioned earlier, illustrates a broader pattern. No authentic choices were presented in the narrowly constrained political system, while propaganda barrages kept the public subdued and confused. The PR system operated overtime to concoct an image of large-scale support for policies the public generally opposed and for the leader of the "conservative revolution," a largely mythical creature whose popularity was a media creation, and who is now among the most disliked figures in public life (see p. 19).

In Britain, the Social Attitudes Survey for 1992 finds that "respondents came out in favour of public spending by bigger margins than ever," the London *Guardian* reports, with 65 percent favoring higher taxes and more spending. Government policy follows a different course. Attitudes towards private enterprise are similarly negative. Asked how profits *should* be distributed, 42 percent chose investment, 39 percent workforce benefits, 14 percent consumer benefits, and 3 percent shareholders/managers benefits. Asked how profits *would* be distributed, 28 percent predicted investment, 8 percent workforce benefits, 4 percent consumer benefits, and 54 percent shareholders/managers benefits. As in the United States, the conviction that the economic system is "inherently unfair" is widely shared, but well beyond the reach of the political system, with the general public largely reduced to a spectator role, as leading democratic theorists have long urged.[95]

The Return to the Fold

The story is much the same in the ruins of the Soviet empire. Hungary was the first great hope for neoliberal success. By 1993, electoral participation declined to under 30 percent, while 53 percent of the population say "it was better before" the collapse of the old system. Casting about for a new success, Western commentators hit upon Poland, where the sharp economic decline throughout the region since 1989 apparently bottomed out in 1993. "Most Poles are much better off socially, politically and economically than they were under the despised communist system," Anthony Robinson writes in an upbeat *Financial Times* supplement. The taste of freedom should indeed be sweet after years of grim dictatorship, but the cheery account offers little evidence of the public share in Poland's "growing prosperity" or popular attitudes towards it, though page after page gives reasons why foreign investors should feel euphoric, among them low wages, tax holidays on profits, the decline of the Solidarity trade union as "mounting unemployment erodes its power base," and the failure of "last-ditch" efforts of unions to "derail" the privatization that is the standard prelude to takeover by foreigners or a domestic kleptocracy.

We also learn that from 1988, incomes have fallen by half for farmers (30 percent of the population), and that "meat production is dropping in response to depressed demand" in the cities, expected to drop further to "below the 1980 level when meat shortages provided the backdrop to the workers' strikes which presaged the fall of communism." During 1992–93, the year of "growing prosperity" that is claimed to have reversed the post-1989 collapse, real wages dropped still further—for those who still have jobs—remaining "very low while prices have soared to world levels."[96]

Elsewhere we discover that the "glowing picture of the Polish economy" that is seen as "an economic success story" in the Western media and as a "vindication of the 'shock therapy' economic policies" advocated by Western advisers looks "less cheerful" on the ground. "Shock therapy has divided Poland, hurt the majority of the population, and paralyzed its political process," a leading Polish journalist reports. Recent polls show that "more than 50% believe that the previous political system—communism—was better." Furthermore, "the generally rosy picture" transmitted to the West overlooks the "awkward fact" that subsidies remain in place for households and industry, Alice Amsden notes. "Without such supports, the human misery would be much greater than it already is," and the "national plight" is much worse than the view from the capital cities throughout Eastern Europe.[97]

Puzzlement over the reaction of the Polish people to their "economic miracle" mounted in the United States as the elections of September 1993 approached. Poland "has been widely praised as a model for Eastern European economies breaking with their Communist past," the *Los Angeles Times* reported on election day as polls predicted "a stunning victory" for "repackaged former Communists." The source of the "wide praise" is unidentified, though the sentence that follows provides an oblique indication: "But the economic miracle has been a harder sell at home," where people seem oddly unappreciative even though "the advances of capitalism abound: Fancy imported cars speed through Warsaw's increasingly stylish streets, and glitzy new shops offer the finest goods from abroad." Ordinary people perceive the "miracle," but say: "We are in despair." The *Wall Street Journal* worries that as "capitalism bloomed" it brought with it "perceived inequalities." This "perception" portends a threat to democracy, perhaps even a "grave threat," as "Poland is sensing the same mood swing that carried the left back to prominence in Lithuania last year" and "may do the same soon in Hungary next year, and in Russia sooner still." The concept "democracy" is understood to mean acceptance of the market discipline favored by Western investors; "democracy" is accordingly threatened if people feel concern for "basic human needs" such as education, health, jobs, and food for their children, not merely "economic rationality" with its store windows featuring consumer goods they cannot buy, profits flowing to Western investors, and a new capitalist *Nomenklatura*. Commenting on the "slick new stores [that] lend a patina of prosperity" to the former industrial city of Lodz, an educated young woman who "theoretically . . . should be one of the winners in Poland's economic shake-out . . . bristles with anger," Jane Perlez reports. "Sure there's some stuff in the stores, but we can't afford it," the woman comments. "Look at those people, they're so crushed psychologically you can see it in their faces." If they stay crushed, "democracy" is safe, but there is always a danger that they may not.[98]

As predicted, the "economic miracle" proved to be a "hard sell at home." "The free-market reform-minded party that has taken Poland through its recent economic 'shock therapy,' winning plaudits from the West, finished third" in the elections, with about a tenth of the vote. Though the parties with a social democratic aura and the left peasant party won, turnout was slim, under 50 percent, "further evidence of disinterest" in what people see as a failed political system, the *Wall Street Journal* commented—assuring its readers, however, that the reforms will continue whatever the population wants. What they want was revealed by polls showing 57 percent opposition to the free market reforms that will continue to be imposed. "Western investors and international bankers were trying to put the best face" on the electoral outcome "by arguing that a return to a command economy was not feasible," the *New York Times* reported as the results came in; also scarcely feasible, given Western controls, are more reasonable choices than the twin absurdities of a command economy or dancing with neoliberal dogmas.[99]

"Public resistance to privatization, especially among workers, has been evident since early in the post-Communist period," the director of Russian and East European studies at George Washington University observes. "A 1990 survey, for example, found that only 13 percent of workers, but 37 percent of directors, favored private ownership of their enterprise," with over one-third of both workers and directors favoring state and employee ownership. But the attitudes of the population are inconsequential in the "new democracies"—one reason, perhaps, why "the Communist era is looking better and better" to Poles, another academic specialist adds.[100]

The population in Russia also shows little enthusiasm for the rapid capitalist reforms advocated by the autocratic former Communist Party boss Boris Yeltsin, a leading democrat by Western fiat by virtue of his advocacy of policies that are beneficial to Western investors. Within Russia, his popularity dropped from 60 percent to 36 percent from 1991 to early 1993 despite rapidly increasing support for a "strong leader." An EC poll in February 1993 found that most Russians, Belarussians, and Ukrainians oppose the move to a free market and feel that "life was better under the old communist system"; "Russians are also hankering after the old political system" (*Financial Times*). A Gallup poll of ten East bloc countries at the same time found that 63 percent opposed "democracy," an increase of 10 percent since 1991. "Generally, the more recent the overthrow of communism in a country, the greater was the enthusiasm for change"—that is, before the effects of "change" set in (AP). Another 1993 U.S. poll (Times Mirror Center) found that Russians favor a "strong leader" over a "democratic form of government" by 51 percent to 31 percent, "almost an exact reversal" of the figures for May 1991; the tepid backing for Boris Yeltsin in the April 1993 referendum he called very likely reflects these sentiments. "Less than a third of the respondents picked capitalism as the future model for Russian society, down from 40 percent 17 months ago," the same poll determined. By August 1993, the *New York Times* reported, "relatively reliable polls indicate that the number of Russians who believe that their lives will be better under capitalism has dropped from 24% to 18%." "Surveys in nearly all countries show a swing back towards socialist values, with 70% of the population saying the state should provide a place of work, as well as a national health service, housing, education, and other services" (*Economist*).[101]

Among those not sampled in the "glowing" reports that hearten Western elites are the women "displayed in windows" in the red light districts of Western cities, brought by criminal organizations from the former Soviet bloc "into the voracious sex industry of Western Europe," where at least they can survive. Or West Europeans, including those who might not be so delighted with the opportunities for profit offered by transfer of jobs to the new Third World in the East, or with the enhanced drug flow to the West as "shock therapy" takes its normal course. Harvard University economist Jeffrey Sachs, who presided over Poland's experiment before moving on to ply his trade in Russia, won his spurs in Bolivia, where he created a much-admired "economic miracle," a macroeconomic success and human disaster; the West applauds the statistics, Bolivians suffer the social reality while voices of concern, like those of the Bolivian bishops, do not penetrate the chambers of the privileged. The statistical successes are based in large measure on sharply increased production of illegal drugs, which may now be the major export earner, several specialists estimate. It is understandable that farmers driven to agroexport by government policy should seek maximum profit, joining international banks and chemical companies in the cocaine racket. The same processes operate in the former Soviet bloc, now becoming a major supplier to the West, notably Poland, which is currently producing the highest-quality illegal drugs in Europe, including 20 percent of the amphetamines confiscated in 1991, up from 6 percent in the late 1980s. Drug use in the region is also increasing rapidly, and the Colombian cartels are hiring Polish couriers to smuggle cocaine to the West. The former Soviet regions of Central Asia are expected to become major drug producers down the road.[102]

There are, so far, few surprises.

In particular, the attitudes expressed in polls throughout the region should come as little surprise. "The IMF–Yeltsin reforms constitute an instrument of 'Thirdworldisation,'" Canadian economist Michel Chossudovsky points out accurately. A "carbon copy of the structural adjustment programme imposed on debtor countries" in the Third World, their goal is to "stabilise" the economy, but their effect in Russia has been to increase consumer prices hundredfold in one year, to reduce real earnings by over 80 percent, and to wipe out billions of rubles of life-long savings. As elsewhere, the program "adopted in the name of democracy" constitutes "a coherent programme of impoverishment of large sectors of the population." "While narrowly promoting the interests of Russia's merchants and business tycoons, the 'economic medicine' kills the patient, it destroys the national economy and pushes the system of State enterprises into bankruptcy"; crucially, it blocks a transition towards "national capitalism," which is as unacceptable to the foreign masters as it was in the "Colossus of the South" fifty years earlier. Official figures report an annual decline of 27 percent in industrial production, but the actual decline is variously estimated at up to 50 percent. Production of most consumer goods has dropped by 20 to 40 percent, according to official figures. Current plans for "privatization" might drive up to half of industrial plants into bankruptcy, leaving what remains largely in foreign hands. Health, welfare, and education are collapsing. On the other hand, there is a rapid increase in capital flight, money laundering, and the market for luxury imports "financed through the pillage of Russia's primary resources." A small sector is enriched, on the Third World model, mostly "compradore elites" linked to foreign capital, with many of the old names and faces in charge. The system retains many totalitarian features in "a careful blend of Stalinism and the 'free market.'" "The collapse in the standard of living and the destruction of civil society engineered through a set of macroeconomic policy propositions is without precedent in Russian history," Chossudovsky observes, reviewing numerous examples.[103]

Reporting from Russia, the outstanding Israeli journalist Amnon Kapeliouk describes desperate misery and pauperization, with 87 percent of the population below the poverty line; sharp deterioration in food consumption from 1989 (apart from bread and potatoes, the food of the very poor), with food purchases taking over 80 percent of family income; collapse of Soviet science, of education, hospitals and welfare, while tuberculosis, diphtheria, and other forgotten diseases rapidly spread; mass graves because people cannot pay for burial; huge inflation; and destruction of social values as the concept "'solidarity' has disappeared from the vocabulary" in a society where "each is for himself."[104]

In Eastern Europe, as throughout the Third World, elites favor the "reforms," from which they benefit; and the West, which holds the power, insists upon them. Accordingly, they will be rammed through in the name of "democracy," properly understood. Recall Lord Bentinck's insight, long ago (see p. 116).

The major beneficiaries, of course, are sectors of Western power. Material and human resources offer wonderful opportunities for profit. Investors are enriching themselves as the *nomenklatura* capitalists of the new Third World sell off its resources at bargain rates. The new labor pool offers a double benefit to Western investors: profitable direct investment exploiting trained and skilled workers at very low wages and with few benefits, and a means to reduce labor costs at home under the threat of shift of production a few miles to the east. In short, the usual Third World amenities.

Other beneficiaries are the Western "experts" and advisers competing for taxpayer subsidies theoretically directed to the East. "When the West recruited an army to mop up after the Cold War," the *Wall Street Journal* observes, "it didn't want aid workers. It wanted a corps of corporate role models—consultants, bankers, and entrepreneurs—to clinch a friendly take-over." Foreign "aid" was designed for that purpose, the leading recipient being Poland, seen as the easiest prize and the most willing to follow the neoliberal rules. Of the $25 billion the West pledged to Poland, under 10 percent reached Poland as "pure gifts," about half the cost of a highway. A large chunk of the aid was "dissipated on Western consultants," who flooded to Poland to take their substantial share of the international capital sent to implement the "friendly takeover." "Aid for Western advice mostly aided Western advisers," the *Journal* notes, and "Western business has been the biggest gainer from the West's business loans." Western advisers can make $1,200 a day, two hundred times the price of their no less competent Polish counterparts. Western consulting firms are doing a booming business, their revenue coming largely from aid agencies (80 percent, one London representative estimates), yet another form of welfare "entitlements" for the rich. The Bush administration's Polish–American Enterprise Fund, "invented to finance small business while maximizing profit for itself and its managers," has succeeded largely in the latter task while retaining its reputation as "the most successful effort in Poland," perhaps rightly. The managers of the Fund have worked out numerous ingenious ways to enrich themselves by tapping the aid and investment flow. As for credits, donors require that more than half "must be spent on Western exports—from corn to economists." Western businesses and experts are doing nicely, while Poles watch with increasing annoyance.

The story in Russia was much the same. U.S. aid has been a "windfall," the *Journal* concludes, but "for U.S. consultants." It has led to "dancing in the streets—though not the streets of Russia." "The chief celebrants" are the "hordes of U.S. consultants who are gobbling up much of the U.S. aid pie," pocketing "between 50% and 90% of the money in a given aid contract" and also doing what they can to ensure that U.S. equipment will be used for any development that might leak through. The newly formed trade groups "use

[U.S.] taxpayer funds to help American businesses expand in Russia," Pillsbury's Green Giant unit, for example, using a $3 million AID grant to expand its presence in the "potentially huge Russian canned good market." The largest of these trade groups, KPMG Peat Markwick, has put together an "all-star agglomeration" including J.P. Morgan, Bechtel, Land O'Lakes, Young and Rubicam, and others eager to use gifts from U.S. taxpayers to lay the basis for new profits. But "Russians won't see much of the AID money that flows through the firm," its manager points out. "The AID money is almost exclusively for consultants who fly in and out."

"Nowhere is the disappointment [in Russia] more acute than in the aid targeted for nuclear disarmament—a field where Russians have considerable unemployed expertise," the *Journal* reports. Of the $1.2 billion U.S. program to implement the project, $754 million has so far gone to the Pentagon, which contracted for U.S. goods and experts. A prime goal of the program, a U.S. Assistant Secretary for Atomic Energy explained to "a group of cheering defense contractors," is to show the Russians "the spirit of free enterprise." If they are good pupils, then, they will learn that "free enterprise," ideally, is a system in which public funds are funneled through the state machinery for private profit, from the taxpayer to U.S. investors and highly paid professionals. Those familiar with the history of aid programs to the Third World will find few surprises here.

To facilitate future profits, Western investors demand that the taxpayer also fund the development of infrastructure. Its poor condition "has hindered Western companies here, making it hard for them to set up distribution systems for their products," the *New York Times* explains. For this reason, Western banks have agreed to relieve 40 percent of the debt that Poland accumulated after the collapse of its economy in 1989. This offer to Poland "is likely to enhance its economic prospects," the *Times* explains—that is, the economic prospects of Western investors and banks that will benefit from the "friendly takeover." The situation was similar in Latin America, the *Times* correctly observes. There too, debt reduction was "tied to market-opening moves" and "helped spur growth and attract foreign investment," the growth being of the kind that benefits the foreign and domestic wealthy, while the population, if lucky, does not suffer still further decline.[105]

In his address as outgoing chairman of the Group of 77 (representing over a hundred of the less developed nations), Luis Fernando Jaramillo of Colombia harshly condemned Western practices, noting in particular that the countries of the South "fail to understand why the international community does not take the measures nor allocate the resources necessary to help the African countries face the acute crisis they are experiencing," a crisis for which the West "is responsible in great part" and which has assumed "sorrowful" and "alarming" proportions in Africa, where "human suffering has reached dimensions unknown in other parts of the world." The question has the usual straightforward answer. Debt relief in Poland aids the rich men in the West; debt relief in Africa does not. The same principles hold for aid.

Taxpayer funds are directed primarily to the needs of wealthy entrepreneurs, investors, and professionals of the Western donors; the needs of starving children are distinctly secondary. That is "the spirit of free enterprise" that U.S. government officials dangle before "cheering contractors," who need little instruction from this source.[106]

Economists J.A. Kregel (Italy) and Egon Matzner (Austria) describe the results of "more than two years of experimentation" with "market shock" in Eastern Europe as "highly disappointing." The approach "not only ignores the lessons of history," they note, but also "fails to provide the social and economic conditions necessary to create a market economy." Their own countries, Italy and Austria, are in fact good examples of the lessons of state-guided development that are ignored. They cite Japan and the "Little Tigers" as recent cases, along with the postwar European economies. The Marshall Plan, they note, "was predicated on the formulation of national accounting and economic planning," just as "the successful operation of any capitalist firm is based on strategic planning within a market system."[107]

A fuller discussion would add that state initiatives and protection are features not only of the "latecomer" economies in "the history of capitalist development" to which Kregel and Matzner refer but of early entries too, as of all contemporary industrial societies; that the "market system" is in large part mythical; and that the "capitalist firms" that engage in strategic planning include TNCs that dwarf many national economies. Furthermore, the failure of such "experiments" has been routine for hundreds of years, with the crucial proviso that holds from Bengal in the eighteenth century to Brazil and Russia today: Adam Smith's observation that the "principal architects" of policy regularly do quite nicely.

The impact of the reforms was reviewed in a UNICEF study that considers them "unavoidable, desirable, and indispensable," though they involved "economic, social and political costs far greater than anticipated." The "shock therapy" confidently designed by the experts, whose arrogance matched their ignorance, "has been shown not to work effectively in practice" and is the cause, the UNICEF analysts believe, for "the largest yearly increases in poverty" and other deleterious social consequences. These have been extraordinary. "The yearly number of deaths in Russia, for instance, is estimated to have increased between 1989 and 1993 by over half a million, a figure which more than starkly illustrates the gravity of the present crisis"—and might stand as a grim footnote to the judgment of former World Bank senior economist Herman Daly, expressed at exactly the same time, that "our disciplinary preference for logically beautiful results over factually grounded policies has reached such fanatical proportions that we economists have become dangerous to the earth and its inhabitants," though he had different human costs in mind. From 1989 to 1993, "crude death rates increased by 17 per cent in Romania, by 12 per cent in Bulgaria, by commensurate amounts in Albania and Ukraine and by 32 per cent in Russia." By 1992, life expectancy for men had diminished by two years in

Russia; the number of suicides had risen by one-third in Poland and one-fourth in Romania. In the first six months of 1993, suicides increased by a third in Russia. Poland also "suffered a considerable surge in poverty and death rates and a deterioration in other demographic and welfare indices" along with still-growing unemployment. Only the Czech Republic, traditionally part of the West, "may slowly be returning to normal conditions."

Prior to the "economic reforms," Eastern Europe had functional though stagnating economies and "substantially lower levels of income inequality and poverty rates than those prevailing in the majority of the middle-income and developed countries, . . . even if account is taken of the privileges of the nomenklatura," many of them now the "nomenklatura capitalists" who are enjoying fabulous wealth in the standard style of Third World collaborators with Western privilege and power. There was also fairly broad provision of benefits and social services. These have collapsed, and poverty rates have "increased massively in the entire region," doubling in Poland from 1989 to 1990 alone with comparable changes elsewhere. In the better-off Czech Republic, the percentage of the population living in poverty rose from 5.7 percent in 1989 to 18.2 percent in 1992; in Poland, from 20.5 percent to 42.5 percent (the criteria are slightly different). Decline in real household net incomes "has been particularly marked in Bulgaria, Poland, Romania, Russia and Ukraine (in 1993)," with average incomes at about 60–70 percent or less of their pre-reform level, and inequality increasing sharply. Food consumption has "dropped significantly" along with decline in child care and pre-school enrollment, reversing the "remarkable results achieved in the past" in Central and Eastern Europe and their well-established "cognitive, developmental and psychosocial benefits." The increase in crime rates is "of precipitous proportions," doubling in Hungary from 1989 to 1992, for example; the proportion of young offenders is growing rapidly.

Other researchers report similar conclusions, anticipating "a 'psychosocial crisis' in which greatly rising insecurity and worry about crime, hardship and change play a large part" (Judith Shapiro, a British academic working with the Russian finance ministry).[108]

With regard to Eastern Europe, Western business reactions are so far mixed. Profits have been slow in coming. "The fact is that reforms are a bust" in Eastern Europe, a leading U.S. business monthly reports, citing a "damning report" of the European Commission which find "the villains" to be the "'shock therapists', such as Harvard's Jeffrey Sachs," who mechanically apply abstract economic principles that lack empirical support without concern for the social realities, bringing "pain" but not "life" to economies that remain "rigid, unreformed and bureaucratic"—hence not profitable enough for foreign investors.[109]

The rich men of the rich nations expect better returns from the "human misery."

The European Institute for Regional and Local Development produced a later report for the European Commission, concluding that the majority of people of the four countries of Eastern Europe sampled "are afraid of their future." The report found that 40 percent of Hungarians found the present government "worse" or "much worse" than the previous one. The director of the Institute "said the human reaction to 'shock therapy' was probably a surprise to experts like Sachs," Linnet Myers reported in the *Chicago Tribune*. Others find it natural, including Nobel Prize–winning economist Jan Tinbergen, who advocates a gradual, social-democratic approach to reform. Dutch economist Jan Berkouwer, an associate of Tinbergen's, says that Sachs is quite wrong in thinking that "there are no poor people and everybody is better off" in Poland. "Over 90 percent have less income and a few percent have more—maybe much more. To a capitalist man like Sachs, that doesn't harm him. But I'm of a different opinion." The European Institute study also found that people are disturbed by the growing gap between rich and poor.

Asked about all this in a telephone interview, Sachs said, "I really don't know what's the matter with the Poles." And he went on: "In Poland they're not rich, but they're also not suffering," a feeling not shared by the average person in Poland, where Sachs' "name alone was already enough to evoke bitterness," Myers reports. "People are reacting [against shock therapy] and correctly so," Berkouwer believes. "They are right," and they are suffering.[110]

Reviewing the record in 1994, Richard Parker of the Harvard Government department concludes that "shock therapy" was a failure. After the much-heralded reforms, "the big public firms—so despised by the therapists as socialist dinosaurs—provide at least 60 per cent of Poland's exports." The market reforms have produced "huge disparities between individual and regional incomes, and "for every two new jobs—often at pitifully low wages and slight benefits—added by the private sector, one worker ends up unemployed." He cites a recent World Bank study that predicts that Poland will not recover Communist-era living standards, let alone approach the West, before the year 2010, while the rest of the region may take still longer to regain the 1989 level. He also points out, as have many others, that "the strongest performers in the past two decades are the Asian economies that least resemble the academic free-market models of the therapists," and that the industrial West does not even come close to accepting "the advice we are giving to the former communists"—that is, to the Third World generally, for whom a stronger word than "advice" is in order, given the relations of power and the weapons available.[111]

5. Looking Ahead

The "affluent alliance" of the postwar era was running on the rocks by the late 1960s. Popular opposition to the Vietnam war prevented Washington from carrying out national mobilization of the World War II variety, which might have made it possible to complete the conquest without harm to the domestic economy. Washington was forced to fight a "guns-and-butter" war to placate the population, at considerable economic cost, while competitors enriched themselves by participating cost-free in the destruction of Indochina amidst sober musings on American bellicosity. The world was becoming economically "tripolar," with a revitalized Europe and a Japan-based Asian region emerging as major economic forces. In the world order established in the 1940s, the United States served, in effect, as international banker, an arrangement that offered great advantages to U.S. investors but that was becoming hard to sustain. In 1971, President Nixon unilaterally dismantled the international economic order; as global hegemon, the United States makes the rules.

Nixon suspended the convertibility of the dollar to gold, imposed temporary wage–price controls and a general import surcharge, and initiated fiscal measures that directed state power, beyond the previous norm, to welfare for the rich. Taxes were reduced along with domestic expenditures, apart from the required subsidies to private enterprise. These have been the guiding policies since, accelerated during the Reagan years. The unremitting class war waged by business sectors was intensified, now increasingly on a global scale.

By 1974, the United States had eliminated all capital controls. As the ideological spectrum was shifted to the right, regulatory structures that inhibit capital flow "were then challenged as 'inefficient' and 'against the national interest' and 'unmarketlike'—and the infrastructure of speculation was rapidly expanded" while "opportunities for profit proliferated," Cambridge University finance specialist John Eatwell writes. At the same time, as we have seen, the rich powers moved towards greater protectionism and other forms of state intervention in production and commerce. GATT economist Patrick Low draws attention to "the sustained assault on [free trade] principle from which the GATT suffered, starting around the early 1970s," a "difficult period economically" until today, in which "the GATT did not fully succeed in holding the line against growing protectionism and systematic decline."

Nixon's initiatives caused the international system to grow more disorderly, political economist David Calleo observed, "with rules eroded and power more significant." There was less "rational control over national economic life," hence great advantages to internationalist business and banking, freed from capital controls and official restraint and secure in the expectation of a state-organized public bail-out if something goes wrong. International capital markets rapidly expanded as a consequence of the decline of regulation and control, the huge flow of petrodollars after the 1973–74 oil price rise, and the information–telecommunications revolution, which greatly facilitated capital transfers. Vigorous bank initiatives to stimulate new borrowing contributed to the Third World debt crisis and the instability of the banks themselves, eased by the socialization of their bad debts.

The breakdown of regulatory structures and the huge increase in unregulated capital have had a large-scale impact on the international economy.

Eatwell notes the striking fact that "in 1971, just before the collapse of the Bretton Woods fixed exchange rate system, about 90 percent of all foreign exchange transactions were for the finance of trade and long-term investment, and only about 10 percent were speculative. Today those percentages are reversed, with well over 90 percent of all transactions being speculative. Daily speculative flows now regularly exceed the combined foreign exchange reserves of all the G–7 governments." From 1986 to 1990, such capital flows rose from under $300 billion to $700 billion daily, and are expected to exceed $1.3 trillion in 1994. One consequence is that "economic performance in the 1970s and 1980s has been poor throughout the industrial nations of the OECD," with growth in each G–7 country about half that of the 1960s, unemployment at least doubled, and productivity growth in manufacturing industry sharply down. Furthermore, "the sheer scale of speculative flows can easily overwhelm any government's foreign-exchange reserves"; repeatedly in recent years, national banks have been unable to protect their currencies against speculative attack. National economic planning is increasingly difficult even for the rich, market instability is increasing, and governments are driven to deflationary policies to preserve market "credibility," driving economies "toward a low-growth, high-unemployment equilibrium," with declining real wages and increasing poverty and inequality.[112]

The World Bank currently estimates the total resources of international financial institutions at about $14 trillion. The rich societies are no longer immune. Not only can European central banks not defend national currencies, but the European Monetary System has "effectively collapsed" as EC governments "have experienced the power of today's free-wheeling global capital markets," the *Financial Times* reports in a review of the world economy and finance. The huge and unregulated international capital market controls access to capital, but "global investors impose a price. If a country's economic policies are not attractive to them" they will use their power to induce changes. Such pressures may not be "fatal" to the very rich, but for the Third World, the international capital market is "no more than an unacceptable arm of economic imperialism," which the countries cannot resist in an era when governments even in the rich countries "are on the defensive and global investors have gained the upper hand."[113]

Even the world's largest economy and most powerful state is facing these problems. The United States can freely disregard IMF "advice," as the Bush administration showed in October 1992 when the IMF prescribed deficit-cutting measures including new taxes and "fundamental" health care reforms—the kind of "advice" that amounts to orders for the Third World. But the United States is not beyond the reach of international bond investors, who "may now hold unprecedented power—perhaps even a veto—over U.S. economic policy," the *Wall Street Journal* reported immediately after the 1992 election. "If bond investors react with even a modest dose of anxiety that sends long-term rates up just one percentage point, the deficit would increase another $20 billion, effectively doubling to $40 billion" the cost of the $20 billion economic stimulus that Clinton advisers were then consider-ing. This consequence of the huge Reagan–Bush debt will serve as a brake on any odd ideas that Clinton advisers might have about spending, the *Journal* indicated; spending of the wrong kind, that is. The complete defeat of Clinton's half-hearted effort to stimulate the economy followed shortly after, as the White House and Congress settled on a deflationary budget not very different from that of the Bush administration, actually reversing the increase in "human capital" expenditure during the Bush years.[114]

Another change in world order brought about by the policy shifts of the early 1970s was a considerable acceleration of the internationalization of production, a new stage in the takeover of the global economy by interna-tional corporations and financial institutions. The end of the Cold War and return of much of Eastern Europe to its traditional service role carries this process a large step further. It also offers new methods to discipline the population at home, as the business press has been quick to point out.

The mechanisms are straightforward. With capital highly mobile and labor immobile, the globalization of the economy provides employers with means to play one national labor force against another. The device can be used to diminish living standards, security, opportunities, and expectations for the great mass of the population, while profits soar and privileged sectors live in increasing luxury. Note that the mobility of capital and immobility of labor reverses the basic conditions of classical economic theory, which derived its conclusions about the benefits of comparative advantage and free trade from the assumption that capital is relatively immobile and labor highly mobile, assumptions that were realistic in Ricardo's day.

General Motors plans to close two dozen plants in the United States and Canada, but it has become the largest employer in Mexico, taking advantage of the "economic miracle" that has driven wages down sharply in the past decade, to much applause; labor's share of personal income in Mexico declined from 36 percent in the mid-1970s to 23 percent by 1992, economist David Barkin reports, while less than eight thousand accounts (including fifteen hundred owned by foreigners) control more than 94 percent of stock shares in public hands—facts that might be borne in mind (throughout the region), along with the uniquely high inequality achieved under U.S. control, when we read of the euphoria among investors about Latin America's prospects with "privatization" offering (often profitable) public assets for purchase, labor costs attractive for investors, and resources available for them.

Now Eastern Europe beckons as well. GM opened a $690 million assembly plant in the former East Germany, where workers are willing to "work longer hours than their pampered colleagues in western Germany" at 40 percent of the wage and with few benefits, the *Financial Times* cheerily explains. The region offers new opportunities for corporations to reduce costs thanks to "rising unemployment and pauperisation of large sections of the industrial working class" as capitalist reforms are instituted. Poland is even better than the former East Germany, with wages 10 percent of those demanded by the pampered west German workers, kept that way "thanks largely to the Polish government's tougher policy on labour disputes," the *Financial Times* reports under the heading "Green shoots in communism's ruins"; not everything is gloomy in the East. Poland is not quite Mexico yet in terms of state repression of labor, but advancing, it is hoped. Solidarity, the darling of the West when struggling against the enemy, is now just another enemy itself, like labor at home—except insofar as union leaders facilitate the reforms, in which case they are increasingly regarded as an enemy by the Polish work force and general population.[115]

Also among the green shoots are the tax holidays for investors noted earlier and other gifts. GM purchased an auto plant near Warsaw, Alice Amsden comments, "on the under-the-table condition that the Polish government provide it with 30 percent tariff protection"—the usual form that "free market" enthusiasms take. Similarly, "VW is capitalizing on low labor costs" to build cars in the Czech Republic for export to the West, but "the tortuous journey towards free markets" includes "a very attractive deal" in which VW was able to reap the profits and "to leave the Government with the debts and with enduring problems like how to clean up pollution," while "stiff tariffs" guarantee the profits of the foreign investors. Daimler-Benz recently worked out a similar "attractive deal" with Alabama.[116]

But the main attraction is cheap labor lacking union protection and welfare benefits. A study by Morgan Stanley International found that average labor costs in Poland were less than one-twentieth those of western Germany, less than one-thirteenth those of Britain, and less than three-quarters those of Hungary, where the German car maker Audi is building a plant having found that production costs would be a third less than in eastern Germany. Executives say that "workers in most Eastern European nations tend to be as well educated and trainable as their counterparts in the West," though not pampered with decent wages and benefits, and increasingly desperate as "market shock" devastates the economies. "Right on our doorstep in Eastern Europe, for the first time, we have a vast pool of cheap and highly trained labor," the president of the Association of German Industry in Cologne observes, arguing that Western labor costs must shrink if West European workers hope to stay in the game at all. The message is reaching the unions, loud and clear. "Every time we're asked to give up a benefit, we're told we're now in direct competition with Taiwan"—where wages are one-third those of Britain, one-fifth those of Western Germany—a British union officer comments, adding: "The message from executives to workers is, if you don't cede on labor costs, we're going elsewhere."[117]

The lessons are spelled out by *Business Week*. Europe must "hammer away at high wages and corporate taxes, short working hours, labor immobility, and luxurious social programs." It must learn the lesson of Britain, which finally "is doing something well," the *Economist* announces approvingly, with "trade unions shackled by law and subdued," "unemployment high," and the Maastricht social chapter rejected so that employers are protected "from over-regulation and under-flexibility of labour" (job security). American workers must absorb the same lessons; their progress in declining towards Third World standards is already perceived by the *Wall Street Journal* to be "a welcome development of transcendent importance," as we have seen. The achievement allows southeastern states with weak unions in the United States to mimic Poland. Daimler–Benz plans to establish a $300 million–dollar auto plant in Alabama to produce high-priced cars for the U.S. market, but only after the state government agreed to provide huge subsidies and tax breaks, for which "Alabama will pay dearly," the *Wall Street Journal* commented, quoting the head of a North Carolina economic development group who described Alabama's victory in the competition with other states as "Pyrrhic": "Something like this can't jumpstart an economy that's so moribund. That state has a Third World economy. They're losing money to invest in their people, their roads, their state in general. For a state like Alabama, which needs money for education, that's a problem." For its people, that is; international investors have no problem with the policies that are bringing the Third World model to the rich societies themselves.[118]

The guiding doctrine is straightforward: profit for investors is the supreme human value, to which all else must be subordinated. Human life has value insofar as it contributes to this end. As the economy becomes globalized, living and environmental standards can be "harmonized" globally, but harmonized down, not up. It is hardly likely that integration into the U.S. economy under NAFTA will lead to any significant rise in wages in Mexico, with its well-established methods of repression of labor and millions of peasants driven off the land as local farming is overwhelmed by U.S. agribusiness under "free trade." "Economists predict that several million Mexicans will probably lose their jobs in the first five years after the [NAFTA] accord takes effect," the *New York Times* reported after the House vote approving the agreement; the effect on wages is predictable. A study carried out by Mexico's leading business journal, *El Financiero*, predicted that Mexico would lose almost a quarter of its manufacturing industry and 14 percent of its jobs in the first two years.

These consequences are anticipated in a country that has lived through a decade of economic reform that has devastated much of the population, while winning much applause in the corporate world and doctrinal institutions. The number of people living in extreme poverty in rural areas has increased by almost a third, and half the total population lacks resources to meet basic needs, a dramatic increase since 1980. Following IMF–World Bank prescriptions, agricultural production was shifted to export and animal feeds, benefiting agribusiness, foreign consumers, and affluent sectors in Mexico while malnutrition became a major health problem, agricultural employment declined, productive lands were abandoned, and Mexico, formerly self-sufficient in agriculture, began to import massive amounts of food. As noted, real wages suffered a severe decline and labor's share in gross domestic product, which had risen until the mid-seventies, fell by well over a third, the standard concomitant of neoliberal reforms. But while further impoverishing the majority and enriching the few and foreign investors, its "economic virtue" has brought "little reward" to Mexico's economy generally, the *Financial Times* observes, reviewing "eight years of textbook market economic policies" that produced little growth, most of it attributable to unparalleled financial assistance from the World Bank and the United States, determined to keep the "miracle" on course. High interest rates partially reversed the huge capital flight that was a major factor in Mexico's debt crisis, though debt service is a growing burden, its largest component now being the internal debt owed to the Mexican rich.[119]

The issues are sharpened by comparison with the formation of the European Community: poorer countries were admitted on condition that their labor and environmental standards "harmonize upwards," and were granted assistance to this end. Not so as "free trade" is brought to North America under NAFTA, by a great power under more effective business control.

The basic goals were outlined by the chief executive officer of United Technologies, Harry Gray, in 1983: we need "a worldwide business environment that's unfettered by government interference," such as "packaging and labelling requirements" and "inspection procedures" to protect consumers. The meaning of his injunction was driven home at once as the World Health Organization voted 118 to 1 to condemn the Nestlé corporation's aggressive marketing of its infant formula in the Third World. The Reagan administration, well aware of the likely toll in infant disease and death, cast the sole negative vote, leading the way in the noble cause of "free market capitalism."[120]

Gray does not, of course, object to "government interference" of the kind that permits his corporation, an offshoot of the Pentagon system, to survive. Neoliberal rhetoric is to be selectively employed as a weapon against the poor, who are required to sacrifice in the name of neoclassical efficiency; the wealthy and powerful will continue to rely on state power, violating the rules as they choose.

It is in this context that the "trade agreements" (GATT, NAFTA, etc.) should be understood. The shift of production to high-repression, low-wage areas will continue independently of these agreements, as will the attack on environmental and health standards. But, as explained by Eastman Kodak chairman Kay Whitmore and a host of other commentators in the press, the business community, and the academic world, NAFTA may "lock in the opening of Mexico's economy so that it can't return to its protectionist ways"—that is, to a course of independent development; in a study of developing countries, the OECD found rates of protection in 1966 to be *lowest in Mexico*, much lower than the next lowest country, Taiwan. NAFTA should enable Mexico "to solidify its remarkable economic reforms," the director of economic studies at the Council on Foreign Relations, Michael

Aho, comments, referring to the "economic miracle" for the rich that has been a catastrophe for the poor majority. The "attraction" of NAFTA for many Mexican government technocrats, the business press reports, is "precisely that it would tie the hands of the current and future governments" with regard to economic policy. It may fend off the danger noted by a Latin America Strategy Development Workshop at the Pentagon in September 1990, which found current relations with the Mexican dictatorship to be "extraordinarily positive," untroubled by stolen elections, death squads, endemic torture, scandalous treatment of workers and peasants, and so on. They did, however, see one cloud on the horizon: "a 'democracy opening' in Mexico could test the special relationship by bringing into office a government more interested in challenging the U.S. on economic and nationalist grounds."[121] The danger is developments that might challenge U.S. state–corporate power, linking up with labor and other popular movements in the United States, which might not agree with international finance on the desirability of "a low-growth, high-unemployment equilibrium."

Once again, the basic threat is functioning democracy. As discussed earlier, there is a spectrum of opinion on the issue, differing on whether the "ignorant and meddlesome outsiders" are permitted to be "spectators," at least aware of what the "responsible men" are doing, or whether even this concession grants them too much, as statist reactionaries of the Reaganite school hold. Agreements of the NAFTA–GATT variety represent a move towards the reactionary end of the narrow anti-democratic spectrum, not only as concerns Mexico. Whatever one's views concerning a "free trade" agreement, it is surely a matter of considerable importance for the people of the United States. The version of NAFTA enacted is an executive agreement, reached on August 12, 1992, just in time to become a major issue in the U.S. presidential campaign. It was mentioned, but barely, and then mainly because a maverick third party candidate, the billionaire Ross Perot, made it a centerpiece of his campaign. The Trade Act of 1974 requires that the Labor Advisory Committee (LAC), based in the unions, must advise the executive branch on any trade agreement. The LAC was informed that its report was due on September 9. The text of this intricate treaty was provided to it *one day before*, ensuring that it could not even formally convene. Furthermore, the LAC notes, "the Administration refused to permit any outside advice on the development of this document and refused to make a draft available for comment," in defiance of the law. The situation in Canada and Mexico was similar. The facts are not even reported.[122]

In such ways, we approach the long-sought ideal: formal democratic procedures that are devoid of meaning, as citizens not only do not intrude into the public arena but scarcely have an idea of the policies that will shape their lives. And, it is hoped, will not even know that they do not know.

It is important that they should not know. As in GATT, property and investor rights are protected in exquisite detail by the executive version of NAFTA, the LAC and other analysts note, while workers' rights are ignored, along with the rights of future generations (environmental issues). Environmental and health standards can be challenged on grounds of interference with "free trade," that is, profits; the challenge will be judged by committees consisting largely of business representatives. The treaty is likely to facilitate the shift of production to regions where regulations are weak and enforcement lax. NAFTA "will have the effect of prohibiting democratically elected bodies at [all] levels of government from enacting measures deemed inconsistent with the provisions of the agreement," the LAC report continues, including measures on the environment, workers' rights, health and safety, all open to challenge as "unfair restraint of trade." Such developments were already underway in the framework of the U.S.–Canada "free trade" agreement. Included were efforts to require Canada to abandon measures to protect the Pacific salmon, to bring pesticide and emissions regulations in line with laxer U.S. standards, to end subsidies for replanting after logging, and to bar a government auto insurance plan in Ontario that would cost U.S. insurance companies hundreds of millions of dollars in profits. Meanwhile Canada has charged the United States with violating "fair trade" by imposing EPA standards on asbestos use and requiring recycled fiber in newsprint. Under both NAFTA and GATT, there are endless options for undermining popular efforts to protect conditions of life, as we "enlarge market democracy" in the intended way under the Clinton Doctrine.[123]

A foretaste of what may lie ahead was given by the attempt of the social democratic governing party of Ontario (the NDP) in 1990 to set up a universal, tax-based (single payer), no-fault auto insurance plan on the model of the Canadian universal health insurance program. NDP governments had instituted such plans elsewhere in Canada prior to the Free Trade Agreement (FTA) with the United States, but this initiative quickly died. The insurance industry charged that the plan violated the FTA, creating a "government monopoly" that would also have an "adverse effect" on U.S. insurance companies operating in the province and would be "tantamount to an expropriation," thus requiring "effective compensation at fair market value." The companies demanded billions of dollars in compensation. Unwilling to face the costs and consequences of a challenge, the government of Canada's largest and most powerful province withdrew the proposal. The implications are large. Commenting on the case, Elaine Bernard observes that under the FTA's successor, NAFTA, as under other trade agreements, governments may privatize—indeed, are under great pressure to do so from private power sectors—but a popular attempt to regain control of industrial, financial, and other resources is very difficult without extensive costs and uncertain prospects, in secret panels dominated by corporate power. It is in such ways that the trade agreements "lock in" arrangements that secure the rights of absolutist power centers, at the expense of freedom and democracy, even if their short-term economic effects are slight.[124]

In general, the LAC concludes, "U.S. corporations, and the owners and managers of these corporations, stand to reap enormous profits. The United

States as a whole, however, stands to lose and particular groups stand to lose an enormous amount." Its report called for renegotiation, offering a series of constructive proposals. A report of the congressional Office of Technology Assessment (OTA) reached similar conclusions. Noting that real wages have fallen to the level of the mid-1960s, declining sharply in recent years, its report concluded that a "bare" NAFTA of the form planned in secret by the executive branch would ratify "the mismanagement of economic integration" and could "lock the United States into a low-wage, low-productivity future." Radically altered to incorporate "domestic and continental social policy measures and parallel understandings with Mexico on environmental and labor issues," a NAFTA could have beneficial consequences for the country.

But the country is only a secondary concern. The masters are playing a different game. Its rules are revealed by what the business press calls "the Paradox of '92: Weak Economy, Strong Profits." As a geographical entity, "the country" may decline, but policy focuses on questions of greater importance for its designers. Again, the Smithian proviso.[125]

Interestingly, the proliferation of grass roots organizations that has expanded since the 1960s allowed an escape from doctrinal control in this case, one factor in the public opposition to NAFTA in its intended form and pressures that the Clinton administration was not able entirely to resist. Side agreements of dubious significance were tacked on, with considerable fanfare; they fall far short of what Clinton promised during his campaign, the *Wall Street Journal* observed, setting up complex procedures that are likely to be unworkable, particularly on labor issues, which are essentially ignored, as unions have bitterly complained. Canadian opinion has been strongly opposed.[126]

U.S. reports regularly described Mexico as wholeheartedly in favor of the accords, but that is because only elite opinion was considered; article after article reported what "many Mexicans" believe, sampling Mexican and U.S. executives and government officials. Historian Seth Fein notes that there were huge demonstrations against NAFTA, "well articulated, if too-little-noticed in the United States, cries of frustration against government policies—involving repeal of constitutional labor, agrarian and education rights stipulated in the nation's popularly revered 1917 constitution—that appear to many Mexicans as the real meaning of NAFTA and U.S. foreign policy here." Realistically. In the *Los Angeles Times*, Juanita Darling reported the great anxiety of Mexican workers about the erosion of their "hard-won labor rights," likely to "be sacrificed as companies, trying to compete with foreign companies, look for ways to cut costs"—a prime reason why the executive versions of NAFTA and other trade agreements, carefully crafted to protect investor but not labor rights, are so appealing to business leaders. Again, the likely effects elsewhere are apparent.

A November 1, 1993 "Communication of Mexican Bishops on Nafta" condemned the agreement along with the economic policies of which it is a part because of their deleterious social effects. They reiterated the concern of the 1992 conference of Latin American bishops that "the market economy does not become something absolute to which everything is sacrificed, accentuating the inequality and the marginalization of a large portion of the population"—the likely impact of NAFTA and similar investor rights agreements. The agreement was also opposed by many workers (including the largest nongovernmental union) and other groups, which warned of the impact on wages, workers' rights, and the environment, the loss of sovereignty, the increased protection for corporate and investor rights, and the undermining of options for sustainable growth. Homero Aridjis, president of Mexico's leading environmental organization, deplored "the third conquest that Mexico has suffered. The first was by arms, the second was spiritual, the third is economic."[127]

Even the Mexican business community was less than enthusiastic, apart from the most powerful elements. At the Congress of International Chambers of Commerce in Cancún, Mexico, in October 1993, the General Director of the Panamerican Institute of Business Executives said that TNCs are demanding a majority share in Mexican companies, threatening to drive them out of the Mexican market through their financial, technological, and economic power if they refuse, prospects that will be accelerated by NAFTA. The president of a major Mexican industrial group warned of a coming economic debacle as "mid-sized and small businessmen . . . are being destroyed by foreign competition and cornered by weak demand, the lack of liquidity and credit," with GDP stagnating, foreign debt increasing along with the trade deficit, and the huge flow of capital into Mexico directed to speculation rather than productive investment. Commentary in Mexico's leading journal as the congressional vote on NAFTA approached denounced "the history of the United States in our country" as "one of unchecked abuses and looting," predicting the same for the new trade initiative, which would benefit "those 'Mexicans' who are today the masters of almost the entire country (15 percent receive more than half the GDP)," a "de-Mexicanized minority" who alone promote the treaty, "praise it and are desperate for it" hoping to "imitate Houston, . . . their present day measure of civilization." "One thing is certain, from treaty to treaty with the United States, Mexico has lost."[128]

With public skepticism rising in the United States despite the near unanimity of government–corporate–media approval for the "bare" NAFTA restricted to investor rights, the issue could not be rammed through to completion in secret as intended in the fall of 1992. But the problems that concerned the LAC, the OTA, Mexicans and Canadians, and other serious critics who called for rethinking of the entire approach remained almost entirely missing from discussion in the press, as did their concrete proposals. The issue was posed as one of free trade—identified as the highly protectionist "bare" NAFTA—"versus a shrieking Ross Perot and Pat Buchanan, near-nativist labor unions and a split environmental movement" (*Globe* liberal columnist Thomas Oliphant). Since "free trade" is recognized to be Good, naturally the shrieking lunatics and nativists must be Bad, and indeed the "arguments" sampled were carefully selected to reinforce that conclusion. So the "debate" continued, largely avoiding all serious topics, with close to unanimous endorsement of what is obviously Good.[129]

Adopting the approach developed by the Advertising Council half a century earlier, the *New York Times*, in a front-page story, graciously provided the foolish masses with "A Primer: Why Economists Favor Free-Trade Agreement." Critics of the executive version of NAFTA are declared to be "malicious" liars, with what they say entirely ignored apart from the easy and irrelevant targets. The *Times* patiently explains the "fundamental insights" about international trade that have not changed for 250 years, citing the "legendary textbook" in which Paul Samuelson quotes John Stuart Mill as saying that international trade provides "a more efficient employment of the productive forces of the world." Who but a lunatic could oppose that?[130]

To be concrete, who but a lunatic could have opposed the development of a textile industry in New England in the early nineteenth century, when British textile production was so much more efficient that half the New England industrial sector would have gone bankrupt without very high protective tariffs, thus terminating industrial development in the United States?[131] Or the high tariffs that radically undermined economic efficiency to allow the United States to develop steel and other manufacturing capacities? Or the gross distortions of the market that created modern electronics? Who could be so silly as to fail to understand that we would be far better off if the United States were still pursuing its comparative advantage in exporting furs, while India produced textiles and ships and, for all we can guess, might have carried out an industrial revolution? Perhaps joined by Egypt, which would not have had to rely on such radical violation of market principles as elimination of the native population and slavery to enable King Cotton to fuel the industrial revolution, as the British and Americans did. And who could be so ridiculous as to contemplate a NAFTA designed to reflect the interests and concerns that are actually articulated by critical voices in all three of the countries to be linked by treaty arrangements?

No reflections on these matters appear in the primer offered to the backward peons.

Despite the drumbeat, opposition to the "bare" NAFTA remained steady, arousing no little concern about the impending "crisis of democracy." President Clinton denounced the "real roughshod, muscle-bound tactics" of organized labor, "the raw muscle, the sort of naked pressure that the labor forces have put on," even going so far as to resort to "pleading . . . based on friendship" and "threatening . . . based on money and work in the campaign" when they approached their elected representatives, a shocking interference with the democratic process. Front-page stories featured the president's call to Congress "to resist the hardball politics" of the "powerful labor interests." Even months after the defeat, the press was still shuddering from the threat of "all the bullying from labor organizations" while reporting Clinton's efforts to "rescue" NAFTA supporters from "labor's revenge," fortunately weak. "Muscle-flexing by the broad antitrade coalition" extended even beyond the labor movement, the *Wall Street Journal* reported grimly, including "upscale environmentalists, suburban Perot supporters and thousands of local activists nationwide," extremists who believe that NAFTA is designed "for the benefit of multinational corporations" and whose "rhetoric is pure down-with-the-rich populism," laced with "conspiratorial, antielitist arguments." At the far left of the spectrum, Anthony Lewis berated the "backward, unenlightened" labor movement for the "crude threatening tactics" it employed to influence Congress, motivated by "fear of change and fear of foreigners."

In a lead editorial the day before the vote, the *New York Times* denounced local Democrats who opposed NAFTA in fear of "the wrath of organized labor" with its political action committees that "contribute handsomely to their election campaigns." A box recorded labor contributions to NAFTA opponents—"an unsettling pattern," the editors ominously observed.[132]

As some aggrieved representatives and others noted, the *Times* did not run a box listing corporate contributions. Nor did it list *Times* advertisers and owners who support NAFTA, raising questions about their editorial stand, perhaps hinting at an even broader "unsettling pattern." Such reactions are misguided, however: conformity to corporate demands is the natural order, hence need not be reported. Furthermore, after much wailing about the terrifying power of labor, the *Times* did run a front-page story revealing the truth: that corporate lobbying utterly overwhelmed the pathetic efforts of the labor movement. Appearing the day after the vote, the story even spoke the usually forbidden words "class lines," referring to the "nasty" and "divisive battle" over NAFTA, now happily concluded.[133]

The same day the *Times* offered its first review of the expected economic impact in the New York City region, giving further insight into the "class lines" and the hysteria as the outcome seemed in doubt. Leading gainers would be sectors "based in and around finance," "the region's banking, telecommunications and service firms." "A vast assortment of professional service firms, from management consultants and public relations to law and marketing, are poised to seek new businesses in Mexico," while "banks and Wall Street securities firms, which would probably draw more benefit from the pact than any other businesses, say that they are itching to buy Mexican businesses or invest in them." Some manufacturers will also gain, primarily in high technology industry and pharmaceuticals, which will benefit from the increased protection for patents and "intellectual property" generally. Other potential gainers include "the region's two largest manufacturing industries," the capital-intensive chemical industry and publishing—more ominous signals, by the logic of the editors.

There will also be a few losers, the report noted in passing, "predominantly women, blacks and Hispanics," and "semi-skilled production workers" generally; that is, most of the population of New York City, where 40 percent of children already live below the poverty line, suffering health and educational disabilities that "lock them in" to a bitter fate. But these are the inevitable concomitants of progress and a healthy economy, not important enough to disturb the upbeat analysis. "Change can indeed be painful," as Anthony Lewis had admonished the labor movement—for some, at least.[134]

The passionate denunciations of labor had a curious impact on public attitudes. As noted, most people continued to oppose the version of NAFTA that was being considered, but about two-thirds criticized unions as unreasonably opposed to change and "too involved in politics," particularly on the NAFTA issue. The propaganda barrage seems to have left opinions on NAFTA relatively unchanged, while causing people to oppose the major popular forces that represented those opinions and sought to protect them in the political arena.[135]

While economic models offer no clear conclusions about job flow, the conclusions about further polarization are widely shared. "Many economists think Nafta could drag down pay," Steven Pearlstein reported in the *Washington Post*, expecting that "lower Mexican wages could have a gravitational effect on the wages of Americans." A study by one leading specialist, Edward Leamer of UCLA, concludes that the kind of globalization that is enhanced by this NAFTA "would add about $3000 a year to the earnings of professional and technical workers by the end of the decade while reducing the income of everyone else by $750—a loss of about $200 a year for the average American." The only negative consequences of NAFTA would be "a slight fall in the real wages of unskilled U.S. workers"—that is, about 70 percent of the work force—the leading trade specialist Paul Krugman observed. The "gravitational effect" is not a consequence of immutable economic laws, but of the specific social policies designed by the powerful, and built into their version of "trade agreements."[136]

The aftermath of the NAFTA vote was no less instructive. In Mexico, workers were fired from Honeywell and GE plants for attempting to organize independent unions, standard practice. The Ford Motor Company had fired its entire work force in 1987, eliminating the union contract and rehiring workers at far lower salaries, protected from protests by brutal repression. VW followed suit in 1992, firing its 14,000 workers and rehiring only those who renounced independent union leaders, again backed by the neoliberal government. These are central components of the "economic miracle" that is to be "locked in" by NAFTA. As the agreement went into effect on January 1, a rebellion broke out among Mayan Indians, the most oppressed sector of the population. The leaders called NAFTA a "death sentence" for Indians, which will deepen the divide between narrowly concentrated wealth and mass misery, and destroy what remains of the indigenous society, though the problems go far beyond NAFTA. After initial efforts to crush the rebellion by force and to attribute it to outside troublemakers, the Mexican government backed off, probably concerned that the pleas of the rebels might evoke broad sympathy. Within a few weeks, in fact, Mexican polls showed that 75 percent of the population approved of the stated motives of the Chiapas uprising and its Zapatista army.[137]

In the United States, immediately after the NAFTA vote the Senate passed an anticrime bill of unprecedented severity, increasing sixfold the federal subsidies to states to fight crime, "the finest anticrime package in history," Senator Orrin Hatch observed from the far right. The bill calls for 100,000 new police, high-security regional prisons, boot camps for young offenders, extension of the death penalty and harsher sentencing, and other onerous conditions. Law enforcement experts doubted that the legislation would have much effect because it did not deal with the "causes of social disintegration that produce violent criminals." Primary among these are the social and economic policies polarizing American society, carried another step forward by NAFTA. The concepts of "efficiency" and "health of the economy" preferred by wealth and privilege offer little to the growing sectors of the population that are useless for profit-making, driven to poverty and despair. If they cannot be confined to urban slums, they will have to be controlled in some other way.[138]

With the acclaim for his NAFTA triumph still reverberating, President Clinton went off to the Asia–Pacific summit in Seattle, where he expounded his "grand vision for Asia," bringing leaders together "to preach the gospel of open markets and to secure America's foothold in the world's fastest growing economic community." This "may be the biggest rethinking of American policy toward Asia" since World War II, David Sanger observed, reporting Clinton's speech outlining the "new vision" before a "cheering throng . . . inside a giant airplane hangar at the Boeing Company," "a model for companies across America" with its "booming Asian business"—and its plans for "multimillion-dollar job-creating investments outside the United States on a scale that would terrify Nafta's opponents."[139]

The choice was apt: Boeing is also the model for radical state intervention to shield private profit from market discipline. It would not be America's leading exporter, nor probably even exist, were it not for a huge public subsidy funneled through the Pentagon and NASA, institutions in large part designed to serve that function for high tech industry. The "grand vision" of a free-market future, then, is that the taxpayer should provide massive welfare payments to investors and their agents, safely protected from interference by public or work force, pursuing profit and market share as they choose, by "job-creating investments" abroad if that suits their interests.

The "model" for the "gospel of open markets" is largely a product of the state-coordinated World War II economy, when Boeing shared in the "astronomical increase" in profits of the aeronautical industry, profiteering from the war, about 92 percent of its investment being Federal funds, Frank Kofsky points out in his study of the early history of America's greatest free market success. Boeing had made virtually no profits before the war, and its "phenomenal financial history" in the years that followed was based on taxpayer largesse, "enabling the owners of the aircraft companies to reap fantastic profits with minimal investment on their part." Boeing increased its net worth from $9.6 million in 1940 to $49.2 million in 1945, doing its patriotic duty. Recognizing that "the aircraft industry today cannot satisfactorily exist in a pure, competitive, unsubsidized, 'free enterprise' economy," as *Fortune* put the problem in January 1948, the government stepped in to sustain and expand the industry through the military system, manipulating "war scares" for the purpose, Kofsky argues, with substantial documentation. The spillover effect for U.S. industry generally was enormous. The Pentagon, later Kennedy's NASA expansion, provided new mechanisms to maintain the "grand vision" of the free market. The contribution of public funding to commercial successes would be difficult to estimate precisely in later years because of the many indirect effects, but there is no doubt that it remained substantial, and still does.[140]

"China alone now buys one of every six of [Boeing's] planes," Sanger continued. And lofty rhetoric aside, Clinton's one achievement at the summit was to open the door to more exports to China, expected to be "the magic elixir that can cure many of the ills of the American economy" (Apple). Clinton arranged for sales of supercomputers and nuclear power generators; the manufacturers (Cray, GE) are also leading beneficiaries of the state-subsidized private profit system. The items sold can be used for nuclear weapons and missiles, Pentagon officials and other experts observed; a problem, perhaps, because of a ban on such exports imposed in August 1993 "after American intelligence agencies produced conclusive proof" that China was engaged in missile proliferation, while also continuing "nuclear cooperation" with Iran, possibly weapons production. But the problem was easily resolved: Secretary of State Warren Christopher informed China that Washington would "interpret an American law governing the export of high technology to China to allow the export of two of the seven sophisticated American-made satellites banned by sanctions imposed on China in August, senior Administration officials said," adding that "there was no linkage" between the new sales and the issue of proliferation. GM's Hughes Aircraft Unit can therefore join Boeing, GE, and Cray as a model of the free market future.

These decisions illustrate the "very different notion of national security" to which Clinton "is drawn . . . with the Communist threat having receded," reported by Thomas Friedman in an adjacent column: "promoting free trade and stemming missile proliferation."[141]

There was also "no linkage" to human rights, another slight problem, if only because of Clinton's impassioned campaign rhetoric denouncing his predecessor for ignoring China's horrendous record in order to enhance private profit ("jobs"). Just as Clinton was preaching the new gospel, a fire killed eighty-one workers in a factory with doors and windows locked "to keep people inside the factory during working hours," a spokesman said. Appended to Friedman's lead story "Clinton Preaches Open Markets at

Summit" the next day was a brief notice of "deadly accidents involving fire and poisonous gas" that had killed one hundred workers, including these, "in booming Guandong Province," widely hailed as a free market miracle.[142]

It could be argued that concern over human rights in China is unfairly selective, since the pattern is so routine in free market miracles. Take Thailand, one of the most lauded, where some 240 young workers, locked inside by security guards, were burned to death and five hundred more injured in a fire in a Kader toy factory on May 10, 1993, reportedly the world's worst factory fire. Hong Kong–based with wealthy Thai and Tai-wanese investors, the corporation employs mostly young women from rural areas, who prefer these options to the flourishing sex industry, one of the major free market triumphs. The factory was a "death trap" in which three earlier fires had been ignored, AFL–CIO president Lane Kirkland com-mented in a press release to business, foreign, and labor editors. This particular factory supplied more than a dozen major U.S. companies, including Tyco, Fisher Price, J.C. Penney, and Hasbro; more than twenty other U.S. companies, including Toys "R" Us and Wal-Mart, purchase goods made in Kader factories in Thailand, where conditions are similar. These companies "cannot deny knowledge or responsibility for the abysmal work-ing conditions in the factories that produce their goods," Kirkland observed. "Indeed, those conditions are the reason they located production in Thailand in the first place. They can literally work people to death" in the course of what "American business executives call . . . 'staying competitive in the world economy.'" Nor can the press or governments deny knowledge. There appears to have been no report in the major U.S. press.[143]

Or consider Indonesia, with some of the worst working conditions and lowest wages in Asia, about half the level of China and far below Thailand and Malaysia, but exempted from human rights conditions by the Clinton administration, with the support of Senate Democrats. Announcing that Washington would "suspend" its annual review of Indonesian labor prac-tices, Trade Representative Mickey Kantor commended Indonesia for "bring-ing its labor law and practice into closer conformity with international standards"—out of concern that Congress might override Indonesia's friends in the White House. "Reforms hastily pushed through by the Indonesian government in recent months include withdrawing the authority of the military to intervene in strikes, allowing workers to form a company union to negotiate labour contracts, and raising the minimum wage in Jakarta by 27%" to about $2 a day, the London *Guardian* reports. The company unions so magnanimously authorized must, to be sure, join the state-run All-Indonesia Labor Union, and to ensure that there is no misunderstanding, authorities also arrested twenty-one labor activists.

"We have done much to change and improve," Indonesia's Foreign Minister said, "so according to us there is no reason to revoke" the trade privileges. "New Democrats" agreed. Senator Bennett Johnston, explaining his opposition to sanctions, noted that he was impressed by "the steps

Indonesia has taken ... to improve conditions for workers." He also explained his leading role in blocking congressional efforts to bar military training and arms sales to Indonesia because of its massive human rights violations in East Timor and elsewhere. Such sales enable us to have a constructive "dialogue" with the Indonesian military and to maintain our "leverage and influence," he informed the public, quoting the Commander of the U.S. forces in the Pacific, Admiral Larson, who observed that "by studying in our schools," Indonesian army officers "gain an appreciation for our value system, specifically respect for human rights, adherence to democratic principles, and the rule of law." Senator Johnston avoided some more pertinent references; for example, Secretary of Defense Robert McNamara's boast to President Johnson that U.S. military assistance to the Indonesian army had "encouraged it" to undertake the "boiling bloodbath" of 1965–66 "when the opportunity was presented." Particularly valuable, McNamara said, was the program that brought Indonesian military personnel to the United States for training at universities. Congress agreed, noting the "enormous dividends" of U.S. military training of the mass murderers and continued communication with them.

Senator Johnston's intervention in the present case merely supplemented White House maneuvers. Congress had cut funds for military training in protest against the atrocities in East Timor, but, on the anniversary of the U.S.-backed invasion, the State Department announced that "Congress's action did not ban Indonesia's purchase of training with its own funds," so it can proceed despite the ban.[144]

Under the heading "Growing Labor Unrest Roils Foreign Businesses in China," Sheila Tefft reported from Beijing that "industrial tragedies and labor disputes are stirring tensions between Chinese workers and their foreign bosses," referring to the November fire that killed eighty-one women trapped "behind barred windows and blocked doorways" and another a few weeks later that killed sixty workers in a Taiwanese-owned textile mill. More than eleven thousand Chinese workers were killed in industrial accidents in the first eight months of 1993, double the 1992 rate, the Labor Ministry reported. "Chinese officials and analysts say the accidents stem from abysmal working conditions, which, combined with long hours, inadequate pay, and even physical beatings, are stirring unprecedented labor unrest among China's booming foreign joint ventures." "The tensions reveal the great gap between competitive foreign capitalists lured by cheap Chinese labor and workers weaned on socialist job security and the safety net of cradle-to-grave benefits." Workers fail to comprehend that after their rescue by the Free World, they are to be "beaten for producing poor quality goods, fired for dozing on the job during long work hours" and other such misdeeds, and locked into their factories to be burned to death.[145]

While such matters are routinely ignored, China's labor practices do figure prominently in the debate over its human rights record: namely, the use of prison labor. The distinction is clear. The latter is state industry, yielding no profit to private power, indeed interfering with its prerogatives.

Prison exports have greatly exercised Washington and the press, the sole labor rights issue to have achieved this status. "U.S. Inspections of Jail Exports Likely in China," a front-page story by Thomas Friedman was headlined in the *New York Times*. The Chinese "agreed to a demand to allow more visits by American customs inspectors to Chinese prison factories to make sure they are not producing goods for export to the United States," he reported from Beijing. U.S. influence is having further benign effects, "forcing liberalization, factory by factory," including contract, bankruptcy, and other laws that are "critical elements of a market economy," all welcome steps towards a "virtuous circle." Unmentioned are a few other questions about economic virtue, such as the horrifying conditions that contribute to private profit, helping U.S. business executives "stay competitive in the world economy," in the preferred terminology.

Underscoring the basic point, the rules allow the United States to sell prison goods—for export: they are not permitted to enter U.S. markets. California and Oregon export prison-made clothing to Asia, including specialty jeans, shirts, and a line of shorts quaintly called "Prison Blues." The prisoners earn far less than the minimum wage, and work under "slave labor" conditions, prison rights activists allege. But their products do not interfere with the rights that count, so there is no problem here.[146]

Though there was "no linkage" to human rights issues or proliferation, it would be unfair to suggest that the New Democrats have no qualms about China's bad behavior. "Clinton administration officials are considering imposing trade sanctions against China," the *Wall Street Journal* reported a few weeks after the Asia–Pacific summit. The reason is China's "resolve to withstand U.S. pressure" to cut its textile exports. "Washington is angry over what it claims are more than $2 billion of Chinese-made textiles and apparel shipped illegally to the U.S. each year through third countries."

December 31 was the deadline for Chinese submission to U.S. protectionist demands, vigorously imposed immediately after the GATT agreement of mid-December, and also "for China to meet promises made to the U.S. in 1992 to open up its market." After China failed to live up to these paired obligations, "the Clinton administration is set to slash China's textile quotas by as much as a third while also lifting a ban on the sale of two communication satellites to Beijing," the *Journal* reports further, describing this as the "good-cop, bad-cop style": the "bad-cop" will punish China for its brazen defiance of U.S. barriers to free trade, and the "good-cop" will sell them satellites (despite the ban) to show that the United States is "ready to reward China if it makes demonstrable progress"—also, incidentally, rewarding GM's Hughes Aircraft unit, which is looking forward to $1 billion in future business. Careful students of free trade gospel will have no difficulty seeing how all this hangs together.

The punishment was duly administered, Thomas Friedman reported in the lead story the next day. U.S. trade representative Mickey Kantor announced harsher quotas that should cost China over $1 billion, "to insure that

China abides by its commitments to follow fair, nondiscriminatory trade practices" and to show the administration's determination "to stand up for U.S. jobs" as demanded by the textile manufacturers' lobby, noted for its single-minded dedication to "jobs." China soon conceded.[147]

The closing months of 1993 shed much light on the "grand vision" opening before us.

While staunchly upholding the banner of free trade by employing GATT-violating measures to compel China to stop exporting to the United States, the Clinton administration also carried the battle for free trade to the shores of Japan, threatening yet another resort to the GATT-violating methods of retaliation available to a powerful economy with a huge market (Super 301) unless Japan agreed to "managed trade" with qualitative and quantitative criteria on outcome that the United States demands. Other countries did not find this defiance of GATT rules very amusing, immediately after the successful conclusion of the Uruguay Round on December 14. "U.S. finds itself friendless in Gatt," a headline read in the *Financial Times*, reporting the concerns voiced by "more than 20 rich and poor countries, among them European Union States, Mexico, Australia, Canada, South Korea and Poland ... over U.S. demands for numerical targets for Japanese imports and threats of trade retaliation." The European Union ambassador to GATT said these threats highlighted "the doubtful and disquieting nature" of the U.S. aims. Others condemned "Washington's attempt to manage bilateral trade with Japan, to the detriment of other nations and the multilateral system as a whole." A GATT report on U.S. trade policies, published on February 17, also warned that U.S. actions threaten the openness of the multilateral system. Japan once again argued that the problem underlying the trade balance was the U.S. failure to deliver on earlier assurances to reduce the federal budget deficit; the GATT report agreed that improper U.S. fiscal policies were contributing to protectionism, and took "a dim view" of the latest U.S. moves, noting also the rise in its "anti-dumping and anti-subsidy actions, increasingly labelled the protectionists' weapon of choice," often based on dubious industry-based claims. The editors described Clinton's post-GATT maneuvers as "almost perfect examples of the mercantilist fallacy," and urged Japan to reject them, "because the alternative would be dreadful."[148]

So GATT was celebrated in the first few weeks after its approval in mid-December. As for China, in the months that followed it gave President Clinton little help in his task of evading the human rights issues that, by law, stand in the way of renewing China's Most Favored Nation (MFN) trade status in June 1994. Clinton's executive order in this regard was issued in "fear that Congressional Democrats might otherwise have forced an even more stringent approach," Thomas Friedman reported, and because Clinton "did not want to appear to be going back on another campaign promise," having "strongly criticized President Bush for 'coddling' China." The problem reached the front pages as Warren Christopher visited Beijing in

March to express Washington's concerns on human rights, which, the State Department hastened to explain, are quite limited—in fact, limited to finding means to evade congressional pressures. John Shattuck, U.S. assistant secretary of human rights, clarified to the Chinese leaders that Clinton's requirements for improvement are "very narrow," that pledges of progress may be enough: "What the president is looking for is an indication of direction . . . that is generally forward looking." The administration was virtually pleading for some straw, so that it could respond to the needs of its constituency in the corporate sector. The Chinese, however, seemed to enjoy watching their partners twist in the wind.[149]

As Christopher left for China, the administration announced that it would once again relax the sanctions on high technology transfers, this time by allowing the Hughes Aircraft Company to launch a satellite from China. This "gesture of good will toward Beijing" is one "part of the strategy to engage China rather than to isolate it," political correspondent Elaine Sciolino reported from Beijing. Asked about this decision while China is under pressure on issues of missile proliferation and human rights, Christopher responded that it "simply sends a signal of even-handed treatment." The "good will gesture," as usual, is directed towards a leading segment of the publicly subsidized "private enterprise" system, much like those of the Asia–Pacific summit. The Pentagon also sent high officials with Christopher "to discuss ways to upgrade the two countries' military relationship," Sciolino reported, another part of the "strategy."[150]

Christopher did not return empty-handed. At a White House session, Thomas Friedman reports, he "presented a chart . . . showing that on many fronts China was making some progress toward meeting the terms of the President's executive order, but that forward movement had been obscured by the confrontational atmosphere of his visit." On leaving Beijing, Christopher had stated that his discussions with the Chinese leaders were "business-like and productive." "The differences between China and the U.S. are narrowing somewhat," Christopher informed the press, though he "was hard put to point to examples of specific progress on the vexed human rights issue beyond a memorandum of understanding on trade in prison labour products," the *Financial Times* commented. China did agree (once again) to restrict exports from prison factories to the United States.[151]

The Clinton administration "has been quietly signaling Beijing that if it met Washington's minimum human rights demands, the United States would consider ending the annual threat of trade sanctions to change China's behavior," Friedman reports. The reason is that the old human rights policy imposed by congressional (ultimately popular) pressures is "outmoded and should be replaced." This is a "major shift in policy which reflects the increasing importance of trade to the American economy." The human rights policy "is also outmoded, other officials argue, because trade is now such an important instrument for opening up Chinese society, for promoting the rule of law and the freedom of movement there, and for encouraging" private property. The device finally hit upon was "a selective withdrawal of current trade status from China's state-owned enterprises instead of an across-the-board penalty if Beijing failed to make sufficient progress on human rights." That is a welcome idea, Assistant Secretary of State Winston Lord explained to the U.S. Chamber of Commerce, because it "would help preserve private enterprise in China and protect American investments there," Steven Greenhouse reported. It might even "encourage some state enterprises to become private," with further benefits to Western investors.[152]

The hypocrisy is stunning, though hardly more than the "human rights" policy that is now "outmoded," which was always carefully crafted to avoid endangering profits and to somehow "not see" huge atrocities carried out by U.S. clients under Washington's sponsorship. Human rights concerns have been a passion in the case of Nicaragua and Cuba, subjected to crushing embargoes and terror. In such cases, trade is not "an instrument" that induces good behavior. The criminals have to be restored to their service role; if cynical posturing about human rights contributes to that end, well and good. Vastly worse atrocities that the United States was supporting and organizing right next door were never a candidate for sanctions, naturally. The same was true of the Soviet empire. Until it was returned to its traditional Third World role, trade was not "an instrument" to help lift the chains. Similarly China, until it began to open its doors to foreign investment and control, offering wonderful opportunities for profit.

6. The Contours of the New World Order

Structures of governance tend to coalesce around domestic power, in the last few centuries, economic power. The process continues. In the *Financial Times*, BBC economics correspondent James Morgan describes the "de facto world government" that is taking shape: the IMF, World Bank, G–7, GATT, and other structures designed to serve the interests of TNCs, banks, and investment firms in a "new imperial age." At the other end of the bludgeon, the South Commission observes that "the most powerful countries in the North have become a *de facto* board of management for the world economy, protecting their interests and imposing their will on the South," where governments "are then left to face the wrath, even the violence, of their own people, whose standards of living are being depressed for the sake of preserving the present patterns of operation of the world economy"—that is, the present structure of wealth and power.[153] A particularly valuable feature of the rising de facto governing institutions is their immunity from popular influence, even awareness. They operate in secret, creating a world subordinated to the needs of investors, with the public "put in its place," the threat of democracy reduced. This reversal of the expansion of democracy over the past centuries is a matter of no slight importance, alongside the new forms of perversion of classical liberal doctrine in the international economy.

These developments are naturally regarded with much concern throughout the South, and the growing Third World at home should be no less concerned. In his last address to the Group of 77, Chairman Luis Fernando Jaramillo contemplated the "hostile international environment" and the "loss of economic and political standing" of the developing nations "in the so-called New World Order . . . at the dawn of the 21st century," factors that cause real adversity that contrasts sharply with the "euphoria" engendered by the end of the Cold War, economic liberalization programs, and the GATT agreement. The strategy of the rich, he observed, is "clearly directed at strengthening more and more the economic institutions and agencies that operate outside the United Nations system," which, with all its serious flaws, remains "the only multilateral mechanism in which the developing countries can have some say." In contrast, the Bretton Woods institutions (World Bank, IMF, etc.) that are being made "the centre of gravity for the principal economic decisions that affect the developing countries" are marked by "their undemocratic character, their lack of transparency, their dogmatic principles, their lack of pluralism in the debate of ideas and their impotence to influence the policies of the industrialised countries"—whose dominant sectors they serve, in reality. The new World Trade Organization established by the latest GATT agreements will align itself with the World Bank and IMF in "a New Institutional Trinity which would have as its specific function to control and dominate the economic relations that commit the developing world," while the industrialized countries will make "their own deals . . . outside normal channels," in G–7 meetings and elsewhere.

A similar perception was expressed by the conference organized by Jesuits in San Salvador in January 1994, already discussed (p. 53). Its report concludes that "Central America today is experiencing globalization as a more devastating pillage than what its people underwent 500 years ago with the conquest and colonization," a comment that generalizes to much of the "developing world." The new dominant force is not the market but rather "a strong transnational state that dictates economic policy and plans resource allocation. The IMF, World Bank, Interamerican Development Bank, U.S. Agency for International Development, European Community, UN Development Program and their ilk are all state or interstate institutions of a transnational character that have much greater economic influence over our countries than the market."[154]

Moreover, the institutions of the transnational state largely serve other masters, as state power typically does; in this case, the rising transnational corporations in the domains of finance and other services, manufacturing, media and communications—institutions that are totalitarian in internal structure, quite unaccountable, absolutist in character, and immense in power. Within them, a participant takes a place in a fairly rigid hierarchy of domination, implementing orders from above, transmitting them downwards. Those outside may try to rent themselves to the masters and may purchase what they produce, but few other options are open to the great mass of the population.

One may imagine what classical liberals would have thought of this new form of unaccountable, absolutist power, with its extraordinary scale;

Thomas Jefferson, for example, with his scorn for a "single and splendid government of an aristocracy, founded on banking institutions and moneyed incorporations," through which the few would be "riding and ruling over the plundered ploughman and beggared yeomanry"—a nightmare realized beyond anything he might have dreamed. Or even Adam Smith, in a pre-capitalist era, with his skepticism about "joint stock companies" (corporations), particularly if they would become in effect immortal persons—entities with the rights of persons, without time limit—rights that were accorded them through the nineteenth century, largely by judicial decision. We may recall in the same connection Smith's belief that under "perfect liberty" there would be a natural tendency towards equality, a condition for efficient market function.[155]

One consequence of the globalization of the economy is the rise of new governing institutions to serve the interests of transnational economic power. Another is the spread of the two-tiered Third World social model to the industrial world. The United States is taking the lead, another consequence of the unusual power and class consciousness of the business sector, which has been able to resist the social contract that popular struggle has achieved elsewhere. Increasingly, production can be shifted to low-wage areas, and directed to privileged sectors in the global economy. Large parts of the population thus become superfluous for production and perhaps even as a market, unlike the days when Henry Ford realized that he could not sell cars unless his workers had a decent wage in a more national economy.

GATT, NAFTA, and the like are called "free trade" agreements. That is a misdescription. Firstly, the term "trade" hardly applies to a system in which some 40 percent of U.S. "trade" is intrafirm, centrally managed by the same highly visible hands that control planning, production, and investment. Over half of U.S. "exports" to Mexico, for example, do not enter the Mexican market, consisting of transfers from one to another branch of a U.S. corporation, to maximize gains from lower labor costs and environmental standards. Such internal operations (including pricing policies aimed at tax benefits and the like) also introduce various market distortions that amount to non-governmental non-tariff barriers (NTBs), of no small scale, though not considered in the trade agreements and the neoliberal fetishism that accompanies them. Calculations of alleged trade efficiencies overlook numerous other factors. Former World Bank senior economist Herman Daly notes that they do not take into account such matters as the artificial reduction of transport costs by government subsidy of energy through investment tax credits and research, as well as military expenditures that ensure access to petroleum and control its price, a large part of the function of the Pentagon system. Environmental costs of fuel-burning are also "externalized," another factor that would greatly reduce the alleged advantages of trade. In the case of U.S.–Mexico trade, he observes, "U.S. corn subsidized by depleting topsoil, aquifers, oil wells and the federal treasury can be freely imported" to Mexico, so that "it is likely that NAFTA will ruin Mexican peasants when 'inexpensive'" U.S. agribusiness exports, subsidized in such ways, undercut them and drive them to the cities, lowering wages there, and indirectly in the United States as well.[156]

A UN report on transnationals (UNCTAD *World Investment Report 1993*, *WIR*) estimates that TNCs control one-third of the world's private sector productive assets, while their overseas investment is "a bigger force in the world economy than world trade," Tony Jackson reports in the *Financial Times*, with $5.5 trillion in sales outside the country of origin compared with $4 trillion of total world exports (including the huge flow of intrafirm "exports"). These figures, trade analyst Chakravarthi Raghavan adds, "do not reflect the number of firms that carry on transnational activities and, with little or no [foreign direct investment, FDI], exert control over foreign productive assets through a variety of non-equity arrangements—subcontracting, franchising, licensing, etc.—as well as through strategic alliances." The *WIR* reports that FDI is highly concentrated, with about one percent of TNCs owning over half of the FDI stock or total affiliate assets. It notes further that the 1993 GATT agreements increase the rights of TNCs to pursue their activities, which are "advancing the economic integration of the global economy on a scale and at a pace that is unprecedented," Raghavan observes. In contrast, they impose no corresponding obligations on TNCs. Similarly, the World Bank publishes guidelines for treatment of private FDI by host governments, but "they do not deal with the obligations of foreign investors, except in very general ways," the *WIR* points out. Attempts to develop a Code of Conduct for TNCs broke down in July 1992; "This brings to a formal end the most comprehensive effort to create a global and balanced framework for FDI," the *WIR* notes.[157]

As in GATT and NAFTA, investor rights are to be protected and enhanced. People are incidental to "market democracy," in its current perversion.

From 1982 to 1992, the two hundred top corporations enhanced their share of global Gross Domestic Product from 24.2 percent to 26.8 percent, doubling combined revenues to almost $6 trillion, with the leading ten taking almost half the profits of the top two hundred—an underestimate of concentration, since it does not take account of privately owned giants such as Cargill, UPS, and others. Meanwhile the world's top five hundred firms "have shed over 400,000 workers yearly over the past decade notwithstanding the upsurge of their combined revenues," Frederic Clairmont and John Cavanagh observe. The phenomenon is reflected within the United States. In 1992, the first year of a mild recovery, the business pages reported that "America is not doing very well, but its corporations are doing just fine," with corporate profits "hitting new highs as profit margins expand." "Paradox of '92: Weak Economy, Strong Profits," the headline read, capturing the quite non-paradoxical consequences of a bitter and successful class war, extended successfully through the first Clinton year. *Forbes* magazine, in its annual review of corporate welfare, found that corporate profits rose 13.8 percent in

1993 to $204 billion for the top five hundred firms, assets expanded 10.2 percent to $8.9 trillion, and market value rose 6.9 percent to $3.6 trillion; and total employment declined about 1 percent, extending the cutback of jobs, now reaching nearly 10 percent of total employment, 1.8 million jobs, since 1991. Profits grew four times faster than sales among the 785 companies in the *Forbes* list.[158]

The strength of private power and the shadowy character of "trade" is illustrated further in a suggestion of the National Academy of Sciences that "exports" from the United States be calculated in terms of total sales of U.S.-based firms, wherever the factories are located. "Using that method," the *Wall Street Journal* reports, "Commerce Department economists calculated that the U.S. would have posted an overall trade surplus in goods and services of $164 billion in 1991, rather than a $28 billion deficit," another indication of how the nation's "economy" can thrive while its people suffer.[159]

In an important critical analysis of the GATT, World Bank economists Herman Daly and Robert Goodland point out that in prevailing economic theory, "firms are islands of central planning in a sea of market relationships." "As the islands get bigger," they note, "there is really no reason to claim victory for the market principle"—particularly as the islands approach the scale of the sea, which departs radically from free market principles, and always has, because the powerful will not submit to these destructive rules.[160]

Apart from not being remotely "free," the "free trade" agreements are only partially related to "trade," not only because they enhance the power of TNCs and thus reduce "trade" (in any meaningful sense). The agreements go far beyond trade. One leading feature is the demand for liberalization of finance and services, which means allowing international banks to displace domestic rivals so that no country can carry out the kind of national economic planning that enabled the rich countries to develop. And, needless to say, Adam Smith's principle that "free circulation of labor" is one of the cornerstones of free trade, while constantly invoked by the Third World, is dismissed out of hand by the champions of neoliberalism, who also have little use for their hero's conclusion that working people will be devastated by market forces "unless government takes some pains to prevent" this outcome, as must be assured in "every improved and civilized society." Furthermore, the rich powers, and dominant elements within, remain opposed to free trade as they commonly have been, except when they feel they can prevail in competition.

In other ways as well the current trade agreements reflect the hostility of the "rich nations" to the neoliberal doctrines that are imposed on the poor to ensure more efficient plunder. One primary U.S. objective is increased protection for "intellectual property," including software and patents, with patent rights extending to process as well as product. The U.S. International Trade Commission estimates that U.S. companies stand to gain $61 billion a year from the Third World if U.S. protectionist demands are satisfied at GATT (as they are in the NAFTA), a cost to the South that will dwarf the huge debt service flow when extrapolated to other industrial countries. Such doctrines—which the United States and other rich countries never accepted when they were developing, up to recent years—are designed to ensure that U.S.-based corporations control the technology of the future, including biotechnology, which, it is hoped, will allow state-subsidized private enterprise to control health and agriculture, and the means of life generally, locking the poor majority into dependence on high-priced products of Western agribusiness, biotechnology, the pharmaceutical industry, and so on.

It is important to ensure that India not produce drugs at a price that its people can afford. The Indian pharmaceutical industry, one of the most advanced in the developing world, relied on the restriction of patents to processes, not products, opening the way to new and more economical design. These principles, on which today's wealthy powers had insisted as they were developing, are now to be eliminated by the new protectionism, carefully crafted to preserve the power of the TNCs. The same procedures also hamper technological innovation, as does the increased protection of patent rights itself. "The prohibitive costs of international patents will also deter even those individuals/research establishments that may wish to get into the business of patenting," a leading biologist of the Indian Institute of Science observes, noting that his institution lacks the resources to deal with more than two patents a year. By accepting these features of the GATT agreements, the director of a major Indian pharmaceutical company adds, "we have compromised on two crucial areas of the country's well-being— food and health," placing "ourselves at the mercy of multinationals," which will be able to destroy Indian pharmaceutical corporations and raise drug costs to prohibitive levels. These measures are "in sharp contrast to the principles of 'free trade' so sanctimoniously proclaimed by the West," a leading Indian journal comments, and are "a serious impediment to our scientific and technological advance," undermining progress and independence, steps towards "rule by transnational corporations and a mockery of people's sovereignty and parliamentary democracy."[161] More generally, U.S. corporations must control seeds, plant varieties, drugs, and the means of life generally; by comparison, electronics deals with frills. The same measures are being employed to undermine Canada's annoyingly efficient health services—a "rotten apple" right next door—by restricting the production of generic drugs, thus sharply raising costs, and profits to U.S. corporations.[162]

The executive version of NAFTA also includes other protectionist features, some already discussed, and was supported by industry for just such reasons. The only respect in which it is a genuine North American Free Trade Agreement is that it applies to North America: it is not "free," it is not about "trade," and it is surely not based on an "agreement" among the irrelevant public. The "free trade agreements" impose a mixture of liberalization and protection, going far beyond trade, designed to keep wealth and power firmly in the hands of the masters of the "new imperial age."

U.S. attitudes towards "free trade" are illustrated further by its reliance on embargo and sanctions as weapons against its Third World enemies from democratic capitalist Guatemala and Chile to Cuba, Vietnam, Nicaragua, and other transgressors. Of 116 cases of sanctions used since World War II, 80 percent were initiated by the United States alone. These measures, which radically violate free trade doctrine, have often received international condemnation, including decisions of the World Court and GATT council. GATT rules do offer recourse to victims of such measures: they may retaliate in kind. Thus the United States may retaliate if it feels that Nicaragua discriminates against it, and Nicaragua can impose sanctions on the United States and even demand the reparations called for by the World Court, abandoned by Nicaragua under U.S. threat. As recognized by the founders of the Chicago school before it was taken over by ideological extremists, "freedom without power, like power without freedom, has no substance or meaning"—another truism drowned out in the enthusiastic "free market" chorus.[163]

Reviewing Chile's "economic miracle," Latin Americanist Cathy Schneider comments that, quite apart from the standard economic features of market reforms—sharply increasing poverty rates, inequality, and so on—

> the transformation of the economic and political system has had a profound impact on the world view of the typical Chilean. Most Chileans today, whether they own a small, precarious business or subcontract their labor on a temporary basis, work alone. They are dependent on their own initiative and the expansion of the economy. They have little contact with other workers or with neighbors, and only limited time with their family. Their exposure to political or labor organizations is minimal, and with the exception of some important public-service sectors such as health care [which the fascist rulers were unable to demolish in the face of popular resistance], they lack either the resources or the disposition to confront the state. The fragmentation of opposition communities has accomplished what brute military repression could not. It has transformed Chile, both culturally and politically, from a country of active participatory grassroots communities, to a land of disconnected, apolitical individuals. The cumulative impact of this change is such that we are unlikely to see any concerted challenge to the current ideology in the near future.[164]

Exactly as intended, market reforms have undermined the basis for functioning democracy, leaving people isolated, "each for oneself," if not yet "crushed" as in Eastern Europe and other places mired more deeply in Third World misery. One finds much the same in American working-class communities, where people who once struggled courageously and successfully for social justice and human rights are now often hopeless, demoralized, and alone. Among the more deeply impoverished of America's growing Third World, criminal violence and other forms of social pathology have reached shocking proportions as human values erode under the impact of selective marketization.

Where there was a lively social democratic tradition as in New Zealand and Costa Rica, the effect of the reforms is to undermine its basic values, to extend to everyone the reach of the vile maxim: "All for ourselves, and nothing for other people"—or in the version of Clinton humanists, "What is in it for us?" "Economic rationality" and "efficient use of resources," interpreted to serve the needs of the rich and powerful, must become *the* dogma of fundamentalist religious faith, suppressing such evil departures from orthodoxy as the "empathy" and "feeling of obligation" and sympathy that "bind people together" in livable societies. So we discover century after century, and today in country after country: from the rich Western societies to the occasional Third World exception such as Costa Rica and Chile, their heresies now beaten down, to the festering sores of the South and increasingly the East. The triumphalism of the secular priesthood in the West can readily be appreciated.

Neither at home nor abroad does the real world resemble the dreamy fantasies now fashionable about history converging to an ideal of free markets and democracy, "a future for which America is both the gatekeeper and the model."

A more accurate description would bring together the features that have come more vividly into view over the past twenty years. In the New World Order, the world is to be run by the rich and for the rich. The world system is nothing like a classical market; the term "corporate mercantilism" is a closer fit.[165] Governance is increasingly in the hands of huge private institutions and their representatives. The institutions are totalitarian in character: in a corporation, power flows from top down, with the outside public excluded. In the dictatorial system known as "free enterprise," power over investment decisions, production, and commerce is centralized and sacrosanct, exempt from influence and control by workers and community as a matter of principle and law. With the rapid growth of TNCs to a level at which their foreign sales already exceed all of world trade, these systems of private governance gain undreamed-of power. They have naturally used it to create the "de facto world government" described in the business press, with its own institutions, also insulated from public inspection or influence. As for "world trade," well over a third is already "intrafirm," that is, centrally managed commercial interactions, not trade in any serious sense. The great concentrations of private power demand powerful states that protect and enhance their interests in numerous ways. Their ability to transfer production to the most repressed areas and to direct it to the rich sectors of the global system extends the two-tiered Third World model to the rich societies themselves, processes accelerated by the end of the Cold War, with the new weapons it offers for use against "pampered Western workers" who have won some rights in long struggles. The processes are enhanced by the huge expansion of unregulated international capital, and the radical shift of capital from productive investment and trade to speculation. These factors have also contributed to the slowdown of economic growth and have undermined national economic planning. National governments, which in varying ways involve some measure of public participation, are constrained by such external factors to serve the interests of the rich and powerful even more than in the past.

The present era evokes memories of important periods of the past. The enthusiastic resort to classical (now "neoliberal") economic doctrine as a weapon of class war is a striking example. Another is the resort to new technology to create a form of "progress without people," not as a consequence of the nature of technology or the pursuit of efficiency and cost-effectiveness, as David Noble has shown in important work—noting, for example, that the extreme inefficiencies of automation had to be masked through the usual resort to the Pentagon system of public subsidy and market distortion. As in the early industrial revolution, the technology is designed to increase profit and power, ownership and managerial control at the expense of meaningful work, freedom, human life, and welfare; other social arrangements could develop its liberatory potential. Similarly, current debates about welfare–workfare can hardly fail to evoke memories of Malthus and Ricardo, whose new "science" allegedly showed that the poor majority could only be harmed by efforts to help them—a demonstration with the certainty of the "principle of gravitation," Ricardo declared.[166] Someone who lacks independent wealth "has no claim of right to the smallest portion of food, and, in fact, has no business to be where he is," apart from what his offer of labor will bring in the market, Malthus proclaimed in highly influential work. Efforts to mislead the poor into believing that they have further rights are "great evils" and violations of "natural liberty," Ricardo held, as shown by the economic science of which he was the leading figure, and the unchallengeable moral principles on which it was based.

As Karl Polanyi observes in his classic study of these developments, "nothing could be more obvious than that the wage system imperatively demanded the withdrawal of the 'right to live' as proclaimed" in earlier legislation, reflecting pre-capitalist mentality. "To later generations nothing could have been more patent than the mutual incompatibility of institutions like the wage system and the 'right to live.'" The latter therefore had to go, in the interests of all.[167]

By the 1830s, the results of the "science" were becoming established in law, and the "right to live," an outmoded relic of earlier delusion, succumbed to the wage system and the workhouse-prison. "Thus was mankind forced into the paths of a utopian experiment," Polanyi writes. "Never perhaps in all modern history has a more ruthless act of social reform been perpetrated; it crushed multitudes of lives while merely pretending to provide a criterion of genuine destitution in the workhouse test." But "almost immediately the self-protection of society set in," he continues: "factory laws and social legislation, and a political and industrial working class movement sprang into being . . . to stave off the entirely new dangers of the market mechanism. . . ." Widespread despair and suffering led to disorder and upheaval, first riots, later the rise of organized social movements that began to challenge the principles that raised capital accumulation to the supreme human value— and ominously for the master, to challenge their right to rule. "The implicit submission with which men resign their own sentiments and passions to those of their rulers," the foundation of government as Hume had written, was being eroded. The same happened in the United States as the industrial order became established, with its "free labor" that workers saw as "wage slavery." In the face of riots and disorder—and worse, Chartist and socialist organizing—elite opinion shifted, and the "science" took new forms based on the discovery that the "right to live" had to be preserved. Laissez-faire doctrines fell into further disrepute as the new rulers came to understand that they still required state power, as in the past, to enhance their privilege and to protect them from market discipline. We move on to various forms of welfare state capitalism, at least in those societies that had won their place in the sun by terror, oppression, and robbery.

This history has, in fact, been relived over and over. There is little that is new in neoliberal programs, trickle-down theories, and the rest of the doctrinal baggage that serves the interests of privilege and power. The ideology of oppression may differ in form when applied to Third World service areas and domestic populations, but similarities are apparent, and current enthusiasms are hardly more than a recapitulation, often sordid, of earlier devices to justify the privilege of those who hold the reins. As in the early nineteenth century, we are now once more to understand that it is a violation of natural liberty and even science to deceive people into thinking that they have some rights beyond what they can gain by selling their labor power. Any effort to depart from such right thinking leads directly to the Gulag, leading thinkers soberly explain. The present era is highly reminiscent of the moments of enthusiasm before the unseemly noises of the rabble had become too threatening to overlook, a fact that carries lessons that are not too obscure.

Amidst an atmosphere of general dismay and fear, there are also signs of resistance, taking varied forms. Compare two cases: the 1992 riots in south-central Los Angeles, and the Mayan uprising in Chiapas, Mexico, on January 1, 1994. In both cases, the uprisings reflected the increasing marginalization of people who do not contribute to profit-making under prevailing institutional arrangements, and therefore lack human rights or value. People who live in the slums of Los Angeles once had jobs, in part in the state sector that plays a critical role in the "free market capitalist" society, in part in factories that have been shifted to places where labor can be more savagely exploited and destruction of the environment can proceed unhampered. By absolute measures, they are considerably wealthier than the Mayans of Chiapas, who recognize that what remains of their lives faces destruction as the investor rights agreements (NAFTA, GATT) extend their sway. But the Los Angeles riots proceeded quite differently from the Chiapas rebellion. The contrast reflects the difference between communities that have become demoralized and devastated by external forces and others that have retained their inner cohesion and vitality. The specific problems that lie ahead are quite different; the crying need for solidarity and constructive participation could hardly be more clear, in the face of the "global experiment" now underway.

The nature of the experiment is graphically illustrated by a report of the International Labor Organization, which estimates that about 30 percent of the world's labor force was unemployed in January 1994, unable to earn enough to sustain a minimum standard of living. This "long-term persistent unemployment" is a crisis of the scale of the Great Depression, the ILO concludes. Vast unemployment persists alongside of huge demands for labor. Wherever one looks, there is work to be done of great social and human value, and there are plenty of people eager to do that work. But the economic system cannot bring together needed work and the idle hands of suffering people. Its concept of "economic health" is geared to the demands of profit, not the needs of people. In brief, the economic system is a catastrophic failure. Of course, it is hailed as a grand success, as indeed it is for a narrow sector of privileged people, including those who declare its virtues and triumphs.[168]

How far can this go? Will it really be possible to construct an international society on something like the Third World model, with islands of great privilege in a sea of misery—fairly large islands, in the richer countries—and with controls of a totalitarian nature within democratic forms that increasingly become a facade? Or will popular resistance, which must itself become internationalized to succeed, be able to dismantle these evolving structures of violence and domination, and carry forth the centuries-old process of expansion of freedom, justice, and democracy that is now being aborted, even reversed? These are the large questions for the future.

3

History's
"Greatest Prize"

Reviewing briefly, the New World Order constructed from the ruins of World War II kept closely to the Churchillian guidelines, amended by the crucial footnotes. The world is to be ruled by the "rich nations," which are in turn to be ruled by the rich men within them, in accord with the maxim of the Founding Fathers of American democracy that "the people who own the country ought to govern it" (John Jay). As Adam Smith observed, they pursue "the vile maxim of the masters," using state power to ensure that the interests of the "principal architects" of policy will be "most peculiarly attended to," whatever the effect on others. Their minions meanwhile cloak social reality in the guise of benevolence and harmony, laboring to keep the "ignorant and meddlesome outsiders" in their place: far removed from the political arena though granted a periodic choice between representatives of the business party, with little danger of much deviation in any event, given the constraints imposed on policy by concentrated private power, increasingly international in scale, with financial power (and its low growth, low wage impact) gaining unprecedented importance.

As the process takes its natural course, it tends towards globalization of the economy with its consequences: globalization of the Third World model of two-tiered societies, now reaching to the core industrial economies themselves; and a "de facto world government" that represents the interests of the TNCs and financial institutions that are to manage the international economy. The global system meanwhile becomes a form of "corporate mercantilism," with centrally managed commercial interactions and planning within a framework of liberal internationalism, crafted for the needs of power and profit, subsidized and supported by state authority. The "hungry nations" and the Third World at home are to observe the doctrines of neoliberalism, which the powerful are free to discard at will. The end of the Cold War, restoring large parts of the domains of Soviet tyranny to their traditional Third World status, offers new opportunities for profit and

Israel and bordering countries

(*Source*: Foundation for Middle East Studies)

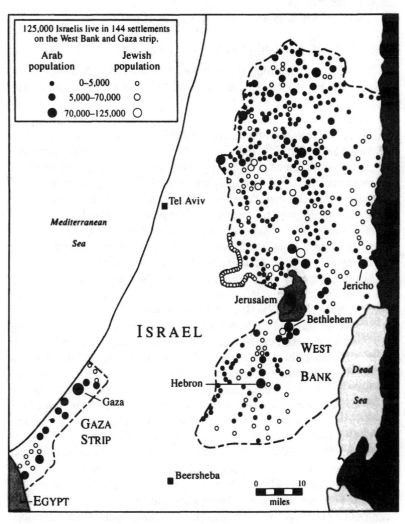

Israeli settlements just before the May 4, 1994, peace agreement
(*Source*: Associated Press, *Boston Globe* staff map)

improved weapons for the bitter one-sided class war that is fought unceasingly by the masters.

These remain, in essence, leading features of world order.

1. Updating the Monroe Doctrine

In discussing the outlines of Grand Area planning for the postwar era, I put to the side the role of the Middle East. Let's now turn to that.[1]

Here, the major interest was (and remains) the incomparable energy reserves of the region, primarily in the Arabian peninsula. The central policy goal was to establish U.S. control over what the State Department described as "a stupendous source of strategic power, and one of the greatest material prizes in world history," "probably the richest economic prize in the world in the field of foreign investment"—the most "strategically important area in the world," as Eisenhower later described the peninsula. As in Latin America, it was necessary to displace the traditional imperial powers: France was unceremoniously expelled, though Britain was accorded a considerable role in this region, gradually declining as power relations dictated.

U.S. corporations gained the leading role in Middle East oil production, while dominating the Western hemisphere. Within "our little region over here," as Secretary of War Henry Stimson termed the Western hemisphere, rival powers were expelled. Venezuela is the most important case, remaining the world's leading oil exporter until 1970, when it was displaced by Saudi Arabia and Iran, also U.S. clients. After World War I, the United States supported its violent and corrupt dictator Juan Vicente Gómez, who opened the country to American corporations while barring British concessions under U.S. pressure. In the New World Order after World War II, the U.S. oil industry took control over the country's economy. Relations were particularly close, and profitable for U.S. corporations, during the 1949–58 dictatorship of Pérez Jiménez, who surpassed Vicente Gómez in brutality and rapacity; he was awarded the Legion of Merit by President Eisenhower, in recognition that "his wholesome policy in economic and financial matters has facilitated the expansion of foreign investment, his Administration thus contributing to the greater well-being of the country and the rapid development of its immense natural resources"—and, incidentally, to huge profits for U.S. corporations, including by then steel companies and others. About half of Standard Oil of New Jersey's profits came from its Venezuelan subsidiary, to cite just one example. The Kennedy administration followed its standard Latin American policy of support for the military to suppress labor and other popular forces. The policies and results were, not surprisingly, rather as in Brazil, the other jewel in the Latin American crown.[2]

The basic policy guidelines were outlined in a State Department memorandum of April 1944 entitled "Petroleum Policy of the United States." It called for "the preservation of the absolute position presently obtaining [in the Western hemisphere], and therefore vigilant protection of existing concessions in United States hands coupled with insistence upon the Open Door principle of equal opportunity for United States companies in new areas." In brief, "really existing free market doctrine": what we have, we keep, closing the door to others; what we do not yet have, we take, under the principle of the Open Door. The policies were implemented, much to the dismay of the major competitor: "Declining power led Britain to accept an arrangement that reserved a privileged position for the U.S. domestic oil industry," David Painter writes, "while exposing all of Britain's oil production, which was in other countries, to the competition of the powerful U.S. international oil companies."

Washington was thus able to extend to the Middle East the "closed door" policy that had been successfully imposed in the Western Hemisphere, outlined most succinctly by the Woodrow Wilson administration in 1918: "Department considers it most important that only approved Americans should possess oil concessions in the neighborhood of the Panama Canal," Secretary of State Lansing informed Central American officials when he learned of British efforts to obtain concessions, which must be barred. This "aggressive American policy met with extraordinary success," Jeffry Frieden notes, rapidly increasing the share of U.S. oil companies "entirely at the expense of the Anglo–Dutch companies." In the Middle East a generation later, he continues, "the principled American stand on the open door in petroleum lasted precisely as long as it took for American oil men to be let in; once this aim was accomplished, the United States was perfectly content to see the door slam shut."[3]

That U.S. planners should extend the Monroe Doctrine to the Middle East as soon as this became feasible is entirely understandable. Justifications were readily at hand, familiar back to colonial days. The U.S. minister to Saudi Arabia, Alexander Kirk, observed that it only made sense for the United States to displace Britain: "Needless to say a stable world order can be achieved only under the American system," which would "help backward countries to help themselves in order that they may lay the foundation for real self dependence," the kind that the United States had already brought with such success to the Caribbean–Central America region and the Philippines— the latter an example constantly invoked with pride, and little regard for the realities.

A State Department memorandum approved by President Roosevelt in 1944 concluded that U.S. aid to the Saudi monarchy would "demonstrate the difference between the American and British approaches to the problems of backward nations, and emphasize the greater capacity of America for providing continuous and constructive material assistance." To ensure that British conniving would not "lead either Ibn Saud or his successors to diddle [American companies] out of the concession and the British into it," William Bullitt, a leading foreign policy adviser, recommended that the United States provide Lend Lease assistance. The president recognized the Saudi Arabian monarchy as one of the "democratic allies" fighting the Nazis, making it eligible for Lend Lease aid, including scarce construction materials; "the defense of Saudi Arabia is vital to the defense of the United States," Roosevelt declared—the "aggressor" being Great Britain. The Saudi royal family merited U.S. support because Ibn Saud was a "man of vision and executive ability ready to lead his people in keeping with the progress of the world" (Roosevelt's special representative to the Middle East, Patrick Hurley). Ibn Saud was depicted as a progressive and far-sighted monarch who, under U.S. tutelage, would ensure that Saudi Arabian riches were properly deployed in the U.S.-dominated New World Order.[4]

The United States did not need Middle East oil for itself. Rather, the goal was to ensure that the enormous profits from the energy system flow primarily to the United States, its British client, and their energy corporations, not to the people of the region, and that oil prices stay within the range most beneficial to the corporate economy, neither too high nor too low. A related goal was to dominate the world system. The case of Japan is instructive. Though Japanese prospects were generally disparaged until the 1960s, some far-sighted analysts recognized that problems of insubordination might arise even here. George Kennan proposed in 1949 that the United States keep control over Japanese oil imports, so as to hold "veto power" over Japan's military and industrial policies. Japan was helped to industrialize, but the United States maintained control over its energy supplies and oil-refining facilities, though after the "shock" of the early 1970s, Japan's programs of diversification of energy resources and improving efficiency have reduced the power of the "veto" considerably.

2. Containing the Internal Enemy

As elsewhere, the primary concern in the Middle East was independent nationalism, in the region itself as well as southern Europe. The alleged Soviet threat was brandished, but largely as a pretext (as now conceded; see p. 70), though the threat was real insofar as the USSR interfered with U.S. designs by posing a deterrent and, for its own cynical reasons, supporting targets of U.S. attack. The first major postwar counterinsurgency campaign, in Greece, was motivated in part by the danger of the "rotten apple" effect of a victory by the peasant- and worker-based forces that had fought the Nazis under Communist leadership. The "rot" might "infect" the Middle East, Dean Acheson grimly warned Congress while seeking to garner support for the Truman Doctrine. "Although Acheson had reference to the oil of the Middle East deleted from the president's address" announcing the Truman Doctrine, David Painter observes, "concern over U.S. access to the region's chief resource played an important role in the 'revolution' in U.S. foreign policy."[5] A CIA study warned of "the possible loss of the petroleum resources of the Middle East" if the revolt against the right-wing government imposed by British military force were not crushed. Though Stalin was in fact adhering to the "spheres of influence" agreement he had reached with Churchill, a Soviet threat was concocted in the routine manner, and Greece was "pacified" by a bloody campaign of terror and torture that took 160,000 lives, restored the old order including Nazi collaborators, and opened the country to U.S. investment and control, with consequences that persist until today.

Italy, a prime target of U.S. subversion from the 1940s, aroused similar concerns. The threat of a Communist victory in the 1948 elections was taken very seriously by U.S. planners. The first Memorandum of the newly formed National Security Council in 1947 secretly called for support for paramilitary operations in Italy along with national mobilization in the United States "in the event the Communists obtain domination of the Italian government by legal means"; democratic processes are not acceptable, and must be overturned by violence or other means, unless the proper outcome is assured. George Kennan urged still stronger measures, suggesting that the Communist Party be outlawed to forestall its electoral victory, though this would probably lead to civil war and U.S. military intervention, he recognized. He was overruled, on the assumption that other means of coercion would suffice, as proved to be the case. The United States was able to subvert the election by methods similar to those employed in Nicaragua in 1990, including a very credible threat of starvation if people voted the wrong way. Here too, the Middle East was a major concern. "U.S. strategic interests" required control over "the line of communications to the Near East outlets of the Saudi-Arabian oil fields" through the Mediterranean, a 1945 interagency review observed. These interests would be threatened if Italy were to fall into "the hands of any great power"—in translation: if it were to escape from the hands of the proper great power.

The threat of independent nationalism led to the CIA coup restoring the shah in Iran in 1953, overthrowing the conservative parliamentary Mossadegh government. Nasser was viewed in similar terms, later Khomeini, leading the United States to provide Saddam Hussein with decisive support in the Iran–Iraq War. The tyrant shifted overnight from favored friend to reincarnation of Genghis Khan when he broke the rules in August 1990 by invading Kuwait, a U.S.–British client. The primary fear throughout has been that nationalist forces not under U.S. influence and control might come to have substantial influence over the oil-producing regions. The family dictatorships, in contrast, are considered appropriate partners, managing their resources in conformity to basic U.S. interests, and helping to fund U.S. projects of terror and subversion throughout the Third World.

Underlying attitudes sometimes reach the general public. Thus after the restoration of the shah and the takeover by U.S. companies of 40 percent of the British oil concession, the *New York Times* commented editorially that this was "good news indeed," however costly "to all concerned"—Iranians in the shah's torture chambers, for example. "The affair may yet be proved worth-while if lessons are learned from it," the editors observed. The primary lesson is stark and simple: "Underdeveloped countries with rich resources now have an object lesson in the heavy cost that must be paid by one of their number which goes berserk with fanatical nationalism. It is perhaps too much to hope that Iran's experience will prevent the rise of Mossadeghs in other countries, but that experience may at least strengthen the hands of more reasonable and more far-seeing leaders," who have a better grasp of our priorities.

As is the norm, media coverage kept to government policy guidelines with precision. Mossadegh became a devil when the United States determined to overthrow him. As the U.S.-backed terror regime took command after the coup, the *New York Times* praised it for its "highly successful campaign against subversive elements" and its "long record of success in defeating subversion without suppressing democracy," noting with particular pleasure the suppression of the "pro-Soviet Tudeh party," formerly "a real menace" but "considered now to have been completely liquidated," and the "extreme nationalists" who had been almost as subversive as the Communists—all liquidated without suppressing "democracy." The shah remained a hero until the Peacock Throne began to totter in 1978. Human rights concerns suddenly became an issue when the United States lost control in 1979, having been "missed" before (as was the CIA coup, long known, but suppressed). Furthermore, the shameful media record, exposed in readily available work, teaches no "lessons" and was quickly forgotten, if ever noticed. Lessons are drawn for policy, however: we should think more carefully about the likely staying power of tyrants we impose.[6]

The dominant lines of thinking are often articulated with particular clarity at moments of crisis. When popular demonstrations on July 21, 1953, undermined British efforts to subvert the parliamentary Mossadegh regime, British chargé George Middleton reported in panic that the court had been "fatally weakened," describing the day as "a turning point in Iranian history. Previously the small ruling class determined the prime minister, with [the shah] as umpire. Now the consent of the mob is the decisive factor."

Another instructive example is the U.S.–U.K. reaction to the military coup by nationalist officers in Iraq in July 1958, the first serious break in Anglo–American control of the oil-producing regions (Iran having been returned to the fold). Concerns were high, sufficiently so that Washington apparently considered the use of its nuclear arsenal. President Eisenhower was referring to nuclear weapons, William Quandt concludes, when he ordered the chairman of the Joint Chiefs of Staff to "be prepared to employ, subject to [Eisenhower's] approval, *whatever* means might become necessary to prevent any unfriendly forces from moving into Kuwait" (Eisenhower's emphasis); the issue was "discussed several times during the crisis," Quandt adds. He concludes further that the United States intended "to help look after British oil interests, especially in Kuwait" when it landed Marines in Lebanon after the Iraqi coup. The major irritant at the time was Egypt's Gamal Abdel Nasser and his independent nationalism.[7]

Immediately after the Iraqi coup, British foreign secretary Selwyn Lloyd consulted in Washington with Secretary of State John Foster Dulles. In a secret telegram to the prime minister, Lloyd discussed several policy options. One possibility would be "immediate British occupation" of the semi-dependency of Kuwait; "The advantage of this action," he noted, "would be that we would get our hands firmly on the Kuwait oil." Nevertheless, he recommended against military occupation because it might arouse nationalist feelings in Kuwait and "the effect upon international opinion and the rest of the Arab world would not be good." It would be more sensible, he proposed, to offer Kuwait a form of nominal independence, turning the protectorate into "a kind of Kuwaiti Switzerland where the British do not exercise physical control," but without relinquishing actual control—rather like what Saddam Hussein planned after invading Kuwait, top U.S. government officials feared (see pp. 12–14).

Crucially, Britain must recognize "the need, if things go wrong, ruthlessly to intervene, whoever it is has caused the trouble." Lloyd stressed "the complete United States solidarity with us over the Gulf," including the need to "take firm action to maintain our position in Kuwait" and the "similar resolution" of the United States "in relations to the Aramco oilfields" in Saudi Arabia. The Americans, he continued, "agree that at all costs these oilfields [in Kuwait, Saudi Arabia, Bahrain, and Qatar] must be kept in Western hands"—meaning, in U.S.–U.K. hands, and outside the hands of the only serious challengers, namely indigenous elements. Six months before the Iraqi coup, Lloyd had noted that "minor changes in the direction of greater independence are inevitable" for Kuwait, while summarizing "the major British and indeed Western interests in the Persian Gulf":

> (a) to ensure free access for Britain and other Western countries to oil produced in States bordering the Gulf;
> (b) to ensure the continued availability of that oil on favourable terms and for sterling; and to maintain suitable arrangements for the investment of the surplus revenues of Kuwait;
> (c) to bar the spread of Communism and pseudo-Communism in the area and subsequently beyond; and, as a pre-condition of this, to defend the area against the brand of Arab nationalism under cover of which the Soviet Government at present prefers to advance.

Declassified U.S. documents outline U.S.–U.K. goals in similar terms: "the U.K. asserts that its financial stability would be seriously threatened if the petroleum from Kuwait and the Persian Gulf area were not available to the U.K. on reasonable terms, if the U.K. were deprived of the large investments made by that area in the U.K. and if sterling were deprived of the support provided by Persian Gulf oil." These British needs, and the fact that "an assured source of oil is essential to the continued economic viability of Western Europe," provide an argument for the United States "to support, or if necessary assist, the British in using force to retain control of Kuwait and the Persian Gulf." The disadvantage is that "U.S. relations with neutral countries elsewhere would be adversely affected." In November 1958, the National Security Council recommended that the United States "be prepared to use force, but only as a last resort, either alone or in support of the United Kingdom," to insure access to Arab oil.[8]

The general goals were stated succinctly by the British Foreign Office in 1949: Kuwait must remain under British supervision even if granted nominal independence, because "if the way . . . were opened to Egyptian and Iraqi penetration there would be a real danger that Kuwait would be rapidly infected with all the ultra-nationalist maladies from which those two countries are at present suffering." The perspective and even the terminology is standard in U.S. internal documents along with the recognition that "it was long the British policy to keep the people flanking the sea route to India in a state of primitive economy," and they "remain for the most part ignorant, poverty-stricken and diseased," as the State Department put it—"minor irritants in the exercise of foreign policy," historian Mark Curtis comments. What is important is to protect them from the malady of independence and control over their own resources.[9]

By the early 1970s, the United States was coming to rely on Gulf oil and riches for its own increasingly troubled economy. Capital flow from Saudi Arabia, Kuwait, and the other Gulf principalities to the United States and Britain has provided significant support for their corporations, banks, and the national economy generally. These are among the reasons why the United States and Britain have often not been averse to increases in oil price. The 1973–74 price rise—preceded by comparable increase in price of U.S. coal, uranium, and agricultural exports—yielded temporary advantages for the U.S. and British economies, providing windfall profits for the energy corporations, primarily U.S. and British, and inducing them to bring into production high-cost oil (Alaska, North Sea) that had been withheld from the market. For the United States, rising energy costs were substantially offset by military and other exports to the Middle East oil producers and huge construction projects for them. Their profits also flowed to Treasury securities and investment as local managers carried out their primary responsibility: to support the economies of the United States and Britain.

The stable policy guidelines expressed in the secret diplomatic record underlie the decision of the United States and Britain "ruthlessly to intervene" in response to Saddam's invasion of Kuwait in August 1990, blocking the threat of a negotiated Iraqi withdrawal that would "defuse the crisis," while other powers were only reluctantly dragged into this unilateral military operation. The record also lays out clearly the basic interests and the perceived threat to them, a special case of much more general policy perspectives, as we have seen. It is understandable that it was so rigorously suppressed in 1990–91, when it was so clearly pertinent and informative.

As in Latin America, "economic nationalism" was unacceptable in the Middle East, which must keep to the principle of comparative advantage, sacred because it guarantees subordination, under prevailing conditions. Governments of the region requested assistance to develop manufacturing industry, but the United States insisted on "sound economic principles," which required that they specialize in raw materials production while the United States and Europe monopolize industry and technology.

The case of Egypt is again instructive. With the British yoke being removed in the postwar period, Egypt once again sought to industrialize. The U.S. reaction was not unlike Palmerston's a century earlier.[10] The director of the American Economic Mission in the Middle East, James Landis, commented in a December 1944 speech that the United States would not aid Egypt if it followed a path of "mercantilism, uneconomic and political subsidies, narrow nationalism, group preferences"—that is, if Egypt were to adopt any of the measures that have led to development elsewhere, including the United States. U.S. advisers recommended that economic aid be contingent on Egyptian assurances that "such assistance would not result in strengthening Egyptian nationalism, with all its resultant restrictions and controls." Egyptian industry should confine itself to "a series of simple operations within the capacity of the Egyptian worker," another report advised. The country should remain a primary producer if it hoped to receive financial or technical assistance, British and American advisers recommended.

These instructions were harmful enough, but still harsher strictures made them impossible to follow. Under pressure from domestic cotton interests, the United States moved to protect its cotton production from Egyptian competition. This "arbitrary quota" was the chief cause of Egypt's dollar shortage, the National Bank of Egypt alleged, criticizing the United States for "not fully practising the principles of commercial non-discrimination which she is preaching to others." As always, the principles we honor are fetters for the weak that do not bind the powerful. The basic point—captured in the State Department "Petroleum Policy of the United States" and Clinton's National Export Strategy, among many other policy initiatives—was expressed in simplified form by U.S. oil magnate Howard Pew, a firm advocate of free trade, who explained in 1949 that American tariffs should be seen as a "defense mechanism, rather than as a barrier to free trade."

Lacking dollars and unable to obtain what it needed from Britain in its postwar straits, Egypt entered into a barter arrangement with the USSR in 1948, earning quick condemnation from the State Department, which patiently explained that such measures "divert trade into uneconomic channels and reduce the volume and benefits of world trade," the lessons now taught to Americans by the *New York Times* "primer" discussed earlier. "Egyptian requests for capital aid from the United States fell on deaf ears," Godfried notes, in the light of Egypt's lack of understanding of sound economic principles. Private investment followed the same guidelines. Lebanese diplomat George Hakim complained that private foreign investment was "not directed towards the general development of the Middle Eastern countries, but towards the export of crude oil to the European market." The region aspired to economic development; the West, to its subordination on grounds of the conveniently flexible truths of economic theory (rationality).[11]

3. The Structure of Power

Now largely in U.S. hands, the Middle East region was to be organized along the lines established by late British imperialism, which recognized by World War I that direct colonial rule was no longer feasible. Local management, therefore, would be delegated to an "Arab Facade" of weak and pliable rulers, with "absorption" of the colonies "veiled by constitutional fictions as a protectorate, a sphere of influence, a buffer State, and so on," a device more cost-effective than direct rule (Lord Curzon and the Eastern Committee, 1917–18). But we must never run the risk of "losing control," John Foster Dulles warned. The Facade would consist of family dictatorships that do what they are told, and ensure the flow of profits to the United States, its British client, and their energy corporations. They are to be protected by regional enforcers, preferably non-Arab (Turkey, Israel, Iran under the shah, Pakistan). British and U.S. muscle stand in reserve, with military bases from the Azores through North Africa to the Indian Ocean and the Pacific. The system has operated with reasonable efficiency over a considerable period, and has new prospects today.[12]

Successes have been dramatic. Cheap oil fueled the "golden age" of postwar development. "Profits beyond the dreams of avarice" enriched Western corporations,[13] also helping to keep the ailing British economy afloat, later the U.S. economy as well. The postwar settlement perpetuated the separation of the large population concentrations of the region from the oil wealth, retained in the hands of the Facade with sparse populations to share it. Apart from its unfairness, this "outrageously skewed ownership of property in the world's most heavily armed region, with a long history of volatility and violence, is an ongoing recipe for destabilization and violent upheavals," Dilip Hiro warns. "An increasing number of Arab intellectuals and religious leaders," he writes, are coming to share the viewpoint articulated by Saddam Hussein on August 10, 1990, however they may despise the author of the sentiment. In Saddam's words:

> Through its partitioning of the [Arab] lands, western imperialism founded weak mini-states and installed the families who rendered it services that facilitated its [exploitative] mission. Thus it prevented the majority of the sons of the people and the [Arab] nation from benefiting from their own wealth. As a result of the new wealth passing into the hands of the minority of the [Arab] nation to be exploited for the benefit of the foreigner and the few new rulers, financial and social corruption spread in these mini-states . . . [and from there to] many quarters of the majority of the Arab countries.

The United States opposes democracy in the region, Hiro writes, because "it is much simpler to manipulate a few ruling families—to secure fat orders for arms and ensure that oil price remains low—than a wide variety of personalities and policies bound to be thrown up by a democratic system," with elected governments that might reflect popular calls for "self-reliance and Islamic fellowship." Hence the persistence of Washington's policy of "supporting dictatorships to maintain stability" (Ahmad Chalabi), and the admitted preference for the "iron fist."[14]

Hiro's analysis is persuasive. The roots of policy lie deep in firmly established institutional structures of power, with effects that have long been evident worldwide. The basic policy thrust is occasionally recognized with some regret by world leaders. Reflecting on British policy in the Middle East, Prime Minister Harold Macmillan found it "rather sad that circumstances compel us to support reactionary and really rather outmoded regimes because we know that the new forces, even if they begin with moderate opinions, always seem to drift into violent revolutionary and strongly anti-Western positions."[15] We need only add the usual gloss: a "violent revolutionary position" may be nothing more than one that seeks an independent pau, becoming "strongly anti-Western" when that path is barred by Western power, a tragedy that has been enacted over and over again.

Rights accrue to regional actors by virtue of their position within the three-tiered strategic conception. At the local level, the Facade of managers have rights, as long as they do their job; otherwise they will be crushed. For internal "stability," the "iron fist" has often been preferred, exactly as the State Department currently explains through the medium of the *Times* chief diplomatic correspondent. The regional guardians also have rights, as does the British assistant. And the United States naturally has rights without qualifications. As for Kurds, Palestinians, slum-dwellers in Cairo, and others who contribute nothing to the basic structure of power—they have no rights, by the most elementary principles of statecraft. Perhaps they can occasionally be used in one or another power play, but that is where their rights end. Much of the modern history of the Kurds reflects these realities, as when they were supported in their revolt against Iraq in the early 1970s in the interests of Washington's Iranian client, then left to be slaughtered when that episode was successfully terminated, leading Henry Kissinger to comment acidly, in response to criticism, that foreign policy is not to be confused with missionary work. Contemporary events, reviewed earlier, add another ugly chapter to the story.

Today, it is not hard to understand Eisenhower's lament that "the problem is that we have a campaign of hatred against us, not by the governments but by the people" (p. 79). One might ask, however, why that should have already been true in July 1958, when the words were spoken, not long after the United States had expelled Britain, France, and Israel from the Egyptian territory they had conquered in their 1956 invasion, and well before the "special relationship" with Israel was in place. It is easy to explain the hatred in Iran five years after the restoration of the shah. Washington's rejection of attempts to undertake independent development was also unlikely to have elicited warm feelings. A decade of CIA operations in Syria may shed further light on the matter.

Syria had traditionally been pro-American, but clandestine U.S. intervention "helped reverse a century of friendship," Douglas Little observes in a review of these operations. In 1948, the CIA approached Chief of Staff Husni Zaim to discuss the "possibility [of an] army supported dictatorship," a result achieved when Zaim overthrew the government a few months later. Zaim approved the Aramco oil pipeline (TAPLINE) concession in accord with U.S. wishes, and called for peace talks with Israel, offering to resettle 250,000 Palestinian refugees, a diplomatic opening that Israel chose not to pursue. Zaim was overthrown a few months later. In 1951, Col. Adib Shishakli overthrew the government once again and set up a military dictatorship, with clandestine U.S. support. Matters drifted out of control again, and in March 1956, Eisenhower approved Project OMEGA, which aimed to overthrow the increasingly pro-Nasser regime in Syria as part of a more general plan to undermine Nasser. Operation Straggle, organized jointly with British intelligence to overthrow the government of Syria, was timed (apparently, at British initiative) for the day of the invasion of Egypt, which France and Britain had kept secret from Washington. Possibly Britain's goal was to keep the United States preoccupied elsewhere. In any event, Syrian counterintelligence had uncovered the plot, and it quickly unraveled. Several further clandestine operations sought to subvert the government of Syria, leading finally to a bungled CIA effort again penetrated by Syrian intelligence.

The "Eisenhower Doctrine," approved by Congress in March 1957, authorized the president to provide assistance, including U.S. troops, "to secure and protect the territorial integrity and political independence of such [Middle Eastern] nations, requesting such aid, against overt armed aggression from any nation controlled by international communism." While Egypt was the publicly designated culprit, U.S. officials believed that Syria was more "nearly under the control of international communism," Douglas Little concludes. The end result of a decade of such machinations was hostility to the United States, close Syrian relations with the USSR, and much hysteria in Washington about "losing the whole Middle East to Communism."[16]

The similarity to Cold War history in Latin America, Southeast Asia, and Africa is unmistakable, and its sources in U.S. policy are easy enough to detect.

4. The Regional Actors

American relations with regional actors developed within the context of the strategic thinking just outlined, in most cases successfully from the standpoint of U.S. strategic and economic interests. Successes include the autocracies of the Gulf, Iran under the shah's tyrannical rule for a quarter of a century after the CIA coup, Israel's expansion and military dominance, and the mass of superfluous people, effectively subdued. Sometimes efforts misfired, as in the case of Syria.

Egypt is an example of particular importance because of its unique position in the region and the complexity of the case. Initially, the United States faced two problems in integrating Egypt into the New World Order of the postwar era. The first was the Egyptian interest in development in violation of the principles of comparative advantage and international specialization: the problem of "economic nationalism," already discussed. The second problem was the role of Britain. The U.S. economic mission was somewhat annoyed that Britain was blocking sterling balances and otherwise impeding U.S. commercial activities.[17] Dissatisfaction with British policies continued; by the late 1950s, the United States had largely displaced Britain in the region.

The United States may have supported the 1952 revolution in Egypt, and was initially disposed rather favorably towards the Nasser regime. By the mid-1950s, that attitude was changing because of Nasser's neutralist and independent stance, which inevitably led him to accept Russian assistance in response to Western hostility; U.S. intelligence recognized that the USSR was reacting to Western initiatives.

At Eisenhower's request, Dulles prepared a memorandum (March 28, 1956) that became the basis for Project OMEGA, which aimed to displace Nasser by supporting the Gulf dictatorships, scuttling the Aswan Dam project, and withholding aid. Commenting on Dulles's memorandum in a diary entry, Eisenhower noted that "the growing ambition of Nasser" is the fundamental problem, which could be overcome, he hoped, by "build[ing] up some other individual as a prospective leader of the Arab world. . . . My own choice of such a rival is King Saud." The United States "could not be unsympathetic to the British and French" intention to overthrow Nasser by force, Dulles informed congressional leaders in August 1956. He warned that "fulfillment of Nasser's ambitions would result in reducing Western Europe literally to a state of dependency," the usual apocalyptic reaction to loss of some degree of control.

The United States nevertheless opposed the British–French–Israeli invasion of late October 1956, partly, it is reasonable to suppose, because of uneasiness over the reassertion of an independent French and British role in a region that the United States was taking over for itself, but more specifically because of the timing. A few weeks earlier, Eisenhower had opposed internal U.S. government proposals to overthrow Nasser because there was "so much hostility at present" in the Arab world. It would be necessary to delay until after his re-election in 1956, Eisenhower felt. When that was past, "a time free from heated stress holding the world's attention would have to be chosen." The invasion also disrupted the planned U.S. coup in Syria. In December, shortly after forcing Britain and France to abandon their effort, Eisenhower wired Dulles at a NATO meeting to make sure that the allies "know that we regard Nasser as an evil influence," but the British and French "chose a bad time . . . in which to launch corrective measures."[18]

By January 1958, Washington had become seriously concerned about Arab reactions to U.S. policies. The National Security Council recognized that "in the eyes of the majority of Arabs the United States appears to be opposed to the realization of the goals of Arab nationalism. They believe that the United States is seeking to protect its interest in Near East oil by supporting the *status quo* and opposing political or economic progress." The perception is difficult to counter, the NSC recognized, since "our economic and cultural interests in the area have led not unnaturally to close U.S. relations with elements in the Arab world whose primary interest lies in the maintenance of relations with the West and the status quo in their countries." It is difficult, in short, to counter perceptions that are plainly accurate. Britain hoped to convince Washington of the need to use force to maintain Anglo–American control: "Anything that brings home to them the problems of an administering or protecting power is to be encouraged. We can all agree that force is to be deprecated and that it solves no problems permanently (perhaps because superior force is brought to bear on the other side). But theories of this kind are not a very helpful guide when the mob is battering at the gates."[19]

The implication is that force is a legitimate means to control the mob if counterforce need not be feared, another theme that persists into the post–Cold War era.

By then, Lebanon too was becoming a problem, with the Chamoun regime facing serious internal problems. Dulles informed President Chamoun in May 1958 that U.S. troops would be available if his government could not control rising popular opposition. Dulles also gave Chamoun careful instructions on how the request for troops should be formulated. It would not be possible to appeal to the Eisenhower Doctrine, Dulles explained, since there was no way to conjure up "armed aggression" from a Communist-controlled nation. U.S. combat forces could, however, be sent on the "dual mission of (a) protecting American life and property and (b) assisting the GOL [Government of Lebanon] in its military program for the preservation of the independence and integrity of Lebanon which is vital to the national interests of the United States and to world peace." Request for U.S. troops "should be couched in the terms indicated," Dulles instructed, adding that as a cover, the Lebanese government should also file a complaint with the UN alleging outside interference in its internal affairs. The British felt that "armed attack" should indeed be alleged to rebut the argument that it is the U.S. intervention itself that threatens peace.

As for the "extremely dangerous fanatic" who was considered responsible for the difficulties faced by Washington and its clients in maintaining internal control, Gamal Abdel Nasser, he was "moved by a dream of pan-Arabism, something like Hitler's pan-Germanism," Dulles informed Israeli ambassador Abba Eban, complaining that there are "no international practices for dealing with his type of intervention" (May 1958). It is much like the "economic and ideological infiltration" from the East that the British Foreign Office had described as "something very like aggression" ten years earlier. Once again, a "rotten apple" was inciting the poor to "plunder the rich," their age-old crime.

Other allies felt much the same way. British and French leaders had fallen prey to virtual hysteria as they planned their 1956 invasion. Israeli prime minister David Ben-Gurion felt that the Lebanon crisis of 1958 was "perhaps last opportunity for U.S. to act in manner that will prevent all of ME from being engulfed by Soviets," the U.S. ambassador to Israel cabled Washington on May 16. "Israel believed that objectively the security of Lebanon and

Israel were equivalent," Israeli ambassador to Washington Abba Eban explained: "If Lebanon fell, Jordan would be next, and the momentum of Nasserism would gather force" (May 15). Israel offered to withdraw forces from the Lebanese border, which would permit the Chamoun government to deploy its army more efficiently for internal repression. Visiting Washington on July 1, the shah of Iran urged military intervention "to save Lebanon from falling into the hands of the communists or Nasser," with an inevitable domino effect beyond. Communism, he informed Eisenhower, "must find means constantly of expanding. Like an octopus, if one tentacle were covered, others become even more active. Communism and Nasserism were constantly probing for weak spots. If Lebanon should fall, Iraq and Jordan would be in grave danger. The current problem [in Lebanon], now being aggravated by Syrians and Egyptians, was a worry to all of us."[20]

At the time, a UN investigating team in Lebanon and U.S. analysts were unable to find any credible evidence of the large-scale intervention from Egypt or Syria that was alleged, though President Chamoun had already lost 80 percent of his territory to the internal opposition.

The shah regarded Nasser's *Philosophy of the Revolution* as akin to *Mein Kampf*. The United States should not, however, cater to his whims. "Egypt represented nothing but a few million unhappy and impoverished beggars" led by a fanatic with exalted ambitions. Nasser aimed "to gain control of large areas in the Middle East," the shah held, agreeing with Dulles that Hitler was his role model and that he intended to subjugate Western Europe through control of oil—as the United States had in fact intended a century earlier, through its control of cotton.

The CIA, meanwhile, contended in a July 12 report that Nasser was neither "a Communist or sympathetic to the Communist doctrine." Nasser suppressed domestic Communists, the CIA recognized, and regarded the USSR as a great power with interests that happened to mesh with his own. "The Arab objectives of maintaining independence and of utilizing the profits of Arab oil are compatible with two crucial U.S. interests—denial of the area to Soviet domination and maintenance of Western access to Middle East oil" (July 12, 1958). But this point of view was not welcome to the White House.

On July 7, Dulles emphasized that the United States must seek a solution "avoiding any victory for Nasser through a political compromise of Chamoun with the rebel elements." A week later, the Marines landed in the wake of the Iraq coup. The outcome is described in a Marine Corps history:

> The presence on their soil of American troops sobered the Lebanese and evoked from them a spirit of responsibility. Thanks to this spirit, a workable political compromise was arranged. . . . The new chief executive [Gen. Chehab] soothed the suspicious Moslems by agreeing to increase the number of representatives in the national parliament and by appointing certain prominent ex-rebels to his cabinet. These reforms, however, would not have been carried out voluntarily. The implied threat that the US would use its troops to enforce a dictated settlement was the goad that started the Lebanese along the path towards political stability.

There is no need to comment on the political stability that ensued. In the rhetoric affected in the post–Cold War era, the Marine landing might be called an exercise of "new style humanitarian intervention," which responds to popular pleas for assistance with less respect for national boundaries than heretofore.

Relations between the United States and Israel, unique in world affairs, developed within the same general context. Israel's military successes in the 1948 war impressed the U.S. Joint Chiefs of Staff, who described the new state as the major regional military power after Turkey, offering the United States means to "gain strategic advantage in the Middle East that would offset the effects of the decline of British power in that area." As for the Palestinians, U.S. planners had no reason to doubt the assessment of Israeli government specialists in 1948 that the refugees would either assimilate elsewhere or "would be crushed": "some of them would die and most of them would turn into human dust and the waste of society, and join the most impoverished classes in the Arab countries." Accordingly, there was no need to trouble oneself about them. These basic interpretations have remained stable until today, taking concrete form as events unfolded.[21]

In January 1958, the National Security Council concluded that a "logical corollary" of opposition to growing Arab nationalism "would be to support Israel as the only strong pro-Western power left in the Middle East." Through the 1960s, U.S. analysts saw Israeli power as a barrier to Nasserite pressures and influences in the Arabian peninsula and Jordan. Israel's successes in the 1967 war reinforced the conception of Israel as a "strategic asset" that could serve U.S. interests by undermining independent nationalist forces. This thesis received further support as Israel acted to deter Syrian intervention in support of the Palestinians in 1970, regarded by Washington as a potential threat to the Hashemite kingdom and U.S. clients beyond. The "strategic asset" thesis by then found its natural place within the Nixon Doctrine, which recognized that the United States could "no longer play policeman to the world" and would therefore "expect other nations to provide more cops on the beat in their own neighborhood" (Defense Secretary Melvin Laird)— though police headquarters, it was understood, remains in Washington. In Henry Kissinger's phraseology, already cited, other states must pursue their "regional interests" within the "overall framework of order" managed by the United States. The two main cops on the beat in that particular precinct were Israel and Iran, secretly allied.

Robert Reppa, a Middle East analyst for the Defense Intelligence Agency, writes that the Israeli–Iranian relationship, well established by the 1970s, contributed to the stability of the region, securing U.S. interests by keeping any potential radical nationalists in line. In May 1973, the Senate's ranking expert on oil and the Middle East, Henry Jackson, emphasized "the strength and Western orientation of Israel on the Mediterranean and Iran on the Persian Gulf," two "reliable friends of the United States," who, along with Saudi Arabia, "have served to inhibit and contain those irresponsible and radical elements in certain Arab States ... who, were they free to do so, would pose a grave threat indeed to our principal sources of petroleum in the Persian Gulf"—sources that the United States scarcely used at the time, but that were needed as a reserve and as a lever for world domination, and primarily for the vast wealth they yield, which is to flow primarily to the United States and Britain. The formal conflict between Saudi Arabia and both Iran and Israel was a technicality, as was the theoretical opposition of the shah's regime to Israel's policies.

With the fall of the shah, Israel's role as a regional gendarme only increased. It comes as no surprise that immediately after the overthrow of the shah's regime and the failure of Carter administration envoy General Robert Huyser to inspire a military coup, the United States, Israel, and Saudi Arabia joined in clandestine efforts to restore the tripartite alliance, with Saudi Arabia funding sales of U.S. arms via Israel to elements in the Iranian military who, it was hoped, would overthrow the regime.[22]

Throughout, Israel had been pursuing its own complementary "periphery policy," forming alliances with Turkey, Iran, and Ethiopia, with the support of the United States after Israel's considerable assistance to U.S. intervention in Lebanon (with a spillover to Jordan) in mid-1958.[23]

Meanwhile, Israel was enlisted to perform secondary services for the United States. In the 1960s, Israel made inroads in Black Africa with a large CIA subsidy, helping to establish and maintain the rule of Mobutu in Zaire, Idi Amin in Uganda, and others, and also offering the United States a way to evade the UN embargo against oil shipments to Rhodesia. Israeli relations with South Africa probably fall within the same framework, in part at least. Israel also served U.S. interests in Asia, for example sending U.S. jet fighters to Indonesia in the course of the murderous aggression in East Timor, when the Carter administration was blocked by Congress from doing so directly.

The major services, however, were in Latin America, particularly after congressional human rights legislation prevented the U.S. executive from providing direct assistance to the most brutal tyrants. Israel maintained close contacts with the neo-Nazi regimes of the southern cone, undeterred by the virulent anti-Semitism of the ruling generals. It supported Somoza until virtually the last days of his bloody rule, through the period when his National Guard had slaughtered some forty thousand people while Carter's ambassador Lawrence Pezzullo advised that the bloodbath should continue, and the administration sought to keep the Guard in power even if Somoza could not be sustained. Israel also lent valued support to the terrorist rulers of El Salvador in the 1970s, until the United States took over the task of organizing the massacre directly. Perhaps the most significant services were in Guatemala, where Israeli assistance was instrumental in near-genocidal slaughters and repression at a time when the U.S. government was inhibited by popular pressures, reflected in congressional legislation, from direct participation. Israel also joined other clients in the training and support of the terrorist forces attacking Nicaragua. In these efforts, Israel functioned within the extraordinary international terrorist network that the United States designed, particularly during the Reagan years, including Taiwan, Saudi Arabia, South Africa, Argentine neo-Nazis, and an intricate system of arms suppliers, military trainers, and funders worldwide.

At the same time, Israel forged close links with U.S. intelligence and the Pentagon, both in military production and in the testing of advanced weapons under battlefield conditions or against defenseless targets, again providing valuable services for U.S. power. Israel also has offered the United States a form of "export promotion," as grants of arms to Israel helped stimulate huge arms sales to the Arab states, recycling petrodollars to U.S. industry.

The U.S.–Israel alliance has been based primarily on the perception of Israel as a "strategic asset" fulfilling U.S. goals in the region in tacit alliance with the Arab Facade in the Gulf and other regional protectors of the family dictatorships, and performing services elsewhere. One may debate the validity of the doctrine, as many do, but that is a separate matter. It is largely independent of the Cold War, and there is every reason to expect it to continue in force, as prominent Israeli analysts anticipate, if it continues to be seen as serving U.S. power interests.

Many Israelis have regarded this relationship as both dangerous and degrading. Expressing widely-held attitudes, Israeli satirist B. Michael defined the reigning doctrine with characteristic insight: "My master gives me food to eat and I bite those whom he tells me to bite. It is called strategic cooperation." As one Israeli analyst put the matter when the Iran–Contra affair erupted: "It's like Israel has become just another federal agency, one that's convenient to use when you want something done quietly." The Israeli press describes Israel as "the Godfather's messenger," undertaking the "dirty work" for the Godfather, who "always tries to appear to be the owner of some large respectable business." But Israel's dependence on the United States is so extreme that no domestic opposition can gain much credibility unless it has backing from within the United States, and that has been almost completely lacking in this case.[24]

The general strategic conception has its grim logic. While information from the Arab dictatorships is sparse, it is not unlikely that it is shared by their ruling elites.

5. Seeking Peace: Stage One

After the June 1967 war, the U.S.–Israeli alliance was firmly in place, with Iran a close partner and the oil monarchies probably lending tacit support. The war had brought the world dangerously close to a superpower confrontation. Years later, then–Defense Secretary Robert McNamara commented that "we damn near had war" when the U.S. fleet "turned around a [Soviet] carrier in the Mediterranean"; he gave no details, but it was probably during Israel's conquest of the Golan Heights after the cease-fire, an act that elicited severe warnings from the USSR. There were several "hot line" communications during the war, apparently of a threatening nature; Soviet premier Kosygin at one point warned President Johnson that "if you want war, you'll have war," according to McNamara. Though by no means the only source of tension in the region, the Arab–Israel conflict was recognized to be too dangerous to be ignored, and diplomatic efforts to resolve it were undertaken with renewed seriousness.[25]

From 1967 to 1971, there was a broad international consensus on the general terms for a settlement, expressed in Security Council Resolution 242 of November 1967. The document "emphasiz[es] the inadmissibility of acquisition of territory by war and the need to work for a just and lasting peace in which every state in the area can live in security." It calls for "withdrawal of Israeli armed forces from territories occupied in the recent conflict" and "termination of all claims or states of belligerency and respect for and acknowledgment of the sovereignty, territorial integrity and political independence of every state in the area and their right to live in peace within secure and recognized boundaries free from threats or acts of force." It calls for an agreement among *states*; Palestinian rights are mentioned only in the reference to "a just settlement of the refugee problem," left unspecified. UN 242 is therefore thoroughly *rejectionist*, if we understand the concept of rejectionism as denial of the right to national self-determination of one of the two contending parties in the former Palestine.

With varying degrees of ambiguity, UN 242 was accepted by the contending states of the region over the next few years, though their interpretations differed. The Arab states rejected full peace, Israel rejected full withdrawal.

Little documentary evidence is available, to my knowledge, on the Arab positions. The Israeli record under the Labor Party (1967–77) is most fully discussed in a review of cabinet records by Labor Party functionary Yossi Beilin. He reports a secret offer transmitted via the United States after a divided (11–10) cabinet decision of June 19, 1967, calling for a settlement at the international borders with Syria and Egypt (Israel keeping Gaza), but no mention of Jordan and the West Bank. This proposal, which Foreign Minister Abba Eban later described as "the most dramatic initiative that the government of Israel ever took before or since," was canceled a year later, when Israel proposed a settlement in terms of the Allon Plan, which at the time accorded Israel control over the Golan Heights, Gaza, a strip of Eastern Sinai from the Mediterranean to Sharm al-Sheikh, and about 40 percent of the West Bank including the Jordan valley and a greatly expanded area around Jerusalem. With various modifications, this has been the basis for Labor Party policies since, including the 1992 Rabin government. Israel has forcefully rejected other proposals apart from the Camp David arrangements, which the (Likud) government interpreted as granting it effective control over the occupied territories.[26]

The phrase "withdrawal from territories" has been a particular bone of contention. In most of the world (including Europe), it has been understood to imply Israeli withdrawal from *all* of the territories occupied during the war, with at most minor—and mutual—adjustments. Through the early period (1967–71), that was also Washington's interpretation. UN ambassador Arthur Goldberg informed King Hussein that the United States insisted that "there must be a mutuality in adjustments," a classified State Department history observes: to both Israel and the Arab states, "U.S. officials emphasized that any territorial adjustments would be limited in nature and would not, of necessity, be detrimental to the Arab states"; there would be at most "minor reciprocal border rectifications" with no "substantial redrawing of the [pre-war] map." It was on this understanding, explicitly conveyed by U.S. government mediators, that the Arab states accepted the resolution, and the United States itself unequivocally held to this interpretation until 1971. At that time, Israel was alone among major actors in rejecting this interpretation of the document, contrary to standard U.S. versions and claims by American advocates of Israeli policies.[27]

The disagreements over interpretation came to a head in February 1971, when UN mediator Gunnar Jarring presented a proposal to Egypt and Israel that called for full peace between them in return for full withdrawal from Egyptian territory, in accord with the general consensus on UN 242. President Sadat accepted the proposal. While officially welcoming Egypt's expression "of its readiness to enter into a peace agreement with Israel," the government of Israel rejected the agreement, stating that "Israel will not withdraw to the pre–June 5, 1967 lines," a position that it maintains until today.

In his memoirs, Yitzhak Rabin, then Israel's ambassador in Washington, describes Sadat's acceptance of the "famous" Jarring proposal as a "bombshell." Egypt's positive reaction was a "milestone," he writes, though it contained "bad news" as well as "good news." The "good news" was that "in return for an Israeli withdrawal from the Sinai and the Gaza Strip, Egypt was prepared to enter into a peace agreement with Israel." The "bad news" was that "Sadat's evasive imprint" remained, implying a "conditional link" between the peace agreement and Israel's withdrawal to the pre–June 1967 borders. Rabin informed Secretary of State William Rogers that "our reply to Jarring will be earnest and responsible. It has been decided to state clearly that Israel will not withdraw to the June 4, 1967, lines."

Israel's official response made that condition explicit, thus effectively terminating Jarring's initiative. The reasoning was outlined by Haim Bar-Lev of the governing Labor Party:

> I think that we could obtain a peace settlement on the basis of the earlier [pre–June 1967] borders. If I were persuaded that this is the maximum that we might obtain, I would say: agreed. But I think that it is not the maximum. I think that if we continue to hold out, we will obtain more.

Prevailing thinking was elaborated a few weeks later by General Ezer Weizmann, now president, discussing the decision to go to war in 1967. If Israel were to withdraw from the conquered territories, he explained, it could not "exist according to the scale, spirit, and quality she now embodies."[28]

The crucial question was how the United States would react. The Jarring–Sadat agreement was consistent with official U.S. policy, stated most explicitly in the Rogers Plan of 1969, approved by President Nixon, which held that "any change in the pre-existing lines should not reflect the weight of conquest and should be confined to insubstantial alterations required for mutual security." There was, however, a conflict between the State Department and National Security Adviser Henry Kissinger, who was then engaged in a campaign to undermine and displace Rogers, as he was soon to do. Kissinger insisted that the United States must reject the international consensus to which it had previously conformed, and insist upon "stalemate": no diplomacy, no negotiations. His position prevailed, and Sadat's peace offer was dismissed.

In his 1979 memoirs, Kissinger puts forth his alleged reasons for preferring military confrontation to diplomacy. It was necessary to insist upon "stalemate until Moscow urged compromise or until, even better, some moderate Arab regime decided that the route to progress was through Washington." "Until some Arab state showed a willingness to separate from the Soviets, or the Soviets were prepared to dissociate from the maximum Arab program, we had no reason to modify our policy" of stalemate. These comments are remarkable. Of the two major Arab states, Egypt was plainly showing "a willingness to separate from the Soviets," and the question doesn't arise for Saudi Arabia, which did not even have diplomatic relations with the hated Russians—who had, furthermore, never associated themselves with the "maximum Arab program" but kept well within the international consensus. As Senate Foreign Relations Committee Middle East specialist Seth Tillman pointed out, "the official Soviet position has been consistent since 1948 in support of Israel's right to exist and consistent since 1967 in support of Israel's right to a secure national existence, as called for in Security Council Resolution 242, within its 1967 borders." Thus both the USSR and Egypt had adopted the official U.S. policies that Kissinger rejected. In fact, a few months later (November 1971), Leonid Brezhnev secretly proposed to Nixon that the Rogers Plan be the basis for a great-power agreement to settle the conflict, a proposal relayed to Rabin by Kissinger, Rabin records.

That Kissinger might have held such beliefs in 1971 is perhaps imaginable, though they are so astonishing as to suggest that his primary motive may have been personal ambition and vindictiveness: his desire to undermine his despised rival at the State Department. That he should be willing to repeat these fantasies eight years later is even more revealing, as is the fact that they pass with little or no comment in the huge literature on Kissinger's career—along with other absurdities that are no less remarkable.[29]

The record leaves little doubt, as Beilin observes, that Israel could have had a peace settlement in terms of the prevailing international consensus, offering nothing to the Palestinians, by 1971. Indeed it is possible that that would have been the outcome, avoiding much subsequent tragedy, had

Kissinger not succeeded in wresting Middle East policy from the State Department. Beilin also notes that Israel's "security problems with regard to terror," including Katyusha rockets, became serious from mid-1971, that is, after the rejection of the Egyptian peace proposals. But, Beilin observes, security considerations were secondary throughout in the ten-year record of internal deliberations that he reviews. Far more significant was the "demographic problem"—that is, the problem of how to take over substantial parts of the occupied territories without accepting responsibility for their population. The question of the water resources of the West Bank is also repeatedly raised.

It should be borne in mind that for Israel, the problem posed by an independent Palestinian state has never been security. Prime Minister David Ben-Gurion noted in his diaries in December 1948 that "an Arab state in Western Palestine [that is, west of the Jordan] would be less dangerous than a state linked to Transjordan, and maybe tomorrow to Iraq." The reasoning is obvious and compelling, and remains unchanged. The Labor Party's preferred option of assigning parts of the West Bank to Jordanian rule hardly increases Israel's security. The problems lie in the barrier an independent state would pose for expansion and access to resources, particularly water.[30]

The importance of this factor can hardly be overemphasized. One of Israel's leading specialists on the topic and a consultant for the U.S. Defense Department, Hebrew University professor Haim Gvirtzman, takes note of "a 'little secret', which has been hidden for two decades": "the criterion guiding Ma'arach [the Labor coalition] in establishing the first settlements prior to its electoral defeat in 1977 was—their location in critical regions for controlling Israel's water sources." "Any beginning hydrologist" could draw a map of these critical regions, he points out, reviewing the settlement pattern that was determined by this criterion. The result by mid-1993 is that of the 600 million cubic meters of water taken annually from the sources in "Judea and Samaria," Israeli citizens use almost 500 million, which satisfies about a third of "the total water requirements of citizens of Israel" (for urban communities, irrigation, etc.). These conditions must be maintained under any impending "autonomy," Gvirtzman concludes, arguing that Israel's use of these sources for nineteen years grants it rights to them under international law. As is well known, a large part of the significance of the Golan Heights has been control over the headwaters of the Jordan.

In an earlier interview, Gvirtzman had expressed his relief that the new minister of interior, Yossi Sarid of the dovish Meretz Party, had come to understand "the hydraulic system of the entire Land of Israel," and the implications under "autonomy." His own view is that "the autonomy authorities must never be given any power over the water resources of their areas," just as Palestinians were never permitted to sink more than the shallowest wells under the occupation. The only realistic alternatives, he suggests, are expensive purification of sea water or diversion of the Litani river in southern Lebanon. Under autonomy, he explains,

Israel must care only for a minimal Palestinian standard of living, nothing more, which means water supply for them only for urban needs. That amounts to about 50–100 million cubic meters per year. Israel is capable of suffering that loss. Therefore we should never allow the Palestinians to develop any new agricultural areas, because such development will come at the expense of Israeli agriculture. We must certainly never allow the Palestinians to supply the water needs of the Gaza Strip from the mountain aquifer. If purifying sea water is a realistic solution, then let them do it for the needs of the residents of the Gaza Strip.

Before the issue of autonomy arose, Gvirtzman continues,

Israel proved that it had the ability to turn any conflict over water into a casus belli. It is difficult for me to imagine a situation in which we will grant autonomy without there being binding rules made in advance to allow us to control the issue of water. We shall never allow Palestinians "to rob" the water and sit with tied hands. The Kibbutzim will never agree that we will do nothing while Palestinians would drill and steal their water!

—nor would urban residents stand by silently and permit such theft of West Bank water.

Washington economic analyst Thomas Stauffer, who has written for years on these matters, estimates that 40 percent of Israel's water depends on territories occupied in 1967, and that it would cost Israel $1 billion or more annually if a peace settlement diverted these resources to residents upstream in Lebanon, Syria, Jordan, and the West Bank. He argues further, as have others, that control of the Golan Heights and southeast Lebanon "enables Israel to protect the system of canals, pumps, and pipelines which move Jordan River water through Israel as far as the northern Negev desert."[31]

Recall that the rejected 1971 Jarring–Sadat peace proposal offered nothing to the Palestinians. In this respect, it was more in conformity with Israel's perceived self-interest—however one evaluates this perception—than the proposals that established Sadat as a "man of peace" on the occasion of his visit to Jerusalem in 1977, when he called for a Palestinian state. The rejection of the 1971 peace offer underscores the conclusion that the issue of Palestinian self-determination, like security, has not been the stumbling block for a negotiated political settlement. Rather, the primary strategic motivation for Israeli rejectionism, whether of the Likud or Labor variety, is control over the territories and their resources. And for the United States, since Kissinger's takeover of Middle East policy, the primary motivation for consistent rejectionism and support for Israeli expansionism (personal idiosyncrasies aside) has been the general strategic conception that was raised to a principle within the Nixon–Kissinger Doctrine. In the mood of triumphalism after Israel's 1967 victory, it was assumed that Israel could achieve its longer-term goals by the traditional method of "building facts" and evading firm diplomatic and political commitments, with U.S. support— Kissinger's "stalemate." After the 1973 war, such assumptions were less persuasive. Hence Sadat could be disregarded in 1971, but became a beloved figure for offering a less forthcoming proposal in 1977; and official history can accommodate the 1977 initiative, which could be modified to conform to U.S. intentions of that period, but not the 1971 events, which reveal far too much about the policies of the United States and Israel.

Excision of the 1971 events from the record has been accomplished with startling efficiency. Though a "famous milestone" for peace in Israel, the Jarring–Sadat agreement is effectively barred from discussion of the "peace process," while Sadat's 1977 initiative, which the United States was then willing to accept (after eliminating its call for recognition of Palestinian national rights), is regularly hailed as a historic breakthrough that established him as an American folk hero. The standard version is that "even Mr. Sadat admittedly did not accept [Israel's] existence until he decided to come to Jerusalem" in 1977, and even then his "program called for peace on the most extreme Arab terms, except for those Arab extremists who would be satisfied with nothing but the total destruction of the state of Israel" (Theodore Draper, a scholar who is generally scrupulous about facts when Israel is not concerned). Similarly, the two-page obituary for Sadat by *New York Times* Middle East specialist Eric Pace not only suppressed the facts but explicitly denied them, stating that until his 1977 trip to Jerusalem, Sadat was unwilling "to accept Israel's existence as a sovereign state." *Newsweek* even refused to print a brief letter correcting falsehoods on the matter by their columnist George Will, though their research department privately conceded the facts. The story is repeated in an endless litany, corrected only at the margins or in scholarly monographs, often not even there. Much the same story is now being repeated with Yasser Arafat, a matter to which we return.[32]

After the 1971 failure, Sadat tried in every way to catch Kissinger's eye. He expelled Soviet advisers, and announced repeatedly that if all diplomatic paths were blocked he would be compelled to resort to war, particularly after the Labor government extended its policies of expulsion and settlement in northeastern Sinai. Rejecting ample evidence from U.S. ambassadors, oil companies, and other sources, Kissinger blindly dismissed all such moves with contempt, as did Israel, both assuming that Israel's military power was so overwhelming that it could not possibly be challenged.[33]

Egyptian and Syrian successes in the 1973 war came as a great shock. Recognizing that Egypt could not simply be discounted as a basket case, Kissinger changed course, deciding to accept Sadat's implicit offers to convert Egypt into a U.S. client. In this fallback strategy, Egypt would not be ignored but rather neutralized by a settlement that would leave Israel free to pursue its goals elsewhere in the region, with U.S. backing. There followed a period of "shuttle diplomacy" and partial agreements consummated finally at Camp David in 1978–79.

Kissinger outlined his thinking in a private 1975 meeting with Jewish leaders organized by the dovish Philip Klutznik, later released under the Freedom of Information Act. Even discounting for the circumstances, much of what he says rings true. His strategy, Kissinger explained, was based on the desire "to ensure that the Europeans and Japanese did not get involved in the diplomacy concerning the Middle East," "to keep the Soviets out of the diplomatic arena," "to isolate the Palestinians" so that they would not be a factor in the outcome, and "to break up the Arab united front," thus allowing Israel "to deal separately with each of its neighbors" while of course remaining dependent on the United States. During the 1973 war—for which he bears major responsibility—his goal was to help inflict "the most massive Arab defeat possible," so as to be able to implement these plans. Kissinger also claimed, whether accurately or not, that Jordan offered to make peace after 1973 if Israel would yield "about one-half of the territory called for in the old Allon Plan," thus keeping about 20 percent of the West Bank along with the ambiguously expanding area of Jerusalem. The strategic goals Kissinger outlined are a natural modification of policy in the light of the consequences of his gross miscalculations with regard to the military balance.[34]

The Camp David agreements removed the major Arab deterrent, leaving Israel free, with a huge increase in U.S. military and economic aid, to proceed with its plans to integrate the occupied territories and attack its northern neighbor. As summarized by Israeli strategic analyst Avner Yaniv, the effect of the "Egyptian defection" was that "Israel would be free to sustain military operations against the PLO in Lebanon as well as settlement activity on the West Bank."[35]

Since the Camp David agreements were U.S.-brokered, they must be understood to be a diplomatic triumph, despite their consequences, obvious at the time, impossible to miss in retrospect. This stance is uniform in American journalism, though some correspondents are surely aware of the realities. Thus in an interview in Israel, *New York Times* Middle East correspondent David Shipler recognized that "on the Israeli side, it seems to me that the [Camp David] peace treaty set up the situation for the war in Lebanon. With Egypt no longer a confrontation state, Israel felt free to initiate a war in Lebanon, something it probably would not have dared to do before the peace treaty. . . . It is an irony that the war in Lebanon could not have taken place without the peace treaty"—hardly an "irony," and quite remote from the picture presented in the *New York Times*, or elsewhere in the media and journals of opinion. Editing a volume of essays on the tenth anniversary of Camp David, William Quandt, a government insider at the time, rejects the fears then expressed in the Arab world "that Israel would become more aggressive once Egypt was neutralized," exactly what happened. His grounds are that "Egypt was not the only available brake on Israel's aggressive policies" in Lebanon and the West Bank, which is surely true, but irrelevant to the issue: no one claimed that Egypt was the *sole* deterrent to Israel's actions. Another contributor who was also involved in the Camp David negotiations, Harold Saunders, observes more realistically that "although the Camp David Accords gave lip service to Palestinian interests, they actually freed the Likud government in Israel to consolidate its hold on the West Bank and Gaza. . . . In the same vein, the Egyptian–Israeli peace freed Israel to invade Lebanon in 1982 [as it had in

1978] to destroy or drive out the PLO." Quandt himself had recognized earlier that "the Israeli operational planning for the invasion of Lebanon against the PLO seems to coincide with the consolidation of the Egyptian–Israeli peace treaty," not surprisingly.[36]

With the major Arab deterrent neutralized, and U.S. support reaching new heights under Carter, then Reagan, Israel proceeded with its takeover of the territories and its attacks on Lebanon, which were linked. In the United States, the official line is that Israel was responding to PLO terror and other Arab threats, though a review of the record of interactions in preceding years completely undermines this thesis.

The actual reasons for the 1982 invasion have never been concealed in Israel, though they are rated "X" in the United States. A few weeks after the invasion began, Israel's leading academic specialist on the Palestinians, Yehoshua Porath, pointed out that the decision to invade "flowed from the very fact that the cease-fire had been observed" by the PLO, a "veritable catastrophe" for the Israeli government because it endangered the policy of evading a political settlement. The PLO was gaining respectability thanks to its preference for negotiations over terror. The Israeli government's hope was to compel "the stricken PLO" to "return to its earlier terrorism," thus "undercutting the danger" of negotiations. As Prime Minister Yitzhak Shamir later stated, Israel went to war because there was "a terrible danger. . . . Not so much a military one as a political one." The invasion should be called "the war to safeguard the occupation of the West Bank," having been motivated by Begin's "fear of the momentum of the peace process," according to Israeli Arabist and former head of military intelligence Gen. Yehoshaphat Harkabi. Chief of Staff Rafael ("Raful") Eitan described the operation as a success: "We destroyed the PLO as a candidate for negotiations with us about the Land of Israel." U.S. backing for Israel's aggression, including the vetoing of Security Council efforts to stop the slaughter, was presumably based on the same reasoning.[37]

Extending the analysis, Yaniv observes that "several developments in the summer and fall of 1981 may have heightened Israel's anxieties concerning the PLO," most ominously, the threat that the PLO would observe the cease-fire agreement and PLO efforts "to convince the Saudi government to promote" a diplomatic two-state settlement. In the following year, Israel attempted with increasing desperation to evoke some PLO response that could be used as a pretext for the planned invasion of Lebanon, designed to destroy the PLO as a political force, establish Israeli control over the occupied territories, and—in its more extreme versions—to establish Defense Minister Ariel Sharon's "New Order" in Lebanon and perhaps beyond. These efforts, including bombing of civilian targets in Lebanon with many casualties, failed to achieve their objective. Israel then used the pretext of the attempted assassination of Ambassador Argov by Abu Nidal—who had been at war with the PLO for a decade and did not so much as have an office in Lebanon—to launch Operation Peace for Galilee.

Again, all of this is completely falsified in what reaches the American public. The standard version has been that "Operation Peace for Galilee—the Israeli invasion of Lebanon—was originally undertaken" to protect the civilian population from Palestinian gunners, and that "the rocket and shelling attacks on Israel's northern border" were ended by the operation, though "if rockets again rain down on Israel's northern border after all that has been expended on Lebanon, the Israeli public will be outraged" (Thomas Friedman, 1985); all sharply at odds with the historical record, which is unchallenged and immaterial.

A few years later, it was clear that southern Lebanon had not been pacified, so the story was revised slightly: "Israel's two military forays into Lebanon [1978, 1982] were military disasters that failed to provide long-term security for Israel's northern border" (*Times* Middle East specialist Elaine Sciolino, 1993). Security had been at risk only as a result of Israel's unprovoked attacks from 1981, and to a certain extent before. The phrase "military disaster" does not refer to the killing of some twenty thousand Lebanese and Palestinians in 1982, overwhelmingly civilians, the destruction of much of southern Lebanon and the capital city of Beirut, or to Shimon Peres's "Iron Fist" operations and other atrocities in Lebanon through the mid-1980s. Rather, to Israel's failure to impose the "new order" it had proclaimed for Lebanon, and its inability to maintain its occupation in full because of the casualties caused by unanticipated resistance ("terror"), forcing it back to its "security zone." More careful commentators write that after the U.S.-mediated cease-fire of July 1981, "the Lebanese–Israeli border was quiet" (William Quandt), meaning that the PLO adhered to the cease-fire scrupulously while Israel continued its violations: bombing and killing civilians, sinking fishing boats, violating Lebanese air space thousands of times, and carrying out other provocations designed to elicit some PLO reaction so that the planned invasion could proceed. The border was "quiet" in that the cross-border terror was Israeli, tacitly supported by the United States, and only Arabs were being killed.[38]

The occasional reports during 1981 reflected the common understanding. Thus in April 1982, Israel bombed alleged PLO centers south of Beirut, killing two dozen people, in retaliation for what it called a PLO "terrorist act": an Israeli soldier had been killed when his jeep struck a land-mine in illegally occupied southern Lebanon. The *Washington Post* thoughtfully observed that "this is not the moment for sermons to Israel. It is a moment for respect for Israel's anguish—and for mourning the latest victims of Israeli–Palestinian hostility." Typically, it is *Israel*'s anguish that we must respect when still more Arabs are killed, to be seen as victims of mutual hostility, no agent indicated. The same attitudes prevail today. After Israel's July 1993 attack on Lebanon, foreign affairs editor H.D.S. Greenway of the *Boston Globe*, who reported the 1978 invasion graphically, commented that "if shelling Lebanese villages, even at the cost of lives, and driving civilian refugees north would secure Israel's border, weaken Hezbollah, and promote peace,

I would say go to it, as would many Arabs and Israelis. But history has not been kind to Israeli adventures in Lebanon. They have solved very little and have almost always caused more problems," so the murder of civilians, expulsion of hundreds of thousand of refugees, and devastation of the south is a dubious proposition. Imagine the reaction if someone were to approve a comparable attack on Israel or the United States, if only it could secure Lebanon's border and promote peace.[39]

In the real world, the "fundamentally strategic approach to the question of the PLO" recognizes that "a moderate—political rather than terrorist—PLO . . . could become far more dangerous than the violent PLO of the previous years," Yaniv explained (approvingly) in 1987. It was Arafat's moderation and turn towards diplomacy that "alarmed the Israeli government more than anything else," and it was therefore necessary to conduct "the fiercest military pressures" to "undermine the position of the moderates within [the PLO] ranks," to block "the PLO 'peace offensive,'" and to prevent Arafat from gaining PLO support for "a 'grand gesture,'" presumably a qualified acceptance of UN Resolution 242." This has been a matter of great significance for U.S.–Israeli propaganda. The primary goal of the 1982 invasion of Lebanon, Yaniv continues, was "to halt [the PLO's] rise to political respectability"; "dealing a major blow to the PLO as a political force was the raison d'etre of the entire operation." As long as the PLO held to its nationalist demands, it could not be a partner for negotiations.

Facing unexpected resistance and unwilling to bear the costs, Israel withdrew to its "security zone," reserving the right to attack the rest of Lebanon at will, as it regularly does, most recently in July 1993, when a week of intensive bombing destroyed dozens of Lebanese towns and villages and drove hundreds of thousands of people to the north. Prime Minister Rabin informed the Knesset (Parliament) that after Israeli forces killed Hezbollah leader Sheikh Abbas Mussawi [and his wife and child] in February 1992 well north of the "security zone," Hezbollah changed "the rules of the game, adopting the policy that in response to our strikes north of the security zone—it reacts by firing on Israel." The goal of the Israeli military operation was not simply destruction, Rabin explained, "but moving the population north, in the hope that this will signal something to the central authorities. . . ." The "wave of flight" is to pressure the government to keep Hezbollah to the old "rules of the game," and to negotiate a separate peace with Israel, high Israeli officials added.[40]

The familiar and understandable principle is that Israel must retain the right to use violence throughout Lebanon without fear of retaliation, and that separate state-to-state arrangements will advance the goals of U.S.–Israeli rejectionism.

Mainstream U.S. coverage of Israel's 1993 attack on Lebanon, while initially reporting the clear pronouncements of Israeli leaders, gradually shifted gears, finally adopting the preferred version that "the Israelis launched the assaults last Sunday in response to the killing of seven soldiers in the security zone earlier this month and rocket attacks on settlement towns in northern Israel."—rocket attacks which, as the press knew, were a *response* to the Israeli assaults. This "Big Lie," as Nabeel Abraham terms it, was established step-by-step, and now enters history. Out of history are the "women and children shrieking with pain in the hospital wards, their bodies plastered with burns from Israeli phosphorous shells" made available by U.S. largesse and tolerance, observed by Robert Fisk, one of the few reporters to have covered the assault from Lebanon, where he heard President Clinton blaming the events on Hezbollah and urging "all sides" to exercise "restraint."[41]

Even in the face of such explicit official pronouncements as those cited, foreign apologists for Israeli terror continued to depict their favored state as the innocent victim. In England, Conor Cruise O'Brien wrote that "Israel's action was one of retaliation for bombardments from Lebanese territory," excising the background for these bombardments outlined by Prime Minister Rabin and other high Israeli authorities. If the IRA regularly bombed England from Dublin, O'Brien continued, Britain would surely "use air strikes" to force the government of Ireland "to bring the bombardments to an end." Adding the facts he chooses to suppress, suppose that British troops were to occupy and terrorize a "security zone" within the Republic of Ireland in violation of orders from the UN Security Council, and after attacks on these troops by an Irish resistance, were to bomb Ireland at will, evoking retaliatory IRA shelling of England itself. Then according to the O'Brien doctrine, Britain would be entitled to destroy large parts of Ireland and drive hundreds of thousands of people to Dublin, to pressure its government to restore the "rules of the game" it stipulates. A performance of this kind is particularly revealing in London, where far more diversity is tolerated on this issue than in the United States, and there can be no doubt that the facts of the matter are well known.[42]

Regular Israeli bombing of Lebanon continued, generally ignored as usual. Sometimes there was no stated reason, as when Israeli warplanes bombed guerrilla bases in May 1992, killing twelve people, including a woman, her teenage son, and a nine-year old girl, police reported. The practice continued after the July 1993 attack and the signing of the Israel–Arafat agreement shortly after, on September 13. A week later, Israeli warplanes attacked alleged Hezbollah bases north of its "security zone." Hezbollah, AP reported, "opposes the peace accord between Israel and the Palestine Liberation Organization and seeks the destruction of the Jewish state," the standard U.S. version. That Hezbollah opposes the peace accord is correct; that it seeks to destroy Israel would, if true, also provide no justification for the bombing, but Israeli commentators, to whom we return, take quite a different view, regarding Hezbollah's goals as restricted to the Israeli occupation of their country. The bombing was in retaliation for the shelling of two outposts of Israel's mercenary army, the SLA (South Lebanon Army), which controls the region by terror. A few weeks later the

Financial Times ran a Reuters picture of two boys looking out of the ruins of their house after an Israeli helicopter raid on their village. In March 1994, Israel bombed and shelled villages in the UN-patrolled area with many casualties, including a Fijian UN peacekeeper, in retaliation for a bomb explosion in Israeli-occupied southern Lebanon. A few weeks later, Israeli shelling of the market town of Nabatiyeh killed a schoolgirl, wounding twenty-two other schoolchildren, in retaliation for an attack on Israeli occupying forces in southern Lebanon. The next day Katyusha rockets were fired into northern Israel.[43]

The attacks on Lebanon, like the settlement and repression in the occupied territories, depend crucially on military and diplomatic support by the United States. For that fundamental reason they proceed with at most mild reprimands and tactical criticism from the U.S. government and media.

U.S.–Israeli policies with regard to the occupied territories and Lebanon have been intimately related to their opposition to political settlement, except on their strictly rejectionist terms. From 1971, the United States systematically blocked a peaceful resolution in terms of the international consensus. Despite U.S. obstructionism, diplomatic efforts continued. By the mid-1970s, the terms of the international consensus had changed to include a Palestinian state in the West Bank and Gaza, at which point the PLO and the major Arab states joined, sometimes with ambiguity, sometimes more clearly. Israel and the United States, meanwhile, vehemently opposed such a settlement. Their diplomatic isolation thus increased, but that was a matter of indifference, given the global distribution of power.[44]

In January 1976, the "confrontation states" (Egypt, Syria, Jordan) proposed a settlement in the terms of the international consensus at the United Nations, with the support of most of the world, including the USSR and the PLO; according to former president Haim Herzog, then Israel's UN ambassador, the PLO not only publicly supported the resolution but actually "prepared" it. The proposed Security Council resolution called for a settlement on the pre–June 1967 borders, with "appropriate arrangements . . . to guarantee . . . the sovereignty, territorial integrity and political independence of all states in the area and their right to live in peace within secure and recognized boundaries," including Israel and the new Palestinian state; the wording of UN 242, supplemented with recognition of Palestinian political rights.

Israel strongly opposed this proposal and refused to attend the session. The United States vetoed the Security Council Resolution, as it did again in 1980, effectively removing the UN Security Council from Middle East diplomacy.[45] The General Assembly continued to advance peace proposals in its annual winter meetings. In December 1990, the General Assembly voted 144–2 (United States and Israel) to call an international conference. A year before, the Assembly voted 151–3 (United States, Israel, Dominica) for a settlement incorporating the wording of UN 242, along with "the right to self-determination" for the Palestinians. The record is similar in earlier years.

The NATO allies, the Soviet bloc, the Arab states, and the nonaligned countries had long been united in advocating a political settlement along these lines, but the United States would not permit it. Like the Security Council, the General Assembly has also been eliminated from the diplomatic scene by the U.S. "veto." After 1990, overwhelming U.S. power simply drove the issue off the international agenda; and out of history, given the worldwide conquests of the U.S. doctrinal system, a notable feature of modern culture that reached a remarkable level by the 1990s.

In keeping with its shift of policy towards a more extreme position on the Middle East, the Clinton administration lost little time in finding new ways to disrupt efforts to advance a nonrejectionist peace process. At the December 1993 UN session, the United States sought to restrict or terminate UN activities with regard to Israel–Palestine, claiming that past resolutions were "obsolete and anachronistic" in the light of the recent Israel–PLO agreement, to which we return. Washington called for abolishing the special committee on Palestinian rights, which it termed "biased, superfluous and unnecessary," and refused to condemn Israel's settlement activity because it is "unproductive to debate the legalities of the issue." Most important, Clinton reversed long-standing U.S. support for UN Resolution 194 of December 11, 1948, which affirms the right of Palestinian refugees who had fled or had been expelled during the fighting to return to their homes. For the first time, the United States joined Israel in opposing the resolution, reaffirmed by a vote of 127–2 (abstentions included the Russian Federation). As usual, the vote passed without report or comment.[46]

Resolution 194 was a direct application of Article 13 of the Universal Declaration of Human Rights, adopted unanimously by the United Nations the day before (Dec. 10, 1948). Article 13 states that "everyone has the right to leave any country, including his own, *and to return to his country*" (my italics). The Universal Declaration is recognized in U.S. courts and elsewhere as "customary international law," and as the "authoritative definition" of human rights standards. Article 13 is surely its most famous provision, invoked annually on Human Rights Day, December 10, with demonstrations and angry appeals to the Soviet Union to let Russian Jews leave. To be exact, half of Article 13 achieved this status; the words italicized—their significance enhanced by the passage of UN 194 the following day—were regularly omitted, and were always rejected by those who most passionately condemned the Soviet Union for failing to adhere to the Article, another fact kept in the shadows. At least that hypocrisy is now behind us: the first half of Article 13 has lost its relevance, and the United States now officially rejects the second half, so inconsistencies have been overcome.

As mentioned earlier (pp. 60, 62), the United States also flatly rejects other crucial articles of the Universal Declaration (including Article 14 on political asylum, and the articles on social and economic rights), while striking impressive poses as it leads the denunciation of Third World countries who challenge the sacred principle of universality of the Universal

Declaration. That charade too proceeds with much self-adulation, and scarcely a critical note.

After the massacre of some thirty Palestinians by an American-Jewish settler in Hebron on February 25, 1994, the UN passed Resolution 280, which called for measures to protect Palestinian civilians (March 18). Apart from the United States, all fourteen Security Council members voted for the Resolution without qualifications. The Clinton administration, which had delayed the resolution for three weeks by various objections, abstained from several paragraphs, including the one that says that the massacre "underlines the need to provide protection and security for the Palestinian people." The administration also again "reversed traditional U.S. policy," Donald Neff observes, "by abstaining on two paragraphs ... identifying occupied land as Palestinian and including East Jerusalem in the occupied territories." Previously, the United States had joined the world in referring to "all the Palestinian territories occupied by Israel since 1967, including Jerusalem" (Resolution 694, 1991, the most recent reiteration). Two changes are noteworthy: on Jerusalem, and on the status of the territories conquered by Israel in the June 1967 war. These are no longer to be considered "occupied Palestinian territory," U.S. ambassador Albright declared. They are merely "disputed territories" according to the new Clinton doctrine.[47]

The U.S. record in blocking diplomatic initiatives scarcely skims the surface of its disruption of international forums. As noted earlier, the United States is far in the lead in the past quarter century in vetoing Security Council resolutions on matters of peace and human rights, a large number of these cases having to do with Israel (others with South Africa, or UN condemnation of actions of the United States itself). To cite merely one case, in the winter session of 1989, while again blocking the UN call for a diplomatic settlement of the Middle East crisis, Washington also vetoed a Security Council resolution (14–1, no abstentions) calling on Israel to "lift its siege" in the occupied territories, return the vast amount of property confiscated from the village of Beit Sahour in retaliation for tax resistance, and admit a fact-finding mission for on-site monitoring (and, as noted, vetoed two resolutions condemning its own aggression in Panama, along with a General Assembly resolution and other international condemnations).

The United States naturally expects payment in return for its services, and receives it. Thus in the same winter 1989 UN session, the General Assembly addressed U.S. terrorism in Central America. The recent Tela Accords of the Central American presidents had called upon Washington to dismantle the terrorist forces attacking Nicaragua by December 5. The date was ignored in the United States; as serious people understand, the appeal of the presidents was invalid because Washington is self-authorized to violate these and all other agreements. But the United Nations took notice, passing yet another resolution vainly calling on the United States to obey the ruling of the World Court and cease its funding of the contras. The resolution passed by 91 to 2, Israel alone supporting its patron's open contempt for international law. The press maintained its familiar deafening silence. Still more striking perhaps, the press unanimously followed the party line that declared U.S. aid to its terrorist forces to be "humanitarian aid," completely suppressing the explicit determination of the World Court rejecting that contention.

Like Washington's torpedoing of the UN on the Middle East, its defiance of the UN, the Central American presidents, and the World Court in the 1989 session was part of a more general pattern, which tells us a good deal about the New World Order taking shape as the Berlin Wall fell. After the U.S. rejection of the World Court decision in 1986, Nicaragua, still pursuing the peaceful means that all states are obliged to follow under international (and U.S.) law, brought the matter to the Security Council, where the United States vetoed a resolution calling on all states to observe international law. Nicaragua then turned to the General Assembly, which passed a resolution 94 to 3 calling for compliance with the World Court ruling; two client states, Israel and El Salvador, joined the United States in opposition. A year later, the General Assembly again called for "full and immediate compliance" with the World Court decision. This time only Israel joined the United States in opposing adherence to international law. Virtually none of this was reported by the *New York Times*, the *Washington Post*, or the three TV networks. Subsequent World Court proceedings on the matter of reparations to Nicaragua for U.S. crimes also rarely reached threshold; the same was true of Washington's arm-twisting that compelled the Nicaraguan government to abandon the request for reparations to which it was entitled under the World Court judgment, and the still more shameful aftermath, already discussed.[48]

In brief, U.S. attitudes towards diplomacy and violence in the Middle East cannot sensibly be divorced from a more general context. Washington's deep commitment to the rule of force in world affairs may have become more glaringly obvious as the Soviet Union collapsed, but the guiding principles did not change. True, the doctrinal system faced new challenges as the familiar mechanisms of deceit disappeared along with the Soviet Union, but that challenge was met with impressive success, worldwide. It is not, of course, that the United States is unique in this contempt for international law and institutions. Rather, it is more powerful, and therefore more free to do what it wishes; and, given the general obedience of the educated classes in the West, to do so with confidence that its image will remain untarnished, indignation being focused on more suitable targets. It is difficult to imagine that the world would be a better place if some other country were to have had a comparable position of power.

6. Seeking Peace: The Interests of the Actors

To understand the subsequent course of events and the prospects, it is important to be clear about the essential concerns of the major actors; that is to say, the United States and its allies and clients.

The conventional picture of U.S. policy is that it is guided by "protecting national interests," which have three major components in the Middle East:

1) "the great fear of Soviet dominance in the region" and "military confrontation," 2) access to oil, and 3) "Israel's security" (William Quandt).[49]

Several clarifications are in order. Concerning (1), U.S. analysts recognized from the 1950s that the Soviet Union was a passive player in the region, entering largely in response to U.S. initiatives. Soviet dominance was never remotely in the cards. Military confrontation was doubtless a grave danger from the 1950s, but a danger often exacerbated by U.S. initiatives. As now conceded, Cold War pretexts having lost their utility, the "threats to our interests [in the Middle East] could not be laid at the Kremlin's door" (p. 70). "Security" and "Soviet dominance" are conventional masks for something quite different, here and elsewhere, as already discussed.

Turning to oil (2), the problem was not access but control, as the record makes clear back to World War I. David Painter's remarks summarizing his scholarly study are surely accurate:

> Divisions within the government masked overall agreement that some form of U.S. control over world oil reserves was necessary, . . . the idea that the United States had a preemptive right to the world's oil resources [having been] well entrenched by World War II. . . . Thus to maintain an international environment in which private companies could operate with security and profit, the U.S. government became actively involved in maintaining the stability of the Middle East, in containing economic nationalism, and in sanctioning and supporting private arrangements for controlling the world's oil. . . . Foreign oil policy was shaped not only by the structure of the oil industry but also by the "privileged position of business" in the United States. Corporate power influenced the outcome of specific decisions, and, more importantly, significantly shaped the definition of policy objectives . . . ; alternative policies for the production and consumption of oil clashed with well-organized political and economic interests, deep-seated ideological beliefs, and the "structural weight of an economic system in which most investment decisions are in private hands."[50]

Note that this is only a special case of the demand for "preponderance," the guiding doctrine "that America must maintain what is in essence a military protectorate in economically critical regions to ensure that America's vital trade and financial relations will not be disrupted by political upheaval," a doctrine borrowed from the "Leninist" critique of imperialism that the "American foreign policy elite" is now "more candid in articulating" after "the USSR's demise" (see pp. 30ff.).

With regard to (3), it is only necessary to take note of the power of rejectionist assumptions: "security" for the indigenous population of the former Palestine, or others in the region, is not a "main interest." More interesting, the assumptions are so firmly entrenched as to disappear into the background, beyond perception, simply framing thought and discourse. Reflexively, commentators describe "America's own greatest interest" in negotiations as "enhanced security for Israel and a durable regional peace." Rights and welfare of others are, once again, "an incident, not an end."[51]

The second of the major actors is Israel, only to a limited extent an independent state, having become, in part by choice, an appendage of U.S. power and wealth, its economy almost entirely dependent on capital inflows from abroad and its policies constrained generally by U.S. requirements. Keeping now just to the post-1967 period, Israeli policies fell within the range determined by the two major political groupings, Labor and Likud. Labor adhered to versions of the Allon Plan; Likud to extension of Israeli sovereignty over the territories in an unspecified form. Both parties have advocated some form of "autonomy" for the population of the occupied territories, but in the sense described by Israeli journalist Danny Rubinstein, one of the most acute observers of the occupation. As the current phase of the "peace process" was about to open in Madrid in October 1991, he wrote that the "autonomy" that the United States and Israel are proposing is "autonomy as in a POW camp, where the prisoners are 'autonomous' to cook their meals without interference and to organize cultural events." Palestinians are to be granted little more than what they have: control over local services. Rubinstein adds the important point that even advocates of Greater Israel had not called for literal annexation of the territories, which would require Israel to provide the "restricted services" available to Israel's second-class Arab citizens, at enormous cost. Far preferable is some variant of the system then prevailing: Israeli access to the cheap labor, controlled markets, resources, and selected regions for settlement, including desirable suburbs for Tel Aviv and Jerusalem, but no responsibilities for the bulk of the population, left to fare as they can under conditions that offer limited prospects.[52]

It has been assumed with some confidence that such privileges will remain in effect after "autonomy" is granted. There is no reason to expect voluntary abandonment of them unless the costs of occupation become too high, as happened in Lebanon a decade ago and more recently in the Gaza Strip. And pressures from the United States are unlikely as long as the American taxpayers who subsidize the practices are kept in the dark, as they effectively are.

The specific modalities of control have been highly beneficial to the Israeli economy in ways that have often been detailed, notably by critics of the practices within Israel. To mention only one example, recently exposed, Israel has extracted at least $1 billion from workers from the territories for social benefits that they never received (pensions, unemployment payments, and so on); the funds end up in the State treasury. In addition to "deduction of social insurance payments without parallel allocation of insurance rights," Hebrew University labor law specialist Frances Radai observes, Palestinian employees are punished by "punitive" income tax procedures. They are also kept at the status of day laborers, even if they work at the same job for twenty years, thus reducing standard workers' rights. On June 24, 1993, the Knesset passed by initial vote an Equalization Levy Law that legalized the past practices, and will, presumably, perpetuate them.[53]

The policy spectrum with regard to the occupied territories is illuminated in a study by Israel's Peace Now organization, which compares four different plans for the territories from 1968 to 1992, asking how many Palestinians would be within areas annexed by Israel if these plans were enacted in 1992: 1) the 1968 Allon Plan (Labor); 2) the 1976 Labor Party Settlement Plan (never officially adopted, though "it has informed practical decision-making and action"); 3) the Ariel Sharon Plan of 1992 (Likud), which created eleven isolated and discontinuous "cantons" for Palestinian autonomy; 4) the Defense Establishment Plan of 1992 (Labor), which deals only with the West Bank:

1) Allon Plan: 385,000 (91,000 in the West Bank and the rest in Gaza)
2) Labor Party Settlement Plan: 603,000 (310,000 in the West Bank)
3) Sharon Plan: 393,000 (378,000 in the West Bank)
4) Defense Establishment Plan: 204,000 in the West Bank, Gaza unspecified

To these figures must be added the 150,000 Palestinians of East Jerusalem, to be annexed under all plans, the Peace Now study notes. "The Labor Party plan of 1976 would annex the greatest number of Palestinians from the West Bank and Gaza," while the Sharon Plan "is the maximalist plan with regard to the West Bank," though ceding self-rule to more Gaza Palestinians than the Labor plans. The reasons for the increasing willingness—indeed, determination—to withdraw from central parts of Gaza have been entirely explicit. As Gaza has declined to utter catastrophe under the military occupation, the costs of direct Israeli rule became too high, particularly after the Intifada broke the pattern of submission. Israel has "practically lost the war" in Gaza, the leading military commentator Ze'ev Schiff wrote in April 1993: "What is going on today in the Gaza Strip is, in fact, a battle for the conditions of the future withdrawal"—partial withdrawal, already planned when he wrote, soon to be consummated.[54]

With regard to Jerusalem, whatever may have been envisioned in the past, current understanding is that it extends to "Greater Jerusalem," "a metropolis with much wider borders than the area annexed to Israel in 1967," Nadav Shragay points out in a discussion of the expanding concept of "Jerusalem"; the occasion for his article was the achievement of a Jewish majority in East Jerusalem (already overwhelming in West Jerusalem) as a result of building programs carried out largely by the Labor Party. The jurisdictional area of Jerusalem itself tripled after Israel's conquest and annexation of the city in 1967. But when Prime Minister Rabin speaks about Jerusalem, Shragay continues, "he means really Greater Jerusalem, a big metropolitan area created by Israel south, north and east of the present boundaries of jurisdiction," including settlements in surrounding areas "where construction work is going on at full speed, in fact, much more rapidly than under Shamir." Highways, sewage disposal, and water networks are designed to incorporate a region extending to Ramallah and Bethlehem, including many Arab villages. "In fact, a large metropolitan area of Greater Jerusalem, with borders drawn according to the decision of Israeli governments, exists already," inhabited by 750,000 people, half of them Arabs.[55]

There is no intention of relinquishing any of this system to Palestinian jurisdiction.

In 1993, another plan was reported, this one authored by Tel Aviv University orientalist Yitzhak Beilin, published in *Ha'aretz* with an accompanying map. The plan, not officially adopted but in fact being implemented by the Rabin–Peres Labor government, brings up to date the "cantonization" proposals for the territories that have taken various forms over the years. The basic idea is to leave areas of Palestinian "autonomy" separated from one another and isolated from the main highway system and the developed economy generally. The Beilin plan envisions three such enclaves in the West Bank; Palestinians would also remain in East Jerusalem, already annexed by Israel. The Palestinian enclaves include less than half the territory of the West Bank. The remainder, including almost all current Jewish settlements, would fall under Israeli sovereignty, presumably to be annexed at some future date. The cantons are to be administered by Jordan according to the Beilin plan, which, in fact, conforms rather closely to the official U.S.–Israeli plan that was the basis for the phase of Middle East diplomacy that led to the Oslo Agreement of August 1993.[56]

In January 1993 the Rabin government formally approved a plan of road building, development, and settlement that effectively implements such proposals, with the expectation that the U.S. government would continue to provide required funds and would allow the loan guarantees to be adapted to these purposes. The goal is to complete the de facto cantonization of Palestinian areas, and the integration within Israel of territories intended to be retained ("Greater Jerusalem" extending virtually to Jericho, the Jordan Valley, the more valuable parts of the Gaza Strip), before any agreement on Palestinian autonomy is reached through negotiations.[57]

The elaborate development programs of past years have laid the basis for further implementation of these plans, with or without "autonomy." In a detailed review, Anthony Coon, Head of the Center for Planning at the University of Strathclyde (Glasgow), reports estimates of Israeli and Palestinian analysts that about 60 percent of West Bank land had been taken by Israel by mid-1991, "with a substantial additional area subject to blanket restrictions on use and access falling short of outright expropriation." Much of this land, partially used for Jewish settlement, is termed "state land," "the implication being that the land is unused and that there are no adverse consequences for the Palestinians." But in fact, Coon notes, about 95 percent of land under the control of Jewish settlements was privately owned. The road system has been designed to serve the needs of the Jewish settlements and "to integrate the West Bank and Israel physically and economically," with Palestinian villages isolated and the population in disconnected enclaves, linked primarily via Israel and Israeli-annexed East Jerusalem.[58]

As the Peace Now analysis indicates, the policy spectrum has been narrow, and invariably rejectionist. Traditionally, a central component of the Labor movement (Ahdut Avodah, the largest sector of the Kibbutz movement) was as expansionist as Menachem Begin's Herut party (the core of Likud).[59] The political blocs have differed on West Bank Arab population concentrations, Labor being more concerned than Likud to exclude them from areas scheduled for Israeli takeover. The August 1993 Oslo Agreement falls within the policy spectrum just outlined.

Prior to the Clinton administration, Washington had favored Labor Party rejectionism, which is more rational than the Likud variety. The latter had no real provision for the population of the occupied territories except eventual "transfer" (expulsion), while the Labor plans (all versions of the original Allon Plan) would leave Arab population concentrations either stateless or under Jordanian administration, or perhaps in something called a "state" for cosmetic reasons but without even limited independence. Labor's style has also been better attuned to the norms of Western hypocrisy. The United States has much preferred Labor's technique of quietly "building facts" that will determine the eventual outcome to Likud's brazen and often absurd building programs, sometimes implemented in ways that were deliberately insulting to the superpower patron.

Tactical disagreements occasionally led to conflict, including the Bush–Shamir conflict of late 1991 over loan guarantees, temporarily withheld. But the conflict was over timing and modalities, not principle. It was resolved with Israel's acceptance of U.S. preferences; Labor's electoral victory a few months later was in no small measure a reflection of Washington's clearly expressed demands. Along with the traditional huge subsidies, the $10 billion loan guarantees, theoretically intended for settlement of Russian immigrants, are being used for infrastructure and business investment, it is frankly conceded, contributing to Israel's record growth for 1992–93. Israel's finance minister Avraham Schohat observed that the government "had been considerably helped, especially in its expanded infrastructure programme, by the $10bn U.S. loan guarantees," which drew investment capital.[60] And while Jewish settlement continued to flourish and expand, the Palestinian inhabitants of the occupied territories sank more deeply into misery and despair, the decline sharply accelerated by Rabin's closure of the territories in March 1993, which threatened even survival in a region that had been denied any possibility of independent development under the military occupation. The "closure" exempts Jewish settlers in the territories, and was rarely discussed in the United States, being in accord with Washington's long-term plans to assist Israel's programs of quiet expansion and integration of the territories.

It should be emphasized that it is misleading to call these "Israeli policies." Though formed and implemented by Israeli authorities, they are, in effect, U.S. policies, given the extraordinary relations of dependency.

Other major U.S. allies include the local managers of oil wealth. The tacit alliance between this "Arab Facade" and the regional gendarmes that help protect it from nationalist currents is now coming closer to the surface, even receiving some media notice. In the *New York Times*, Thomas Friedman reports Saudi preference for Israel over the PLO or Jordan's Hussein "for controlling the progressive, potentially radical Palestinians," Israel being "a more efficient policeman."[61] That seems a fair assessment. These preferences are likely to remain in force as the "more efficient policeman" supervises Palestinian surrogates under the Oslo Agreement.

Other regional actors are for the most part under control; their interests are secondary, with only indirect impact on U.S. policy as long as "stability" is maintained, however brutally. The human rights record compiled by Saddam Hussein was never a matter of much concern in Washington or London, nor that of Saudi Arabia, Kuwait, Egypt, Turkey, Pakistan, or others. Syria's Hafez al-Assad was readily absorbed into the American system when that proved useful for regional control, despite extreme human rights violations, and was tacitly authorized to extend control over Lebanon, just as he had been supported by the United States (and Israel) in 1976 when his targets in Lebanon were Palestinians and the national movement. As for democracy in the Arab world, that has always been regarded as disagreeable or intolerable, for reasons already discussed, though a formal electoral facade would be acceptable as long as it conforms to the required "top-down forms of democratic change" that leave U.S. clients in power. With secular nationalism in utter disarray, having largely failed or been destroyed, the current threats are seen to be Islamic fundamentalism (of the wrong variety; not, say, that of Saudi Arabia) and the "rogue states": Iraq, Iran, Libya, and the Sudan. The latter are not under control, therefore enemies on standard principles. The fundamentalist wave is perceived as an unacceptable form of "ultranationalism," appealing to popular forces and perhaps responding to their interests in some manner, hence analogous to secular nationalism, capitalist democracy with an independent flair, democratic socialism, liberation theology, etc.: all enemies, irrespective of their internal features, for reasons already discussed.

7. Seeking Peace: The Recent Phase

Returning to Middle East diplomacy in the post-1967 period, along with UN initiatives, those of the Arab states, the PLO, the USSR, and the European allies were regularly rebuffed. These initiatives shared two crucial features that were unacceptable to Washington. First, they made at least some gesture towards Palestinian national rights; second, they called for meaningful international participation in a settlement. The reason for U.S. rejection of such proposals has already been discussed. The Palestinians perform no services for the United States, indeed are an irritant in that their plight stirs up Arab nationalist sentiments; they therefore lack rights. And the United States is unwilling to accept outside interference in a region effectively drawn under the Monroe Doctrine, much as Kissinger had explained (see pp. 212–13).

By 1988 it was becoming difficult for the U.S. government and the media to conceal PLO and other Arab initiatives for a political settlement. By December, the U.S. government had become something of an international laughing-stock with its increasingly desperate efforts to deny the obvious.

Washington grudgingly agreed to "declare victory," claiming that at last the PLO had been compelled to utter George Shultz's "magic words." The purpose of the exercise, Shultz explained to Reagan, was to ensure maximum humiliation. In his much acclaimed apologia, *Turmoil and Triumph*, Shultz reports that he told Reagan in December 1988 that Arafat was saying in one place "'Unc, unc, unc,' and in another he was saying, 'cle, cle, cle,' but nowhere will he yet bring himself to say 'Uncle,'" in the style expected of the lesser breeds. Similarly Shultz required that the PLO not only condemn terrorism but "renounce" it, thus conceding that it had engaged in terrorism— though at a level barely detectable in comparison to the record compiled by Shultz and his predecessors, another unmentionable fact. Again, the purpose was to grind a weak and defenseless adversary under foot, something that commonly gives great pleasure to the powerful, and earns them much respect. PLO calls for renunciation of violence "on a mutual basis" have always been dismissed out of hand, as ridiculous.[62]

It is, incidentally, next to inconceivable that U.S. news reporting or commentary might take note of the major UN resolution on terrorism, which states "that nothing in the present resolution could in any way prejudice the right to self-determination, freedom and independence, as derived from the Charter of the United Nations, of peoples forcibly deprived of that right . . . , particularly peoples under colonial and racist regimes and foreign occupation or other forms of colonial domination, nor . . . the right of these peoples to struggle to this end and to seek and receive support [in accordance with the Charter and other principles of international law]." The resolution passed 153–2, U.S. and Israel opposed, Honduras alone abstaining. It is therefore vetoed, and banned from history.[63]

Naturally, Washington denies any right to resist the terror and oppression imposed by its clients. Since Washington's stand is taken to be obviously valid by U.S. commentators, indeed axiomatic, there is no need to report the facts, or what they imply about the occupied territories or southern Lebanon, which is obvious enough. On these matters, silence has been total, apart from margins of the usual margins, and the most elementary conclusions would by now be virtually unintelligible to a U.S. (indeed, Western) audience.

It is only fair to note, in this connection, that Israeli practice is far more honest. After four hundred Hamas activists were deported in December 1992, a lead article in the Israeli press observed that "we cannot accuse [Hamas] of practicing random terror which hits innocent women and children, because they don't"; "we should pay heed to the fact that . . . all Hamas guerrilla operations prior to the expulsion [were] targeted at soldiers." The same point was made with regard to Hezbollah by Uzi Mahanaimi, a respected hawkish commentator on Intelligence and Arab Affairs. Commenting on Israel's attack on Lebanon in July 1993, he asserted that "Hezbollah is not a terror organization," since it avoids striking civilians except in retaliation for Israeli attacks on Lebanese civilians. Furthermore, "Hezbollah differentiates between the Israeli conquest of Southern Lebanon and the existence of the State of Israel," taking its task to be only that of reversing the conquest, that is, legitimate resistance against an army occupying foreign territory in violation of Security Council orders. Other commentators ridicule the U.S. State Department, "which knows no better than to give Hezbollah greater prestige by declaring it 'the most conspicuous terror organization in the world.'" American commentary, in contrast, keeps strictly to State Department doctrine.[64]

Mahanaimi's analysis, surely correct, at once raises the question of why Israel has insisted on occupying southern Lebanon. Not for security reasons, as both the history and his accurate observations make clear. A widespread suspicion is that this has to do, once again, with long-term plans for control over water resources of the region, much as in the case of the "little secret" about Labor Party settlement programs from the 1970s revealed by Haim Gvirtzman. But in the absence of any closer inquiry, the questions remain open.

Returning to the antics of December 1988, the record shows clearly that the gap between the U.S. and PLO positions remained about as before on every major issue. But the farce proceeded smoothly in the public arena. Having declared victory, the United States could then impose its own interpretation of what had happened and proceed on course, without fear of contradiction.

As a reward for saying "uncle" in properly humble tones, the PLO was offered the right to take part in a "dialogue" with the U.S. ambassador in Tunis. Publishing leaked protocols of the first meeting, the *Jerusalem Post* could hardly contain its pleasure over the fact that "the American representative adopted the Israeli positions." Ambassador Robert Pelletreau stated two crucial conditions that the PLO must accept: it must abandon the idea of an international conference, and call off the "riots" in the occupied territories (the Intifada), "which we view as terrorist acts against Israel." In short, the PLO should ensure that the former status quo is restored, so that Israel's repression and expansion in the territories with firm U.S. support could again proceed unhindered. The ban on an international conference follows from the fact that the world is out of step, so that participation of outside parties beyond the United States and its clients would lead to unacceptable pressure for a nonrejectionist political settlement. Britain might be allowed, later Russia, but no voice that might prove too independent. The characterization of the Intifada as "terrorism" (for example, tax resistance in Beit Sahour, effectively declared illegitimate by the United States at the Security Council a year later) follows from the U.S.–Israeli rejection of the otherwise unanimous international consensus on the right of resistance to military occupation, already discussed. The "sheer accumulation of endless humiliations and casually committed brutalities" that close Israeli observers regard as the "crucial factor" eliciting resistance (p. 135) has been removed from the record along with the international consensus on "terror."

A few weeks later, in February 1989, Rabin had a meeting with five Peace Now leaders in which he expressed his satisfaction with the U.S.–PLO dialogue. He described it as a "successful operation," journalist Nahum Barnea reported, involving only "low-level discussions" that avoid any serious issue. The Americans are "now satisfied, and do not seek any [political] solution, and they will grant us a year, at least a year" to resolve the situation in our own way. This way is force. "The inhabitants of the territories are subject to harsh military and economic pressure," Rabin explained. "In the end, they will be broken," and will accept Israel's terms.[65]

Endorsing the essentials of this view, a high-level U.S. official urged Israel to put an end to its public objections to the dialogue, which "only add significance" to it, thus interfering with its intended goal: to displace attention from the forceful repression of the Intifada. Bush administration proposals in early March, offering "suggestions" to Israel and the PLO, underscored the point. Israel was urged to limit the repressive measures instituted to suppress the Intifada; and the PLO to terminate the "violent demonstrations" and the distribution of "inflammatory leaflets." The proposal, then, is that the PLO cooperate with Israel in establishing a somewhat harsher—but not *too* harsh—version of the former status quo.[66]

The tactics adopted in December 1988 worked like a charm. News coverage of the occupied territories declined further, thus granting Israel the opportunity to resort to still harsher measures so that "they will be broken"— as eventually, they were; there is a limit to what flesh and blood can endure, when any hope of help from the outside is gone. Attention was focused on the U.S.-managed "peace process," not the repression that was intensifying with U.S. backing. Nonviolent resistance was finally displaced by violence, much to the relief of U.S. and Israeli authorities, who have always been particularly concerned about the threat of moderation, as Israeli commentators have long recognized.

The violence of the Israeli reaction to the Intifada received some general notice, but neither these reports, nor the occasional accounts in earlier years when atrocities passed beyond the norm, give an accurate picture of the "sheer accumulation of endless humiliations and casually committed brutalities" that finally led to the uprising.[67] More illuminating are the innumerable cases considered too insignificant to report, for example, an event in Gaza a few weeks before the Intifada broke out there. A Palestinian girl, Intissar al-Atar, was shot and killed in a schoolyard by a resident of a nearby Jewish settlement. The murderer, Shimon Yifrah, was arrested a month later and released on bail because the courts determined that "the offense is not severe enough" to warrant detention. In September 1989 he was acquitted of all charges except causing death by negligence. The judge concluded that he only intended to shock the girl by firing his gun at her in a schoolyard, not to kill her, so "this is not a case of a criminal person who has to be punished, deterred, and taught a lesson by imprisoning him." Yifrah was given a seven-month suspended sentence, while settlers in the courtroom broke out in song and dance.

Though below the threshold of attention in the United States, these events left some memories among Israelis. As settler violence against Arabs mounted in the months after the Oslo Agreement along with the "demand that the Israeli-Jewish public, and especially the government, should understand the religious settlers in these hard times they are going through," Olek Netzer suggested another look at a photograph of the settlers "who danced in a circle of joy with Uzi [rifles] on their shoulders" after Yifrah's release, and who now "fear that they will no longer be able to kill people, especially children, and be immune from punishment." Such cases and the reaction to them in the United States provide a good deal more understanding than the occasional massacre that is too violent to ignore. They also provide insight into the values that inspire U.S. leaders to reject the right of resistance and declare it to be terrorism against U.S. clients, standing alone against the world.[68]

While Rabin's "harsh military and economic pressure" was having the intended effects on the subject population, Washington supervised a version of the "peace process" that would satisfy the two basic requirements: no meaningful outside interference, and no Palestinian rights. On May 14, 1989, Israel's coalition Labor–Likud (Peres–Shamir) government adopted a detailed "peace plan," with three basic principles:

1) There can be no "additional Palestinian state in the Gaza district and in the area between Israel and Jordan" (Jordan already being a "Palestinian state");
2) "There will be no change in the status of Judea, Samaria and Gaza other than in accordance with the basic guidelines of the [Israeli] Government," which reject an "additional Palestinian state";
3) "Israel will not conduct negotiations with the PLO," though it may agree to speak to certain Palestinians other than their chosen political representatives.

On these conditions, "free elections" were to be held under Israeli military control, with much of the Palestinian leadership in prison without charge or expelled.[69]

The United States endorsed the Israeli proposal, while keeping its essential content under wraps. There appears to have been no official reference to the May 14 plan, nor any report in the press, though it was the operative policy statement, and this was understood in Washington, where the May initiative was lauded for its "great promise and potential."[70] Secretary of State James Baker announced in October that "our goal all along has been to try to assist in the implementation of the Shamir initiative. There is no other proposal or initiative that we are working with." A different "Shamir initiative" had been proposed in April, then superseded by the May 14 Shamir–Peres Election Plan, which was the only "proposal or initiative" that Israel had presented officially, and was therefore the only "Shamir initiative" that Baker or anyone else was working with.

In December 1989, the Department of State released the five-point Baker Plan, which stipulated that Israel would attend a "dialogue" in Cairo with Egypt and Palestinians acceptable to the United States and Israel. These Palestinians would be permitted to discuss implementation of the Israeli proposals, but nothing else: "The Palestinians will come to the dialogue prepared to discuss elections and the negotiating process in accordance with Israel's initiative and would be free to raise issues that related to their opinions on how to make elections and the negotiating process succeed."[71]

In short, the Palestinian delegation would be permitted to express opinions on the technical modalities of Israel's proposal to bar any meaningful form of Palestinian self-determination—and even this right was accorded only to Palestinians who convince Israel and its patron that they are free from any taint of association with the PLO. The purpose of the latter condition was again little more than humiliation. It has been understood on all sides that these associations exist, and that the PLO was directing the negotiating process.

The Bush–Baker plan, then, was to have the Intifada crushed by force while attention was diverted to a "peace process" that bars Palestinian rights. While pursuing this two-part program to deal with the Israel–Palestinian problem, the Bush–Baker team pressed forward with their policies in the Gulf, extending still further their support for Saddam Hussein, quite oblivious to his appalling record of atrocities. In October 1989, as the Baker Plan was being given its final form, the White House intervened in a highly secret meeting to ensure that Iraq would receive another $1 billion in loan guarantees, overcoming Treasury and Commerce department objections that Iraq was not creditworthy. The reason, the State Department explained, was that Iraq was "very important to U.S. interests in the Middle East"; it was "influential in the peace process" and was "a key to maintaining stability in the region, offering great trade opportunities for US companies." A few weeks later, as U.S. invasion forces were bombarding slums in Panama, the White House announced plans to lift a ban on loans to Saddam, implemented shortly after—to achieve the "goal of increasing U.S. exports and put us in a better position to deal with Iraq regarding its human rights record . . . ," the State Department explained with a straight face.[72]

Once again, to understand the functioning of American democracy it is worth noting that virtually nothing that has just been reviewed concerning the Bush–Baker programs reached the public, apart from the dissident margins, where a record of the ongoing events was available to a minuscule fraction of the population.

Bush administration aid to Saddam Hussein continued until the day of his invasion of Kuwait in August 1990. At that point, policy shifted in the manner already discussed, as the administration seized the opportunity to establish even more firmly U.S. control of the oil-producing regions by a show of force.

The aftermath of the war provided both a need and an opportunity to revitalize the "peace process." The need arose from the sordid spectacle in the Gulf: huge destruction and casualties, the human rights catastrophe escalating under the effect of sanctions; the Gulf tyrannies safeguarded from democratic pressures; Saddam Hussein firmly in power, having demolished popular rebellions with tacit U.S. support. All in all, hardly a scene that could be left in public memory, particularly after the frenzy of jingoist hysteria and awe for the Grand Leader that had been whipped up by the doctrinal institutions.

The opportunity arose from the international context. Europe had at last fully conceded the Middle East to the United States; Europeans would henceforth refrain from independent initiatives, limiting themselves to implementation of U.S. rejectionist doctrine, as Norway indeed did in 1993. The Soviet Union was gone, its remnants now loyal clients of Washington. The UN had become virtually a U.S. agency. Whatever space the superpower conflict offered for independent nonalignment was gone, and the catastrophe of capitalism that swept the traditional colonial domains of the West in the 1980s left the Third World mired in general despair, disciplined by forces of the Western-managed "market." With Arab nationalism dealt yet another crushing blow by Saddam's aggression and terror and PLO tactics of more than the usual ineptitude, the Arab rulers had less need than before to respond to popular pressures with pro-Palestinian gestures. The United States was therefore in a good position to advance its rejectionist program without interference, moving towards the solution outlined by James Baker well before the Gulf crisis while satisfying the basic conditions stressed by Henry Kissinger years earlier, now modified by changed conditions. Europe, having abandoned any independent role, was less of a threat. Russia could now be welcomed rather than excluded, being powerless and obedient. The PLO approached the same status, for similar reasons, by mid-1993.

The "peace process" was renewed with great fanfare at Madrid in the fall of 1991. The "remarkable tableau" in Madrid revealed "that a very great deal had changed," *Times* diplomatic correspondent R.W. Apple observed, as "George Bush and the United States today plucked the fruits of victory in the Persian Gulf war." The reason why Bush could now "dream such great dreams" about Middle East peace, Apple explained, is that his "vision of the future" can be implemented with no fear that "regional tensions" might lead to superpower confrontation, and "no longer must the United States contend with countries whose cantankerousness was reinforced by Moscow's interest in continuing unrest"—the standard reference to Soviet adherence to the international consensus that the United States rejects, in splendid isolation.[73]

U.S. diplomats naturally agreed. As the Madrid negotiations opened, Alfred Leroy Atherton, in charge of Near East affairs in the State Department under Ford and Carter and a participant in the Camp David negotiations, observed that "no significant Arab–Israeli agreement, at least since 1967, has been reached without an active U.S. role, and this need still exists." Now, he continued, "the U.S. task will surely be easier in the absence of a Soviet spoiling role." That an active U.S. role has been essential is absolutely correct. Just as in the affairs of the Caribbean, nothing else is permitted by the reigning superpower; that, after all, is the basic meaning of the Monroe Doctrine, realized for Latin America in 1945 and extended to the Middle East. It is also true that the former Soviet Union had played a "spoiling role," joining the rest of the world (including Europe) in objecting to U.S. rejectionist designs.[74]

Analysts found "great inspiration" in Bush's statement that "the time has come to put an end to the Arab–Israeli conflict," words "spoken with commitment by an American president at the height of his powers" and forming part of his "broad vision of Middle East peace-building" (Helena Cobban). Even critics were impressed. Anthony Lewis wrote that the president is "at the height of his powers" and "has made very clear that he wants to breathe light into that hypothetical creature, the Middle East peace process." The reasons why the creature remained hypothetical are unarticulated, unthinkable. Palestinian Middle East scholar Walid Khalidi, an adviser to the Jordanian–Palestinian delegation, hailed "the personal commitment of the president of the US . . . to a just and comprehensive settlement." In the occupied territories, well-informed Palestinians reported, there were great expectations and hope.[75]

Something else that "had changed," the press exulted, was "the birth of a new pragmatism among the Palestinians," now raised "another important notch" through Baker's benign influence at Madrid (Thomas Friedman). Until Madrid, Friedman continued, "both sides have hidden behind [the] argument . . . that there is no one on the other side with whom to negotiate"— the official version of the fact that the PLO called on Israel to negotiate but the United States and Israel refused. The Palestinian delegation at Madrid called "explicitly for a two-state solution," Friedman wrote admiringly—so different from the despised PLO, which supported (or perhaps "prepared") the Security Council resolution calling for a two-state solution fifteen years earlier. The great achievement of Madrid was "the Palestinian self-adjustment to the real world," Palestinian acceptance of "a period of autonomy under continued Israeli domination," during which Israel can build the facts of its permanent domination with U.S. aid, as it proceeded to do after Madrid. This willingness to follow U.S. orders—the real world—has "tossed the negative stereotypes out the window," Times journalist Clyde Haberman observed approvingly. With their "new pragmatism," Palestinians are at last willing "to talk to Israel, to set aside all-or-nothing demands, to accept half a loaf in the form of interim self-rule under Israeli domination."[76]

The Madrid conference was organized under unilateral U.S. leadership, an obsequious Russian partner offering a fig-leaf of internationalism. The Palestinian delegation, after passing U.S.–Israeli tests of legitimacy, was informed by James Baker that the negotiations would be based solely on UN 242, which offers nothing to the Palestinians: "Anything else, the president noted, would fail the twin tests of fairness and security." The modifications in the international consensus through the 1970s, as reflected in the vetoed Security Council resolutions and other blocked initiatives, were completely off the agenda, though Baker did relax the demand in his December 1989 five-point plan that Palestinians must keep strictly to the technical details of Israel's program for integration of the territories.[77]

As was reasonably clear from the outset, the goal of the latest phase of the "peace process" has been to establish a peace settlement among the states of the region, with Palestinian national rights excluded. The best outcome from Washington's point of view would be a settlement that entrenches the traditional strategic conception and gives it a public form, raising tacit understandings to a formal treaty. If some version of local autonomy can remove the Palestinian issue, well and good. Meanwhile security arrangements among Israel, Turkey, Egypt, and the United States can be extended, perhaps bringing others in if they accept the client role. There need be no further concern over independent European or Third World initiatives, or Soviet support for attempts within the region to interfere with such designs.

While the negotiations were proceeding without issue, Israel stepped up the harsh repression in the territories, following the thinking outlined by then–Defense Minister Yitzhak Rabin in February 1989. These U.S.–Israeli measures achieved much success, extended with Rabin's "closure" of the territories, which administered a crushing blow to the staggering Palestinian economy and also took an important step towards the intended "cantonization" by effectively barring West Bank Palestinians from their institutions (hospitals, etc.) in East Jerusalem, and preventing travel from the northern to the southern part of the West Bank, since the main road connections pass through East Jerusalem.

The current situation is assessed—plausibly, in my opinion—by General (res.) Shlomo Gazit, formerly head of Israeli military intelligence, a senior official of the military administration of the occupied territories, and a leading participant in the secret meetings that developed the security arrangements for implementing the Oslo Agreement. With the collapse of the Soviet Union, he wrote,

> Israel's main task has not changed at all, and it remains of crucial importance. Its location at the center of the Arab Muslim Middle East predestines Israel to be a devoted guardian of stability in all the countries surrounding it. Its [role] is to protect the existing regimes: to prevent or halt the processes of radicalization and to block the expansion of fundamentalist religious zealotry[78]

—or any other form of "radical nationalism" that comes along. In this task it is to be joined by U.S. allies, perhaps more openly than in the past. These are basically the conclusions that had been articulated by American planners thirty-five years earlier. What has changed is that they no longer have to contend with a possible "spoiling role" of outsiders who might lend support to indigenous efforts to bring about changes unwelcome to the rulers.

Subsequent shifts in U.S. policy add credibility to Gazit's assessment. Israeli analysts quickly recognized the Clinton administration to be even more extreme in rejection of Palestinian rights than the government of Israel itself. Political correspondent Amnon Barzilai observed that the proposals presented by the new Clinton administration to Israel and the Palestinians broke new ground in rejectionism: for the first time, they stipulated that "all the options will be left open," including even "the demand for full annexation of the territories" under "Israeli sovereignty." In this respect, he notes, Clinton went well beyond the governing Labor Party, "which never demanded that all the options be kept open," only "territorial compromise." The U.S. initiative will therefore "strengthen the suspicion among the Palestinians that there is reason to fear an Israeli conspiracy with American support," he writes; though in reality, neither the United States nor the Israeli political blocs would consider annexation of the territories, for reasons already mentioned.[79]

Reporting from Washington, Ron Ben-Yishai developed the point further. He described the Clinton administration's new Middle East policy as "revolutionary," "a completely different diplomatic stance from those of preceding Administrations," and one that is "completely positive" from Israel's point of view. Senior U.S. government officials have made it clear that Arabs "will not be able to obtain concessions from Israel through American pressure, diplomatic or economic." Similarly, Ben-Yishai continued, security relations were enhanced, including arrangements kept secret. "Never have we had such good relations with an American administration," a senior Israeli official observed. The disappearance of the Soviet Union, eliminating any alternative options for the Arab states, is one of several factors leading American policy in this direction, according to Washington thinking. Clinton insiders "see the [increased] support for Israel as part of a much broader global conception that includes a new view of the Middle East in the era after the Cold War and the Gulf war," now that U.S. domination of the region is more firmly established than before. The new approach to "Israel and its neighbors," "the western part of the region," is complemented by the new approach to "the eastern part": the policy of "dual containment" aimed at both Iraq and Iran, formerly played one against the other. "It is important to stress that there is no political leader in Israel, and also not in Riyadh or Kuwait, who would take any exception to this global conception."[80]

The same may well be true of Cairo and other capitals, which have their own reasons to pin the blame on malign outsiders (Iran, Sudan, and others) for violence and disruption that result in large measure from their own social and economic policies.

Ben-Yishai pointed out the significance of Clinton's appointments for the Middle East, notably his choice as chief Middle East adviser and "one of the central figures of the peace team, Martin Indyk, until [January 1993] the head of the Washington Institute for Near East Policy." Before Clinton's inauguration, "Indyk and the deputy director of the Institute, Robert Satloff, had presented to Clinton's transition team a policy memorandum on a new Middle East policy," now being implemented under Indyk's direction. Indyk, an Australian who was granted citizenship a few days before his appointment, was an employee of the Israeli lobby (AIPAC), largely representing the hawkish right-wing of the policy spectrum. Indyk left AIPAC to found the Institute in order to counter the influence of Washington think tanks that the lobby considered pro-Arab and anti-Israel, some even having recommended that the United States consider joining the international consensus on a peaceful diplomatic settlement.[81] The Institute has played an interesting role in American cultural life. It enables reporters to present U.S.–Israeli propaganda while preserving their fabled objectivity, "merely reporting the facts" while citing some "expert" provided by the Institute to provide the opinions they wish to propagate.

Clinton policies conformed to the picture presented by Israeli analysts. One of the administration's first tasks was to deal with the embarrassment caused by Israel's deportation of four hundred Palestinians in December 1992. The deportees were accused of responsibility for "terrorist acts," namely attacks against the Israeli occupying army that cannot be termed "terrorist," as recognized in the Israeli press (see p. 228). Danny Rubinstein observed that about half the alleged "Hamas activists" worked in Islamic religious institutions, including preachers, teachers, "a large number of young people who serve as missionaries for increasing religious practice," and professionals who "helped establish the Islamic movement's network of educational and welfare institutions which includes clinics, kindergartens, kitchens for the needy, and organizations providing aid to prisoners' families, invalids, and orphans." "Members of the military wing of Hamas and the Islamic Jihad organization are not among those deported," he added. The analysis was confirmed in a study by Middle East Watch, which found that half the deportees were imams, religious scholars, or *shari'a* (Islamic law) judges, including the head of the Palestine Religious Scholars Association, an imam at al-Aqsa Mosque, while others are university professors, doctors (sixteen on the UNRWA staff), school teachers, businessmen, students, and manual workers. *Four* had been convicted by courts, eight others had been in administrative detention (jailing without charge or trial). A "significant proportion of the deportees had never been convicted of offenses," something of an understatement. Middle East Watch described conditions in the "snake-pit" where they had been deposited in Lebanon as disgraceful and harmful, and once again called upon Israel to terminate this "grave breach of the Fourth Geneva Convention."

Israeli intelligence agreed with these assessments. *Ha'aretz* quoted a "senior government official" who said that the intelligence services (Shabak) provided Prime Minister Yitzhak Rabin with *six names* of Hamas activists, adding one more when they were asked "to increase the number." Israeli intelligence was "astonished" to learn that more than four hundred had been expelled—without any relevant intelligence information.[82]

The American press had no use for any of this, preferring the version presented in the *New York Times* by Israeli Arabist Ehud Yaari, an associate of Indyk's Washington Institute. According to Yaari, who ignores the intelligence reports and other Israeli sources, "About 300 of the 413 deportees constituted Hamas's command network in the West Bank and Gaza Strip."

His account makes some sense on the assumptions expressed by Cabinet Legal Advisor Yosef Harish, arguing for the expulsion before Israel's High Court: asked how many residents of the occupied territories are members of terrorist organizations, he responded "I think all of them."[83]

The Security Council passed a resolution demanding that the deportees be returned forthwith. Israel refused, stating that it would allow them to return as it chose. The Clinton administration then determined that Israel was honoring the Security Council resolution by flagrantly violating it, and the issue was declared closed, and promptly disappeared from press coverage, which returned to the "peace process." The Washington Institute's much-quoted expert Robert Satloff explained that Palestinians should be heartened by the administration's decision to back Israel's defiance of the UN: "It's to the Palestinians' negotiating advantage that the US and the Israelis have the relationship they have now."[84]

While not as revolutionary as Ben-Yishai indicates, the policy changes are interesting and instructive nonetheless. The traditional strategic conceptions and objectives are not being abandoned with the disappearance of the Soviet Union; rather, as General Gazit observed, they are being pursued more vigorously, the deterrent having disappeared and the Third World becoming even more defenseless for this and other reasons. The pattern is exactly what we have seen elsewhere in the world. It is radically inconsistent with decades of propaganda about the Cold War, but quite in accord with both planning and history—with the basic thinking that has undergirded policy, and the way events have unfolded.

8. Conquering History

The treatment of the diplomatic record in the doctrinal system is yet another triumph of propaganda. In this case, the usual subordination to state–private power was amplified by the affection that Israel won among American intellectuals, notably in the left–liberal spectrum, when it demonstrated its military prowess in 1967. This is an important matter that is much too little discussed, the facts being unattractive.[85] A much more useful image for propaganda purposes is that "supporters of Israel" are an embattled few, desperately trying to stem the assault on Israel by its armies of enemies in the press and intellectual community. The PLO was "the darling of many Western liberals," Thomas Friedman writes—meaning, presumably, that some Western liberals regarded them as at least semi-human. The fabrication is so extreme as to be comical, but it is functional for power, therefore quite admissible.[86]

A whole new vocabulary has been designed to disguise reality. Thus the term "peace process" does not refer to the process of seeking peace: rather, to whatever the United States happens to be doing, often blocking peace initiatives. The diplomatic record—including Sadat's "famous" offer of 1971 and Palestinian and other Arab proposals later, those advanced by Europe and the USSR, and the entire record at the United Nations since the

United States dismissed it in 1976—are therefore not part of the "peace process," indeed, not part of history. Failed U.S. initiatives qualify for entry; initiatives blocked by the United States do not. The doctrine, which extends to other regions as well, is convenient: by definition, the United States is always advancing the peace process, trying to bridge the gap between "extremists" on all sides.

The terms "moderate" and "extremist" obtain their meanings within this framework, moderates being those who conform to U.S. plans, extremists those who have their own ideas. The moderates can also be called "pragmatists," the extremists "radicals" or "hard-liners." The conventions are in fact quite general. In the present case, the moderates are those who accommodate to U.S. rejectionism. Thus we read that a Soviet draft presented to Secretary of State Cyrus Vance in 1977 was "remarkably balanced [for a Soviet document]. It did not include calls for a Palestinian state or participation by the PLO," and deviated from the U.S. stand only in "a reference to Palestinian rights, which went a step beyond the standard American reference to Palestinian interests." The U.S. stand does not "lack balance," indeed could not, by definition.[87]

Note that the Middle East is unusual in that, since 1967, the American intellectual community has been loyal to *two* states, not just the usual *one*. This sometimes leads to departures from the norm. Thus in October 1977, President Carter agreed to a Soviet–American statement calling for "termination of the state of war and establishment of normal peaceful relations" between Israel and its neighbors, as well as for internationally guaranteed borders and demilitarized zones, arousing strong criticism from the government of Israel. Instead of reflexively adopting Washington's position as the basis for discussion, the media highlighted the Israeli position, treating Carter in the manner of some official enemy. Israeli premises framed the issues, and Israeli sources generally dominated coverage and interpretation (Arab views scarcely entered the discussion). Under sharp media attack, the Carter administration backed down, and the "peace process" resumed its rejectionist course.[88]

The terminological conventions permit marvels of reportage. Thus, as the Baker Plan was taking form in late 1989, a *New York Times* correspondent in Israel noticed a difficulty lurking in the background: "with the exception of the United States, not one nation has endorsed the [Israeli peace] plan" that was the only one on the table, Baker made clear. A few days after the Baker Plan was announced, another *Times* report perceived some signs of improvement in world behavior. Under the headline "Soviets Trying to Become Team Player in Mideast," Alan Cowell wrote that "the Soviet Union has moved away from a policy of confrontation with the United States and now indicates that it prefers partnership with Washington in the diplomacy of the region." This "shift away from confrontation" brings the Soviet Union "closer to the mainstream of Mideast diplomacy." To translate from Newspeak: the Soviet Union may be moving towards U.S. rejectionism, thus joining the

United States off the spectrum of world opinion. This will make it a "team player"; in "the mainstream" because "the team," by definition, is the United States and "the mainstream" is the position occupied by "the team," however the world may be out of step. A person who has not internalized these conventions can scarcely be taken seriously; accordingly, such commentary, which abounds, does not even evoke an amused smile in cultivated circles.[89]

The term "rejectionism" is used, by now quite unthinkingly, in a strictly racist sense, referring to those who reject the right of national determination of Jews, not Palestinians. That usage is, indeed, a necessity: were the term used properly, it would be necessary to conclude that the United States leads the Rejection Front, joined by both Israeli political groupings and various elements in the Islamic world, mostly peripheral in recent years, and justly termed "extremist." The conclusion is quite unacceptable, and, fortunately, need not be drawn, thanks to the rigid norms of Political Correctness. The facts have been "vetoed" along with numerous peace initiatives that interfere with the "peace process."

A related notion is "mutual recognition" of Israel and Palestinians. As proposed over the years, it has referred to recognition by Palestinians of Israel's rights as stipulated in UN 242, and Israel's recognition of comparable rights of Palestinians to national self-determination in their own territory, from which Israel is expected to withdraw in accord with the international consensus (which the United States shared, pre-1971). Within the U.S. ideological system, "mutual recognition" was long dismissed as an option totally, with such force that Palestinian calls for "mutual recognition" have been banned from major media and history, as we see directly. As Israel and the United States came to the conclusion that the PLO leadership in Tunis might be more willing than local Palestinians to forfeit Palestinian rights, "mutual recognition" came to be a thinkable option, and we thus read of a dazzling breakthrough: steps towards "mutual recognition by Israel and the Palestine Liberation Organization."[90] But this is not the kind of "mutual recognition" that the PLO has been proposing for many years with overwhelming international support, all under a rigorous ban in the Free Press. Rather, in this breakthrough, the PLO is to "renounce terrorism" (once again crying "uncle") and formally recognize "Israel's right to exist," a right accorded to no other state in the international system, designed to ensure that Palestinians officially recognize not only the fact but also the justice of their displacement. In return Israel will "recognize" the PLO, but no Palestinian national rights. Recognizing the PLO means allowing it to administer local "autonomy" under Israeli supervision. That may or may not be a step forward for Palestinians, but plainly it constitutes no meaningful mutuality.

Other terms of art include "territorial compromise" and "land for peace," which have a nicer sound than "rejectionism," but mean exactly that. The terms refer to the form of rejectionism preferred by Washington, basically, some version of Israel's Allon Plan, modified to accommodate a form of "autonomy."

Also available is an array of terms that can be used to cancel deviant thoughts generally. Thus it is fine for the Joint Chiefs, the National Security Council, government intelligence analysts, congressional leaders, Israeli generals, and others to outline Washington's use of Israel as a counter to "radical Arab nationalism." But for a critic of U.S. policy to review such evidence and the policies that accord with it—even worse, to place all of this within the more general framework of policy planning and implementation worldwide—is to indulge in "conspiracy theory," "stale leftist rhetoric," "Marxist dogma," and other such old-fashioned nonsense. The terms in the arsenal are the intellectual equivalent of four-letter words, mere invective, lacking any substance, but enough to dismiss anything that might depart from respectable orthodoxy. The crucial doctrine that must be safeguarded is that, unlike other states past and present, the United States has no coherent policies apart from a generalized benevolence, and no domestic power structure that interferes with the democratic pluralism from which policy decisions flow as a reflection of popular will.

The exercise of doctrinal management on Middle East issues falls within the general project of disciplining the enemy within, discussed earlier, though with some special features. The achievements in imposing this regimen have been most impressive, as documented in detail elsewhere.[91] As the Newspaper of Record, the *New York Times* has had to be more careful than most to safeguard the preferred version of history. To cite a few additional (and typical) examples, one priority has been to preserve the image of the United States and Israel as moderates seeking peace, faced with the terror and unremitting rejectionism of their Arab adversaries, particularly the unspeakable Palestinians. Accordingly, public PLO support in 1976 for Israel's "sovereignty, territorial integrity and political independence" and its "right to live in peace within secure and recognized boundaries" is down the memory hole, even more deeply buried than Sadat's "famous milestone" of 1971. Similarly, when Yasser Arafat issued several calls for negotiations leading to mutual recognition in April–May 1984, the *Times* refused to print not only the facts but even letters referring to them. When its Jerusalem correspondent Thomas Friedman reviewed "Two Decades of Seeking Peace in the Middle East" a few months later, the major Arab (including PLO) initiatives of these two decades were excluded, and discussion was restricted to the official "peace process": various U.S. rejectionist proposals. Four days later, the *Times* editors explained that "the most important reality is that the Arabs will finally have to negotiate with Israel," but Yasser Arafat stands in the way "and still talks of an unattainable independent state" instead of adopting a "genuine approach to Israel" to "reinforce the healthy pragmatism of Israel's Prime Minister Peres" by agreeing to accept King Hussein as the spokesman "for West Bank Palestinians." Shortly after, in yet another review of the "peace process" under the heading "Are the Palestinians Ready to Seek Peace?" diplomatic correspondent Bernard Gwertzman asserted—again falsely—that the PLO has always rejected "any talk of negotiated peace with Israel." It was unnecessary for him to ask whether the United States is seeking peace, that being true by definition, since "genuine peace" is whatever it happens to be seeking—"pragmatically" and "moderately," also by definition.

The contributions that won *Times* Middle East correspondent Thomas Friedman his second Pulitzer prize for "balanced and informed coverage," and his promotion to chief diplomatic correspondent, are particularly noteworthy in this regard. To cite a last example, on December 10, 1986, Friedman reported from Jerusalem that Israel's Peace Now organization has "never been more distressed" because of "the absence of any Arab negotiating partner." A few months later (March 27, 1987), he quoted Shimon Peres as bewailing the lack of a "peace movement among the Arab people" such as "we have among the Jewish people"; the PLO cannot take part in negotiations "as long as it is remaining a shooting organization and refuses to negotiate." Recall that this is almost three years after Israel's rejection of Arafat's offer for negotiations leading to mutual recognition, eleven years after the PLO supported the Security Council resolution calling for a settlement based on UN 242 modified to include a Palestinian state alongside Israel, not to speak of the record through these years—all safely buried.

Six days before Friedman's December 10 article, a headline in the mass-circulation Israeli journal *Ma'ariv* read: "Arafat indicates to Israel that he is ready to enter into direct negotiations." The offer was made during the tenure of the "healthy pragmatist" Shimon Peres as prime minister. Peres's press advisor confirmed the report, commenting that "there is a principled objection to any contact with the PLO, which flows from the doctrine that the PLO cannot be a partner to negotiations." Yossi Beilin, who is close to Peres, observed that "the proposal . . . was dismissed because it appeared to be a tricky attempt to establish direct contacts when we are not prepared for any negotiations with any PLO factor." Yossi Ben-Aharon, head of the prime minister's office and Yitzhak Shamir's political adviser, went much further, stressing that "there is no place for any division in the Israeli camp between Likud and the Labor Alignment" on this matter. All agree that "the PLO cannot be a participant in discussions or in anything. . . . If there is any hope for arrangements that will solve this problem, then the prior condition must be to destroy the PLO from its roots in this region. Politically, psychologically, socially, economically, ideologically. It must not retain a shred of influence." He added that "no journalist may ask questions about the PLO or its influence. The idea that the PLO is a topic for discussion in the Israeli press—that is already improper. There must be a consensus here, and no debate, that the PLO may not be a factor with which Israel can develop any contact."

There was no hint of any of this in the mainstream U.S. media, though Friedman was alone in using the occasion to issue one of his periodic laments over the bitter fate of the only peace forces in the Middle East, which lack any Arab negotiating partner.

Given the success in shaping history for many years, it is not surprising that when Arafat finally accepted U.S.–Israeli terms in August 1993 (the Oslo

Agreement), the press should laud his sudden abandonment of his firm dogma that Israel must be destroyed, or smirk self-righteously about it. A typical example is a political cartoon in the liberal *Boston Globe* depicting a supine Arafat, a dove with an olive branch resting on his (very long) nose, saying "O.K., O.K. You win. I give up." The *New York Times* editors sympathized with Israel's reluctance "to trust the P.L.O., a group that had long epitomized Arab vows to sweep Israel and its Jewish inhabitants into the sea" and that has, until now, proclaimed "that 'armed struggle is the only way to liberate Palestine'"— always refusing to consider peaceful means, we are to understand, unlike Israel and the United States. But at last, the PLO may have "evolved into a more realistic organization," with which Israel might consider a settlement. In the *Times*'s major historical review, Thomas Friedman wrote that "For almost 100 years the Israeli–Palestinian conflict has proven insoluble because the two sides would not recognize the other as legitimate enemies. Israel dismissed the Palestinians as either terrorists or individuals, not a nation with legitimate claims on historic Palestine; the Palestinians dismissed the Israelis as either 'colonizers' or members of a religious community, not a nation with rights in the land of Israel." Now all has changed, thanks to the PLO's sudden willingness to consider a political settlement.

As Arafat and Rabin proceeded to Washington to ratify the Oslo Agreement, the lead story in the *Times* reported that a photograph of Arafat shaking hands with Rabin and Clinton would be a "dramatic image" that "will transform Mr. Arafat into a statesman and peacemaker," who has "finally brought prestige to an organization that Washington refused to deal with for years" (Elaine Sciolino); Rabin and Clinton are already "statesmen and peacemakers," since, unlike Arafat, they have not dedicated their every waking moment to destruction of the adversary, refusing to contemplate any compromise. The next day, her lead story opened: "After a lifetime of violent struggle for a Palestinian homeland, Yasir Arafat set foot on American soil today and expressed hope that an agreement with Israel would bring peace to the Middle East," a dramatic reversal for this man of pure violence. The journal's leading dove Anthony Lewis, boycotted by Jewish organizations for years as a defender of Palestinian rights, wrote that Palestinians "said no" in 1947, "as they had repeatedly rejected compromise before and have since," but now, for the first time, they are willing to "make peace possible."[92]

Their colleagues elsewhere sang the same song, without a false note. Once again, we see the great importance of maintaining a totalitarian-style intellectual culture, in accord with Hume's maxim—particularly in societies in which governments are the "most free and most popular," and public opinion can more easily make a difference.

9. The Berlin Wall Falls Again

From the early days of the Intifada, if not before, it was becoming clear that the PLO leadership was losing its popular support in the occupied territories. Local activists from the secular nationalist sectors, while still recognizing the PLO as the sole agent for negotiations, spoke with open contempt of its corruption, personal power plays, opportunism, and disregard for the interests and opinions of the people it claimed to represent. By all indications, the disaffection increased in the years that followed, while the fundamentalist opposition that Israel had initially nurtured gained popular support, feeding on this growing discontent and on the demoralization as the program of violent suppression that Rabin had outlined in February 1989 was implemented, with constant U.S. support at all levels: economic, diplomatic, and ideological.[93] With its popular support in decline and its status deteriorating in the Arab world, the PLO became more tolerable to U.S.–Israeli policymakers, particularly as the growing fundamentalist movement evoked memories of the resistance that had driven Israel out of much of Lebanon. Informal Israel–PLO contacts were increasingly reported, reaching their culmination with the agreements of summer 1993.

The growing crisis in the PLO was naturally observed with close attention by the Israeli press. In late August 1993, Danny Rubinstein reported that the PLO had reached "bankruptcy." Its crisis was in part financial, but "even more important" was the criticism of Arafat's methods, which had evoked "a large wave of protests" and threats of resignation. "All the dams had broken in internal Palestinian politics," he reported, as dozens of activists and community leaders in the territories and the Palestinian diaspora abandoned the principle of not "washing dirty laundry in public," and expressed sharp protests and denunciations of the PLO leadership. PLO officials described Arafat as personally responsible for the "deterioration" of the organization, and announced that they would call for a "National Palestinian Congress," even over his objections. On August 22, Faisal Husseini of the Palestinian negotiating team, close to Arafat's Fatah, called for a "government of national salvation that will prevent the general collapse of Palestinian institutions." The next day, the military leader of Fatah in Lebanon called upon Arafat to resign. Within the occupied territories, Palestinians described a new feeling among the leadership that in the light of Arafat's "difficult position," the time had come to move towards democratizing the PLO. In Arab East Jerusalem, Nadav Ha'etzni reported, "the evaluation was spreading that the days of the PLO, Fatah, and the leadership of Yasser Arafat are numbered." "The amusing fact is that the center of support for Arafat is passing to [Jewish] West Jerusalem," he added, noting that the "big question" for the impending negotiations in Washington is: "Is there anyone to talk to," with the PLO and Arafat disappearing from the scene?

"This is the critical moment," Israeli journalist Hami Shalev observed. "Just as the Gulf War compelled the Palestinians to come to the negotiating table"—as they had been requesting for years, while Israel refused—"so their current crisis is forcing them to agree to conditions that are exceptional from Israel's point of view."[94]

Israeli doves too followed the decline of the PLO with mounting interest. In mid-August 1993, Shmuel Toledano, a Labor specialist on Arab affairs and representative of the dovish left, described the split developing between the PLO in Tunis and the Palestinian negotiators, who "were not prepared to accept the PLO's orders to respond positively to the US proposal"—referring to the Clinton administration proposal that the Israeli press had described as even more antagonistic to Palestinian rights than those of the Israeli government itself, as we have seen. Toledano asked: "Is this not another good reason to prefer direct talks with the Tunis PLO," who seem ready virtually to surrender Palestinian rights in order to salvage some authority by gaining U.S.–Israeli recognition?

Toledano noted further that as far back as January 1991, the PLO had officially praised a U.S.-sponsored proposal that recognized that "there will be no collective return, that the refugees will be settled in the Palestinian state only, and that equal rules will apply when it comes to compensation for Jews who left the Arab states and for Palestinians, something which Israeli governments have said for decades," and which the world community had rejected because of the obvious asymmetries. No one denies that flight of Jewish refugees followed the flight or direct expulsion of Palestinians, and that it was enthusiastically welcomed and facilitated (indeed, stimulated) by the new Jewish state, which hoped to shift the demographic balance. Even if we put aside such crucial facts, a symmetrical response would call for implementing the right of all refugees to return to the place of their origin, and if this is refused, to receive compensation, a proposal that the United States and Israel would dismiss out of hand. But with the PLO capitulating on all fronts, this leading Israeli dove advised that the time had surely come to deal with it directly, before it had disintegrated, leaving behind only people who call for Palestinian rights.

Reporting at the same time from Amman, Lamis Andoni wrote a perceptive account of the collapse of the PLO, which is "facing the worst crisis since its inception" as "Palestinian groups—except for Fatah—and independents are distancing themselves from the PLO" and the "shrinking clique around Yasir Arafat." "Two top PLO executive committee members, Palestinian poet Mahmoud Darwish and Shafiq al-Hout, have resigned from the PLO executive committee," the Palestinian negotiators are offering their resignations, and even groups that remain inside are distancing themselves from Arafat. The leader of Fatah in Lebanon called on Arafat to resign, while opposition to him personally and to PLO corruption and autocracy are mounting in the territories. Along with "the rapid disintegration of the mainstream group and Arafat's loss of support within his own movement, ... the speedy disintegration of the PLO's institutions and the steady erosion of the Organisation's constituency could render any breakthrough at the peace talks meaningless." For such reasons, she observed, Arafat is advancing the Jericho–Gaza option, which he hopes "will assert the PLO's authority, especially amid signs that the Israeli government could go the extra ten miles by talking directly to the PLO," thus salvaging for it the legitimacy it is losing internally.

"At no point in the PLO's history has opposition to the leadership, and to Arafat himself, been as strong," Andoni observed, "while for the first time there is a growing feeling that safeguarding Palestinian national rights no longer hinges on defending the PLO's role. Many believe that it is the leadership's policies that are destroying Palestinian institutions and jeopardising Palestinian national rights."

Israeli authorities were surely aware of these developments. Under these conditions, they came to appreciate that it made good sense to deal with those who are "destroying Palestinian institutions and jeopardising Palestinian national rights" before the population turns elsewhere to realize its national goals.

The August 1993 articles of Toledano and Andoni are entitled, respectively, "Talking to the PLO" and "Arafat and the PLO in crisis." The two concepts are obviously related, as was to become clear a few weeks later when the secret talks were announced. Unknown to the authors, the government of Israel had seen the light, and was "talking to the PLO" to help Arafat reestablish his authority and preside over the anticipated abandonment of Palestinian national rights.[95]

The tragicomedy spun by the shapers of history took new forms as these developments proceeded. Recall that as the "peace process" was launched at Madrid in October 1991, the Palestinian negotiators had received high marks for their "pragmatism" and "realism," as government and media perceived signs that they were more willing to accommodate to U.S.–Israeli demands than the outrageous PLO. But by mid-1993, it was becoming clear that Arafat was moving to undercut them by becoming even more "pragmatic" and "realistic" than they. In the past, the *New York Times* explained, Arafat had "always appeared to be a hawk holding out for the hardest Palestinian positions"—true enough, if we keep to the "appearance" designed by the Newspaper of Record. But now he seemed willing to make compromises that the local population regards as "selling out." His image accordingly began to improve, even more so as a proper form of "mutual recognition" began to take shape, undercutting the Palestinian delegation, now considered too "hard-line" to be taken seriously.[96]

By the end of August an agreement was reached in Oslo between Israel and Yasser Arafat, in a personal initiative. The Oslo Agreement was welcomed in the United States with great acclaim,[97] marred only by skepticism as to whether it could hold. "America's own greatest interest," the twin goals of "enhanced security for Israel and regional peace," "both . . . seem closer to achievement this morning than ever before," the *Times* editors observed as the agreement was announced. Apart from omission of the tacit understanding that "regional peace" must ensure U.S. control, their identification of Washington's highest priorities is accurate, though automatic identification of U.S. government policy with "America's greatest interest" reflects the standard mystification; it requires argument, not mere assertion, to show that ignoring Palestinian national rights and the security of others is in the interest of the American people.

One would have to search far to find any deviation from these fundamental assumptions about "America's interest." Palestinians may have problems, but they are not our business. The only question that arises is whether the risks are acceptable for Israel. "Those opposed to the historic agreement toward peace in the Middle East argue that it will lead within a few years to a Palestinian state and therefore to the fatal undermining of Israel," U.S. Middle East diplomat Roger Harrison writes. But the critics are wrong, he argues; though Israel faces risks, it is to its interest to accept them, and no other question even arises. H.D.S. Greenway, a foreign correspondent with extensive Middle East experience who has reported the travail of Palestinians with sympathy, writes that the agreement looks promising, but remains problematic:

> In the end the question will always be what it has always been. Is it safer to keep control of occupied territories and more than a million unhappy Arabs who can never be absorbed if Israel is to remain a Jewish state? Or is it safer to rid the state of the occupation that is sapping Israel's energy and seek security through compromise? There is great risk in either course.

That someone might rationally question the Oslo Agreement on grounds of risks to the Palestinians is unworthy of mention, perhaps unintelligible.

The leaders of Iran and Hamas are doubtless aware of their rejectionist assumptions. Their Western counterparts cannot perceive the comparable facts in their own case, a remarkable and important fact. The fundamental commitments are illustrated symbolically by a series of maps that the *Times* displayed under the heading: "Shifting Borders: A History of Conflict in Israel and the Middle East." The second in the series depicts Palestine under the British Mandate; the three that follow, later stages. The first delineates the "Kingdom of David and Solomon, 10th Century B.C."[98]

The guiding assumptions were revealed again as the background planning for the Oslo Agreement was made public. In a lead story, the chief political correspondent of *Yediot Ahronot* reported from Washington that Israel's police and intelligence services were meeting with their PLO counterparts to arrange for close cooperation in ensuring security in the Gaza Strip—meaning, security for Israelis and the PLO authorities who are to take over local administration under their supervision. A few weeks later, the *Boston Globe* reported that similar meetings had taken place under the auspices of the American Academy of Arts and Sciences in Cambridge and Harvard professor Everett Mendelsohn, a well-known dove. In these meetings, General Gazit, former senior Mossad official Joseph Alper, and military correspondent Ze'ev Schiff met with top PLO officials to arrange methods to ensure that Israeli security would not be endangered by actions originating in areas under PLO supervision. No discussion is reported about security for Palestinians under Israeli military rule. There is no reported discussion of any supervision of the Israeli army or Border Guards, or the secret police and intelligence, or the Jewish settlers. The security of Israeli Jews is a matter of importance, that of Palestinian Arabs is not; the strong have rights, the weak do not. The assumption is so deeply entrenched in the Western consciousness as to be quite beyond awareness."[99]

We return to the Israeli reports of these meetings directly.

The editors of the *New York Times* may well be right in thinking that long-standing U.S. policy goals have been advanced. The intended eventual outcome falls well within the bounds of traditional U.S.–Israeli rejectionism, adopting essential features of the rightwing extremist Sharon Plan as well as the Labor Party's Allon Plan (see p. 224). That much was spelled out the same day on the facing page of the *New York Times* by Israel's deputy foreign minister Yossi Beilin. He informed the American audience that

> the permanent solution will be based on Israeli withdrawal from Gaza and from most of the West Bank. We agree to a confederated formula between Jordan and the Palestinians in the West Bank, but we will not return to pre-1967 borders. United Jerusalem will remain the capital of the State of Israel.

In return, "after years of rejection of Israel as part of the Middle East, the Arabs will accept and recognize Israel's right to exist as a sovereign state within secure and defined borders in this region"—as they did, for example, in the vetoed Security Council resolution of January 1976, gone from history along with much else like it, so that Beilin's statement rings true to American ears. The reasons for preferring "confederation" to independence are the traditional ones, already discussed. "United Jerusalem" is a concept of broad and as yet undetermined scope. "Withdrawal from Gaza" and other territories is constrained by the condition that "subsequent to the Israeli withdrawal, Israel will continue to be responsible for external security, and for internal security and public order of settlements and Israelis," while Israeli military forces "may continue to use roads freely within" areas subject to withdrawal, thus presumably leaving in place something resembling the Yitzhak Beilin and Ariel Sharon plans now being implemented in essentials (see pp. 223–25).[100] And even this "permanent settlement" lies well down the road.

It is understandable, then, that the *Times* editors, expressing the prevailing view, should see the "historic deal" as a great opportunity. It is "the Middle East equivalent of the fall of the Berlin wall," Thomas Friedman proclaimed; a reasonable metaphor, given that the "historic deal" represents Palestinian capitulation on the major issues that had caused Washington to block international efforts at diplomatic settlement. Though the projected arrangements may not reach Friedman's personal recommendation—that Israel should run the territories in the manner of its "security zone" in South Lebanon—nevertheless they represent the "triumph of realism over fanaticism and political courage over political cowardice." "Realists" understand that in this world, you follow U.S. orders. Those who are not convinced of the justice of traditional U.S.–Israeli rejectionism are not only wrong but are "fanatics" and "cowards." The rhetoric suggests that more is understood than appears on the surface.[101]

The draft agreement makes no mention of Palestinian *national* rights, the primary issue that separated the United States and Israel from the international consensus for almost two decades. Throughout these years, there was general agreement (including the PLO from the mid-70s) that a settlement should be based on UN 242 (and 338, which endorses 242). There were two basic points of contention: 1) Do we interpret the withdrawal clause of 242 in accord with the international consensus (including the United States, pre-1971), or in accord with the position of Israel and U.S. policy from 1971? 2) Is the settlement based *solely* on UN 242, which offers nothing to the Palestinians, or 242 *and other relevant UN resolutions*, as the PLO had long proposed in accord with the nonrejectionist international consensus? Thus, does the settlement incorporate the Palestinian right to national self-determination repeatedly endorsed by the UN (though blocked by Washington), or the right of refugees to return and compensation, as the UN has insisted since 1948 (with U.S. endorsement, long forgotten)? These are the crucial issues that have stood in the way of a political settlement.

On both major issues under dispute, (1) and (2), the agreement explicitly and without equivocation adopts the U.S.–Israeli stand. Article I, outlining the "Aim of the Negotiations," specifies that "the negotiations on the permanent status will lead to the implementation of Security Council Resolutions 242 and 338"; nothing further is mentioned. Note that this refers to the *permanent* status, the long-term end to be achieved. Furthermore, as Beilin made explicit, UN 242 is to be understood in the terms unilaterally imposed by the United States (from 1971), entailing only partial withdrawal, as Washington determines. In fact, the agreement does not even preclude further Israeli settlement in the large areas of the West Bank it has taken over, or even new land takeovers. On such central matters as control of water, it refers only to "cooperation in the management of water resources in the West Bank and Gaza Strip" and "equitable utilization of joint water resources" in a manner to be determined by "experts from both sides," some of them already cited. The outcome of cooperation between an elephant and a fly is not hard to predict.

Both sides agree that it is only the resources of the occupied territories that are to be subject to such "cooperation," consistent with the general framework of U.S.–Israeli rejectionism, which demands—and in Oslo achieved—a relation of subordination between a region of Palestinian local autonomy and an expanded Israel, the precise terms and boundaries of that subordination remaining ambiguous.

The victory of the rejectionists is complete, in the ideological sphere as well; given U.S. global power, the version of history designed by its doctrinal institutions becomes the general framework for discussion in most of the world, including most of Europe, which has drifted towards becoming a cultural colony of the United States in recent years. While Yossi Beilin is surely right in concluding, in his review of the documentary record, that Israel could have had peace in 1971, his Labor Party colleagues and Henry Kissinger were also proven correct in their conviction that "if we continue to hold out, we will obtain more." So they did.[102]

The extent of the rejectionist victory became even clearer with the exchange of letters between Yasser Arafat and Yitzhak Rabin.[103] Recall that the United States opposed the international consensus on a third crucial point: the right of resistance to military occupation, which the United States and Israel alone reject. Accordingly, the United States has demanded that the PLO terminate the Intifada, which it views as "terrorist acts against Israel." On that issue too, the United States achieved its goal. Arafat's letter listed a series of substantive commitments, including (once again) recognition of "the right of the State of Israel to exist in peace and security" in the wording of UN 242. Arafat also (once again) "renounces the use of terrorism," thus again "crying uncle" in accord with the George Shultz requirement of maximal humiliation. More crucially, Arafat's letter states that the PLO renounces "other uses of violence and will assume responsibility over all P.L.O. elements and personnel in order to assure their compliance, prevent violations and discipline violence." Here the term "violence" is understood very broadly, as was emphasized in the accompanying commentary by the United States and Israel, who, holding power, determine the content of the words exchanged. "The Israelis said Mr. Rabin was adamant that the intifada be curtailed," Clyde Haberman reported from Jerusalem. "It was a measure of Mr. Arafat's determination to reach an agreement that he yielded on this point even though most Palestinians in the territories consider the uprising an indispensable tool to resist the Israeli occupation."

In brief, those who matter, and who set the terms, understand that the PLO is committed to suppress any form of resistance to the Israeli military occupation. It must agree to a return to the *status quo ante*, as the United States and Israel had been demanding since resistance to the violent repression and endless humiliation of the occupation became hard for Israel to contain in December 1987. The Palestinian police, disbanded as collaborators under the pressure of the Intifada, are to be restored. Their function now, even more than before, is to keep the population controlled and passive under the occupation. If they fail in this duty, the United States and Israel can determine that the agreement has been violated, and react as they choose.

The Palestinian police who will be brought in for pacification of the territories are to a large extent foreigners, without roots in the communities where they will serve. They are elements of the Palestine Liberation Army, whose lives were spent abroad, trained as soldiers. The United States and Israel are thus moving towards more rational forms of imperial control, those used by the British in India, the Soviet Union in Eastern Europe, Nazi Germany in occupied France, the United States in Latin America, and so on. Ninety percent of the British forces that held India were native mercenaries; Czech security forces and Vichy police controlled the domestic populations, not the foreign overseer; official U.S. policy from the 1940s has been that the Latin American military must be under firm U.S. control, doing the dirty work with its own hands as much as possible. Imperial domains have typically been controlled by local forces, often brought in from other regions of the subject countries; a typical modern example was China's Tiananmen Square massacre with troops brought from the remote countryside. The current U.S.–Israeli plans for Gaza, and such portions of the West Bank as may eventually be released, are similar in conception, and far more rational than direct Israeli control, costly for the occupying power and occasionally bringing international condemnation when atrocities become too extreme to ignore entirely.

Control by indigenous forces backed by foreign troops carries ideological advantages as well. The inevitable harshness is sure to be used for a great show of anguish by Western commentators, brought forth as a proof of the inherent unworthiness of the native peoples and a retrospective justification for what shreds may still be recalled of the Israeli military occupation, now to be depicted as tender and merciful in comparison with what the backward natives do to one another. As a model, recall the current rehabilitation of the wondrous days of European colonialism.

In return for Arafat's explicit concessions on such matters, Yitzhak Rabin's letter in exchange conceded nothing of any substance. It states tersely that "in the light of the P.L.O. commitments, the Government of Israel has decided to recognize the P.L.O. as the representative of the Palestinian people and commence negotiations with the P.L.O. within the Middle East peace process." In response to Arafat's commitment to suppress any resistance to Israel's military occupation, Rabin did not make the slightest gesture towards alleviating its harshest features. There is no commitment to "renounce" torture, killing of children, or collective punishment, to release prisoners held without charge—even to relax the "closure." There is no commitment to slow down the rapid expansion of Greater Jerusalem, or of settlement, land confiscation, and construction elsewhere in areas designated for eventual annexation. Indeed, to do anything.

To be precise, there is one "concession" in the Rabin letter: recognition of the PLO as representative of the Palestinian people. As the Israeli press was careful to emphasize, the Oslo Agreement itself includes "no direct recognition of the PLO." Rather, it states (in the preamble) that "the Government of Israel and the Palestinian team (in the Jordan–Palestinian delegation to the Middle East peace conference) representing the Palestinian people agree. . . ." Rabin's letter, then, would represent the first recognition of the PLO, now regarded as a more suitable negotiating partner than the local Palestinian delegation, given its willingness to concede more and the loss of nationalist credentials with the "growing feeling that safeguarding Palestinian national rights no longer hinges on defending the PLO's role."[104]

It is interesting that Israel decided to implement traditional Labor Party rejectionism through Norway rather than Washington. The decision might have been motivated by the Clinton administration's shift to rejectionist positions more extreme than those of the governing Labor Party, which Washington had supported in the past. As discussed earlier, commentators in Israel felt that this "revolutionary" change in the U.S. stance would "strengthen the suspicion among the Palestinians that there is reason to fear an Israeli conspiracy with American support." Peres may have sensed that the chance to realize long-standing Labor Party plans would be jeopardized if he contributed to such suspicions by working through Washington. To maintain any credibility with his Palestinian interlocutors, then, it would be more reasonable to select intermediaries who could help implement traditional U.S. rejectionism rather than the extremist version now being promulgated.[105]

Summarizing, for some twenty years there were three major issues on which the United States opposed the international consensus, virtually alone, relying on its dominance in the diplomatic, military, economic, and ideological arenas to bar a peaceful negotiated settlement of the Israel–Palestine conflict: 1) withdrawal, 2) rejectionism, 3) the right of resistance. On the first issue, the United States rejected full withdrawal from the territories, abandoning its early support for the international consensus in February 1971, when Egypt agreed to a full peace treaty in the terms of the then-official U.S. position. On the second issue, the United States has always led the rejectionist camp, rejecting the right to national self-determination of one of the two claimants for national rights in the former Palestine, the indigenous population. On the third issue, the United States denies the right of resistance to "colonial and racist regimes and foreign occupation or other forms of colonial domination," in the words of the United Nations. On all three issues, the United States stood alone (apart from Israel), with only occasional and marginal exceptions. On all three issues, the United States won hands down. The Israel–PLO Agreements adopt the U.S. position on 1) partial withdrawal, 2) denial of Palestinian rights, and 3) denial of the right of resistance. Not only Yasser Arafat, but the entire world, capitulated in the "historic deal," recognizing, after the Gulf War, that the United States now felt able to extend the Monroe Doctrine to the Middle East, and would use arbitrary force, if the occasion warranted, to establish that "What We Say Goes"— George Bush's slogan as he announced the New World Order while the bombs and missiles were flying.

The Clinton administration is now carrying the rejectionist victory several steps beyond, abandoning the former U.S. support for the international consensus on the right of Palestinian refugees to return or compensation, the status of the territories as "occupied" (rather than "disputed"), and the inclusion of Arab Jerusalem in the "disputed" territories. Given U.S. power, those departures too are likely to become the conventions of the future, the facts securely hidden from view. See pp. 219–20.

A closer look at Gaza helps explain the meaning of what is contemplated: not withdrawal, but modification to satisfy Israel's needs. The point is made quite forcefully and prominently in Israeli commentary. A major interview with Chief of Staff Ehud Barak in the journal of the governing Labor Party takes as its headline, running across the top of the page: "We are not leaving Gaza and we will be in any place where it is necessary that we be."[106]

General Barak's announcement is based firmly in the text of the Oslo Agreement, which secures Israel's rights to control the settlements and access to them. Israeli settlements in Gaza include a large part of the coastline, the most valuable areas; Israel might estimate the proportion it holds at about 40 percent, depending on how it chooses to draw the boundaries around the settlements it is committed to maintain and protect. These areas include a small section in the north bordering Israel as well as the Gush Katif region running from the Egyptian border northward, established by the Rabin–Peres Labor government of 1974–77. These settlements, surrounded with concertina wire and an electrified fence, "convey a more established sense of permanence" than the ones in the north, Middle East specialist Geoffrey Aronson wrote after a recent visit, with their "plentiful grass, larger trees, more public buildings and commercial services." Some four thousand Israeli settlers use much of the limited water of this desert area for agriculture and for such benefits as a huge artificial lake in front of a luxurious tourist hotel. Their "Garden of Eden," as the Labor Party press described it in March 1993, exports almost half of Israel's tomatoes and a substantial part of its flowers, grown with labor-intensive cultivation at enormous profits, given the super-cheap Arab labor available. Construction continued to boom after the Labor government returned to power in mid-1992, including water pipes from Israel to the Gush Katif settlements, new villas, and roads that allow access without passing through Arab-settled areas. Prime Minister Rabin has confirmed that the Gaza settlements are entitled to top priority development assistance.

"We have continued to steal the Strip's water, even though its quality deteriorated from year to year," military correspondent Ze'ev Schiff wrote in March 1993, and "to steal the Strip's tiny land resources, in order to found there more and more [Jewish] settlements, as if we deliberately wanted to make the inhabitants despair, and in their despair think in terms of having nothing to lose." He regarded this as absurd from the point of view of Israel's security. Though figures are secret, Israeli and Palestinian economists conclude that the yearly per capita budget allotted by Israeli authorities to the Gaza Strip was about $30 (compared to $120 in the West Bank, $825 in Jordan, $2,113 in Israel). Throughout its rule, "the Israeli government has refused to allocate a single cent from its own budget for the Arabs in the territories," Alex Fishman reported. Taxes collected locally were mostly used for the military administration. With fishing barred and Arab fruit and citrus cultivation dwindling, the population of the Gaza Strip was compelled to rely on work under intolerable conditions at miserable pay in Israel or subcontracting for Israeli industries by women and children at home, as in the early days of the industrial revolution, Danny Rubinstein reports. Meanwhile a new wealthy Palestinian elite has been arising from these and similar forms of integration into Israel's economy. The territories have been "a huge laboratory for testing the military government's successive theories" for control and economic integration, Fishman observes.[107]

Consistent with General Barak's pronouncement, after the Oslo Agreement the Israeli civil administration continued to offer forty-nine–year leases to Jewish settlers and developers, a clear indication of intentions, Gaza researcher Sara Roy observes. They also established industrial zones "on fertile agricultural lands, a blow to local agriculture, despite the availability of barren lands," she adds. The development plans and projects, she concludes, express Israel's plan to establish "a restructured form of integration ... insuring Israeli state control over Palestinian land and water." The accords merely provide "a protective guise for the deepened integration the state is pursuing." The situation in Gaza "took a dramatic turn for the worse in the fall of 1992 under the newly installed Labor-led government of Yitzhak Rabin," deteriorating further in the following year. Rabin "closed" the territories, meaning that everything remains open to Israeli Jews while Palestinians are locked in, a severe economic blow because they had been made dependent on employment under harsh conditions in Israel.

Rabin's government also imposed onerous constraints on exports of Gaza oranges, the main cash crop, causing much of it to rot, along with new requirements that all produce be purchased by Israeli agents for sale in Israel or export through Israeli enterprises (for example, about half of Israel's exports of strawberries, which Gaza Arab farmers are not permitted to export directly). Other forms of independent development, such as a banking structure, continue to be barred. The goal, Roy and other observers conclude, is to turn parts of Gaza into a "branch plant" economy designed "to serve Israeli interests ... primarily," with Israel retaining control over land, zoning, water, and any development that may take place in the areas released to local self-administration.[108]

Steps towards effective annexation of parts of the Gaza Strip also proceeded. In negotiations in Cairo in November 1993, the Israeli press reported, "the Palestinians accepted Israel's security conception, which stipulates defense of three large blocs of settlements in the Gaza Strip," Gush Katif and two others, while the Israeli navy controls the coastline. The issue under dispute was just what the army (IDF) would control: Only the Jewish settlements themselves, as a literal reading of the Oslo Agreement suggests? Or, as Israel demanded, a "bloc" that includes the settlements? IDF control of access is assumed in either case. The difference is crucial; the Israeli version is a step towards annexation of the "blocs." Palestinian concessions on this matter come as no surprise, the head of the Israeli negotiating team, General Amnon Shahak, explained on Israeli radio: "One must remember that there is no mutuality in the discussions." Israel will grant "what we think it is proper to give, and we will retain what we think it is necessary to hold." The head of the Gaza Council (of settlers) meanwhile alleged that in the months following the Oslo Agreement, sixty new families were absorbed in Gush Katif.[109]

The security situation in Gaza continued to deteriorate, Sara Roy reported from the scene, as the local population faced "two oppressors: Israel *and* the

PLO." The PLO is establishing an authority that favors Arafat loyalists from Fatah over people with grass-roots support, and that also includes collaborators with Israel, a decision that has led to "outrage and disbelief." As anticipated, "Fatah is increasingly seen as a reactionary, regressive force promoting dissension and discord"; it is, in short, playing very much the role of local forces subordinated to the dominant power in the classic pattern of imperial control. Roy also confirms reports in the Israeli press that the IDF is allowing weapons to be brought into Gaza, another factor in the "total lack of authority and increased lawlessness, the emergence of guns and armed youth gangs, the reemergence of drug dealing, the rapid devolving of the economy and growing pauperization, the disintegration of the community as a social and political actor, the lack of unity, and a diminished psychological capacity"—all classic techniques of imperial domination.

Meanwhile the military occupation itself continued to be "brutal" and its practices "malicious," Roy continues. "Between the signing of the peace accord and Dec. 31, for example, 30 Gazans were killed by Israeli forces and 1,100 were wounded, 500 of whom were children. Of the wounded, about half were shot with live ammunition." The security forces in Gaza (as in the West Bank) also continued to employ undercover assassination units (death squads, in the Latin American sense), a practice that sometimes led to publicity and even apologies when the wrong targets were hit; to use massive force to demolish houses and kill suspects within; and otherwise to rule with an iron hand. It is "standard procedure" for undercover units to open fire on armed men distributing leaflets, and in general to shoot without warning at any armed Palestinian, an IDF spokesperson informed the press after six PLO loyalists ("Fatah Hawks") had been killed without warning in Gaza while riding in cars handing out leaflets; a mistake, the government acknowledged. The official reason is "the protection of our own soldiers," the spokesperson said, but "privately, however, military officials acknowledge that massive overkill operations also have the advantage of scaring Palestinians and deterring them from sheltering wanted men," Peter Ford added.[110]

Standard procedures in the West Bank are the same, a fact illustrated dramatically at the time of the Hebron massacre of Feb. 25, 1994. The day before the massacre, soldiers fired antitank rockets and grenades at a stone house near Jerusalem, killing one Palestinian and wounding another, both "accused by the army in the slaying of an undercover agent" and other actions, the press casually reported. In the first eight days following the massacre by settler Baruch Goldstein and the army killings that followed, thirty-three more Palestinians were shot dead by the IDF, with "no danger to soldiers' lives" in at least twelve of these killings, according to the Israeli human rights group B'Tselem. After the massacre, the Arab population was placed under still more harsh confinement, "kept under lock and key," correspondent Graham Usher observes, while "the town's settlers are free to walk, drive and go about their business, armed to the teeth and under army escort."[111]

The Oslo Agreement speaks of elections, but history suggests skepticism about their significance, even if they take place. Well-informed Israeli commentators suggested that the reference to elections concealed "a tacit understanding" between Israeli and PLO negotiators "to the effect that no autonomy in the West Bank and the Gaza Strip can possibly materialize even if the Oslo Agreement mandates it" (Uzi Benzamin). Outlining the "tacit understanding" further, Benzamin observes that Israeli and PLO leaders agree in opposing democratization of the "autonomous" regions. It would be preferable, they agree, to leave them under the direct rule of PLO authorities, who in turn are under Israel's supervision. The agreement "is built on a tacit assumption that it will never be carried into effect," Benzamin alleges. "Today all knowledgeable persons in Jerusalem" speak of a regime that "will not be an elected autonomy but a PLO-appointed administration," established "not as a result of any elections but by an Israeli grant." "Israel supports a process which is intended to prevent any chance for a democratic Palestinian entity (or a state) to form at its side," preferring "an autocratic form of regime, similar to those existing in the Arab states." Benzamin considers this the likely outcome of the Oslo Agreement, given the shared interest in suppressing popular democracy on the part of the signers. Commenting, Israel Shahak observes accurately that the opposition to popular democracy in the Arab world reflects long-standing commitments of the United States in the entire region, of the Zionist movement from its origins, and of the PLO leadership, all for understandable reasons, often discussed. For such reasons, these predictions seem not implausible.[112]

Three months later, as intentions had become clearer through ongoing practice, Benzamin reiterated his early assessment more forcefully. To Israeli political leaders, he wrote in early December, "it is already clear now that the [planned] July 13 '94 elections for the Autonomy Council will not take place. It is clear to them that the PLO will rule over all of Gaza (except for the [Israeli] settlements) in the manner in which it is to take control of Gaza and Jericho, that is: by an accelerated transfer of authority from the Israeli military and civilian administrations." "Secretly Israeli leaders hope that a 'season' will break out in the territories"; the term "season" refers to Haganah operations in 1945 to suppress Menachem Begin's Irgun in tacit cooperation with the British authorities. "Their assumption is that unless it destroys Hamas opposition, the PLO will not be able to rule the Gaza Strip (in the first phase) and the West Bank (later on)." Israel's negotiating tactics and its support for well-armed PLO security forces are based on this assumption. "The recognition that the PLO is better able than Israel to identify rejection front activists in the territories may improve the prospects for successful conclusion of the affairs," and also "creates a common interest" between Israel and Arafat "to reach an earlier agreement."[113]

The reports of Israeli participants in the secret meetings in Cambridge under the auspices of the American Academy lend credibility to these skeptical assessments. At a press conference in Tel Aviv on September 10, Joseph Alper reported agreement between the two sides that the Israeli army (IDF) should withdraw only from "peaceful areas." The Palestinian participants "explicitly requested that the IDF evacuate areas of tension in the refugee camps only after [the PLO forces] succeed in gaining control over them." "Evacuate the refugee camps only at the end," Alper quoted them as saying. Both sides agreed that the PLO should have dominant military force, including armored personnel carriers and machine guns. They need "impressive military force" to ensure that there is no challenge to their control. They also requested joint patrols with the IDF, Alper reported. General Gazit "expressed hope that the internal security forces of the Palestinians will be an 'efficient Shabak,'" referring to Israel's dreaded secret police. "He did not rule out the possibility of cooperation between them and Israeli intelligence services," the press reported. Gazit added that "there are in the Arab world excellent specialists in internal security and one should not underestimate the ability of the Palestinians to take responsibility for the matter."[114]

Barring of elections if they threaten to come out "the wrong way," or their control by force, would be entirely in keeping with Western doctrine on "democracy," which defines it in terms of acceptability of *outcome*, not of process and conditions, as demonstrated by a long history of the kind already discussed, amply documented.

Israel's political leaders were forthright in explaining what they had achieved. The day the accords were announced, Shimon Peres stated over Israeli television that "there has been a change in *them*, not *us*. We are not negotiating with the PLO, but only with a shadow of its former self," effectively gaining Israel's traditional demands. His conclusion was underscored by the prime minister. Interviewed about the accords a month later, Rabin suggested that "maybe the greater part of wisdom is to skip the second phase in nine months because maybe Arafat does not want elections, and go straight to a territorial solution where you separate Israeli and Palestinian populations permanently"—without ceding anything significant to the Palestinians, he made clear. The idea that large numbers of refugees might return to the areas of Palestinian autonomy is "nonsense," he said. "If they expect tens of thousands, they live in a dream, an illusion." Perhaps some "increased family reunification," nothing more. There might be "a Palestinian entity which is less than independent"; Israel can "do many things to prevent" a Palestinian state from coming into being.

Speaking to the political council of the Labor Party on October 2, Rabin outlined his expectations about security. Palestinian forces, he said, should be able to "deal with Gaza without problems caused by appeals to the High Court of Justice, without problems made by [the human rights organization] B'Tselem, and without problems from all sorts of bleeding hearts and mothers and fathers." Other "dreams and illusions" were also summarily dismissed.[115]

10. After the Agreement

Events followed a parallel course. Israeli military operations in the territories were accelerated at once, with fifteen Palestinians killed and nine houses destroyed in September. The "recent increase in the number of Palestinians killed by Israeli forces," including children, was noted in the U.S. press parenthetically, and the careful reader might discover that Israel TV "showed rare pictures of a Palestinian being shot in the head after he taunted soldiers on a street corner"—one of many similar cases. IDF death squad activities continued, targeting people "suspected" of terrorist acts. Among them was grocer Abdul-Rahman Yusif Aruri, "the victim of what the human rights organization, Al-Haq, described as 'premeditated execution,'" his cousin, University of Massachusetts professor Naseer Aruri, reported. "He was shot and killed by two bullets fired from a silent revolver at a close range in front of his own home as his eight-months pregnant wife, three children, and relatives watched out the window in horror and disbelief." He had made a "suspicious move," the IDF spokesperson said. The executioners were disguised as Arabs, a regular practice.[116]

Settlers continued to rampage, attacking people and destroying property under the eyes of the army—"so that the Arabs will understand who the true rulers are in Hebron," a religious settler from Kiryat Arba explained. "Our beautiful women light the candles and the men light up the locals," a Rabbi from a nearby settlement added, referring to the regular Friday evening riots of the religious settlers in and near Hebron. A petition to the Defense Ministry by the officers of an IDF paratrooper unit serving in the area blamed the settlers for violence, humiliations, provocations, and sabotage. "The Arab population is quiet now, only the settlers are active," an officer said. "Most of the time we deal with them," though they know they have virtual impunity. To quiet the situation, the Arab population of Hebron is kept under a dusk-to-dawn curfew, yet another burden to bear along with unemployment and despair. The settlers riot at will.

U.S. political leaders and media commentators issue stern warnings to desist, directed to Palestinians. The practice is consistent with the basic assumptions of the Oslo Agreement and what preceded it: the concerns and security of a powerful ally matter, not those of their victims.

The IDF also began "to detain Palestinians for incitement against Arafat or the Agreement," the Hebrew press reported, the first case being a Ramallah lawyer brought to a military court for possession of "seditious leaflets." Suspected opposition to the "peace process" is also an element in the "license to kill" granted undercover units, as regular reports make clear, without explicit comment. Prisoner release is also conditioned on this political stand. "Hamas prisoners will not be released because they are against peace," chief Israeli negotiator General Amnon Shahak stated frankly.[117]

As noted earlier, the "brutal" and "malicious" practices of the security forces go back to the earliest days of the occupation, and settler violence, with impunity, is nothing at all new. As it increased after the Oslo Agreement, the earlier history was occasionally recalled in Israel. *Ha'aretz* correspondent Yossi Torpshtein reported from Hebron in November on what had happened there since the first religious settlers took over a section of the old city in the mid-1970s. Palestinian fear of the settlers "is real and substantive," he commented, "and was not born in the last few weeks." In the old city, there had been twenty-five thousand Palestinians, but "as a result of systematic pressure, daily provocations and imposition of terror by the 'foreign settlers,' many of them abandoned the old quarter, leaving their houses to the settlers." Settler atrocities included destruction of property and "wild shooting," along with "attacks on women and children and on Muslims praying in the Cave of the Machpelah," where the February massacre took place three months later. Palestinian anger at the prevailing pogrom-like atmosphere was heightened by the reaction of the army, "which may be described as standing perplexed on the side." The IDF continues to look the other way, he reports, as settlers try to burn down property, fire their weapons at Palestinians, and terrorize them in other ways. The army did not react, he writes, when settlers stoned Palestinians right next to an IDF installation, severely wounding a schoolgirl, the daughter of a faculty member of Bir Zeit University. In contrast, any Palestinian action elicits a brutal response. In the two months after the signing of the Oslo Agreement, he reports, eighteen Palestinians were killed by soldiers and settlers, while settlers rampaged freely.

"The simple truth is that an Arab who attempts to shoot a Jew forfeits his life—and justly," Amnon Denkner wrote in early January, "but a Jew who attempts to shoot an Arab is immune from the wrath of the soldiers, if they act according to the army's orders. They will not hinder him or prevent him from murdering an Arab, they will not shoot over his head or shoot at his legs, and certainly will not shoot to kill before he commits his dastardly crime." No secret to anyone familiar with the territories, these army orders were made public in the first days of January by a Lieutenant Colonel who commanded a military unit there. Asked how he was permitted to respond if he saw a Jew aiming a rifle at an Arab with the obvious intent of murder, the Colonel stated that he would be permitted to "rush and cover the Arab with my own body, but under no circumstances am I allowed to open fire on a Jew." These standing orders "invite all the settler fanatics to shoot Arabs, guaranteeing to them that in the course of the action not a hair on their heads will be harmed," Denkner adds. Television viewers in January "were shocked . . . to see film of Israeli soldiers running away as settlers shot at Palestinians in Hebron," Peter Ford reported after the February massacre.[118]

After the massacre, great shock was expressed at the revelation of the "double standard" that had prevailed for the twenty-seven years of the occupation, and "the army's open-fire rules," which "forbid shooting at Israelis involved in violent disturbances," Joel Greenberg reported, while recalling a December 1993 army document stating: "It should be emphasized that a soldier shall not use a weapon against an Israeli." The shock and surprise were unwarranted. The facts were well known before, from regular practice over many years and even explicit statement. It also comes as no surprise that well after the February massacre, General Barak "underlined that the army's continuing top priority in the occupied territories was the battle against Palestinian terrorism. Its second most important task, he added, was securing the roads for Israeli travellers" (David Horovitz).[119]

General Barak was speaking after the IDF killed four Palestinians in Hebron in a gun battle in which they used heavy weapons to demolish the building in which they were found—"suspected gunmen of the militant Hamas group," the *New York Times* reported, quoting General Danny Yatom who said that "one of the gunman believed to have been inside the apartment houses had been involved in the slaying" of two Israelis from Kiryat Arba. The IDF reported that the men were "wanted" for "complicity" in that killing. Chief of Staff Barak stated that they "were on a retribution mission" and "were among the most important Hamas men in Hebron." A pregnant Palestinian woman was killed, by Israeli army fire according to witnesses and "Palestinian hospital sources." The IDF commandeered a children's hospital and fired from it, eliciting a rare public protest from the ICRC (Red Cross) for this "violation of one of the most sacred principles of international humanitarian law." They then declared the entire Hebron area a closed military zone, another blow to the Arab population confined under the curfew imposed after the February massacre, which in turn followed long curfews that had made life intolerable for the eighty thousand inhabitants. The Red Cross for the first time felt compelled to supply food aid to three thousand of Hebron's inhabitants, but that was prevented by the IDF on grounds that it "might lead to disturbances." Prime Minister Rabin said that he felt "uncomfortable" about the plight of the Palestinians in Hebron.[120]

A few days later, when eight Israeli Jews were killed by Arab assassins, the entire occupied territories were closed off for an indefinite period while Israel moved to bring in eighteen thousand new "guest workers" from Romania, Bulgaria, Thailand, and Turkey, increasing their numbers to over thirty-five thousand. The Palestinians, of course, have no recourse: for example, those left destitute when the only source of employment that has been allowed them is eliminated, the Arab doctors and nurses barred from Arab hospitals in East Jerusalem and their patients, and so on. But for government ministers, "the potentially harmful impact on Palestinians took a distant second place to their main goal of reassuring Israelis about their security after several lethal attacks."[121] The "closure" has the usual porous character: Jews are exempt. And the reaction to atrocities has its usual consistency: when an Arab murders Jews, the entire Arab population is subjected to collective punishment; when a Jew murders Arabs, exactly the same is true. The standard practices are considered acceptable among those who foot the bills, on the familiar racist assumptions.

The Israeli human rights group B'Tselem presented a report to the Shamgar Commission investigating the February massacre in which it accused the government of having shown "utter disdain regarding the lives of Palestinians." Chairperson Gila Svirsky charged that "Goldstein's act did not take place in a vacuum but was the result of ongoing incitement to hurt Palestinians," conducted with almost complete impunity in the light of the government's "protracted impotence in dealing with violence perpetrated by settlers," even murder. The B'Tselem report reviews longstanding practices of the security forces and the courts. The former refuse to pursue Arab complaints or even accept them, while the courts are "extremely lenient where the punishment of Israeli civilians convicted of crimes against Palestinians is concerned." Meanwhile they continue to tolerate treatment of Palestinians by methods that "certainly constitute ill-treatment and correspond to most accepted definitions of torture," a 1992 B'Tselem report concluded, leading to a conviction rate of over 95 percent, usually by "confession." At the same time, the ICRC, in another highly unusual statement, called upon the Israeli government to "put an immediate end to the ill-treatment inflicted during interrogation on detainees from the occupied territories," expressing its conclusion from many interviews that "means of physical and psychological pressure are being used that constitute a violation of the [Fourth Geneva] Convention" and that "preclude any fair trial."[122]

After the early revelations of the Shamgar Commission, Israeli journalist Haim Baram wrote that "only radical Israeli racists can dispute the conclusion that the Palestinians are absolutely defenseless confronting armed, bloody-minded settlers and their loyal partners, the Israeli army and the Border Police." The facts have long been available, though ignored or denied in the United States, as continues to be the case. One reason for the behavior of the "partners," the Israeli press adds, is that a large number of the officers and soldiers serving in the territories are from the Jewish settlements there. The fact was reported by the commander of a military unit, Yisrael Blumenthal of Kiryat Arba, in a television broadcast in which he described the perpetrator of the February 25 massacre, Baruch Goldstein, as "a soldier who fell in battle"—one of the milder commendations widely expressed, particularly from religious and American sectors.[123]

Construction in the occupied territories continued at the record levels instituted by Rabin, who "boasted that more housing in the territories is being built during his tenure than at any time since 1967," the Washington *Report on Israeli Settlement* observed, noting that under the new Rabin government, housing starts have shifted from Israel proper to the territories while total government-financed housing dropped. In October 1993, Housing Minister Binyamin Ben-Eliezer announced in Israel and Washington that construction in formerly Arab East Jerusalem would continue "despite US and Palestinian demands it be halted," the *Jerusalem Post* reported, the concept "Jerusalem" being understood in the usual lax fashion. A new government plan announced a month later called for development "from the eastern borders of Jerusalem to the outskirts of Jericho." The intention is to settle seventy thousand Jews in this new Gush Adumim bloc, which will effectively divide the remaining Palestinian areas of the West Bank and extend Israeli control of the large Jerusalem region. A report in *Ma'ariv* estimated the actual number of living units at fifteen thousand, not the thirteen thousand announced. The building pace is far beyond that of the ultra-right Ariel Sharon, whose construction projects caused some friction with Washington. The plans extend well beyond the borders of Jerusalem in all directions. Givat Ze'ev, "an urban concentration seven km. north of Jerusalem" is to be more than doubled. To the east, the population of Ma'ale Adumim, which has doubled in recent years, is to be more than doubled again under the new plans. "Ma'ale Adumim, according to all views, is part of Jerusalem," Deputy Defense Minister Mordechai Gur said.

Ben-Eliezer's announcement in Washington of "expansion of construction in Jerusalem"—a "particularly sensitive matter" that had been kept secret previously, the Hebrew press reported—aroused little interest in the United States. Nor does the further elaboration. All of this is again consistent with the wording of the Oslo Agreement; and, we can only assume, the intentions of the effective rulers.[124]

The Israeli press gave many further details. Michal Sela described the rapid construction of Givat Ze'ev and the highway to it. There has been no proposal to allot any housing "to Palestinians suffering from a severe housing shortage," Sela added. "Israel's intention at this stage is to keep out of the negotiations not just the city of Jerusalem, but also anything the [Israeli] Housing Ministry may fancy to set up in 'Greater Jerusalem.'" This rapidly growing urban area separates the northern and southern halves of the West Bank (Samaria and Judea), undermining any prospects for meaningful autonomy, Sela observes; Arab towns and villages within it "begin to look like scattered islands in the midst of a sea." Israel "insists on keeping an arrangement" that requires a long and difficult drive between Bethlehem and Ramallah—for Arabs, barred from direct access through East Jerusalem. "Israeli construction intended exclusively for Jewish habitation in what is already called 'Greater Jerusalem' can be seen as a continuation of the well-known plans of Ariel Sharon to split the areas of Palestinian habitation into enclaves, which he called 'the pockets of autonomy.' No fairness and no solution satisfactory to the two peoples is possible if Sharon's plans are applied to urban development of Jerusalem," as has been rapidly underway since the agreements were signed.

A few weeks later the government announced the annexation of lands linking Givat Ze'ev to the Jerusalem border. A government official "said the plan reflects the government's often stated policy of strengthening the country's control of 'greater Jerusalem,' in particular in the direction of Givat Ze'ev and Ma'aleh Adumim." New construction to the east and west of Givat Ze'ev was also announced.[125]

The Rabin–Peres enclave strategy is similar in principle to Sharon's plans, but more acceptable in style and manner to the United States, which ultimately foots the bill.

In the Israeli journal *Challenge*, two researchers of Israeli settlement policies estimate the area of "the greater Jerusalem zone of influence," extending from Ramallah to Hebron to the border of Ma'ale Adumim near Jericho, at 30 percent of the area of the West Bank. "The aim of the current settlement drive is to finish creating circles of contiguous Jewish settlements in the greater Jerusalem zone of influence, so as to further surround the Palestinian communities, limit their development, and prevent any possibility that East Jerusalem could become a Palestinian capital. With control of land that reaches almost to Jericho, the settlements are also designed to cut the West Bank into two geographically separated areas, one north of Ramallah, and one including Hebron and the south." At the same time, "a vast network of roads has been under construction, forming the backbone of the settlement pattern." There are also plans for a Palestinian settlement northeast of Jerusalem, to be named "al-Quds," the Arabic name for Jerusalem. "We need to find a capital for the Palestinians, we have to find a site for al-Quds," explained Uzi Veksler, chairman of the Authority for the Development of Jerusalem.

In early October, *Hadashot* reported a visit to the Jordan Valley by Aryeh Mizrachi, director of the settlement bureau, who announced new construction there for hundreds of settlers on the express orders of the prime minister to ensure Israeli control of that area. Inducements include "an especially low price" and generous subsidies for construction and schooling (ten times what is offered within Israel).

A comprehensive review in *Hadashot* two months after the Oslo Agreement was reached found that the government of Labor and the dovish Meretz party had scarcely reduced expenditures for settlement, employing many devices to attract Jews to the territories. Settlers there, who constitute 2.4 percent of the population of Israel, receive 12 percent of the domestic budget. The analysis also shows that the furor over Washington's reduction of loan guarantees as a settlement penalty was, as usual, largely feigned. Unlike its predecessors, the Clinton administration left the calculations to the government of Israel, which presented an estimate of $430 million, omitting Jerusalem; the "bombshell" was that Clinton added $7 million to show its concern for Israel's expanding settlements in and around East Jerusalem. The Israeli treasury estimates actual expenditures beyond Israel's borders at $700 million. The review finds "no change in the expenditures flowing to the settlements" after the Oslo accords, with new plans for 1994 throughout the West Bank and Gaza (Gush Katif). "Rabin will continue not to dry out the settlements," the report ends, ironically using Rabin's phrase for settlement beyond the borders. "And the Americans? They will understand."[126]

A plausible conjecture, with ample historical precedent.

The Settlement Ministry continued its efforts to stimulate emigration to the occupied territories. Along with the various subsidies and other inducements, the ministry engages in such activities as hiring buses to bring Ethiopian immigrants living near Netanyah in Israel to tour West Bank settlements where the ministry wants them to rent apartments. In January, the Israeli press and radio reported secret government plans to extend the integration of greater Jerusalem virtually to Jericho, with vast construction projects, plans for tourist sites along the northern shore of the Dead Sea, some $700 million of investment in new roads to connect settlements with Israel and each other, bypassing Palestinian villages and towns, and steps to effectively obliterate the official border (the Green line) by settlement and road building. Confiscation of Palestinian lands continues for road construction, ensuring "territorial continuity" between Jewish settlements, and for related ends. Housing Minister Ben Eliezer confirmed that "there are no limitations on building" in the area of greater Jerusalem, extending well south of Bethlehem, where settlements are "an integral part of Jerusalem's defensive perimeter." Deputy Defense Minister Gur stated that the purpose of new development programs is to consolidate the existing "territorial continuity running from [the settlement of] Vered Jericho overlooking Jericho through Ma'ale Adumim to Jerusalem, an achievement which Israel will present to Palestinian negotiators as a geographic fact." After the February massacre, Gur assured settlers that the government was not considering evacuation from the Hebron vicinity or elsewhere. In the Oslo and later Cairo accords, he said, "it was agreed that all the Jews would stay where they are, and they are going to stay where they are." The general principle was explained by Prime Minister Rabin: "What is important is what is within the boundaries, and it is less important where the boundaries are, as long as the State [of Israel] covers most of the territory of the Land of Israel [Eretz Israel, the former Palestine], whose capital is Jerusalem."[127]

The status of the Syrian Golan Heights is to be settled in negotiations with Syria, but here too it seems that Israel plans to keep a major presence. The Council of Golan Settlements announced in late December that Finance Minister Avraham Shochat had authorized 40 percent of the Council's plans for 50 million shekel (about $17 million) expenditures in the 1994 budget, with the intent of increasing the Jewish population there by about half within the next four years. Along with 1,700 new dwellings, new industrial installations are planned with government funding, extending the 117 million shekel investments of 1993, including 50 million shekel in state funds. In January, Minister Ben Eliezer dedicated a new neighborhood in the "capital city" of Katzrin, with 550 dwellings, 20 percent already occupied. Just before the Oslo Agreement was announced, the press had reported major new constructions, quoting the head of the Golan Council, Yehuda Wallman, who described the new building drive as beyond anything seen for twenty-six years. The program continues, perhaps accelerated, after the agreement, as in the West Bank and Gaza Strip. The August 1993 report was headlined "Quiet, We're Building," referring to the traditional Labor Party strategy of "building facts" while others "do not see," or at least pretend not to see, notably the U.S. authorities who ensure that the huge flow of aid, and now loan guarantees, will enable these programs to proceed unhampered.[128]

Despite the achievements in "historical engineering," there is always the danger that discipline might erode and the actual historical record might someday come to light, with all that it implies about the Oslo Agreements. It only makes sense, then, to purify the record by official fiat, eliminating offending facts. A useful step in this direction was announced amidst the euphoria over the "historic agreement" in Oslo. "Egypt, Russia and the United States have agreed to work with Israel to eliminate, revise or defer many resolutions on Middle East affairs that the United Nations General Assembly has adopted," *New York Times* UN correspondent Paul Lewis reported. "The countries plan to press for the wholesale revision of the 32 resolutions, most of them critical of Israel." The step is unprecedented, but useful for two reasons: first, for interring the corpse of history; and second, because the concerns that elicited the resolutions have not been addressed. The goal is to eliminate resolutions on Palestinian national rights, human rights violations under the military occupation, Israeli settlements, Israel's refusal to renounce nuclear weapons, Israel's (virtual) annexation of the Golan Heights, etc. It is time to "get rid of obsolete, anachronistic and counterproductive resolutions, which are irrelevant to the new Middle East situation," Israel's UN representative Gad Yaacobi said in an interview. In *Times* lingo, this worthy effort of eliminating past irrelevancies is part of "the drive to bring the United Nations positions in line with the new status"—as the "new status" is construed by the United States, Israel, and the *New York Times*. Plainly, the issues that fall under these resolutions remain quite alive, exactly as under the "old status." Nothing material has changed in this regard. Equally plainly, that fact is doctrinally unacceptable, as are the circumstances that gave rise to the resolutions that the United States blocked, and in the Security Council, regularly vetoed.[129]

Clinton administration initiatives at the December 1993 UN session, reviewed earlier, are a step towards implementing these plans.

In his commentary on the Rabin–Arafat letter exchange in "The Brave New Middle East," Thomas Friedman described Arafat's letter as "not simply a statement of recognition. It is a letter of surrender, a typewritten white flag, in which the P.L.O. chairman renounces every political position on Israel that he held since the P.L.O's foundation in 1964." In return, Arafat received a few words with no substantive commitment. Friedman's account is partially accurate; as noted, in the real world, PLO willingness to recognize Israel's rights in the context of a two-state settlement, and its calls for negotiations leading to mutual recognition, date back many years, though they do not enter into the official version of history as conveyed by the *Times* and other doctrinal organs. But Friedman's recognition of the "surrender" is realistic, and it is understandable that the reaction to it should be so exultant on the part of a correspondent for whom Israel "is like an old flame.... We're in love—there's no two ways about it."[130]

Reactions elsewhere varied. Danny Rubinstein noted that in the agreement, "there isn't even a hint of a solution to the basic problems which exist between Israel and the Palestinians," either in the short run or down the road. *Financial Times* Middle East correspondents Julian Ozanne and Andrew Gowers describe Arafat's acceptance of the accords as "a desperate last throw by a weakened leader to secure a part of Palestine before all is lost"— and, perhaps, to save something of his personal prestige and influence in whatever fiefdom may be granted him, from which he can disburse largesse to loyal supporters, which, it is hoped on all sides, will bribe the population into accepting the abandonment of their rights and hopes. "From Israel's point of view the deal is a dream," Ozanne and Gowers continued: "it leaves Jewish settlements in the territories intact, preserves full Israeli control over its security and borders, does not broach the thorny subject of Jerusalem (claimed by Israel as its 'eternal, indivisible capital'), and does not concede a Palestinian state." "For the Palestinians, the fruits are more bittersweet. . . . The danger, as they discovered through hard experience, was that—like Bosnia's Moslems—they would get nothing" if they insisted on what were "good arguments for holding out for more."[131]

The analogy that Ozanne and Gowers drew to Bosnia has some merit, despite many differences. A settlement may come in Bosnia too, recognizing the weight of conquest. In that case, the Belgrade press will resemble American media in September 1993. In general, those with the guns tend to win, to exult about their victory, and to praise themselves for their integrity, honor, and virtue rewarded.

Some of Israel's more extreme American advocates remained dissatisfied, warning that the Palestinians might use their territorial gains "as a launching pad for a final assault" in "Phase 2" of their nefarious design (Norman Podhoretz, A.M. Rosenthal). One Harvard professor, lamenting Israel's "terrible mistake," said that "it's the first time that an Israeli Government is doing something for which I, as an American Jew, would not like to bear moral responsibility" (Ruth Wisse); an interesting comment, when one thinks of the actions over the years for which the problem doesn't arise. But the more rational and perceptive understood what had been achieved. The PLO had been forced "to become more reasonable," *Times* columnist William Safire wrote, recognizing that its leadership had acceded to Israel's demands. A self-described "pro-Israeli hawk," Safire observed with pleasure that "Arafat finally appears to be ready to accept [Menachem] Begin's approach [of 1978], adding the Gaza–Jericho twist, . . . having been softened by 15 years of Israeli hard line," not to speak of U.S. intransigence.[132]

For Palestinians in refugee camps and elsewhere outside the territories, the agreement offers little hope, and they have expressed understandable bitterness. Jordan, Syria, and Lebanon also "criticized the PLO for making concessions with Israel that could jeopardize Palestinian national rights and undermine the joint Arab negotiating strategy," giving "Israel the upper hand in imposing its conditions on each Arab country separately" in the negotiations to follow.[133]

If Israel reacts intelligently to the "white flag," it will drop the restrictions that have prevented any development in the territories. It will, that is, abandon its official doctrine, familiar from American practice and Western imperialism generally, that "no permits will be given for expanding agriculture and industry which may compete with the State of Israel."[134] The rational stance now would be to encourage an inflow of foreign funds, which can be used to establish a service sector for Israeli industry. It would be profitable for Israel to move assembly plants a few miles away, where there is no need to be concerned about such matters as labor rights, pollution, and the presence of unwanted Arabs within Jewish settled areas. Plants in the Gaza Strip and the cantons left for Palestinian administration in the West Bank can provide super-cheap and easily exploitable labor, yielding profits for foreign investors and helping to control the population. Israel is under considerable U.S. pressure to liberalize its economy, largely an artificial construct dependent on American grants and aid. The result will likely be to integrate Israel more fully into the international economy dominated by TNCs, in this case even more U.S.-based than the norm for historical and sociocultural reasons. That will only increase the pressures to integrate the occupied territories as well; the Caribbean Basin and Mexican border provide a possible model. Another likely consequence will be the dismantling of Israel's social democratic features, much as the United States has been accomplishing in the case of Costa Rica (see p. 136).

Israeli industrialists have been considering these matters for some time. While "a whole generation of Israeli manufacturers tried to crush every possibility of capitalist industrial development in the territories," correspondent Asher Davidi wrote in the Labor Party journal *Davar* in February 1993, with the increasing likelihood of some form of "autonomy," that way of thinking was changing. There is "complete agreement between representatives of the various sectors (banking, industry and large-scale commerce) and the government that the economic dependence of the 'Palestinian entity' must be preserved," including Israel's $1 billion-a-year export market in the territories. Large Israeli manufacturers, at least, see advantages in a shift to a U.S.–Mexico NAFTA–style model. "The realization of the Israeli industrialists' demands and their acceptance by the representatives of the Palestinian bourgeoisie would amount to a transition from colonialism to neocolonialism," Davidi observes, "a situation similar to the relations between France and many of its former colonies in Africa." Meanwhile, Israel's policy "is clear." "As Lieutenant-Colonel Hillel Sheinfeld, the Israeli coordinator of operations in the territories, put it, the declared goal of his work is to 'integrate the economy of the territories into the Israeli economy.'"[135] It can hardly be doubted that these plans remain in force. Under current conditions, they are likely to be realized.

Steps towards their implementation were taken in the Cairo agreement between Israel and the PLO (May 4, 1994). "Whether by choice or compulsion," the *Wall Street Journal* observed, "the PLO agreed in essence to keep the territories it will govern squarely within Israel's economic fold, forswearing, for now, any serious market integration with the surrounding states." Israeli companies "will continue to enjoy near-captive markets," "Palestinian consumers will continue to pay higher prices than their Arab neighbors, and Palestinian laborers will continue to work in Israel in large numbers," as Israel allows. Israel's high tariff structure is extended "to cover nearly everything entering the Palestinian market from abroad," and though prices in Jordan are a third of those in the West Bank and Gaza, according to the World Bank, "Palestinians in those areas will continue to be barred from importing most Jordanian goods." "Palestine will be treated as an Israeli market," an executive of a Jordanian multinational drug company observes. The agreements, the *Journal* continues, reflect Arafat's "desire to develop a state under Israeli, rather than Arab, tutelage." They contradict "some key terms that the PLO had agreed upon with Jordan," notably in financial matters, of much significance because of the expected inflow of foreign aid. "Most upsetting of all to neighboring Arabs, however, is the dimming prospect of trade," a particular disappointment to merchants in Jordan, most of whom "are Palestinian by descent, with family and economic ties to the West Bank."

The text released by the Israeli Foreign Office emphasizes again that the "permanent status" will be based on UN 242 alone, with no reference to Palestinian national rights. Israel will withdraw from the town of Jericho and parts of Gaza, but not from "the Gush Katif and Erez settlement areas, as well as the other settlements in the Gaza Strip"—the blocs it apparently intends to keep—or from the Egyptian border area. Military forces will be "redeployed" to ensure that "Israelis, including Israeli military forces, may continue to use roads freely within the Gaza Strip and the Jericho area," and Israel retains all "necessary legislative, judicial and executive powers and responsibilities," broadly construed and exercised "through its military government." Both sides agree to block "incitement, including hostile propaganda against each other," acting "to prevent such incitement by any organizations, groups or individuals within their jurisdiction"; such conditions can hardly apply within Israel, but they may be imposed on the Palestinian "authority." As before, there are provisions only for the security of Israelis, not Palestinians under Israeli occupation.

The agreements allow Palestinians to open banks, collect taxes, and carry out some trade, and offer prospects of economic development on the Third World model. The World Bank announced a $1.2 billion three-year aid program, mainly for badly needed infrastructure. The Bank "says the Israeli-run civil administration of the occupied territories for 27 years had an unusually low rate of investment, only 3 per cent of gross domestic product," Julian Ozanne reports, leaving infrastructure "in disrepair and chaos," compounding earlier Egyptian neglect. As for elections, he continues, "it is already clear [they] will be long delayed and might even be indefinitely postponed." The inflow of foreign funds should facilitate "the transition from colonialism to neo-colonialism" that Israeli industrialists and Palestinian investors anticipate.

Other Palestinians found little to celebrate. "The provisions of the agreement have alarmed even the most moderate Palestinians, who worry that the accord consolidates Israeli control in the territories," Lamis Andoni reports. Saeb Erekat, a senior Palestinian negotiator, commented that "apparently this agreement aims at reorganizing the Israeli occupation and not at a gradual termination." Even Faisal Husseini, who is close to Arafat, said that the accord "is definitely not the beginning that our people were looking for." Centrist Palestinian leaders, including the former head of the Palestinian delegation, Dr. Haidar Abdel Shafi, again criticized the PLO leadership for accepting an agreement that permits Israel to continue settlement, land appropriation, "annexation and Judaization" of its expanded Jerusalem area, and its "economic hegemony" over Palestinians. Particularly grating is what Palestinians saw as "the shabby behavior of the P.L.O. leadership, including a pattern of ignoring Palestinians who have suffered through 27 years of Israeli occupation in favor of exiles coming from Tunis to take power" (Youssef Ibrahim, reporting that PLO representatives "were pelted with stones by Palestinian youths as they rode into [Jericho] in Israeli Army jeeps"). Arafat's provisional list for his governing authority reveals "that he is determined to stack it with loyalists and members of the Palestinian diaspora," Ozanne reports from Jerusalem, including only two Palestinian "insiders," Faisal Husseini and Zakaria al-Agra, both Arafat loyalists. The rest come from Arafat's "loyal political factions" from outside the territories.[136]

All pretty much as expected.

A separate matter entirely is whether the parties are well-advised to accept the Cairo and Oslo agreements. For the United States and Israel, the question hardly arises: the agreement incorporates the basic terms on which they have insisted. For the Palestinians, the question is more complex. The agreement entails abandonment of their hopes for national self-determination and independence, at least for the foreseeable future. Nevertheless, realistic alternatives may be much worse.

Given U.S. power, refusal to accept U.S.–Israeli terms is at once translated into a demonstration of the worthlessness of such "fanatics" and "cowards," who thereby cede any remaining rights and are rightfully subject to the whims of the powerful. That consideration aside, the Israel–Arafat agreement should offer Palestinians some relief from the barriers to development imposed by the military administration, no small matter. And it moves beyond Rubinstein's "autonomy of a POW camp" in that Palestinians are assigned control over some economic affairs, including direct taxation. How much this might help the Palestinian economy one can only guess, since economic figures are secret, but a possible indication is given in a statement by Finance Minister Avraham Shochat, who said, in an interview with the *New York Times*, "that Israel would transfer some of the tax revenues it currently received from the Occupied Territories to help finance the Palestinian civil administration," a move that "could provide several hundred million dollars more to the Palestinians over the next decade."[137] An Israeli-supervised "strong police force" of Palestinians might, at worst, be the local counterpart of Israel's South Lebanon Army, subduing the population by terror and threat while the masters observe closely, ready to move if the iron fist is needed. But it might turn out that Palestinian police will treat the population less harshly than the Israeli forces, and settler depredations should reduce. Though the agreements say nothing about the matter, there may be a decline in construction for Jewish settlers in the territories and in the development programs designed to integrate them into the Israeli economy, leaving Palestinians on the side.

Many issues can be debated, but not—at least not seriously—within a doctrinal framework that identifies "realism" as what the United States and Israel demand, dismisses critical analysis in advance as "fanaticism" and "cowardice," and declares that only "extremists on both sides" might question an agreement that fully accepts long-standing U.S.–Israeli rejectionist principles.

Once again in the present case, we find that "historical engineering" has served effectively to contain perception of critically important developments within a mold that serves the interests of power and privilege, yet another example of the workings of a disciplined intellectual culture in a very free society. Unless these patterns of control are somehow dismantled, the prospects for peace and justice are not very bright.

It is, however, of no small significance that in this case too, much of the American population appears to be "out of control," though unorganized and inarticulate, hence without impact on policy. Despite the constraints on information and discussion, unusually severe in this case, the population has tended to favor a Palestinian state by roughly two to one. One historic failure of the PLO in the days when it had ample resources, international status, and loyalty within the territories is that it showed no interest in developing "people-to-people contacts" and support among the general American population. The roots of this failure merit exploration, including self-examination. With a concentrated effort of education and organizing, it might have been possible to weaken or overcome the effect of doctrinal barriers, as was done, to an extent, in the case of Indochina and Central America, among recent examples. Popular opinion, if organized and articulated, might have brought about a shift in U.S. policy towards the international consensus, which happened, in this case, to be favored by powerful domestic interests, including the oil companies. The doors are by no means closed, even now; there is sure to be a continuing struggle over the long-term meaning of the 1993 agreements. Efforts to defend Palestinian human and political rights could draw from, and also help stimulate, similar forces in Israel, which have been politically marginalized because of lack of U.S. support. There are common interests among the great mass of the population in the Arab world,

Israel, and the United States. The case is a striking example of the need for international solidarity, to the benefit of all.

The respected head of the Palestinian delegation, Haidar Abdel Shafi, had some observations on these matters in a talk in Bethlehem on July 22, 1993, just as Arafat was secretly moving to take matters into his own hands, undercutting local Palestinians. He held out little hope for the "peace process," which excludes entirely the possibility "that Palestinians must be the main authority in the interim period for the people and for the land," leading to true national self-determination. He stressed, however, that

> the negotiations are not worth fighting about. The critical issue is transforming our society. All else is inconsequential. . . . We must decide amongst ourselves to use all our strength and resources to develop our collective leadership and the democratic institutions which will achieve our goals and guide us in the future. . . . The important thing is for us to take care of our internal situation and to organize our society and correct those negative aspects from which it has been suffering for generations and which is the main reason for our losses against our foes.[138]

The Arab world is passing through a crucial moment in its history. It has rich human resources, cultural and intellectual. It also has rich material resources—notably oil, a wasting resource that will be gone in a few generations. If these resources are used to enrich sectors of the West and local elements that serve their interests, the people of the region will face a tragedy of incalculable proportions in the not-too-distant future. If resources are used to develop a domestic basis for sustained development, the future could be promising. A prerequisite for any serious progress in this direction is the dismantling of authoritarian and repressive structures, creation of an atmosphere of tolerance and defense for freedom of expression, organization of constructive popular forces, and, in general, substantial steps towards meaningful democracy.

These choices have to be faced seriously before too long, or it will be too late.

As for the New World Order, it is very much like the old, in a new guise. There are important developments, notably the increasing internationalization of the economy with its consequences, including the sharpening of class differences on a global scale, and the extension of this system to the former Soviet domains. But there are no fundamental changes, and no "new paradigms" are needed to make sense of what is happening. The basic rules of world order remain as they have always been: the rule of law for the weak, the rule of force for the strong; the principles of "economic rationality" for the weak, state power and intervention for the strong. As in the past, privilege and power do not willingly submit to popular control or market discipline, and therefore seek to undermine meaningful democracy and to bend market principles to their special needs. Within the culture of respectability, the traditional tasks remain: to reshape past and current history in the interests of power, to exalt the high principles to which we and our leaders are dedicated, and to file away the flaws in the record as misguided good intentions, harsh choices inflicted on us by some evil enemy, or the other categories familiar to the properly educated. For those who are unwilling to accept this role, the traditional tasks also remain: to challenge and unmask illegitimate authority, and to work'with others to undermine it and to extend the scope of freedom and justice.

Both tendencies exist, as they almost always have. Which prevails will determine whether there will be a world in which a decent person would want to live.

EPILOGUE: MIDDLE EAST DIPLOMACY

Chapter 3 carries the review of the diplomacy of the Israel-Arab conflict to signing of the Declaration of Principles in September 1993 (Oslo I) and the further implementation through the Cairo agreement of May 1994. The next major step was the signing of the September 1995 Interim Agreement (Oslo II).[1]

1. The Framework of Rejectionism

To appreciate the significance of these events, let us recall the context and backgrounds discussed in chapter 3.[2] In brief, after the June 1967 war, a diplomatic framework was established (UN 242) that called for Israeli withdrawal from conquered territories in return for peace. UN 242 was strictly rejectionist, according no rights to one of the contending parties, the Palestinians, apart from a reference to "just settlement of the refugee problem." Withdrawal was understood by the authors of UN 242 (including the United States) to mean *complete* withdrawal, with at most minor and mutual border adjustments. That remained official U.S. policy until February 1971, when it was accepted by President Sadat of Egypt, who offered Israel full peace in return for Israeli withdrawal from Egyptian territory. Israel recognized Egypt's "readiness to sign a peace agreement with Israel in an official document" to be a "far-reaching development"—a "famous . . . milestone" on the road to peace, in the words of Yitzhak Rabin's memoirs. Israel rejected the offer, reaffirming that "Israel will not withdraw to the pre-June 1967 lines." Washington then shifted policy, abandoning the international consensus it had helped to forge and joining Israel in rejecting UN 242 in favor of Kissinger's doctrine of "stalemate."

Since that time diplomacy has followed two very different paths: (1) the international consensus based on UN 242, and (2) the U.S.-Israeli program revising UN 242 to require only partial withdrawal. On that issue, the Israeli spectrum has been narrow (cf. pp. 223f.), and remains essentially unchanged today. The basic condition is that Israel should take over the usable lands and resources of the territories, but without responsibility for the population, who are to be marginalized and if possible dispersed. In the

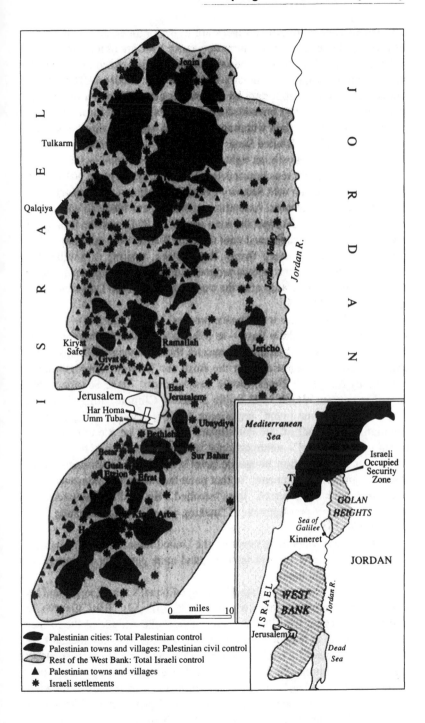

Palestinian cities: Total Palestinian control
Palestinian towns and villages: Palestinian civil control
Rest of the West Bank: Total Israeli control
▲ Palestinian towns and villages
✳ Israeli settlements

U.S.-Israeli conception, the refugees are to be forgotten and their rights, affirmed by the international community since 1948, are of no merit.

By the mid-1970s, the international consensus had shifted to accommodate Palestinian rights. In January 1976, the U.S. vetoed a UN Security Council resolution, supported by almost all other nations in the world, which reiterated UN 242 but added a call for a Palestinian state in the occupied territories after Israeli withdrawal. The two strands of diplomacy separated further, with the United States opposing the withdrawal component of UN 242 as well as Palestinian rights, in virtual international isolation.

With these extreme rejectionist commitments firmly in place, Washington has been compelled to veto Security Council resolutions, vote against regular near-unanimous General Assembly resolutions, and block all other diplomatic initiatives from Europe, the Arab world, the PLO, and the nonaligned countries. So matters continued until the Gulf War of 1991 established U.S. power in the region more firmly than before, making it possible for Washington to implement its own program unilaterally. That process, beginning at Madrid a few months after the war's end, led to Oslo I, the subsequent agreements, and Oslo II.

In U.S. discourse, the term "peace process" is used routinely—not only with regard to the Middle East[3]—to refer to whatever Washington advocates. To take a typical example, consider the comments of Dennis Ross, chief Middle East negotiator for the Bush and Clinton Administrations, reported by *New York Times* Middle East specialist Elaine Sciolino. Ross describes how in March 1993 Rabin presented Clinton with a "brilliant, cogent, clear-cut argument" explaining "exactly why the delegates then negotiating on behalf of the Palestinians would not be able to deliver"— meaning: "to deliver" a nonrejectionist settlement recognizing the rights of the indigenous population alongside Israel's. But the PLO refused to accept Rabin's compelling argument: "at that point they hadn't demonstrated they were prepared to make peace," Ross "recalled." His recollection is accurate, as the news report presupposes, if "making peace" means accepting U.S.-Israeli terms.[4]

Given the overwhelming power of the United States, these terminological conventions have by now been adopted quite generally, a propaganda victory of no slight import.

Washington's increasingly open backing of Israel's rejectionist stand has aroused some surprise in Israel (cf. pp. 235–36, 251–52). "Bill Clinton is the first U.S. President who liberated himself from the attitude of the former Presidents, who at least pretended that their attitude toward Israel and the Arabs is 'balanced'," a leading columnist (Nahum Barnea) observed under the headline "Clinton, the last Zionist." At home, a different picture is preferred. The history has been suppressed in favor of renditions of the kind reviewed in chapter 3, and the United States is depicted as an "honest broker" that is keeping "its critical distance" from both sides, perhaps unfair to Israel in its efforts to achieve "balance," critics object. Only when U.S. support for Israeli actions risks international opprobrium is this posture modified—for example, when Washington qualified its initial support for Israel's bombing of Tunis in 1985, killing 75 people, after the UN Security Council unanimously denounced the bombing as an "act of armed aggression" (the U.S. merely abstaining). More recently, when Clinton's support for Israel's renewed atrocities in Lebanon in 1996 began to contrast too prominently with the bitter condemnation internationally and even within Israel, the *New York Times* reported concerns "among Middle East specialists that America is losing something crucial—its critical distance from Israel—and thereby damaging its ability to play the 'honest broker' for Israelis and Arabs," the "traditional American role."[5]

2. "The Peace of the Victors"

Commenting on the May 1994 Cairo agreement, Meron Benvenisti, one of the most knowledgeable and astute analysts in the Israeli mainstream, observed that "Arafat once again bowed his head before the infinitely stronger opponent." The Cairo interpretation of Oslo I placed over half the West Bank under "absolute Israeli control," leaving the status of most of the rest ambiguous so that Israel could continue to use U.S. subsidies to "create facts," including settlements and infrastructure. Benvenisti predicted that the essential structure of Israel's military occupation would remain intact, but that "Israeli control will become less direct: instead of running affairs up front, Israeli 'liaison officers' will run them via the clerks of the Palestinian Authority." Israel will no longer insist on using its own military forces and administrators to control the subject population, adopting instead the more rational mechanisms that have been the traditional modality of Western domination for centuries. Benvenisti reiterated these conclusions after Oslo II established more firmly what he called "the peace of the victors," pointing out that its map conforms to the most extreme Israeli proposal of past years—that of the ultra-right General Ariel Sharon in 1981.[6]

Israeli leaders recognized what had been achieved. In the Oslo II agreements "we screwed the Palestinians," President Ezer Weizmann informed the Chinese Ambassador. Asked how Israel expects the Palestinians to accept such terms, Foreign Minister Ehud Barak answered simply: "We are the ones with the power."

Barak, formerly army Chief-of-Staff, had been appointed by Shimon Peres, who became Prime Minister when Rabin was assassinated a few weeks after the signing of Oslo II. Like his predecessor, Peres dismissed the idea that the permanent settlement might involve a Palestinian state. Explaining the Oslo II accords to a gathering of Ambassadors in Jerusalem, Peres stressed that "this solution about which everyone is thinking and which is what you want will never happen." Peres also responded with a "resounding 'No,'" Amnon Barzilai reports, when asked at a meeting with *Newsweek* editors whether a Palestinian state might be the eventual outcome. He had begun a "learned explanation," but it was never completed; it was interrupted by the broadcast verdict in the O.J. Simpson trial, which brought the meeting to a stop. Afterward the *Newsweek* editors were "too excited about the verdict" to return to his thoughts on the final outcome of the "peace process."[7]

The Rabin-Peres rejection of a Palestinian state is pointless from Israel's point of view, and may well be modified as events proceed. If so, that will confirm the expectations of Israeli commentators who have compared the settlement to South Africa's Bantustan program.[8] The comparison is not entirely apt, however. The Bantustans were much more viable politically and economically than any fragments that might eventually be called a "Palestinian state," and South Africa provided them with substantial subsidies. In contrast, Israel provides nothing to the cantons it is relinquishing to Palestinian administration. Another crucial difference is that South Africa's Bantustans were not recognized internationally, but rather condemned. In contrast, an eventual "Palestinian state" that has considerably less legitimacy will be hailed by international opinion as yet another "historic compromise" under the benign tutelage of the "honest broker." It would only make sense for the Israeli leadership to adopt the terminological convention of "statehood."

The more dovish Israeli leadership is accurate in its assessment of the victory that has been achieved. They have not had to depart in any meaningful way from the official stand of Israel's Labor-Likud coalition government of 1989, ratified by the Bush administration in the 1989 Baker plan, which stipulated that there will be no "additional Palestinian state in the Gaza district and in the area between Israel and Jordan" and "no change in the status of Judea, Samaria and Gaza other than in accordance with the basic guidelines of the [Israeli] Government" (cf. p. 231). Oslo II establishes these principles still more firmly, and the Likud government that took office in the May 1996 elections is likely to keep to them, in essentials.

The extent of the victory is revealed further by comparison of the Oslo Agreements with the traditional Labor stand. At the peak of U.S.-Israeli rejectionism in 1988, when both parties refused to recognize any Palestinian rights, Rabin called for Israeli control of 40 percent of the West Bank and Gaza Strip, reiterating the basic stand of his Labor Party from 1968.[9] At Oslo II in 1995, as we will see shortly, Rabin settled for Israeli control of about twice that much, along with ratification of whatever Israel and its sponsor have done and may choose to do.

It would, again, be pointless for Israel to insist on such extensive control of mostly useless territory, and if rational, it will rearrange jurisdictional matters in subsequent imposed agreements, calling whatever is left a "state."

Israeli political scientist Shlomo Avineri points out that "In one sense [Oslo II] is a major victory for Israel and a minimalist settlement for Arafat," who "has done a relatively good job given the impossible circumstances under which he is working."[10] One qualification is in order. Bear in mind other features of the traditional models of Western domination: Arafat, his associates, and rich Palestinians generally can expect to do well in the client relationship, whatever the effects on the population. And the enormous security apparatus that his Israeli-backed regime has put in place can also be expected to follow the norms, continuing to carry out the harsh repression and abuses that have been sharply condemned by human rights organizations and the Israeli press.[11] But Avineri is correct in tacitly recognizing that the outcome lends credence to the most cynical appraisals of the peace process.

3. The Interim Agreement: Jurisdiction

The Oslo II Agreement is impressively detailed, running to 314 pages in the official (Israeli) version. But while spelling out many specific arrangements, the text is interspersed with more general and abstract verbiage that is subject to varying interpretations. It is the kind of agreement that would be crafted by intelligent law students assigned the task of constructing a document that would allow U.S.-Israeli authorities the option to do as they please, while also leaving room for speculations about more forthcoming outcomes. When these remain unrealized, the blame can be laid on the extremists who have undermined the promise.

The Interim Agreement deals primarily with the West Bank. In Gaza, Israel maintains control of the blocs surrounding its settlements, the borders with Egypt and Israel, and the infrastructure linking these to Israel and isolating the Arab population.[12] The West Bank is divided into three parts: Zones A, B, and C. Zone A is assigned to the (Palestinian) Council, which replaces the Palestinian Authority. Zone C is assigned to Israel. Zone B has the ambiguous status of "autonomy," meaning local administration by Palestinians under Israeli "security control." As for Jerusalem, in theory its status is subject to negotiation; in reality, it has been resolved by Israeli annexation. We return to this important matter in section 6.

Zone A consists of Palestinian urban concentrations, about 2 percent of the West Bank. Zone C covers 70 percent of the territory. Zone B consists of more than 100 sectors of varying sizes scattered through Israel's Zone C. Zones A and B are under the "territorial jurisdiction" of the Council, along with the parts of Gaza that Israel has assigned to local administration. Zones A and B contain 1.1 million Arabs, Zone C 140,000 Jewish settlers and a handful of Arabs. One town, Hebron, has a population of about 500 Jews and 100,000 Arabs; Israel keeps substantial control. In the West Bank areas conquered by Israel in 1967, there are 300,000 Jewish settlers, more than half of them in Arab East Jerusalem, which now has a Jewish majority as a result of policies and regulations to which we will return (sec. 6).[13]

The agreement stipulates that Israelis will remain under Israel's jurisdiction and legislation. Referring presumably to areas outside the territorial jurisdiction of the Council, the agreement states that "the Israeli military government shall retain the necessary legislative, judicial and executive powers and responsibilities, in accordance with international law"—which the United States and Israel have always interpreted as they choose. The same latitude grants these authorities effective veto power over Palestinian legislation. The agreement states that any such "legislation which amends or abrogates existing laws or military orders . . . shall have no effect and shall be void *ab initio*" if it "exceeds the jurisdiction of the Council" or is "otherwise inconsistent" with this or any other agreement; in practice, as the United States and Israel determine.

Furthermore, "The Palestinian side shall respect the legal rights of Israelis (including corporations owned by Israelis) related to lands located in areas under the territorial jurisdiction of the Council"; specifically, their rights related to Government and Absentee land. The latter two categories constitute most of the region, it appears, though the Government of Israel, which determines their boundaries unilaterally, provides no official figures. The Israeli press reports that "unsettled state lands" amount to about half of the West Bank, and total state lands about 70 percent.[14]

Oslo II thus rescinds the decision of virtually the entire world that Israel has no claim to the territories occupied in 1967 and that the settlements are illegitimate. The Palestinian side now recognizes their legality, along with unspecified other legal rights of Israelis throughout the territories, including zones A and B. Oslo II implants more firmly the major accomplishment of Oslo I: UN resolution 242 of November 1967 is dead and buried, along with other resolutions and official declarations concerning the legality of settlements, the status of Jerusalem, the right of return, Palestinian rights in the territories—in fact, virtually the entire record of Middle East diplomacy, apart from the version implemented in the unilateral U.S. peace process. The basic facts are not just out of history, as they have long been in U.S. commentary, but now officially abrogated.

As the text of the agreement indicates, the territorial jurisdiction of the Council is at Israel's whim. The fact was underscored shortly after the signing of Oslo II, when Israeli military forces took over Area B, instituting even more severe measures of collective punishment than in the past: "The term 'closure' was replaced within the Israeli establishment by a new concept, 'strangulation,'" Nahum Barnea and Shimon Shiffer observed, with dire effects on a population already suffering severely, increasingly since Oslo I.[15]

In this case, the "strangulation" was in response to Palestinian terror, but such measures are imposed quite arbitrarily; for example, in response to Jewish terror. Thus after the massacre of Palestinians praying at the Cave of the Patriarchs in Hebron by Baruch Goldstein, a still more punitive curfew was imposed—on Palestinians. The purpose was "to protect the Jewish settlers from revenge," Ori Nir reported, describing how "the Israeli occupation redoubled the oppression" of Palestinians, destroyed the market that was the center for Hebron's economy, and closed roads to Palestinians though not Jewish settlers, who were left free to rampage, destroy, and humiliate the Arab population at will, an "insane reality" enforced by the military that "subordinates their lives to the settlers' interests." A year later, the Arab population of Hebron was again locked up under 24-hour curfew for four days so that settlers and 35,000 Jewish visitors could travel through the city undisturbed by an Arab presence during the Passover holidays, having picnics and dancing in the streets under the protection of extra military forces. The settlers and visitors used the opportunity "to insult the Palestinians imprisoned in their houses and to throw stones at them if they dared to peek out of the windows at the Jews celebrating in their city." The celebration was brought to a close "by settlers rampaging through the Old City, destroying property, and smashing car windows . . . in a city magically cleansed . . . of Palestinians, . . . effectively jailed for days in their homes" but able to watch the "merry dances of settlers" and the "festive processions" on TV while "commerce, careers, studies, the family, love—all are immediately disrupted," and "the medical system was paralyzed" so that "many sick persons in Hebron were unable to reach hospitals during the curfew and women giving birth could not arrive in time at the clinics."[16]

The aftermath of the Goldstein massacre was reviewed by Israel's major human rights organization, B'Tselem. From the February 1994 massacre to September 1995, B'Tselem reports, "security forces further restricted Palestinians' freedom of movement, resulting in substantial harm to the routine of daily life, also killing 27 Palestinians by gunfire (along with others killed in Nablus, Ramallah, and elsewhere). Palestinian homes were demolished. There were 12 curfews of varying length—50 days in all, 29 days immediately following the massacre—in addition to 40 night curfews and numerous partial curfews, all "collective punishment" of Palestinians in part for the acts of an American-Jewish settler who was hailed as a hero by a good part of the religious community.

Jewish settlers are immune from these or other punishments: "The security forces impose curfews on Palestinians for violent acts of Palestinians against settlers and also for violent acts of settlers against Palestinians." The report reviews the closing of Hebron's main roads to Arab inhabitants, their harassment by the security forces, and the destruction of the Arab market in the city center. A section on "Violent Attacks on Residents by Security Forces" reviews some of the reports on how soldiers break into houses, brutally beat residents (including children), and abuse and humiliate Palestinians as they please. Meanwhile "handling of cases where settlers injure Palestinians is still characterized largely by acquiescence, compromise, and mitigation," and attempts by Palestinians to register complaints are rebuffed by the Israeli authorities with contempt and humiliation.[17]

World attention is aroused only when people living in Hebron or the even more miserable and oppressed refugee camps nearby react with terrorist atrocities, demonstrating the criminal streak in Arab culture that makes it so hard for humane and peace-loving people to survive in this "tough neighborhood."

4. The Interim Agreement: Some Applications

Within the territories, the road system is divided into separate categories. Hundred of millions of dollars are being spent on "bypass roads" to allow Israelis, tourists, and Jewish settlers to travel freely through the territories, avoiding any contact with Arab inhabitants, who remain isolated in their villages and towns. These highways are "political facts that have long-term consequences," Benvenisti comments. Their significance is to be understood within the cantonization program designed to "cut the Arab areas into boxes, making *laagers* (encircled camps) out of the West Bank" as part of "a victor's peace, a diktat."[18]

There is also a second category of roads, typically marginal, to be "used only by Palestinian traffic," in the words of the Interim Agreement. Not without restrictions, however. The agreement allows the Palestinian Police 25 stations and posts in Zone B, but they are not permitted to travel from these to other "autonomous" areas—say, if there is a traffic accident in another village. Sometime in the future, perhaps, such "movement of Palestinian policemen" may be permitted on Palestinian roads, though only after they submit a plan in advance with full details and exact schedule, to be ratified by the Israeli authorities. "Uniformed members of the Israeli military forces, as well as vehicles of the Israeli military forces, shall not be stopped by the Palestinian Police in any circumstances," and Israeli civilians "shall not be stopped by the Palestinian police" except for "identification checks" in the Gaza Strip or Area A, or "places in Area B where there is a police station or post."[19]

Though Palestinian authority is narrowly circumscribed both in territory and content, it does extend to local administrative functions, as long as Israel approves. And in some domains, Israel relinquishes all interests and responsibilities:

> The transfer of powers and responsibilities from the Israeli military government and its civil administration to the Council [detailed in a separate 73-page Annex] includes all related rights, liabilities and obligations arising with regard to acts and omissions which occurred prior to such transfer. Israel will cease to bear any financial responsibility regarding such acts or omissions and the Council will bear all financial responsibility for these and for its own functioning . . . [Specifically, if] an award is made against Israel by any court or tribunal [in respect to a] financial claim made in this regard against Israel, . . . the Council shall immediately reimburse Israel the full amount of the award.

Included here are "Israeli statutory agencies and corporations registered in Israel."[20]

As discussed earlier, Israel profited substantially from the occupation and left the territories in a state of ruin. The costs are to be borne by the victims, including any future claims regarding Israel's actions.

The intent and likely consequences are illustrated by particular examples. Consider the fate of the lawsuit initiated by Israeli human rights activists of the workers' rights group Kav La'Oved and the Hebrew University. The plaintiffs requested restitution to Palestinian "guestworkers" of the estimated $1 billion withheld from their salaries for social benefits that they never received (pensions, unemployment payments, and so on). The funds ended up in Israel's State treasury (cf. note 53, chap. 3). In May 1995, Justice Y. Bazak of the Jerusalem District Court issued his ruling on this suit. The Court dismissed the case, accepting the government's contention that Knesset legislation to implement the Oslo I accords retroactively legalized Israel's confiscation of these funds. The Court also accepted the government's argument that Israel's National Insurance Law grants rights only to residents of Israel. The deductions were never intended to ensure equal rights for the Palestinian workers, Justice Bazak ruled, but were designed to keep wages for Palestinians high on paper but low in reality, thus protecting Israeli workers from unfair competition by cheap Palestinian labor. This is "a worthy and reasonable purpose which is recognized by the Court," Justice Bazak explained, "just as the legality of imposing customs taxes is recognized for the purpose of protecting the country's products."[21]

Though the disastrous effects of the occupation had been extensively reported by Israeli journalists, even the most knowledgeable were taken aback when they were able to visit Jordan after the peace agreement. The comparison is particularly apt, Danny Rubinstein observed, since the Palestinian populations were of about the same size in the two areas, the West Bank was somewhat more developed before Israel took it over in 1967, and Jordan is a poor Third World country that lacks Israel's enormous subsidies and other advantages. Rubinstein had reported how the Israeli administration "had purposely worsened the conditions under which Palestinians in the territories had to live," even refusing permits for factories to ensure that Israeli manufacturers would have a captive market; more generally, competitive development was banned by military order. But the effects were brought home more vividly by what he found in Jordan, where the "rate of development is much higher than that of the West Bank, not to mention Gaza," with a well-developed road system, electricity, water projects that "have turned the eastern bank of the Jordan valley into a dense and blooming agricultural area," health services, factories, commerce, hotels, and universities. Israel had allowed nothing similar, apart from "two small hotels in Bethlehem" and universities that "were built solely with private funding and donations from foreign states, without a penny from Israel"; the sole exception was the Islamic University in Hebron, supported by Israel as part of its encouragement of Islamic fundamentalism to undermine the secular PLO, now a Hamas center. "The result is that the backward and poor Jordanian kingdom did much more for the Palestinians who lived in it than Israel," showing "in an even more glaring form how badly the Israeli occupation had treated them."[22]

As Oslo II was announced, journalist Ronny Shaked recalled that in the territories Israeli governments "were only interested in calm and cheap manpower. Decisions about development of infrastructure, industry or agriculture were taken only to promote a specific Israeli interest and were forced on the inhabitants. In Hebron, for example, the Civil Administration refused a request to set up a factory for making nails, fearing competition with a factory in Tel Aviv. Some care was given to the health system, however, because diseases in the West Bank might also endanger residents of Tel Aviv." The Civil Administration was cheap to run, he adds, because its "minuscule" budget was covered by taxes from the local inhabitants.[23]

Oslo I and II are designed to perpetuate these circumstances.

With development banned under the occupation, Palestinians had two options: go elsewhere, or work in Israel. The latter option has been sharply reduced as Israel has turned to other sources of cheap labor: Romania, Africa, Thailand, the Philippines, Latin America, and other places where people live in misery. The Labor Ministry reported more than 70,000 registered foreign workers by March 1995, while only 18,000 entry permits were granted to Palestinians from the territories, down from 70,000 a year earlier. Like the Palestinians before them, they work under miserable conditions and lack basic rights, the press reports, often "living in subhuman conditions," circumstances that "would be the closest thing in our time to slavery" if it were not "an agreed-upon deal," thanks to the alternatives available in their home countries. Among the favorites are Chinese workers, because if they demand the pay that had been promised them, object to beatings and other abuses, or "try to raise their heads" in any way, Israel can turn to the Chinese authorities, who will "deal with them," the Chinese government representative informed the press. By March 1996, Israeli researchers estimated that in addition to the 75,000 licensed foreign workers, another 100,000 were employed illegally, and that the total will reach 200,000 in 1996 for dirty and dangerous jobs "that we Israelis do not want to take," serving as "the threadbare tires on which the Israeli economy races along."[24]

The facts on the ground conform to the principles of the Interim Agreement. As discussed earlier (pp. 261–64), Israeli settlement in the territories accelerated after Oslo I, including new settlements and "thickening" of old ones, special inducements to attract new settlers, and highway projects to cantonize the territory. So matters have continued. Excluding East Jerusalem, building starts increased by over 40 percent from 1993 to 1995, according to a Peace Now report of October 1995, though still not reaching the 1992 level. Government funding for settlements in the territories increased by 70 percent in the year following Oslo I (1994). The Labor Party journal *Davar* reported that the Rabin government kept the priorities of the ultra-right Shamir government it replaced; while pretending to freeze settlements, Labor "has helped them financially even more than the Shamir government had ever done," enlarging settlements "everywhere in the West Bank, even in the most provocative spots," including settlements of the (often American) followers of the racist Rabbi Kahane.[25]

In 1994, the Jewish population in the West Bank increased by 10 percent, in Gaza by 20 percent, the Israeli press reported. Total growth for 1992–94 is estimated at 34 percent. To mid-1995, during the first three years of the Labor government, the number of settlers increased by 31 percent, according to Peace Now. Israel's Central Bureau of Statistics estimated a further 4 percent increase in 1995, a higher growth rate than for any other region in Israel. The figures, which exclude Greater East Jerusalem, are estimates only, considered to be "conservative approximations" by the editor of the authoritative *Report on Israeli Settlements* (Geoffrey Aronson, of the Foundation of Middle East Peace in Washington).

Former West Bank Administrator Gen. Shlomo Gazit observes that the Rabin-Peres Labor government intended to double the Jewish population of the West Bank within the five-year "interim period" following Oslo I. The *Report on Israeli Settlements* concluded in early 1995 that "the Rabin government's construction plans for West Bank and Jerusalem settlements rival and in some respects surpass the settlement construction efforts of the Shamir government during 1989–92," with "a marked increase" planned for the coming years. In June 1995, Ma'ale Yisrael was established as the 145th settlement in the West Bank, against the orders of the government but with its acquiescence. Settlers use heavy equipment and explosives to build access roads near densely settled and heavily patrolled sectors of the West Bank, but the government knows nothing about it, spokespersons tell the press. Recent plans "shatter any remnant of the Palestinians' illusion that the Oslo Accord will bring about either an Israeli withdrawal from significant territories in the West Bank, or that East Jerusalem can ever serve as a Palestinian capital," Danny Rubinstein commented in January 1995. In March 1996, the *Report on Israeli Settlements* added that Prime Minister Peres "continues to invest hundreds of millions of dollars annually to encourage the growth of these settlements, whose population continues to increase at a rate approaching 10 percent annually."

On February 25, 1996, Housing Minister Binyamin ("Fuad") Ben-Eliezer presented a program for the construction of 6,300 new dwellings in the territories (up from 4,100 in 1995), including Ma'ale Adumim (an urban settlement east of Jerusalem), Givat Ze'ev (a suburb north of Jerusalem), and Beitar and Kiryat Safer (ultra-orthodox communities). "It is no secret," he said, "that the government's stand, which will be our ultimate demand, is that as regards the Jerusalem areas — Ma'ale Adumim, Givat Ze'ev, Beitar, and Gush Etzion — they will be an integral part of Israel's future map. There is no doubt about this." On the same day, he announced ground-breaking for the construction of 6,500 housing units for Jews at Har Homa, expropriated mostly from the Arab enclave of Umm Tuba/Sur Bahar in southeast Jerusalem, which has lost 91 percent of its land through town planning since Israel's takeover in 1967.[26]

In an interview in Israel that appeared the day after the signing of Oslo II, Ben-Eliezer described future settlement plans. "Fuad does everything quietly," he said, with "the complete protection of the Prime Minister." He outlined extensive settlement and development plans, including the expansion of Greater Jerusalem to include Ma'ale Adumim, Givat Ze'ev, and Beitar as the "first circle" of settlements surrounding Jerusalem from north to east to south, to which another "chain of settlements" is to be added in a second circle. The term to be used is "natural growth," he explained. He will "build quietly" rather than ostentatiously—the major difference between Labor and Likud over the years, and a large part of the reason why U.S. governments have consistently preferred Labor.

It is, therefore, not entirely false to say that the Rabin Labor government resolved the conflict between Shamir and Bush, "settl[ing] the issue by promising to stop new settlements and allowing, but not encouraging, the growth of existing ones" (Harvard government professor Nadav Safran). The promise may indeed have been made, though if so, it is hard to imagine that the United States government, which provides much of the funding through various channels, has been unaware of the ways it has been fulfilled. Though "quietly," not in the offensive "in your face" style of Shamir.[27]

There have been disagreements between the two major political groupings in Israel, but on these issues they have not been great. Benvenisti was again on target in describing the bounds of the mainstream spectrum, immediately after Oslo II: at one extreme, "a peace which imposes an unconditional surrender on the Palestinians," at the other, "a peace with somewhat more generous terms of surrender"—and we may add, more concern for Western sensibilities in the style of its operations.[28]

5. The Interim Agreement: Water

The Interim Agreement provides the first official Israeli data concerning the allocation of the crucial water resources of the West Bank. In general, these confirm the analyses already cited (pp. 210–11). A little over 10 percent of the total annual recharge is not yet in use. Of the 90 percent now exploited, some 8 percent consists of surface springs used by Palestinians. Of the remainder, seven-eighths is used by Israelis, about 40 percent of the total for settlers, the rest for Israel within the Green Line. This distribution is to continue with little change. Future needs of Palestinians are estimated at about 40 percent more than their current usage, amounting to about 28 percent of the total annual recharge (of which a quarter is uncontrollable surface springs). Existing arrangements for the Gaza Strip remain unchanged.[29]

There should, then, be little amelioration of the situation that has been described by Israeli and foreign journalists. The *Financial Times* reports that "Nothing symbolises the inequality of water consumption more than the fresh green lawns, irrigated flower beds, blooming gardens and swimming pools of Jewish settlements in the West Bank," while nearby Palestinian villages are denied the right to drill wells, and have running water one day every few weeks, polluted by sewage, so that men have to drive to towns to fill up containers with water or to hire contracters to deliver it at 15 times the cost. In summer 1995 the Israeli national water company Mekorot cut supplies to the southern and central parts of Gaza for 20 days because people had no money to pay their bills, though a handful of Israeli settlers run luxury hotels with swimming pools and profit from water-intensive agriculture. The situation is similar in the West Bank, for example, in the village of Ubaydiya, where 8,000 Palestinians were deprived of running water for 18 months while the nearby Jewish settlements are "flourishing in the desert" (though Mekorot did promise to restore service to deter a hearing at the High Court of Justice, with outcome unknown at the time of writing). In Hebron, Amiram Cohen reports, thousands of people had no water from their pipes in "the hot days of summer" of 1995, when each Arab of Hebron received less than a quarter of the water allotment of a resident of the nearby Jewish settlement of Kiryat Arba.[30]

The Israel-Jordan Peace Treaty underscores the basic conception. Its provisions on "achieving a comprehensive and lasting settlement of all the water problems between [Israel and Jordan]" are outlined by David Brooks of Canada's International Development Centre, a specialist on water resources of the region and a member of Canada's delegation to the Middle East Multilateral Peace Talks on water and the environment. He observes that the terms are not "particularly remarkable as water agreements go," with one exception: "what is omitted, or, more accurately, who is omitted. Not a word is said about water rights for the Palestinians, nor about giving them a role in managing the waters of the Jordan valley." "Palestinians are not even party to the negotiations," Brooks observes: "Their omission is staggering given that most of the Lower Jordan River (from Kinneret to the Dead Sea) forms the border between Jordan and what is likely in the near future to be Palestinian, not Israeli, territory," he believes.[31]

Intentions are spelled out further in the first post-Oslo II budget proposal, submitted by Prime Minister Peres in November 1995. Among the inducements to promote new settlement are subsidies for fish ponds in the arid Gaza Strip. The budget also provides almost $40 million for "new Jewish settlements in the Golan Heights, the West Bank, and the Gaza Strip," and extends the inducements to settlers that have given them some of the highest living standards in the country. The sectors of Gaza that Israel intends to keep are assigned by the budget to the Negev, perhaps a prelude to annexation. Not surprisingly, the budget was supported by the right-wing Likud opposition, which came to power six months later.[32]

Needless to say, only the waters of the occupied territories are subject to discussion, consistent with the general framework of capitulation. "The constant references to 'cooperation in the West Bank and Gaza'," Benvenisti points out, "indicate that while Israel is free to act independently in its own sovereign area, it insists on 'coordinating' the usage of natural resources by the Palestinians, so that Israeli interests will not be harmed," thus perpetuating "the existing inequality in the distribution of common natural resources" in this "victor's peace," which, for Israelis, "is a peace without pain or sacrifice, a bargain proposition, compatible with the atmosphere of a de-ideologized consumer society" driven by "pragmatic, even selfish attitudes"—which, we must add, are sustainable only insofar as they accord with the wishes of the real ruler of the area, and the contempt for Palestinians and Arabs generally that animates its dominant culture to such an extent that a rejectionist "victor's peace" is perceived as a "historic compromise" in which both sides abandon their hopes and dreams.[33]

6. Greater Jerusalem

A day after the end of the June 1967 war, Israel began its program to take over the Jerusalem area, expelling 650 Palestinians from the Old City, then bulldozing their homes and two mosques. A few weeks later, Israel expanded the city limits of Jerusalem, more than doubling its size, and effectively annexed the new Greater Jerusalem, claiming it as Israel's capital. These actions were taken over the objections of the UN General Assembly (99–0, with the United States among 20 abstaining, though it declared the actions invalid).[34]

As the U.S.-run peace process was being implemented, Prime Minister Rabin made it clear that Jerusalem will be the "eternal and indivisible" capital of Israel, where by "Jerusalem," the government "means really Greater Jerusalem, a big metropolitan area created by Israel south, north and east of the present boundaries of jurisdiction" (Nadav Shragay). In his report on Oslo II to the Knesset, Rabin outlined "the main changes, not all of them, which we envision and want in the permanent solution." Greater Israel is to incorporate "united Jerusalem, which will include both Ma'ale Adumim and Givat Ze'ev"; the Jordan Valley; and "blocs of settlements in Judea and Samaria like the one in Gush Katif" (the southern sector of Gaza that Israel retains surrounding its settlements). These blocs are to include "Gush Etzion, Efrat, Beitar and other communities" in the West Bank. The press reported that Ma'ale Adumim will be annexed to Greater Jerusalem after increased settlement establishes contiguity between the two urban areas.[35]

These plans fall within the general outline presented on the signing of Oslo II by Housing Minister Ben-Eliezer, already discussed, and will presumably be continued by the new Likud government, perhaps "quietly" if its highly Americanized leadership (Benjamin Netanyahu, Dore Gold) can control the religious and nationalist constituency.

The Greater Jerusalem-Ma'ale Adumim region extends virtually to Jericho and the Jordan Valley, effectively bisecting the West Bank. As Oslo II was signed, efforts were underway to encourage Jewish settlement in lands confiscated from Bedouins in Ma'ale Adumim, where a new bypass road was opened a month later. There, 6,000 new housing units are to be erected by 2005 along with 2,400 new hotel rooms, as well as shopping malls, a new city hall, and other construction. The mayor of Ma'ale Adumim announced in June 1995 that the new housing is expected to more than double the city's population to 50,000.

The map included in the text of the Interim Agreement indicates no distinction between Israel proper and its Zone C in the West Bank. The case of Jerusalem, however, is different. The map makes clear that all of it remains within Israel, including Arab East Jerusalem in its much expanded boundaries. All locations in the West Bank are identified in Hebrew in the official map, and apart from villages, in English as well (there is nothing in Arabic). The Jerusalem area, however, is identified only in Hebrew, and the Hebrew word is placed right across East Jerusalem reaching virtually to the closest autonomous enclave to the East, and extending well to the east of neighborhoods of East Jerusalem to which Arabs are being confined.[36]

The facts are tacitly recognized in published maps of Oslo II. In the Israeli press, Jerusalem is shown as a unified area, but its status is left unclear. The *New York Times* map includes West Jerusalem within Israel, with Greater East Jerusalem given an ambiguous status.[37]

In the expanded East Jerusalem area, Israel has been carrying out programs since 1967 to reduce Arab citizens to a minority with second-class status. These were devised and implemented by former Mayor Teddy Kollek, highly regarded in the West as a democrat and humanitarian, and are being extended under his successor, Ehud Olmert of Likud. Their purpose, Kollek's adviser on Arab affairs Amir Cheshin explained, was "placing difficulties in the way of planning in the Arab sector." "I don't want to give [the Arabs] a feeling of equality," Kollek elaborated, though it would be worthwhile to do so "here and there, where it doesn't cost us so much"; otherwise "we will suffer." Kollek's planning commission advised development for Arabs if it would have "a 'picture window' effect," which "will be seen by a large number of people (residents, tourists, etc.)." Kollek assured the Israeli press in 1990 that for the Arabs, he had "nurtured nothing and built nothing," apart from a sewage system—which, he hastened to add, was not intended "for their good, for their welfare," "they" being the Arabs of Jerusalem. Rather, "there were some cases of cholera [in Arab sectors], and the Jews were afraid that they would catch it, so we installed sewage and a water system against cholera." As noted, similar practices held through the West Bank generally.[38]

Kollek's programs were analyzed by Sarah Kaminker (a City Council member and planner in Kollek's administration) in a June 1994 Report prepared for the High Court on behalf of Arab plaintiffs by the Society of St. Yves, the Catholic Legal Resource Center for Human Rights. In Jewish West Jerusalem, the Report concluded, "there is large-scale illegal construction" which the Municipality does not prevent and retroactively approves. In Arab East Jerusalem, standards are different. There, 86 percent of the land has been made "unavailable for use by Arabs." The remaining 14 percent "is not vacant land but land that has already been developed"; vacant lands are reserved for development for Jews, or kept as "open landscape views" (often for eventual Jewish use). "The dearth of land zoned for Arab housing is a result of government planning and development policy in East Jerusalem," where the Kollek administration conducted "a consistent effort since 1974 to limit the land area available to Arabs for licensed construction." The goal is "demographic balance," partially achieved in 1993 when Kollek's Municipality "was able to announce that the number of Jews residing in East Jerusalem had surpassed the number of Arabs."

The government has provided housing in East Jerusalem: 60,000 units for Jews, 555 for Arabs. Arabs whose homes have been demolished for Jewish settlement often "come from the lowest economic strata of their community" and now "live in makeshift hovels, doubled and tripled up with other families, or even in tents and caves." Those who want to build their own homes on their own lands are barred by law and the houses are subject to demolition if they proceed. The threat is executed, unlike Jewish West Jerusalem, where "the problem of illegal construction . . . is as serious, if not more so, than that in East Jerusalem." "Demographic balance" is advanced further by discriminatory regulations on building heights, far more limited in Arab than Jewish neighborhoods of East Jerusalem. An array of zoning provisions and other legal instruments has been designed to intensify the discrimination between Jews and Arabs, as throughout Israel itself.[39]

In a forthcoming study,[40] Kaminker describes in more detail how Palestinians are to be confined to ever smaller areas (she estimates that only 10 percent of the land may now be used by its Palestinian owners). Though most of the planning is secret, sometimes hints are "inadvertently revealed," as when the City Engineer informed the Jerusalem City Council of the methods used to enforce the "governmental decision to preserve the ratio between the Arab and Jewish populations in Jerusalem as 28% Arabs and 72% Jews": a quota for Arab housing requiring that an increase of units in one Arab neighborhood, even if needed, will be compenstated by decreases in others. Kaminker reviews a variety of measures that are employed to prevent land utilization or any economic development in the Arab areas while fostering it in the Jewish areas; and administrative procedures that "serve to wrest control of most of the land from its owners" and develop it for flourishing Jewish neighborhoods, while "existing Arab communities are to be confined to small areas, isolated from one another . . . ," and kept at the lowest level. Her inquiries also confirm the government plans to integrate Jerusalem and Ma'ale Adumim. In theory the future status of Jerusalem is still to be determined by later negotiations; in practice, the expropriation plans of the Labor government virtually settle the issue.

These actions, substantially funded by American taxpayers, had been undertaken over the rhetorical objections of the United States government prior to the Clinton Administration, which, as already discussed, has dropped any pretense on this and other central issues. These particular subsidies are opposed by the public even more than most foreign aid, and are the one component that is immune from the sharp reductions now being instituted in the United States foreign aid program, miserly by international standards and virtually invisible if Israel and other Middle East interests are excluded. Aid to Israel includes, for example, 25 of "the most sophisticated fighter-bombers in the world," the British press reports, a deal that "slid through Congress with no objections by legislators and virtually no comment in the American media." This is "the first time such high-performance military equipment has been sold unrestricted and unamended abroad since the Second World War" ("sold" generally means funded by U.S. military aid and Ex-Im Bank loans), a "decisive enhancement of Israel's military capabilities, giving it the power to strike at potentially dangerous nations far beyond its borders: Iran, Iraq, Algeria, and Libya for example." The United States "appears to be reappointing Israel as local deputy sheriff, a role which ended with the disappearance of the communist threat in the Middle East"—which was never the real threat, as the extended appointment once again reveals, and is now largely conceded.[41]

7. The Broader Picture

Washington's long-term goals remain as before: to assure its dominance of the world's major energy reserves, "a stupendous source of strategic power, and one of the greatest material prizes in world history." In what the *New York Times* calls "The Brave New Middle East" taking shape after Arafat's "surrender," Washington's Israeli client is to serve as the military, industrial, and financial center of a regional system that links Egypt, Turkey, the Gulf oil producers, and secondary participants.[42]

Oslo I and II take a long step toward that end. Tacit relations among participants are now becoming more overt and efficient. Israel's relations with Turkey are particularly important. Trade between the two is increasing rapidly along with military cooperation. Israel's state military industry is upgrading Turkey's U.S. jets and the Israeli Air Force is now using Turkish air space for training exercises. Jordan may also be incorporated into the alliance. Israel's relations with the Gulf Emirates have also expanded. The director of Jordan's Center for Strategic Studies "sees these changes in the context of what he calls 'the Latin Americanization of the Middle East,'" the *Wall Street Journal* reports, "with the region increasingly coming under U.S. strategic and military hegemony."[43]

These goals were difficult to achieve as long as the Palestinian issue remained a festering sore, a source of unrest in the Arab world. But Arafat's acceptance of "the peace of the victors," in the apparent hope of salvaging some shreds of his waning authority, has helped to suppress the Palestinian issue (there are other factors, including the disintegration of secular Arab nationalism and the disarray of the South generally). One notable consequence of this success is "the real peace dividend for Israel." The *Wall Street Journal* describes how "the barriers are now down in the fastest-growing markets in the world, which are in the Far East, not the Middle East." The United States already has overwhelming influence in West Asia, but for a U.S. outpost to position itself in the contested Asia-Pacific region is a useful further accomplishment.

These consequences of the Oslo peace process are reflected in the rapidly rising level of foreign investment in Israel, which is increasingly seen as "the fulcrum of economic development in the region" (Lord Sterling, chairman of a major UK shipping company). "Israel will look back on 1995 as the year when international finance and business discovered its thriving economy," the *Financial Times* observed—"thriving" in the usual manner of "economic miracles," mimicking its patron by achieving unusually high rates of inequality and dismantling social services. Poverty rates have risen to record heights, a quarter of children now live in families with incomes below the poverty line, and the percentage of elderly among the poor rose by 20 percent from 1993 to 1994.[44]

Another important component of the Oslo diplomatic process is the end of even a gesture toward Palestinian refugees. The settlement effectively abrogates their right of return, endorsed unanimously by the UN General Assembly in 1948 as the direct application of Article 13 of the Universal Declaration of Human Rights (adopted the previous day), and reiterated regularly since. Immediately after Oslo I, Rabin had dashed any hopes that refugees might return to the areas of Palestinian autonomy, let alone anywhere else. While the Clinton Administration offered $100 million to the Palestinian Authority, mostly for security forces (in contrast to $3 billion to Israel, perhaps twice that if we add other devices), it cut by $17 million the U.S. contribution to UNRWA, the largest single employer in the Gaza Strip and responsible for 40 percent of its health and education services as well as for Palestinian refugees elsewhere. Washington may be planning to terminate UNRWA, which "Israel has historically loathed," Graham Usher observed. Breaking with earlier policies, the Clinton Administration voted against all General Assembly Resolutions pertaining to Palestinian refugees in 1993 and 1994, on the grounds that they "prejudge the outcome of the ongoing peace process and should be solved by direct negotiations," now safely in the hands of the United States and its clients. As a step toward dismantling UNRWA, its headquarters are to be moved to Gaza, which should effectively terminate international support for the 1.8 million Palestinian refugees in Jordan, Lebanon, and Syria. The next step may be to defund it completely, UN sources report.[45]

The plight of the refugees is particularly desperate in Lebanon, which became a dumping ground for Palestinians who fled or were expelled by the Israeli army in 1948, and again in 1967. From the early 1970s, Lebanon was drawn into the conflict as a result of cross-border PLO terror and far more destructive Israeli attacks on Lebanon, sometimes retaliatory, often not. Thus in February 1973, Israeli forces attacked north of Beirut, killing many civilians, in a raid justified as preemptive. In December 1975, Israeli bombing killed more than 50 Lebanese in an attack Israel described as "preventive, not punitive"—apparently a reaction to the UN Security Council session debating the diplomatic settlement that Israel opposed and Washington vetoed. There are many other examples.

As the Camp David agreements freed Israel "to sustain military operations against the PLO in Lebanon as well as settlement activity on the West Bank" (Avner Yaniv), its attacks increased, including the 1982 invasion that was intended to overcome PLO moderation, but in doing so created a new problem: the formation of the Islamic fundamentalist group Hezbollah, whose official aim was to drive Israel from Lebanon. Despite massive resort to terror, Israel was forced to withdraw from all but the southern part of Lebanon, where it maintains a "security zone" in violation of orders of the UN Security Council issued in March 1978. Until February 1992, when an Israeli attack killed Sheikh Abbas Mussawi and his family, "not a single Katyusha rocket was fired from Lebanon to Israel," former Defense Minister Moshe Arens reports. But after that act of terror, Hezbollah "changed the rules of the game," Prime Minister Rabin informed the Knesset, retaliating against Israeli attacks north of its "security zone" by rocket attacks on Israel. That change precipitated Israel's 1993 "Operation Accountability," which killed many civilians and drove hundreds of thousands from their homes in an effort to pressure the Lebanese government to force Hezbollah to restore the earlier rules. An informal settlement was reached barring attacks on civilians, but Israel ignored it, continuing to attack north of its "security zone," killing many civilians, sometimes eliciting Hezbollah retaliation.[46]

U.S.-Israeli intentions to maintain those operations was made explicit the day that Shimon Peres assumed his duties as Prime Minister after Rabin was slain. "Peres Sets Tone of Post-Rabin Era," a front-page *New York Times* headline read, introducing a report that "Israeli warplanes shrieked over Lebanon" and "pounded the bases of radical Palestinian guerrillas south of Beirut," well beyond Israel's "security zone." Peres won praise for this demonstration of his intention "to assume Mr. Rabin's soldier's mantle as the scourge of Arabs who reject Israel's offer of peace." The adjacent column condemned the "desperate act, a horrible act, the work of cowards," when terrorists attacked a U.S.-run military training center in Riyadh, Saudi Arabia, the same day. Two weeks later, Hezbollah fired rockets into Northern Israel, wounding several civilians, an act of terrorism that it described as a "warning response" to "Israel's continuing aggressions," including the demolition of homes by the Israeli army in Lebanon and the Israeli Navy's refusal to allow Lebanese fisherman to fish off the Lebanese coast. As the rockets fell, a senior security official of Hezbollah was blown up by a car bomb. Hezbollah's terror was condemned as a violation of the 1993 agreement that Israel violates at will: for example, two weeks earlier as Peres took office, or a month before that, on October 13, when "Israeli artillery bombarded villages outside the security zone," a tiny item reported, with "no immediate word on casualties," in retaliation for the wounding of Israeli soldiers in its Lebanese security zone.

Israeli actions in Lebanon regularly pass with little comment. More than 100 Lebanese were killed by the Israeli army or its local mercenaries in the first half of 1995, the London *Economist* reports, along with six Israeli soldiers in Lebanon. Israeli forces use terror weapons, including anti-personnel shells that spray steel darts (sometimes delayed action shells to maximize terror), which killed two children in July 1995 and four others in the same town a few months earlier, and seven others in Nabatiye, where "no foreign journalists turned up" to describe the atrocities, British Middle East correspondent Robert Fisk reported from the scene. The occasional mention is usually in the context of a denunciation of Hezbollah terror in retaliation. The use of "internationally banned shells which spray steel darts" was justified by Health Minister Ephraim Sneh, a former army commander, who described this as "a very good weapon" that is "completely legitimate" in a war against "terrorists," with no "ethical constraint."[47]

In a review of Israeli and Hezbollah operations, Human Rights Watch compiled a sample of 45 incidents from the July 1993 understandings to the launching of Israel's "Grapes of Wrath" attack in April 1996, a virtual replay of "Operation Accountability." All Hezbollah attacks on Israel in the sample are retaliatory. The standard format is a Hezbollah operation against Israeli forces or their mercenaries in Israel's southern Lebanon "security zone," followed by Israeli attacks north of the zone, then Hezbollah rocketing of northern Israel (also in violation of the laws of war, HRW observes). Other Israeli attacks (also often killing civilians) were not in response to Hezbollah operations. The pattern continued to March 30, 1996, when Israeli shelling killed two civilians in Yater (north of the security zone) with no provocation, leading to Hezbollah retaliation.[48]

After an Israeli soldier was killed in the security zone on April 10, Israel launched Operation "Grapes of Wrath," backed strongly by the Clinton Administration until Israel's actions aroused a storm of protest throughout the world, and U.S. support became more muted. The press pretty much followed the same course. The contrast between the reports in the U.S. and the foreign press, with its vivid eyewitness depiction of Israeli atrocities, was unusually dramatic, but this is not the place to review it.

The preferred U.S. version is that Israel's "strong reply to Hezbollah terror" is "justified," that Peres "only exercised Israel's right to self-defense," and that responsibility for the "senseless casualties on both sides of the border lies squarely with Hezbollah's terrorists and the Governments in Beirut and Damascus" (editorial, *New York Times*; "casualties on both sides of the border" when the operation ended included about 160 deaths to the north, virtually all Lebanese civilians, none to the south). News coverage revised the background in the usual way, stating that the 1993 accord "had largely held until [early April 1996], when Hezbollah resumed its attacks and Israel began to retaliate in force" and that "The guerrillas had repeatedly fired rockets into northern Israel and Israel retaliated with air strikes in Lebanon"; and reporting Washington's speculation "that Hezbollah started firing Katyusha rockets into Israel at the direct instigation of Iran in order to affect the Israeli election."[49]

President Clinton even managed to justify the Israeli massacre of refugees sheltering in the UN base at Qana. He described the killings as a "tragic misfiring by Israel in its legitimate exercise of its right of self-defense" in response to a "deliberate tactic of Hezbollah" to position rockets near civilians. But the international reaction to this and other atrocities was by then so substantial that Washington chose to distance itself. Secretary of State Warren Christopher was sent to try to establish an agreement that would modify the 1993 terms in Israel's favor, barring resistance in Israel's security zone. That got nowhere. Washington was then compelled to adopt the basic outlines of a French proposal that would prevent operations against civilians but allow resistance to the Israeli occupation. The agreement (April 26) was presented as an achievement of U.S. diplomacy by the government and the press. European initiatives were generally condemned, sometimes in curious ways, notably a tirade by Thomas Friedman of the *New York Times* ending with "Advice to the Euros. Get a life. Stick to dealing with problems like a common currency and mad cow disease." I.e., leave international affairs to the big boys.[50]

Israel's attacks north of its security zone resumed at once. Three Israeli air raids and artillery barrages were reported in May, the last wounding five civilians in eastern Lebanon "in apparent retaliation for a guerrilla bombing that killed four Israeli soldiers" in Israel's security zone. A UN source described Israeli bombardment of the village of Tibnit on May 19 as "certainly . . . a violation" of the agreements, because Hezbollah had carefully avoided civilian areas in launching the operation within the security zone to which Israel responded.[51]

The Israeli operations of 1993 and 1996, like those of earlier years, had the openly expressed intent to punish the civilian population so that the government of Lebanon would be compelled to accept U.S.-Israeli demands. It is this "rational prospect" that has always motivated Israel's attacks on civilian populations, Israeli diplomat Abba Eban explained years ago, justifying Israeli terror attacks carried out by the Labor government in which he had served. Not everyone accepts Eban's moral judgments. Describing "the 1996 Lebanon war" as yet another that "will go down in history as a war fought by an army against unarmed civilians," Israeli sociologist Baruch Kimmerling describes "the principle of 'moving the population' and turning them into refugees in order to produce 'political pressure' " as "the kind of policy resorted to by the world's most evil regimes. . . . Only people lacking any moral standards could think up and execute such a policy." Or accept it as legitimate.[52]

But such voices are rare in Israel, or its sponsor.

Israel feels free to carry out terror operations, *Ha'aretz* columnist Ari Shavit commented in a column "adapted" in the *New York Times*, because:

> we believe with absolute certitude that now, with the White House and Senate in our hands along with the Pentagon and the *New York Times*, the lives [of Arabs] do not count as much as our own. Their blood does not count as much as our blood. We believe with absolute certitude that now, when we have

AIPAC [the Israel lobby] and [Edgar] Bronfman and the Anti-Defamation League, when we have Dimona [the nuclear weapons installation][53] and Yad va-Shem and the Holocaust Museum, we truly have the right to tell 400,000 people that in eight hours they must flee from their homes, [which we will then] treat as pure military targets. And that we have the right to rain 16,000 bombs on their villages and towns and populated areas. That we have the right to kill without any guilt.[54]

Shavit's observations are well-taken. Specifically, it is well to remember that Israel's actions, however one assesses them, are essentially costless. As Washington's leading client state, Israel inherits the right to do as it chooses. A dramatic illustration of this right was offered in the home country right in the midst of Operation Grapes of Wrath. On April 19, there was much anguished commentary in the U.S. media on the truck bombing at Oklahoma City a year earlier, when middle America "looked like Beirut," headlines lamented, and commentators called for bombing of any Middle East culprit that might have a hand in the atrocity. Beirut, of course, had looked like Beirut long before; for example, just 10 years before, when the worst terrorist act of the year in the region was perpetrated in Beirut, a car bombing outside a mosque, timed to cause maximum civilian casualties, mostly women and children—an act of terror that was virtually duplicated at Oklahoma City. The facts are well known, but unmentionable. That act of terror was carried out by the CIA, which suffices to remove the incident from history along with much else that suffers the same defect. The implications are of no slight significance in world affairs. Israel's impunity is only one special case.[55]

Another consequence of the Oslo Agreements has been a decline in the ratio of Palestinians to Israelis killed, a tendency described in Israel and the West as an increase in Palestinian terror; not false, but not quite the whole story either, even aside from the matter of international terrorism in Lebanon. In earlier years, the overwhelming majority of deaths, torture, and other abuses were attributable to Israeli security forces and settlers. But that has changed, though the facts are not entirely clear, because killings of Palestinians, or other atrocities and abuses directed against them, receive little attention. A rare report in the U.S. press states that from the signing of Oslo I through 1994, 93 Israelis were killed while "some 187 Palestinians have died mainly at the hands of an increasingly strained Israeli Defense Force (IDF), which bears the burden of protecting Jewish settlers"; by May 1995, the numbers had risen to 124 Israelis and 204 Palestinians, "fewer than in previous years." Middle East correspondent Graham Usher reports that from the signing of Oslo I to mid-1995, "the repressive Israeli regime of containment . . . has killed 255 Palestinians in the West Bank and Gaza, while attacks by Palestinians have claimed 137 Israelis"; Israel also arrested 2,400 Palestinians "for alleged 'Islamist tendencies' between October 1994 and January 1995." According to Amnesty International, more than 80 Palestinians were shot dead by Israeli forces in 1994; in 1995, the numbers rose to at least 99 Palestinians. In both years, the toll includes "children and young people," for example, when a soldier fired into a group of children and killed a 14-year old schoolboy. During 1995, at least 40 people, including 13 civilians, were killed by Palestinian suicide bombers, AI adds. Human Rights Watch reports that Israeli security forces killed 108 Palestinians in 1994 and 34 in the first ten months of 1995.[56]

In November 1995, Hamas, regarded as the primary agency of anti-Jewish terror, proposed negotiations to "remove civilians from the circle of war and violence," the Israeli press reported, but Prime Minister Rabin rejected the offer on the grounds that "Hamas is the enemy of peace, and the only way to deal with it is by a war of extermination." A Hamas truce offer in March 1996 was rejected by Foreign Minister Barak, who refused any negotiations.[57]

AI reports further that "Palestinians under interrogation continue to be systematically tortured or ill-treated," that thousands of Palestinians were detained on such charges as opposing "the peace process," and hundreds tried in military courts in 1995 while more than 200 others were held without charge or trial, among other abuses, many quite serious. Among those under detention without charge or trial in Israeli jails are Lebanese taken prisoner in Lebanon and transferred to Israel, some of whom have "been detained for nine years without trial." AI also condemns new proposals to "legalize torture," extending provisions already in force, as have other human rights organizations. Israel's "systematic torture and ill-treatment of Palestinians under interrogation" has also been condemned by Human Rights Watch, which notes further that for this reason, all U.S. aid to Israel is illegal under U.S. law (as is U.S. aid to Turkey, Egypt, Colombia and many other aid recipients).[58]

Let us turn finally to the public version of the accords. The basic picture is that the longtime adversaries have abandoned their traditional goals, realizing at last that peace requires compromise and sacrifice.

September 28, 1995 was a "Day of Awe" (*Boston Globe*), on which "Israel and the PLO sign agreement extending Palestinian rule to most of West Bank" (Reuters chronology). Rabin had "conquered the ancient lands on the West Bank of the Jordan," but then was transformed to a man of peace and "negotiated the accord to eventually cede Israeli control of them to the Palestinians," Serge Schmemann reported in the *New York Times*, "a process of granting the Palestinians a homeland in exchange for peace." *Times* Middle East correspondent Clyde Haberman wondered at the "evolution" in Rabin's thinking as "his language underwent a remarkable transformation and so did his ideas about peace with the Palestinians"; "it was astonishing how far he had roamed from where he stood in 1992"—or 1988, when he called for Israel to retain half as much as he accepted at Oslo II. *Washington Post* Middle East correspondent Glenn Frankel reported that "when Rabin offered Israelis the possibility of 'separation'—of walling off the Gaza Strip and West Bank and getting Palestinians out of sight and out of mind—the majority responded with enthusiasm"; one can only imagine the response had Rabin proposed anything of the sort. A *Post* editorial added that "the latest Israeli-Palestinian accord is a big one, making the historic move toward accommodation of the two peoples all but irreversible."

Headlines read: "Israel agrees to quit West Bank" (*Guardian*). "Israel Ends Jews' Biblical Claim on the West Bank" in "Rabin's historic trade with Arabs," a "historic compromise" (*Christian Science Monitor*). "Israelis, Palestinians find a painful peace" (*Boston Globe*), establishing an "undeniable reality: The Palestinians are on their way to an independent state; the Jews are bidding farewell to portions of the Holy Land to which they have historically felt most linked." "Those who murdered Rabin, and those who incited them, didn't do so because they opposed plans to create a Palestinian Bantustan," the *New Statesman* correspondent reported from Jerusalem, chiding Edward Said for thinking otherwise. "No: they knew that the course Rabin was charting would lead, unless stopped, to a Palestinian state."[59]

That's a fair sample. A comparison with the facts is instructive.

Another theme is that the grand promise is being undermined by extremists on both sides, mainly Palestinians. Few eyebrows were raised when Israeli novelist Amos Oz wrote in a "Letter to a Palestinian Friend" that "the essence" of the Oslo agreements "is clear and simple: we stop ruling over you and suppressing you, and you recognize Israel and stop killing us. But up until now we have delivered and you haven't."[60] His American readers may not know the facts; he surely does.

One aspect of the general portrayal is not implausible: the Oslo agreements might indeed resolve the conflict. How? Much in the manner advocated by *New Republic* editor Martin Peretz when he advised Israel to invade Lebanon in 1982 to administer to the PLO a "lasting military defeat" so that Palestinians will "be turned into just another crushed nation, like the Kurds or the Afghans," and the Palestinian problem, which "is beginning to be boring," will be finished. These have been the basic guidelines of Washington's peace process, and are hardly without precedent, the most obvious one, perhaps, in North America. To mention another, the conflict between those who had sought a multi-ethnic Bosnia and advocates of a partition between Greater Croatia and Greater Serbia is also moving toward resolution, based as usual on the rule of force.[61]

There is no certainty, of course. No one knows how people will react to becoming "just another crushed nation," subjected to endless humiliation, their voices unheard, their simplest plea for justice drowned in a chorus of self-righteous cynicism. Baruch Kimmerling may yet be proven right in his assessment of the likely consequences of "this 'peace' arrangement," which makes "the infamous Treaty of Versailles seem ideal in comparison." It may be, as he predicts, that "The question of the renewal of the Palestinian uprising—which will make the Intifada seem like child's play—and which, like the [Arab revolt of] 1937–39, will be turned against the actual rulers—is only a matter of time." But history is not kind to the common view that peace and stability are impossible without at least a modicum of justice.[62]

Much will depend on cultural conditions within the United States, the global power that dominates the region and has succeeded in imposing its will. But whatever the outcome, what has taken place, and how it has been interpreted, constitute an impressive testimonial to the rule of force in international affairs, one that should be considered carefully by those who care about the fate of the world.

NOTES

Notes to Chapter 1

1. Weiss, *Boston Review*, February/March 1994; I am flattered to be the chosen target. Fromkin, *NYT Magazine*, Feb. 27, 1994; Kennan, *NYT*, March 14, 1994. See above, p. 27.

2. International terrorism, see, among others, Edward Herman, *The Real Terror Network* (South End, 1982), *The 'Terrorism' Industry* (with Gerry O'Sullivan, Pantheon, 1989); my *Pirates and Emperors: International Terrorism in the Real World* (Claremont, 1986; Amana, 1988; Spokesman (London), 1987) and *Necessary Illusions: Thought Control in Democratic Societies* (South End/Pluto, 1989); Alexander George, ed., *Western State Terrorism* (Polity, 1991). CIA-drug connection, see Alfred McCoy, *The Politics of Heroin* (Lawrence Hill, 1991; revision of 1972 edition); Leslie Cockburn, *Out of Control* (Atlantic Monthly, 1987); Peter Dale Scott and Jonathan Marshall, *Cocaine Politics* (California, 1991). "Drug war," see my *Deterring Democracy* (Verso, 1991), chap. 5; updated paperback edition, Hill & Wang/Vintage, 1992, with an "Afterword" on the Gulf conflict and the Middle East "peace process."

3. Charles Sellers, *The Market Revolution* (Oxford, 1991), 369, 394.

4. *The Challenge to the South*, Report of the South Commission (Oxford, 1990).

5. Churchill, *The Second World War*, vol. 5 (Houghton Mifflin, 1951), 382.

6. *Al-Ahram*, cited by David Hirst, *Guardian* (London), March 23, 1992. The specific reference is to Bush administration maneuvers to set up a confrontation with Qaddafi for domestic political purposes in the routine manner, also "codified" since 1981. See *Pirates and Emperors*, chap. 3.

7. Cited by Paul Drake, "From Good Men to Good Neighbors," in Abraham Lowenthal, ed., *Exporting Democracy* (Johns Hopkins, 1991).

8. For sources and further discussion, see my *Turning the Tide: The U.S. and Latin America* (South End/Pluto, 1985); *Deterring Democracy*, chap. 6. In Britain, the facts were suppressed for years, though discipline broke down slightly during the 1991 Gulf war. See David Omissi, *Air Power and Colonial Control* (Manchester, 1990), on the British reliance on air power. Haiti, my *Year 501: The Conquest Continues* (South End/Verso, 1993), chap. 8, sec. 2.

9. Keegan, cited by Richard Hudson, *Wall Street Journal*, Feb. 5, 1991; Peregrine Worsthorne, *Sunday Telegraph*, Sept. 16, 1990 (reprinted in *National Interest*, Winter 90/91). Christopher Bellamy, *International Affairs*, July 1992.

10. See *Deterring Democracy*, introduction. Bergsten, *Foreign Policy*, Summer 1992. On the spoils of war, see Seymour Hersh, *New Yorker*, Sept. 6, 1993.

11. Bush, January 29, 1991. Baker, "Why America is in the Gulf," address to the Los Angeles World Affairs Council, Oct. 29, 1990. Friedman, *NYT* Week in Review, June 2, 1992.

12. Lars Mjøset, *The Irish Economy in a Comparative Institutional Perspective* (National Economic and Social Council, Government Publications, Dublin, Dec. 1992), 200; an important comparative study of Ireland's development failures and the impact of the colonial legacy on a country that should, otherwise, be comparable to the small wealthy advanced industrial societies of Europe.

13. Joseph Lee, *Ireland 1912–1985* (Cambridge, 1989, 521), cited by Mjøset, op. cit., 29.

14. For review and sources, see *Deterring Democracy*, chap. 6 and "Afterword." The best general account of the Gulf conflict is Dilip Hiro, *Desert Shield to Desert Storm* (HarperCollins, 1992). Howell, cited by Mark Curtis, "Obstacles to Security in the Middle East," in Seizaburo Sato and Trevor Taylor, eds., *Prospects for Global Order*, vol. 2 (Royal Institute of International Affairs and International Institute for Global Peace, London, 1993).

15. Friedman, *NYT*, July 7, 1991.

16. Ibid. For these and other Third World reactions, see my articles in *Z magazine*, Feb., May 1991, and my chapter in Cynthia Peters, ed., *Collateral Damage* (South End, 1992). Also Hamid Mowlana, George Gerbner, and Herbert Schiller, *Triumph of the Image* (Westview, 1992). On the Arab world, see Barbara Gregory Ebert, "The War and Its Aftermath: Arab Responses," *Middle East Policy*, 1.4, 1992.

17. For details, see references of notes 14 and 16.

18. *The Gulf Conflict 1990–1991: Diplomacy and War in the New World Order* (Princeton, 1992). Similar treatment is accorded Israel's invasion of Lebanon and Middle East diplomacy; the views of Iraqi democrats and the population of the region generally; and the illuminating record of U.S. and British documents (see pp. 14f., 194ff., above, for some examples). For a sample of crucial material they avoid or seriously misrepresent, and sources on the above, see references of notes 14 and 16.

19. For details and background, see *Necessary Illusions*, chap. 4 and App. 4.IV; *Deterring Democracy*, chap. 6; my *Letters from Lexington: Reflections on Propaganda* (Common Courage, 1993), chaps. 8, 9; my "World Order and its Rules: Variations on Some Themes," *J. of Law and Society* 20.2, Summer 1993 (U. of Cardiff). Peter Bruce, "missing KIO cash 'used to buy Kuwait liberation,'" *Financial Times*, July 7, 1993.

20. Maureen Dowd, *NYT*, March 2, Feb. 23, 1991.

21. Dionne, *WP Weekly*, March 11; John Aloysius Farrell, *BG* Magazine, March 31; Martin Nolan, *BG*, March 10; Oliphant, *BG*, Feb. 27, 1991. Roosevelt, see *Turning the Tide*, 61, 87.

22. Ropp, "Things Fall Apart: Panama after Noriega," *Current History*, March 1993. *Deterring Democracy*, chap. 5.

23. IPS, Dec. 9, Nov. 23, 1993; *Central America NewsPak*, Documentation Exchange, Austin Texas; *CentralAmerica Report* (Guatemala), Feb. 4; *Mesoamerica* (Costa Rica), March 1994.

24. Woodward, *The Commanders* (Simon & Schuster, 1991), 251–52. Quandt, *Peace Process* (Brookings Institution and U. of California, 1993), 579n. That "no one has disputed [the] facts" of Woodward's account is also noted by Richard Cohen, Chief of Air Force History, 1981–91; *National Interest*, Spring 1994. Freedman and Karsh, op. cit., 67f.

25. See pp. 194ff., above; references of note 14 and citations within for the only exceptions I know of.

26. The views of Iraqi democrats, insofar as I could discover them, were reported in my articles in *Z magazine* (Feb., May 1991); see *Deterring Democracy*. I am aware of nothing else in the American press. For more on their positions (opposing foreign armies, supporting the Palestinian people, advocating independent foreign policies and Arab and Muslim solidarity, etc.), see Curtis, op. cit.

27. See my articles cited in note 16. On Turkish atrocities against Kurds since, see *Desolated and Profaned*, Report of Lord Avebury (chairman, U.K. Parliamentary Human Rights group) and Michael Feeny (Refugee Officer of Catholic Diocese of Westminster) on September 1992 mission to Kurdish region of Turkey; Helsinki Watch, *The Kurds of Turkey: Killings, Disappearances and Torture*, March 1993 (Human Rights Watch, New York). On the cynical coverage of the Kurds over many years, shaped to reflect Western needs, see *Necessary Illusions*, App. 5.3, reviewing studies by the leading Kurdish human rights advocate, Vera Saeedpour.

28. *WP*, June 24; Andrew Whitley, "Saddam's Other Victims," op-ed, *NYT*, June 26, 1993.

29. Special Article, Alberto Ascherio, et al., "Effect of the Gulf War on Infant and Child Mortality in Iraq," *New England Journal of Medicine*, vol. 327, no. 13, 1993. Ekvall, AP, "UN says Shiites flee Iraqi attacks," *BG*, July 24; AP, "Report: US lags on child health," *BG*, Sept. 23; Dalyell, *Scotland on Sunday*, May 23, 1993.

30. See my *Enter a World that is Truly Surreal* (Open Magazine Pamphlet series, Westfield, Sept. 1993), from which some of what follows is taken.

31. Eric Schmitt, Reuters, *NYT*, June 28; Boustany, *WP Weekly*, July 4; Tim Weiner, *NYT*, June 27; Charles Glass, *Sunday Telegraph*, July 4; Paul Quinn-Judge, *BG*, June 28, 1993.

32. Douglas Jehl, *NYT*, June 29; editorial, June 30, 1993. On the trial, see Patrick Cockburn, "The plot thins," *In These Times*, Aug. 9, 1993, excerpted from London *Independent on Sunday*. Seymour Hersh, "A Case Not Closed," *New Yorker*, Nov. 1, 1993.

33. Citing these facts, Alfred Rubin, a well-known specialist on international law, observes that "the law of self-defense has nothing to do with retaliation or reprisals"; letter, *NYT*, July 8, 1993.

34. Editorials, *WP Weekly*, July 5–11; *NYT*, June 28; *BG*, June 28; Stephen Hubbell, *CSM*, June 29; George Jones, *Daily Telegraph*, June 29, 1993. AP, Dec. 20, 1989; Richard Cole, AP, *BG*, Feb. 3, 1990.

35. Steve Coll and Douglas Farah, *WP*, Sept. 20, 1993; *Economist*, March 12, 1994. Also pp. 12–13, above.

36. Craig Whitney, *NYT*, June 28; William Miller, *BG*, June 29, 1993. Russia, *Middle East International*, July 9, 1993. *Guardian*, June 29; *Times*, June 28, 1993.

37. Editorials, *NYT*, June 30; *FT*, June 28.

38. Ruth Marcus and Daniel Williams, *WP–Guardian Weekly*, July 4, 1993; Glass, op. cit. See also Alexander Cockburn, one of the very few dissident journalists with occasional access to the U.S. media, op-ed, *WSJ*, July 1, 1993, making the same point.

39. See *Turning the Tide*, 66f.

40. Justin Lewis and Michael Morgan, "Images/Issues/Impact: the Media and Campaign '92," Summary, U. Mass. Amherst, ms., Nov. 1992.

41. Friedman, *NYT*, June 28, 1993.

42. Safire, *NYT*, June 28; editorial, *NR*, July 19/26, 1993.

43. Reuters, *NYT*, June 27; Youssef Ibrahim, *NYT*, June 29; *Akhbar al-Khalij*, cited in *Middle East International*, July 9, and *Frontline* (India), July 30; F.R. Khergamvala, Bahrain, "Strike at will?," Ibid.; *Al-Alam*, Morocco, cited by Stephen Hubbell, *CSM*, June 29, 1993.

44. *NYT*, June 27; Marcus and Williams, op. cit.; Douglas Jehl, *NYT*, July 4, 1993; Safire, op. cit.

45. Cited by Loch K. Johnson, *A Season of Inquiry: the Senate Intelligence Investigation* (Kentucky, 1985), 53. On invasion fears, see *Year 501*, chap. 6. On recorded assassination plots, see Interim Report of the Select Committee to Study Governmental Operations, Nov. 20, 1975.

46. Friedman, *NYT*, June 28, 1993. See *Pirates and Emperors*, chap. 3, for a review of what the press chose "not to know" in 1986.

47. Friedman, *NYT*, June 28, 1993.

48. For review, see *Year 501*, chap. 5. Almost the only exception, to my knowledge, was Peter Dale Scott, "Exporting Military–Economic Development," in Malcolm Caldwell, ed., *Ten Years Military Terror in Indonesia* (Spokesman, 1975), and other articles in the same volume, unreviewed and unknown. See also my *American Power and the New Mandarins* (Pantheon, 1969), 35.

49. See *Somalia: Human Rights Abuses by the United Nations Forces*, African Rights (London), Rakiya Omaar and Alex de Waal, co-directors, July 1993. As the U.S. mission ended, they estimated that "at least a thousand Somalis were killed and probably many more—the U.S. and UN do not count Somali casualties"—along with

"many human rights abuses, including attacking hospitals, bombarding political meetings, shooting into crowds of demonstrators, and bulldozing homes to make 'free fire' zones" (*Peace and Democracy News*, Winter 1993/94). The U.S. command estimated six to ten thousand casualties in the summer of 1993 alone, two-thirds women and children, casualties "largely overlooked by reporters"; there were 380 U.S.–UN casualties, including eighty-three killed (Eric Schmitt, *NYT*, Dec. 8, 1993). On the operation, see note 133, below.

50. Elaine Sciolino, "U.S. Narrows Terms for Its Peacekeepers: A White House panel asks, What is in it for us?," *NYT*, Sept. 23; John Battersby, "Angolan Strife Endangers 2 Million As Diplomacy Fails, Aid Workers Say," *CSM*, Aug. 26, 1993. The UN Special Envoy estimates deaths at a thousand per day, "the largest death toll in any current conflict," according to Secretary General Boutros Boutros Ghali; ibid., Michael Littlejohns, *FT*, Sept. 17, 1993. See *Pirates and Emperors*, 96. More generally, Elaine Windrich, *The Cold War Guerrilla* (Greenwood, 1992). On UNITA's return to violence after losing the election, with immediate South African support (including arms supplies, the South African press reports), see West Africa specialist John Marcum, "Angola: War Again," *Current History*, May 1993. Africa correspondent Victoria Brittain estimates over half a million Angolans killed and much of the country ruined during Savimibi's post-election "reign of terror." Arms supplies continue to be flown to UNITA airstrips, she reports, quoting a Western diplomat who says that "of course everyone in the aid community knows all about this breaking of sanctions, but no one here likes to buck U.S. policy." *New Statesman and Society*, March 4, 1994.

51. *Foreign Relations of the United States (FRUS)*, 1950, Vol. I, 234–92. For longer excerpts and sources, see *Deterring Democracy*, chap. 1.

52. Such evidence as is offered is falsified for the purposes at hand, but even as presented undermines the conclusions. Ibid., for discussion.

53. Ibid., 90, for this and other examples.

54. Huntington, *International Security*, 17:4, 1993. See Chomsky and Edward Herman, *Political Economy of Human Rights* (South End, 1979), vol. I, 43f.; Herman, *Real Terror Network*, 82f.; Schoultz, *Comparative Politics*, Jan. 1981. See *Turning the Tide*, 157f. The same studies show that aid is not correlated with need, but is correlated with improvements in the climate for business operations, which often involve state violence to eliminate union organizers, dissident political figures and intellectuals, priests working among the poor, and so on.

55. Morgenthau, *The Purpose of American Politics* (Vintage, 1964). See my *Towards a New Cold War* (Pantheon, 1982), chaps. 1, 2, 8 for further discussion.

56. *International Security*, Summer 1981; *National Interest*, Fall 1989.

57. McNamara and Taylor cited by Marcus Raskin, *Essays of a Citizen* (M.E. Sharpe, 1991).

58. On the feats of imagination of policy-makers, and others in their intellectual milieu, see Lars Schoultz, *National Security and United States Policy toward Latin America* (Princeton, 1987). Also Anne Hessing Cahn and John Prados, "Team B: the Trillion Dollar Experiment," *Bulletin of the Atomic Scientists*, April 1993, reviewing the recently declassified "Team B" reports that offered a ludicrous interpretation of Soviet strength. Analysis from the left was often similar, a matter that merits review.

59. See Lynn Eden, "The End of U.S. Cold War History?" *International Security* 18.1 (1993), discussing the valuable study by Melvyn Leffler, *A Preponderance of Power* (Stanford, 1992), and the new consensus on the Cold War it helps to establish among diplomatic historians.

60. Thompson, "Exaggeration of American Vulnerability," *Diplomatic History*, Winter 1992; naval construction, quoting historian Robert Seager. On the alleged German threat, see Nancy Mitchell, "Germans in the Backyard," *Prologue*, Quarterly of the National Archives, Summer 1992.

61. Sellers, op. cit., 279, 92, 393. Adams's recantation, William Earl Weeks, *John Quincy Adams and American Global Empire* (Kentucky, 1992), 193.

62. Christopher Layne, senior fellow of the Cato Institute, and Benjamin Schwarz, international policy analyst at RAND, *Foreign Policy*, Fall 1993.

63. For review, see *Turning the Tide*, chap. 5; my *On Power and Ideology: The Managua Lectures* (South End, 1987), lecture 5.

64. Leffler, op. cit., the most authoritative review, sympathetic to Truman planners. See *Deterring Democracy* and *Year 501* for additional discussion and specific sources. For review of internal estimates of Soviet capabilities and intentions, highly dismissive of the capabilities and "virtually unanimous in concluding that the Soviets currently had no wish to initiate hostilities with the West," see Frank Kofsky, *Harry Truman and the War Scare of 1948* (St. Martins, 1993), Appendix A.

65. See references of note 63, *Deterring Democracy*, 24ff. Warner, *International Affairs* 69.2, April 1993.

66. Gaddis, *Strategies of Containment* (Oxford, 1982), 40, 356–57. See Leffler, op. cit., for close analysis.

67. Ron Suskind, *WSJ*, Oct. 29, 1991. See *Year 501*, 83–84, and on the suppressed history, *Necessary Illusions*, 177f.

68. Gaddis, *The Long Peace* (Oxford, 1987), 43. See *Necessary Illusions*, App. II, for further discussion.

69. Kennan, *Russia Leaves the War* (Princeton, 1956), 352–63. See note 8.

70. Kaplan, *New Republic*, Dec. 28, 1992; Sciolino, *NYT*, July 22, 1993; Landes, *New Republic*, March 10, 1986; Ryan, *CSM*, Feb. 14, 1986. For more on these and other scholarly analyses, see *On Power and Ideology*, 68–69, *Turning the Tide*, 153f. On the events, see Hans Schmidt, *The United States Occupation of Haiti, 1915–1934* (Rutgers, 1971). On U.S.–Haiti relations, see *Year 501*, chaps. 8–9; more generally, Paul Farmer, *The Uses of Haiti* (Common Courage, 1994).

71. *Haiti Info*, May 23, 1993; personal interviews, Port-au-Prince, June 1993. Trouillot, *Haiti: State against Nation* (Monthly Review, 1990), 102f.

72. Lloyd Gardner, *Spheres of Influence* (Ivan Dee, 1993), 176, 207, 235ff., 265.; 240, minutes of Feb. 1945 Cabinet meeting. Leffler, op. cit., 58–59, 15.

73. *Nation*, March 5, 1990.

74. See *Deterring Democracy*, chap. 7, for some comparisons, and comment on the rare attempts to confront the issue. Also *Year 501*, chap. 7, for a closer examination of Brazil and other crucial cases.

75. For sources below where not cited, see *Deterring Democracy*, *Year 501*, and my *Rethinking Camelot: JFK, the Vietnam War, and U.S. Political Culture* (South End, 1993), chap. 1.

76. See *Deterring Democracy*, chaps. 1, 11, for review and sources. Simpson, *The Splendid Blond Beast* (Grove, 1993), chap. 5. Halifax, Gardner, op. cit., 13.

77. Ibid., 67–68.

78. See p. 193. Romero, *The United States and the European Trade Union Movement 1944–1951* (North Carolina, 1989, 1992), 50ff., 143ff., 16, 24. For further discussion and comparison with other cases, see *Deterring Democracy*, chap. 11; *Year 501*, chap. 2.

79. Cited by Drake, op. cit.

80. Ibid. See *Turning the Tide*, chap. 3, secs. 6, 7. Lansing cited by Schmidt, op. cit., 62–63.

81. See William Stivers, *Supremacy and Oil* (Cornell, 1982), 66–73.

82. For more on these matters, see *Deterring Democracy*, chap. 5; *Year 501*, chap. 3. See also pp. 12–13.

83. See, e.g., Lee Hockstader, "Honduras Embattled After Decade of Aid," *WP*, July 13, 1992. On the stand of the national press, see *Necessary Illusions*, *Deterring Democracy*; on evolving policy, these, and publications cited earlier.

84. Abraham Lowenthal, in Lowenthal, op. cit., preface. See *Deterring Democracy*, chap. 10, for review of U.S. and foreign reactions. On earlier elections, see Edward Herman and Chomsky, *Manufacturing Consent* (Pantheon, 1988), chap. 3. Dutch observers, see my introduction to Morris Morley and James Petras, *The Reagan Administration and Nicaragua* (Institute for Media Analysis, New York, 1987). See

William Robinson, *A Faustian Bargain* (Westview, 1992), on U.S. subversion of the 1990 election itself, a relatively minor matter in context, so that this informative study can be recognized within the doctrinal system despite its critical stance, unlike the more fundamental issue, which is under a total ban.

85. Krauss, Review of Pastor, *Whirlpool*, *NYT Book Review*, Feb. 7, 1993. Sanchez, quoted by Christopher Marquis, *Miami Herald*, March 21, 1993. Kinsley, *WSJ*, March 26, 1987; see *Culture of Terrorism*, 77–78 for further discussion and context.

86. World Briefs, *BG*, March 16, 1994.

87. Manlio Tirado, *Excelsior*, Nov. 27, 1993; *Latin America News Update*, Jan. 1994. *Envío* (UCA, Managua), Feb.–March 1994.

88. Edward Oriebar, *FT*, March 22; Howard French, *NYT*, March 22, 1994. Dye, *Latinamerica press* (Peru), March 31; *In These Times*, April 18, 1994.

89. Gene Palumbo, *National Catholic Reporter*, March 25; Rev. Rodolfo Cardenal, vice rector of the Central American University (UCA), *Latinamerica press*, March 31, 1994.

90. See Human Rights Watch/Americas (Americas Watch), *El Salvador: Darkening Horizons, El Salvador on the eve of the March 1994 elections*, VI.4, March 1994. Lauren Gilbert (an investigator for the UN Truth Commission), *International Policy Report* (Center for International Policy, Washington), March 1994. Also Clifford Krauss, *NYT*, Nov. 9; Tim Weiner, *NYT*, Dec. 14, 1993.

91. *ES: Darkening Horizons*, for details.

92. Howard French, *NYT*, March 6, March 22; Gene Palumbo, *CSM*, Jan. 20; David Clark Scott, *CSM*, March 18, 22, 1994.

93. Notimex, Mexican News Agency, *El Nuevo Diario* (Managua), March 20, 1994.

94. Tracy Wilkinson, *LAT*, March 28, 1994.

95. Juan Hernández Pico, *Envío* (UCA, Jesuit University, Managua), March 1994.

96. Lowenthal, op. cit. Carothers, in ibid.; also his *In the Name of Democracy* (California, 1991).

97. Martz, "Colombia: Democracy, Development, and Drugs," *Current History*, March 1994; Steven Greenhouse, *NYT*, March 15, 1994.

98. Americas Watch, *State of War: Political Violence and Counterinsurgency in Colombia* (Human Rights Watch, Dec. 1993); Amnesty International, *Political Violence [In Colombia]: Myth and Reality* (March 1994). *Deterring Democracy*, chap. 4.

99. AP, *BG*, March 14, 1994.

100. WOLA, *The Colombian National Police, Human Rights, and U.S. Drug Policy*, May 1993. On the last three months of 1993, see particularly *Justicia y Paz*, Comisión Intercongregacional de Justicia y Paz, vol. 6.4, Oct.–Dec. 1993, Bogotá.

101. Comisión Andina de Juristas, Seccional Colombia, Bogotá, Jan. 19, 1994.

102. McClintock, *Instruments of Statecraft* (Pantheon, 1992); see *Year 501*, chap. 10, for some discussion. *Deterring Democracy*, chap. 4, on mercenaries.

103. AI, *Political Violence*. Comisión Andina, op. cit.

104. *El Terrorismo de Estado en Colombia* (Brussels, 1992). On the deterioration of the human rights situation in the 1980s, see also Jenny Pearce, *Colombia: Inside the Labyrinth* (Latin American Bureau, London, 1990).

105. *Deterring Democracy*, chap. 4.

106. Justicia y Paz, cited by WOLA, *Colombia Besieged: Political Violence and State Responsibility* (Washington DC, 1989).

107. For details on these and other atrocities, and the general impunity, see references cited above and in *Deterring Democracy*, chap. 4. 1988–92 estimate, *El Terrorismo de Estado*.

108. WOLA, *Colombia Besieged*; WOLA, *The Paramilitary strategy imposed on Colombia's Chucuri region* (Jan. 1993).

109. WOLA, *Colombian National Police*.

110. For another crucial example, see p. 219, above. On posturing in connection with the Vienna conference on the Universal Declaration, and the facts, see my "Letter from Lexington," *Lies of Our Times*, Oct. 1993. For background, see Joseph Wronka, *Human Rights and Social Policy in the 21st Century* (University Press of America, 1992).

111. *Colombia Update*, Colombian Human Rights Committee, Dec. 1989; see *Deterring Democracy*, chap. 4.

112. WOLA, *Colombia Besieged*. Children, Pearce, op. cit.

113. See note 50. Battersby reports that Savimbi is receiving military support from "several nations including Russia, Israel, Portugal, and Brazil, according to diplomatic sources." On "constructive engagement," see p. 131, above.

114. Americas Watch and National Coalition for Haitian Refugees, *Silencing a People* (Human Rights Watch, 1993). Reuters, *BG*, June 18, 1993. On Haiti and the Vienna conference, and the media version of both, see my articles in *Lies of Our Time*, Feb., Sept., 1993, the former reprinted in *Letters from Lexington*. Also *Year 501*, chaps. 8–9; Farmer, op. cit.

115. AP, *BG*, July 18, 27; *NYT*, July 26; Reuters, *BG*, July 27; Reuters, *BG*, Aug. 12, 1993.

116. Pamela Constable, *BG*, Oct. 1; Steven Holmes, *NYT*, Oct. 1; *WSJ*, Oct. 1; Howard French, *NYT*, Sept. 22; Elaine Sciolino, *NYT*, Jan. 15, 1993. On press coverage, see *Boston Media Action Bulletin*, May 1993, reviewing reports of human rights abuses in major media in the months following the September 1991 coup that overthrew President Aristide. The *New York Times* devoted 54 percent of coverage to abuses attributable to Aristide supporters, less than 1 percent of the total. Other journals, though less extreme, reflected the same extraordinary bias, which extends to other aspects of coverage of the recent years as well. See reports of this study in *Extra!* (FAIR), Jan./Feb. 1993; *Z magazine*, March 1993. On the pattern throughout, see references of note 114.

117. French, *NYT*, Sept. 27; Oct. 8, 1992.

118. Canute James, *FT*, Dec. 10, 1992.

119. Douglas Farah, *WP Weekly*, Nov. 1–7, 1993; *Birmingham Catholic Press*, Oct. 15, 1993, citing Father Antoine Adrien, who is close to Aristide.

120. *WP Weekly*, Feb. 17, 10, 1992 (Lee Hockstader, editorial); Barbara Crossette, *NYT*, May 28, 1992. See my "Class Struggle as Usual," *Letters from Lexington* (Common Courage, 1993); reprinted from *Lies of Our Times*, March 1993.

121. Crossette, *NYT*, Feb. 5, 1992.

122. Eyal Press and Jennifer Washburn, letters, *NYT*, March 3, 1994.

123. George Graham, *FT*, Feb. 20, 1994; Report of National Labor Committee Education Fund, Feb. 15, 1994. Note that the increases are not attributable to the rescinding of the embargo from July to October 1993.

124. AP, *NYT*, March 6, 1994.

125. Howard French, *NYT*, Feb. 9; Robert Greenberger, *WSJ*, Feb. 15, 1994. Norman Kempster, *LAT*, Dec. 18, 1993.

126. Christopher Marquis, *Miami Herald*, March 9; Birns, COHA *Washington Report on the Hemisphere*, March 7; Amy Wilentz, *NYT* op-ed, March 24, 1994.

127. Diplomatic correspondent Neil Lewis, *NYT*, Dec. 6, 1987.

128. See *Year 501*, chap. 6.

129. Simes, *NYT*, Dec. 27, 1988.

130. See *Deterring Democracy*, 29–30, for further detail.

131. See note 63.

132. Friedman, *NYT*, Sept. 22; Lake, *NYT*, Sept. 26, 1993. Intervention doctrine, p. 24. On Brazil, see *Year 501*, chap. 7, and sources cited.

133. *Defense Monitor*, CDI, XXI.3, XXII.4, 7 1993. Stephen Shalom, *Z magazine*, June 1993. Evans, *Chicago Tribune*, July 7, 1993. Les Aspin, *The Bottom-Up Review: Forces for a New Era*, Secretary of Defense, Washington D.C., Sept. 1, 1993; his emphasis. On current strategy, see Michael Klare, "Pax Americana: U.S. Military

Policy in the Post–Cold War Era," in Phyllis Bennis and Michel Moushabeck, ed., *Altered States: a Reader in the New World Order* (Olive Branch Press, Interlink, 1993). Somalia, see Stephen Shalom, "Gravy Train: Feeding the Pentagon by Feeding Somalia," *Z magazine*, Feb. 1993; also my article, same issue, and Joseph Gerson, *Peacework*, Jan. 1993; quotes from *WP Weekly*, Dec. 14–20, 1992 (cited by Gerson), Jane Perlez, *NYT Week in Review*, Dec. 20, 1992. For further discussion, see Alex de Waal and Rakiya Omaar, "Doing Harm by Doing Good? The International Relief Effort in Somalia," *Current History*, May 1993; "Somalia: Adding 'Humanitarian Intervention' to the U.S. Arsenal," *Covert Action* 44, Spring 1993; *Somalia Operation Restore Hope: A Preliminary Assessment*, African Rights, London, May 1993.

134. Arkin, *Bull. of the Atomic Scientists*, July–Aug. 1993. Paul Quinn-Judge, *BG*, July 12, 1993.

135. Haberman, "Israel Again Seeks A Deal With an Outcast," *NYT*, July 11, 1993. For more on the matter, see *Necessary Illusions*, 319f., and *Letters from Lexington*, chap. 5. On Israel's "Samson complex" and its manifestations since the 1950s, see my *Fateful Triangle: Israel, the United States, and the Palestinians* (South End, 1983), chap. 7, 4.2.2. On Israeli nuclear policies, see Mark Gaffney, *Dimona: the Third Temple?* (Amana, 1989); Andrew and Leslie Cockburn, *Dangerous Liaison* (HarperCollins, 1991); Seymour Hersh, *The Samson Option* (Random House, 1991).

136. For recent discussion and sources omitted here, see *Deterring Democracy, Year 501*.

137. On its remarkable uniformity, see *Necessary Illusions*, particularly pp. 61–65, on opinion columns in the national press. Kissinger, see Seymour Hersh, *Price of Power* (Summit, 1983), 270, quoting Roger Morris.

138. For further detail, see my *Culture of Terrorism* (South End, 1988), 221f.; *Necessary Illusions*, 71f.

139. Parry, *Fooling America: How Washington Insiders Twist the Truth and Manufacture the Conventional Wisdom* (Morrow, 1992), 300.

140. Hilsman, *To Move a Nation* (Dell, 1967), 85f. John Davies, *A History of Wales* (Penguin, 1993), 160.

141. See references of note 136.

142. P. 30, above, and note 59. Pastor, *Condemned to Repetition* (Princeton, 1987); see *Deterring Democracy*, chap. 8, for the context among the doves.

143. Lansing and Wilson, Lloyd Gardner, *Safe for Democracy* (Oxford, 1987), 157, 161, 261, 242. Britain, Davies, op. cit., 518.

144. See references of note 136. Dulles–Adenauer cited in Warner, op. cit. State Department, Dennis Merrill, *Bread and the Ballot: the United States and India's Economic Development, 1947–1963* (North Carolina, 1992), 123. MacMillan cited by Richard Reeves, *President Kennedy* (Simon & Schuster, 1993), 174. On China and Vietnam, see my *For Reasons of State* (Pantheon, 1973), chap. 1.V; reprinted in James Peck, ed., *The Chomsky Reader* (Pantheon, 1988).

145. Douglas Little, "Cold War and Covert Action: the US and Syria, 1945–1958," *Middle East Journal*, Winter 1990. Steven Freiberger, *Dawn Over Suez* (Ivan Dee, 1992), 167, 156f.

146. See references of notes 14 and 16.

147. *World Development Report 1991: the Challenge of Development* (Oxford, 1991), 14, cited by Michael Haynes, "The New Market Economies and the World Economy," ms, Wolverhampton Polytechnic (U.K.), May 1992. For statistics on decline, see Alice Amsden, "After the Fall," *American Prospect*, Spring 1993. World Bank statement and further discussion, *Year 501*, chaps. 3–4.

Notes to Chapter 2

1. On escape from neoliberal collapse, see Ryutaro Komiya *et al.*, *Industry Policy of Japan* (Tokyo, 1984; Academic Press, 1988); Mjøset, op. cit. (on the smaller countries of Europe); Amsden, *Asia's Next Giant* (Oxford 1989) and Robert Wade, *Governing the Market* (Princeton, 1990) (on the East Asian "tigers"). On the effects

of subordination to neoclassical principles, there are many studies, among them Alejandro Foxley, *Latin American Experiments in Neoconservative Economics* (California, 1983); Carmen Diana Deere *et al.*, *In the Shadows of the Sun* (Westview, 1990) and Kathy McAfee, *Storm Signals* (South End, 1991) (on the Caribbean); Michael Barratt Brown and Pauline Tiffen, *Short Changed* (Pluto, 1992) (on Africa). On Latin America generally, see NACLA, "A Market Solution for the Americas?" *Report on the Americas*, NACLA XXVI.4, Feb. 1993; James Petras and Steve Vieux, "Myths and Realities: Latin America's Free Markets," *Monthly Review*, May 1992; and many studies of specific cases, including Joseph Collins and John Lear, *Chile's Free Market Revolution: A Second Look* (Institute for Food and Development Policy, 1994), and Martha Honey, *Hostile Acts* (Florida, 1994) and Development GAP, *Structural Adjustment in Central America* (Washington DC, 1993), on the interesting case of Costa Rica. An informative review of the record of IMF–World Bank programs of the eighties is Rehman Sobhan, "Rethinking the Market Reform Paradigm," *Economic and Political Weekly* (India), July 25, 1992. On the general issues and problems, see Peter Evans *et al.*, *Bringing the State Back In* (Cambridge, 1985); Tariq Banuri, ed., *No Panacea: The Limits of Economic Liberalization* (Oxford, 1991); Susan George, *The Debt Boomerang* (Pluto, 1992). Among the comparisons of Latin America and East Asia, see Stephen Haggard, *Pathways From the Periphery* (Cornell, 1990); Rhys Jenkins, "Learning from the Gang," *Bulletin of Latin American Research*, 10.1, 1991, and "The Political Economy of Industrialization," *Development and Change* 22, 1991. See *Deterring Democracy* and *Year 501* for further sources and discussion.

2. For more on these matters, see *Necessary Illusions*; *Towards a New Cold War*, chaps. 1, 2; *Deterring Democracy*, chap. 12; *Year 501*, chaps. 10, 11. The very important work of Alex Carey on these topics is collected in a forthcoming book, *Taking the Risk out of Democracy*.

3. For my own views on the topic, including earlier origins, see *Cartesian Linguistics* (Harper & Row, 1966); *Problems of Knowledge and Freedom* (Pantheon, 1971); *Reflections on Language* (Pantheon, 1975); several essays reprinted in Peck, *Chomsky Reader* (some from *For Reasons of State*); *Year 501*, 18f.; and elsewhere.

4. Jefferson, cited by Sellers, op. cit., 269–70, 106. Robert Westbrook, *John Dewey and American Democracy* (Cornell, 1991), 440f., 176f., 225f., 249, 453. On late eighteenth-century articulation of these themes, see references of preceding note and Patricia Werhane, *Adam Smith and His Legacy for Modern Capitalism* (Oxford, 1991).

5. For example, the presidential address to the American Political Science Association in 1934 by William Shepard, who argued in Lasswell–Lippmann style that government should be in the hands of "an aristocracy of intellect and power," while "the ignorant, the uninformed, and the anti-social elements" must not be permitted to control elections as in the past. Westbrook, op. cit., 285.

6. See pp. 103–104. Joyce, "The Revitalization of Civil Society," remarks to Milwaukee Bar Association, June 23, 1993; reprinted in *Wisconsin Interest*.

7. Orwell, unpublished preface for his *Animal Farm*; published by Bernard Crick in *Times Literary Supplement*, Sept. 15, 1972 ; reprinted in Everyman's Library edition. Jo Ann Boydston, ed., *John Dewey: The Later Works*, vol. II, from *Common Sense*, Nov. 1935; see *Necessary Illusions*, chap. 5.

8. See *Letters from Lexington*, chap. 17. On control of radio, see Robert McChesney, *Telecommunications, Mass Media & Democracy* (Oxford, 1993).

9. Carey, op. cit.

10. 1940s campaign, Karl Meyer, Editorial Notebook, *NYT*, Aug. 2; James Perry, *WSJ*, Sept. 23, 1993. Robin Toner, "Poll Says Public Favors Changes in Health Policy," *NYT*, April 6; Elizabeth Neuffer and Richard Knox, "Guide to 'six stars' of health plan debate," *BG*, Sept. 26; Knox, "Many ready to accept care limits," *BG*, Sept. 19, 1993. Toner adds that the 59 percent support for national health care reduces to 36 percent when described as costing an additional $1,000 in taxes while eliminating other premiums, a figure that strongly suggests a misleading question, particularly

when we note that 58 percent were willing to pay additional taxes to improve health care. On current media campaigns, see *Year 501*, chap. 9; FAIR, *Extra!*, July/August 1993.

11. Navarro, in Navarro, ed., *Why the United States does not have a National Health Program* (Baywood, 1992); Navarro, *Dangerous to Your Health* (Monthly Review, 1993), 59, 75.

12. Carey, op. cit. Reich-Brown, cited by Louis Uchitelle, "Union Leaders Fight for a Place in the President's Workplace of the Future," *NYT*, Aug. 8, 1993. For further discussion, see *Turning the Tide*, chap. 5, and sources cited, and references of note 2.

13. BBC1 TV news, 9pm, March 5, 1991. BBC radio, cited by Christopher Hitchens, *Nation*, April 8, 1991. Freedman, "Weak states and the West," in "150 Economist years," *Economist*, Sept. 11, 1993. See chapter 1, note 18.

14. See *Manufacturing Consent* for review of the record over thirty-five years. Shawcross, *New York Review*, Aug. 12, 1993; *The Scotsman*, Dec. 14, 1992. On Shawcross's remarkable record of falsification, see *Manufacturing Consent*, *Political Economy of Human Rights*, vol. II, and Michael Vickery, *Cambodia* (South End, 1983). On the rewriting of history after Tet, see *Rethinking Camelot*, chap. 3. Subsequent efforts to salvage the JFK image have also been remarkable, but not worth discussing here.

15. Sut Jhally, Justin Lewis, and Michael Morgan, *The Gulf War: A Study of the Media, Public Opinion, and Public Knowledge*, Department of Communications, U. Mass. Amherst, 1991. Bruce Franklin, *M.I.A., or Mythmaking in America* (Lawrence Hill, 1992). Also *Manufacturing Consent*, chap. 5; *Necessary Illusions*, chap. 2; *Year 501*, chap. 10; *Rethinking Camelot*, chap. 1.

16. Juliet Peck, *The European* (London); *World Press Review*, Aug. 1993. The U.S. record of crimes against enemy combatants in Vietnam was extensively documented at the time, often casually reported without comment, now forgotten; see, e.g, *For Reasons of State*, viii, citing *NYT*. On Korea, see Rosemary Foot, *A Substitute for Victory* (Cornell, 1990); Pacific war, John Dower, *War Without Mercy* (Pantheon, 1986).

17. *WP-BG*, Jan. 18; *WP Weekly*, Jan. 25, 1993.

18. Antoinette de Jong, *NRC Handelsblad*, *World Press Review*, August 1993; Human Rights Watch 1993 (HRW, New York, Dec. 1992); *Economist*, July 24, 1993.

19. Moore, *WP Weekly*, March 14–20, 1994.

20. *De la Locura a la Esperanza: La guerra de 12 años en El Salvador*, Informe de la Comisión de la Verdad para El Salvador, Belisario Betancur, President (UN, San Salvador–New York, 1992–93), 41.

21. Tracy Wilkinson, *Los Angeles Times*, 29 March; Clifford Krauss, *NYT*, March 26; Reuters, *BG*, March 23; Todd Howland and Libby Cooper, *CSM*, March 25; Tojeira, *CSM*, April 13, 1993.

22. See *Turning the Tide*, 209f.; *Deterring Democracy*, 49; and sources cited. Also Frank Kofsky, *Harry Truman and the War Scare of 1948* (St. Martin's Press, 1993). On NASA, see Walter A. McDougall, . . . *the Heavens and the Earth* (Basic Books, 1985).

23. Cited by Robert Buzzanco, "Division, Dilemma and Dissent: Military Recognition of the Peril of War in Vietnam," in Dan Duffy, ed., *Informed Dissent* (Vietnam Generation, Burning Cities Press, 1992).

24. *Year 501*, chap. 4. *FT*, July 23, 1993; Aaron Zitner, "Arms Across the Sea," *BG*, Aug. 1; Charles Haney, AP, *San Diego Union–Tribune*, Aug. 12, 1993. Feinstein, *Bulletin of the Atomic Scientists*, Nov. 1992. Saudi Arabia, Jeff Gerth, et al., "Saudi Stability Hit by Heavy Spending Over Last Decade," *NYT*, Aug. 22; David Hirst, "Heads in the sand," *Guardian Weekly*, Aug. 29, 1993.

25. Jeff Cole and Sarah Lubman, *WSJ*, Jan. 28; Thomas Friedman, *NYT*, Feb. 17; Leslie Popiel, *CSM*, Jan. 20; Korb, *NYT* op-ed, Feb. 15, 1994. Boeing, Mark Trumbull, *CSM*, Dec. 16, 1993.

26. For some recent revelations, see the important studies of the National Labor Committee Education Fund in Support of Worker & Human Rights in Central America, *Paying to Lose Our Jobs* (1992); *Haiti After the Coup* (1993).

27. *Mandate for Change* (Berkley Books, Jan. 1993). Todd Schafer, *Still Neglecting Public Investment: The FY94 Budget Outlook*, Economic Policy Briefing Paper (EPI, Washington, Sept. 1993). Howard, "The Hidden Welfare State," *Political Science Quarterly*, Fall 1993. Ben Lilliston, *Multinational Monitor*, Jan.–Feb.; James Donahue, "The Corporate Welfare Kings," *WP Weekly*, March 21–27, 1994.

28. DOD-computers, Kenneth Flamm, *Targeting the Computer* (Brookings, 1987). R&D 1958, Flamm, unpublished paper cited by Laura Tyson, *Who's Bashing Whom?* (Institute for International Economics, 1992), 89; 155 on aircraft exports. Lucinda Harper, *WSJ*, Nov. 22, 1993. See also p. 103.

29. Richard Du Boff, *Accumulation and Power* (M.E. Sharpe, 1989), 101–3.

30. *Economist*, Sept. 7, 1985. Lucinda Harper, *WSJ*; *NYT* business section, Oct. 28, 1992. Jeremy Leaman, *Debatte* (Germany), No. 1, 1993. Keith Bradsher, *NYT*, Feb. 15, 1994. Bergsten, *FT*, Aug. 18, 1993; *FT*, Nov. 16, 1992. Low, *Trading Free* (Twentieth Century Fund, 1993), 70ff., 271.

31. Susan George, op. cit., 77.

32. Meller, "Adjustment and Social Costs in Chile During the 1980s," *World Development* 19.11, 1991; Felix, "Privatizing and rolling back the Latin American State," CEPAL Review 46, Santiago Chile, April 1992; Nash, *NYT*, April 4, 1993. See also Collins and Lear, op. cit.

33. EC steel, David Gardner, *FT*, Dec. 2; Ex–Im Bank, *FT*, Nov. 12, 1992.

34. David Gardner, *FT*, Feb. 13/14; William Echikson, *BG*, Feb. 28; Lionel Barber, *FT*, April 16, Bob Davis, *WSJ*, Sept. 17, 1993. Bhagwati, *Foreign Affairs*, Spring 1993. Rules of origin, Michael Aho, *International Affairs*, Jan. 1993.

35. T.R. Reid, *International Herald Tribune* (*WP*), Nov. 21–22, 1992. Scott Pendleton, *CSM*, Jan. 25; Elizabeth Corcoran, *Science*, April 2, 1993. Tyson, op. cit., 152f.

36. Ibid.; her emphasis.

37. Nasar, *NYT*, Dec. 12, 1992. Borrus, *American Prospect*, Fall 1992.

38. Broad, *Science Times*, *NYT*, Nov. 10, 1992. Reich, *NYT*, May 29, 1985. See *Turning the Tide*, 210f. Ralph Winter, *WSJ*, Dec. 28, 1992. Bob Davis, *WSJ*, April 5, 1994.

39. Keith Bradsher, "Administration Plans New Export Initiative," *NYT* business section, Sept. 28; Michael Frisby, *WSJ*, Sept. 29, 30, 1993.

40. Dieter Ernst and David O'Connor, *Competing in the Electronics Industry* (Pinter, 1992), cited in Tyson, op. cit.

41. Sonia Nazario, *WSJ*, Oct. 5, 1992.

42. Howard Wachtel, *The Money Mandarins* (M.E. Sharpe, 1990), 249.

43. For an assessment, see Robert Pear, *NYT*, Jan. 3, 1993.

44. Adam Pertman, *BG*, March 5, 1993. See *Year 501*, chap. 11.

45. Gerschenkron, *Economic Backwardness in Historical Perspective* (Harvard, 1962), a work that can usefully be read alongside an important study at the same time reviewing the other side of the coin, where these methods were blocked by imperial power: Frederick Clairmonte, *Economic Liberalism and Underdevelopment* (Asia Publishing House, 1960).

46. See *Year 501* for fuller discussion and sources, here and below, where not cited. Brenner, *Merchants and Revolution* (Princeton 1993), 45ff., 580.

47. Sellers, op. cit., 101.

48. Ibid., 405, 256. Angolan administrator cited by Neta Crawford, "Decolonolization as an International Norm," in L. Reed and C. Kaysen, eds., *Emerging Norms of Justified Intervention* (American Academy of Arts and Sciences, 1993). On the post–Civil War working class, see Paul Krause, *The Battle for Homestead, 1880–1892* (Pittsburgh, 1992).

49. See Mjøset, op. cit.

50. Merrill, op. cit., 14; Thakur, *Third World Quarterly* 14.1, 1993.

51. Marsot, *Egypt in the Reign of Muhammad Ali* (Cambridge 1984), 169ff., 238ff., 258ff. Peter Gran, *Islamic Roots of Capitalism* (Texas, 1979), 6ff.

52. See Edward Herman, "The Institutionalization of Bias in Economics," *Media, Culture & Society*, July 1982.

53. See *Deterring Democracy*, chap. 7, for estimates, sources, and further discussion.

54. Cumings, *International Organization* 38.1, Winter 1984. Wade, op. cit., 74. Amsden, "The State and Taiwan's Economic Development," in Evans, op. cit.

55. *NYT*, Oct. 24, 1992. See pp. 96–97, above. Manchuria–South Vietnam, see *American Power and the New Mandarins*, chap. 2.

56. Shintaro Ishihara, in Akio Morita and Ishihara, *The Japan That Can Say No* (Konbusha, Tokyo), *Congressional Record*, Nov. 14, 1989, E3783–98.

57. See *Deterring Democracy*, chaps. 1, 11; *Year 501*, chaps. 1–4, 7, for elaboration and sources, here and below.

58. See p. 79. Rabe, *The Road to OPEC* (Texas, 1982). Haines, *The Americanization of Brazil* (Scholarly Resources, 1989). See *Year 501*, chap. 7, for extensive discussion.

59. Stephen Fidler, "Latin America 'chaos' warning," *FT*, Sept. 25/26, 1993.

60. Nathan Godfried, *Bridging the Gap between Rich and Poor: American Economic Development Policy Toward the Arab East, 1942–1949* (Greenwood, 1987), 99. David Painter, *Oil and the American Century* (Johns Hopkins, 1986), 153ff.

61. See among other sources, Tom Barry and Deb Preusch, *The Soft War* (Grove, 1988), 67f.; Borden, *The Pacific Alliance: United States Foreign Economic Policy and Japanese Trade Recovery, 1947–1955* Wisconsin, 1984), 182f.

62. Merrill, op. cit., 145. Latin America, see p. 77; Middle East, p. 198.

63. Merrill, op. cit., 140.

64. Ibid., 61ff., 146f., 158, 170.

65. For further detail, see my "Responsibility of Intellectuals," 1966, reprinted in *American Power and the New Mandarins*, chap. 6, and Peck, *Chomsky Reader*, citing Congressional Hearings, *NYT*, *CSM*.

66. Godfried, op. cit., 194.

67. Chossudovsky, "India under IMF rule," *Economic and Political Weekly*, March 6, 1993. Madhura Swaminathan and V.K. Ramachandran, "Structural Adjustment Programmes and Child Welfare," ms, Bombay, paper presented at the Seminar on New Economic Policy, Aug. 19–21, 1993, Indian Institute of Management, Calcutta. See *Year 501*, chap. 7, on some effects.

68. MP Michael Meacher, *Observer*, May 16, 1993; *Economist*, July 10, 1993.

69. Paul Johnson, "Colonialism's Back—and Not a Moment Too Soon," *NYT Magazine*, April 18, 1993, a particularly vulgar example of the genre.

70. See, e.g., Stuart Auerbach, *Washington Post* Asia specialist, *WP Weekly*, July 26, 1993. See *For Reasons of State*, chap. 1, sec. 5, for examples of errors of fact and logic on these matters in academic scholarship; reprinted in Peck, *Chomsky Reader*. Commerce Department analysis, Wachtel, op. cit., 44f. *BW*, April 7, 1975.

71. Susan George, op. cit., xvf., chap. 3; foreword, Barratt Brown and Tiffen, op. cit. (UNICEF). Meacher, op. cit. Overview of South Commission Report, in South Centre, *Facing the Challenge* (Zed, 1993), 4. Latin America, UN Commission on Latin America, *Report on the Americas* (NACLA), Feb. 1993; *Excelsior* (Mexico), Nov. 21, 1992; *Excelsior*, Aug. 26, 1993; Pastor, "The Effects of IMF Programs in the Third World," *World Development* 15.2, 1987. Africa, Barratt Brown and Tiffen; IMF, 12. World Bank data review, Sobhan, op. cit.; Chile, David Pilling, "Latin America's dragon running out of puff," *FT*, Aug. 19, 1993. For a careful analysis of the case of Chile, see Collins and Lear, op. cit. WHO, *Deterring Democracy*, chap. 7; Reagan in Africa, "Inter-Agency Task Force, Africa Recovery Program/Economic Commission, *South African Destabilization: the Economic Cost of Frontline Resistance to Apartheid* (UN, New York, 1989), 13, cited by Merle Bowen, *Fletcher Forum*, Winter 1991. *Year 501*, chaps. 3–4, for sources not cited here.

72. Swaminathan and Ramachandran, op. cit. Chile, see Jean Drèze and Amartya Sen, *Hunger and Public Action* (Oxford, 1989), 229ff; on the severe deterioration of the health care system, and its sharp polarization, see Collins and Lear, op. cit. On abuse of children, see *Deterring Democracy*, chap. 7; *Year 501*, chap. 7.

73. O'Shaughnessy, *Observer*, Sept. 12, 1993.

74. Cries/Nitlapán team, *Envío*, Jesuit Central American University (UCA), Managua, Sept. 1993. Senate vote, July 29, 1993. CEPAD *Report*, July–August (Evangelical Churches of Nicaragua); *Barricada Internacional*, Oct. 9, 10; *Nicaragua News Service*, Nicaragua Network Education Fund, Washington, Oct. 2–9; *Central America Report* (Guatemala), Oct. 22; Guillermo Fernandez A., *BI*, Sept.; Porpora, *CSM*, Oct. 20; Werner, "Children pay price in Nicaragua's New Order," *Third World Resurgence* (Malaysia) No. 35, 1993. John Haslett Cuff, *Globe & Mail* (Toronto), Nov. 20; O'Shaughnessy, *Observer* (London), Sept. 26, 1993. On similar practices in Latin America and other regions of Western influence, see *Turning the Tide*, chap. 3.8; *Year 501*, chap. 7.7. On the Somoza monetarist model, see the study by Nicaragua's leading conservative economist, Francisco Mayorga, *The Nicaraguan Economic Experience, 1950–1984: Development and exhaustion of an agroindustrial model*, Yale University PhD thesis, 1986; for discussion, see *Deterring Democracy*, 232f.

75. Jeremy Mark, *WSJ*, April 4, 1994.

76. USG and Intifada, see above, p. 229. Rubinstein, "Terror is caused by the humiliations," *Ha'aretz*, April 2, 1993. For a glimpse of the record, see *Towards a New Cold War*, *Fateful Triangle*, *Necessary Illusions*; Geoffrey Aronson, *Creating Facts* (Institute for Palestine Studies, 1987); and particularly Israel Shahak's regular collections. Philip Taubman, *NYT*, Sept. 24, 1984. Representative William Alexander, *NYT*, May 5, 1985; Cranston, U.S. Senate, Committee on Foreign Relations, Feb. 27, 1986. Carlos Argüello Gómez, Agent of Republic of Nicaragua, and State Department Legal Adviser Edwin Williamson, communications to International Court of Justice, the Hague, Sept. 12, 25, 1991; cited by international law specialist Howard Meyer in a letter to the *New York Times* after one of the congressional aid suspensions (Aug. 24, 1993, refused publication). Senate vote, Tim Johnson, Knight-Ridder Service, *BG*, Sept. 24, 1993; the aid ban, initiated by ultra-right Senators Jessie Helms and Connie Mack, did not specifically mention Nicaragua, but all understood its intent and significance. On history, policy, media, see sources already cited, which demonstrate, in particular, how radically the version of events and history presented to the public diverges from the most elementary facts.

77. See particularly Honey, op. cit. For review of the internal record and other sources on the ambivalent U.S. attitudes toward Costa Rican democracy, see *Necessary Illusions*, App. V.1 and text. Ibid., and *Letters from Lexington*, chap. 6, on the rigorous exclusion of Central America' s leading democrat from the U.S. media through the 1980s, even in his obituary notice, a good symbolic indication of the real attitudes "when U.S. efforts to promote Latin American democracy were particularly notable"; see p. 47.

78. See *Year 501*, chap. 7; Haines, op. cit.

79. Paul Kennedy, *New York Review*, Feb. 11, 1993, citing statistics from the Inter-American Development Bank, 1989.

80. See p. 69. Burke, "The Political Economy of NAFTA, the Global Crisis and Mexico," ms, U. of Maine, 1993; "The Beginning of the End of the IMF Game Plan: the Case of Mexico," in Edgar Ortiz, ed., *Public Administration Economics and Finance: Current Issues in the North-American and Caribbean Countries* (Centro de Investigación y Docencia Económicas, Mexico, 1989–90). Meacher, op. cit. South Centre, op. cit., 12.

81. UNDP *Human Development Report*, 1992, 34–35, cited by Ian Robinson, *The NAFTA, Democracy, and Economic Development*, Canadian Centre for Policy Alternatives, 1993, n. 64; *North American Trade as if Democracy Mattered* (CCPA and International Labor Rights Education and Research Fund, 1993), App. 2. Study director Dr. Gregory Pappas, quoted by Robert Pear, "Big Health Gap, Tied to Income, Is Found in U.S.," *NYT*, July 8, 1993.

82. Gilmour, *Dancing with Dogma* (Simon & Schuster, 1992).

83. Thomas Edsall, *WP Weekly*, Aug. 2; Lester Thurow, *Guardian Weekly*, Aug. 22, 1993. Mishel and Bernstein, *Challenge*, Sept.–Oct. 1992. Allen Sinai, "What's Wrong with the Economy," *Challenge*, Nov.–Dec. 1992. Dornbusch, *Economist*, Oct. 24, 1992. Robinson, op. cit. Rothstein, *American Prospect*, Summer 1993.

OECD and other studies of inequality, *Left Business Observer*, Sept. 14, 1993. UNICEF, AP, *BG*, Sept. 23, 1993. Alfred Malabre, *WSJ*, Sept. 13; Judy Rakowsky, "Tufts study finds 12 million children in US go hungry, " *BG*, June 16, 1993. For further discussion, see *Deterring Democracy*, chap. 2; *Year 501*, chaps. 2, 4, 11.

84. Paulette Thomas, *WSJ*, Oct. 5, 1993. Robert Rosenthal, *LAT*, March 31; AP, *Chicago Tribune*, Jan. 26; David Holstrom, *CSM*, Jan. 27, 1994.

85. Labor economists Lawrence Mishel and Jared Bernstein, "The Joyless Recovery," *Dissent*, Winter 1994; Tamar Lewin, *NYT*, March 10; *Fortune* (cover story), Jan. 24, 1994. Robert Hershey, *NYT*, April 2; Jurek Martin, *FT*, April 2, 1994.

86. Gilmour, op. cit. Godley, *London Review of Books*, April 8; Steven Webb and Richard Thomas, *New Statesman and Society*, July 30; David Brindle, *Guardian Weekly*, July 11, 1993. Angelia Johnson, *Guardian*, July 6; David Nicholson-Lord, *Independent*, May 12; Pirt, letter, *Independent*, May 18, 1993. Inequality order as measured by Gini index, computed from Luxembourg Income Study data files; *Left Business Observer*, Sept. 14, 1993.

87. David Nicholson-Lord, *Independent*, Feb. 1; Press release, Action for Children," Jan. 31; Jeremy Laurance, "Workhouse gruel 'too costly for poor today,'" *Times*, Feb. 1; John Palmer, "UK joins poor of Europe," Jan. 30, 1994. David Gardner, *FT*, Oct. 16, 1992.

88. *Business Week*, Feb. 21; Dana Milbank, *WSJ*, March 28, 1994.

89. Manne, "Wrong Way, Go Back, " *ABM*, Nov. 1992; Burchill, "Scenes from Market Life: Neoliberalism in Australia," ms., U. of Tasmania, 1993 (citing P. Kelly, *End of Certainty*, 1992). For informative review and comparative analysis, see Tom Fitzgerald, *Between Life and Economics* (1990 Boyer lectures of the Australian Broadcasting Company, ABC, 1990); John Carroll and Robert Manne, eds., *Shutdown: The Failure of Economic Rationalism* (Melbourne: Text, 1992).

90. Krugman, "The Right, the Rich, and the Facts, " *American Prospect*, Fall 1992.

91. Gordon Campbell, *Listener* (NZ), Jan. 30, 1993. Hazeldine "Taking New Zealand Seriously," Inaugural Lecture, Department of Economics, U. of Auckland, Aug. 10, 1993.

92. Ryutaro Komiya, Yutaka Kosai, and others in Komiya, op. cit.; see Fitzgerald, op. cit., for further discussion. Johnson, *National Interest*, Fall 1989. Amsden, in Evans, op. cit.

93. Overseas Economic Cooperation Fund, "Implications of the World Bank's Focus on Structural Adjustment: A Japanese Government Critique," *Third World Economics* (Malaysia), March 31, 1993.

94. Patricia Corda, *Excelsior* (Mexico), Dec. 4, 1992. Fernando Montes, S.J., of the Chilean Delegation (*Mensaje*, Dec. 1992); Christmas message of Bolivian Bishops Conference; both in *LADOC* (Latin American Documentation), Lima, Mar./ April 1993. Ian Linden, director, Catholic Institute of International Relations, "Reflections on Santo Domingo," *The Month* (Jan. 1993).

95 . See *Turning the Tide*, chap. 4.2.2, summarizing studies by Vicente Navarro; Thomas Ferguson & Joel Rogers, *Right Turn* (Hill & Wang, 1986). Also *Deterring Democracy*, chap. 2; *Year 501*, chap. 11. *British Social Attitudes Survey*, Guardian, Nov. 18, 1992.

96. Jean-Yves Potel, "La Hongrie n'est plus une 'ile heureuse,'" *Le Monde diplomatique*, May 1993. *FT*, June 17, Sept. 16, 1993.

97. Konstanty Gebert, columnist for Poland's largest daily, an "underground journalist" in the eighties, *WP Weekly*, May 10, 1993. Amsden, "After the Fall," *American Prospect*, Spring 1993.

98. Dean Murphy, *LAT*, Sept. 19; Barry Newman, *WSJ*, Sept. 16; Jane Perlez, *NYT*, Sept. 18, 1993.

99. Jonathan Kaufman, *BG*; Barry Newman, *WSJ*; Jane Perlez, *NYT*; Sept. 20, 1993.

100. Sharon Wolchik, Jane Leftwich Curry, *Current History*, Nov. 1992.

101. Abraham Brumberg, op-ed, *NYT*, March 22; Andrew Hill, *FT*, Feb. 25; AP, *BG*, Feb. 25; Times Mirror, *NYT* news service, Jan. 26; Steven Erlanger, *NYT*, Aug. 20; *Economist*, March 13, 1993.

102. Marlise Simons, "In Europe's Brothels, Women from the East," *NYT*, June 9, 1993 . On Bolivia and other "free market successes," see *Year 501*, chaps. 3, 7. Rensselaer Lee and Scott Macdonald, "Drugs in the East," *Foreign Policy*, Spring 1993.

103. "The 'Thirdworldisation' of Russia under IMF rule," *Third World Quarterly*, June 16–30, 1993.

104. "La grande détresse de la société russe," *Le Monde diplomatique*, Sept. 1993.

105. Barry Newman, "Disappearing Act: West Pledged Billions of Aid to Poland—Where Did It All Go?" *WSJ*, Feb. 23; John Fialka, "Helping Ourselves: U.S. Aid to Russia Is Quite a Windfall—For U.S. Consultants," *WSJ*, Feb. 24; Jane Perlez, March 12, 1994. On the general phenomenon of aid programs "as a cash cow for privileged services industries" in the United States, with specific reference to the Egyptian experience, see Robert Vitalis, "The Democratization Industry and the Limits of the New Interventionism," *Middle East Report*, March–June 1994. The basic content of "democratization," Vitalis notes, is captured in the summary and recommendations of a report of USAID's Democratic Institutions Support Project, Near East Bureau: the democracy project aims to operationalize a strategy for "supporting processes of democratic institutional reform that will further economic liberalization objectives."

106. Jaramillo, *Third World Resurgence*, No. 42/43, 1994.

107. Kregel and Matzner, *Challenge*, Sept.–Oct. 1992. On Italy, see Gerschenkron, op. cit.; on Austria, Mjøset, op. cit.

108. UNICEF, *Public Policy and Social Conditions: Central and Eastern Europe in Transition*, Florence (Italy), Nov. 1993. Francis Williams, *FT*, Jan. 27, 1994. Shapiro and other researchers, John Lloyd, *FT*, Feb. 14, 1994. Daly, "The Perils of Free Trade," Scientific American, Nov. 1993. The *New York Times* reported the growing death rate in Russia a few weeks after the foreign press, reviewing possible reasons but with a curious omission: the economic "reforms" it has so strongly advocated; Michael Specter, *NYT*, March 6, 1994.

109. Steve Hanke and Sir Alan Walters, "The high cost of Jeffrey Sachs," *Forbes*, June 21, 1993.

110. Myers, *CT*, Jan. 28, 1994.

111. Parker, "Clintonomics for the East," *Foreign Policy*, Spring 1994.

112. Eatwell, "The Global Money Trap," *American Prospect*, Winter 1993. GATT, Low, op. cit., 242. David Calleo, *The Imperious Economy* (Harvard, 1982). On the Nixon initiatives and their reasons, see also Susan Strange, *Casino Capitalism* (Blackwell, 1986); Howard Wachtel, *The Money Mandarins* (M.E. Sharpe, 1990). Capital flows, Frederic Clairmont and John Cavanagh, *Third World Resurgence*, No. 42/43, 1994. See *Year 501*, chap. 3, for further discussion and sources.

113. Barry Riley, Philip Coggan, "IMF: World Economy and Finance," *FT*, Sept. 24, 1993.

114. IMF, Doug Henwood, *Left Business Observer*, no. 56, Dec. 1992. Douglas Seage and Constance Mitchell, *WSJ*, Nov. 6, 1992. See p. 104.

115. Barkin, "Salinastroika and Other Novel Ideas," Aug. 10, 1992; SourceMex, U. of New Mexico, Latin America Data Base, to appear in new edition of Barkin, *Distorted Development* (Westview, 1990). Andrew Fisher, *FT*, May 20; Anthony Robinson, *FT*, Oct. 20, 1992. Amsden, "After the Fall." See *Year 501*, chap. 2.5, for further discussion.

116. Amsden, "After the Fall." Richard Stevenson, *NYT*, June 22, 1993. Alabama, see below.

117. Richard Stevenson, *NYT*, May 11, June 22; Craig Whitney, *NYT*, Aug. 8; Roger Cohen, *NYT*, Aug. 9, 1993.

118. *BW*, Feb. 15; *Economist*, Feb. 27, 1993. Helene Cooper and Glenn Ruffenbach, *WSJ*, Sept. 30, 1993. On North Carolina's achievements in destroying the labor movement, driving down wages, and attracting industry from Canada and elsewhere, see Linda Diebel, *Toronto Star*, June 6, 1993; see my article in *Lies of Our Times*, Sept. 1993.

119. Tim Golden, *NYT*, Nov. 19, 1993. *El Financiero*, cited by Robinson, *North American Trade*, n. 183. Barkin, *Distorted Development*, and articles by Barkin, Richard Grinspun, Janet Tanski, and James Cypher in *Review of Radical Political Economics*, Dec. 1993. Damian Fraser, *FT*, Oct. 5, 1993.

120. William McGaughey, *A US–Mexico Free-Trade Agreement* (Thistlerose, 1992), 16; Iain Guest, *Behind the Disappearances* (Pennsylvania, 1990), 530, 535.

121. McGaughey, op. cit., 25. OECD, Amsden, in Evans, op. cit. Aho, op. cit. *FT*, March 23, 1993. Workshop, Sept. 26 & 27, 1990, minutes, 3.

122. *Preliminary Report*, Labor Advisory Committee on the North American Free Trade Agreement, submitted to the president and Congress, Sept. 16, 1992.

123. *Year 501*, 57f.; McGaughey, op. cit., 75f.

124. Bernard, ms, Harvard Trade Union Program, Harvard University, Nov. 5, 1993.

125. U.S. Congress, Office of Technology Assessment, *US–Mexico Trade: Pulling Together or Pulling Apart* (U.S. Govt. Printing Office, Oct. 1992). Floyd Norris, *NYT*, Aug. 30, 1992, business section.

126. Of the 60 percent of the U.S. population who had an opinion, two-thirds opposed the NAFTA agreement in the form proposed, figures that roughly persisted despite a huge government–media barrage; Bob Davis, *WSJ*, Dec. 23, 1992. In a review by the Roper Center, in the last poll cited, September 1993, of the 76 percent who had an opinion, 55 percent remained opposed to "the proposed free trade agreement," with a notable class difference, a surprisingly high opposition given the circumstances; Roper Center for Public Opinion Research, *The American Enterprise: Public Opinion and Demographic Report*, Nov.–Dec. 1993. Asra Nomani and Michael Frisby, *WSJ*, Sept. 15; Keith Bradsher, "Side Agreements to Trade Accord Vary in Ambition," *NYT*, Sept. 19, 1993.

127. Fein, *Newsletter*, Society for Historians of American Foreign Relations (SHAFR), March 1993. Darling, *LAT–Chicago Sun-Times*, Oct. 17, 1993; Bishops, electronic communication; Devon Peña, *Capitalism, Nature, Socialism*, Dec. 1993; Dudley Althaus, "Nafta a victory for Salinas, but not all Mexicans happy," *Houston Chronicle*, Nov. 18, 1993; Harry Browne, with Beth Sims and Tom Barry, *For Richer, for Poorer* (Resource Center Press, 1994).

128. *Excelsior*, Oct. 21, 28; Nov. 12, 1993. *Latin America News Update*, Dec. 1993, Jan. 1994.

129. Oliphant, *BG*, Sept. 19, 1993. The OTA study points out the near-meaninglessness of economic models on job projection and the like (the topic that dominated public debate), given the artificiality of assumptions and the huge ignorance about relevant factors.

130. Sylvia Nasar, *NYT*, Sept. 17, 1993.

131. Mark Bils, "Tariff Protection and Production in the Early U.S. Cotton Textile Industry," *J. of Economic History* 44, Dec. 1984. See Du Boff, op. cit., 56; Sellers, op. cit., 277.

132. Gwen Ifill, *NYT*; John Aloysius Farrell, *BG*, Nov. 8. Richard Berke, "Rescuing a Lawmaker From Labor's Revenge," *NYT*, March 15, 1994. Bob Davis and Jackie Calmes, *WSJ*, Nov. 17; Lewis, Nov. 5, 1993. Editorial, *NYT*, Nov. 16, 1993.

133. Michael Wines, *NYT*, Nov. 18, 1993.

134. Thomas Lueck, *NYT*, Nov. 18, 1993. Poverty figures, *Lancet* (Britain), Dec. 4, 1993.

135. AP, *BG*, Jan. 30, 1994.

136. Pearlstein, *WP Weekly*, Nov. 8; Krugman, *Foreign Affairs*, Nov./Dec. 1993. On the category of "unskilled workers," see Robinson, *North American Trade*, n. 224; LAC report.

137. *Labor Notes*, Jan. 1994; Anthony De Palma, *NYT*, Dec. 14, 1993; see *Year 501*, chap. 7. Damian Fraser, *FT*, Jan. 4; Tim Golden, *NYT*, Jan. 4, Feb 26; *Houston Chronicle* news service, Jan. 3; Juanita Darling, *LAT*, Jan. 3, 1994.

138. AP, Krauss, *NYT*, Nov. 20, 1993.

139. R.W. Apple, Thomas Friedman, Sanger, *NYT*, Nov. 21, 1993.

140. See pp. 103–105, 108. Kofsky, op. cit.

141. Elaine Sciolino, Friedman, NYT, Nov. 19, 1993.

142. Reuters, *NYT*, Nov. 19, 1993.

143. Kirkland, press release, May 13, 1993. *Asian Labour Update* (Hong Kong), July 1993. Press Association Newsfile (U.K.), Dec. 6, 1993. *FT*, April 5, 1994.

144. Wage levels, *Economist*, April 2, 1994. *Counterpunch* (Institute for Policy Studies), Feb. 15, March 15; Nicholas Cumming-Bruce, *Guardian*, Feb. 16; Johnston, letter, *Nation*, May 2, 1994. Reuters, *NYT*, Dec. 8, 1993. 1965, see p. 24, above.

145. *CSM*, Dec. 22, 1993.

146. Reese Erlich, *CSM*, Feb. 9, 1994.

147. Lawrence Zuckerman and Asra Nomani, *WSJ*, Dec. 30, 1993; Zuckerman, *WSJ*, Jan. 4; Bob Davis and Robert Greenberger, *WSJ*, Jan. 6; Friedman, *NYT*, Jan. 7, 1994. *WSJ*, Patrick Tyler, *NYT*, Jan. 18, 1994.

148. Francis Williams, *FT*, Feb. 18; editorial, Feb. 10, 1994.

149. Friedman, *NYT*, March 24; Maggie Farley, *BG*, March 7, 1994.

150. Sciolino, *NYT*, March 8, 1994.

151. Friedman, *NYT*, March 24; Tony Walker, *FT*, March 15; Elaine Sciolino, *NYT*, March 15, 1994.

152. Friedman, *NYT*, March 24; Greenhouse, *NYT*, March 30, 1994.

153. *Weekend FT*, April 25/26, 1992; South Centre, op. cit., 13.

154. Jaramillo, op. cit. Pico, *Envío*, op. cit.

155. Jefferson, 1816, cited by Sellers, op. cit., 106. Smith, *Wealth of Nations*, Bk. V, Ch. 1.III.I; Bk. I, Ch. 10.I; E. Cannan, ed., Chicago 1904 (1976), Vol. II, 264ff.; Vol I, 111. See Werhane, *Adam Smith*, 125, 106.

156. Peter Cowhey and Jonathan Aronson, *Foreign Affairs, America and the World*, 1992/93. Sen. Ernst Hollings, *Foreign Policy*, Winter 1993–94. Ian Robinson, op. cit., 63n. Daly, op. cit.

157. Jackson, FT, July 21; Raghavan, "TNCs getting more rights with less obligations, says UN report," *Third World Economics*, 1–15 Aug. 1993.

158. Clairmont and Cavanagh, op. cit.; Floyd Norris, *NYT*, Aug. 30, 1992; Reuters, *BG*, April 11, 1994.

159. "World-Trade Statistics Tell Conflicting Stories, *WSJ*, March 28, 1994.

160. Daly and Goodland, "An Ecological–Economic Assessment of Deregulation of International Commerce Under GATT," Draft, Environment Department, World Bank, 1992.

161. *Third World Economics* (Penang), 1–15 October, 1993. Parvathi Menon and editorial, *Frontline* (India), Jan. 14, 1994.

162. Joel Lexchi, "Pharmaceuticals, patents, and politics: Canada and Bill C-22," *Int. J. of Health Services*, vol. 23.1, 1993; Dennis Bueckert, Terrance Wills, *Montreal Gazette*, Dec. 3, 1992; Linda Diebel, *Toronto Star*, Dec. 6, 1992. See *Year 501*, chap. 4. On the harmful impact of product patents in earlier years, see William Brock, *The Norton History of Chemistry* (Norton, 1992), 308.

163. Mark Sommers, "Sanctions Are Becoming 'Weapon of Choice,'" *CSM*, Aug. 3, 1993, referring to "outlaw regimes"—in practice, those "outlawed" by the United States. Henry Simons, cited by Warren Gramm, "Chicago Economics: From Individualism True to Individualism False," *J. of Economic Issues* IX. 4, Dec. 1975.

164. *Report on the Americas* (NACLA), XXVI. 4, Feb. 1993.

165. Peter Phillips, *Challenge*, Jan.–Feb. 1992.

166. For an insightful account of these developments, see Rajani Kanth, *Political Economy and Laissez-Faire* (Rowman and Littlefield, 1986). Noble, *Progress without People* (Charles Kerr, 1993), and his *Forces of Production* (Knopf, 1984). See also Seymour Melman, *Profits without Production* (Knopf, 1983).

167. Polanyi, *The Great Transformation* (1944; Beacon, 1957), 78ff.

168. *Third World Resurgence*, no. 44, 1994.

Notes to Chapter 3

1. For sources where not given here, see De*terring Democracy*, chap. l; *Year 501*, chap. 2.

2. See pp. 71, 122f., 137f., above; *Year 501*, chap. 7, for review and sources, particularly Stephen Rabe, op. cit. Also Painter, op. cit.

3. Rabe, 64. Petroleum Policy, cited by Gabriel Kolko, *The Politics of War* (Random House, 1968), 302; Painter, 59; Frieden, "The Economics of Intervention," *Comparative Studies in Society and History* 31.55–80, 1989. On the methods by which the principles were applied, see *Multinational Oil Corporations and U.S. Foreign Policy* (*MNOC*), Report to the Committee on Foreign Relations, U.S. Senate, Jan. 2, 1975. See *Towards a New Cold War* for discussion and references.

4. Godfried, op. cit., 158–59. Lend Lease, *MNOC*, 36f.

5. Painter, op. cit., 114.

6. Sam Pope Brewer, "Iran is Reported Subversion Free," *NYT*, Dec. 2, 1956; *NYT*, Aug. 30, 1960. Cited by William Dorman and Mansour Farhang, *The U.S. Press and Iran* (California, 1987), 77, 72. See *Necessary Illusions*, App. V.3, for review and further sources.

7. Mark Gasioworski, "The 1953 Coup d'Etat in Iran," *Int. J. of Middle East Studies* 19 (1987), 265. Quandt, "Lebanon, 1958, and Jordan, 1970," in Barry Blechman and Stephen Kaplan, eds. *Force without War* (Brookings Institution, 1978), 247, 238.

8. See *Deterring Democracy*, chap. 6, for sources and further discussion.

9. Mark Curtis, *The Ambiguities of Power: British Foreign Policy Since 1945* (Zed, 1959).

10. See chapter 2, sec. 2. See Godfried, op. cit., for an in-depth review.

11. Ibid., 152f., 68, 134, 109.

12. British, Dulles, see Stivers, *Supremacy and Oil*, 28, 34; *America's Confrontation with Revolutionary Change in the Middle East* (St. Martin's, 1986), 20f.

13. John Blair, analyst of the international petroleum cartel for the Federal Trade Commission, *The Control of Oil* (Pantheon, 1976).

14. Hiro, "The Gulf between the rulers and the ruled," *New Statesman and Society*, Feb. 28, 1993. Pp. 9, 23, above.

15. 1962 remarks cited by Michael Bishku, *Middle East Policy* I.4, 1992, from Macmillan's *At the End of the Day* (Harper & Row, 1973).

16. Little, op. cit., Freiberger, op. cit.

17. Godfried, op. cit., 152f.

18. Freiberger, op. cit.

19. NSC 5801/1, Jan. 24, 1958; *FRUS* 1958, Vol. XII, Near East, 17ff. (Washington, 1993). British Joint Intelligence Committee report, Feb. 20, 1958. Both cited by Irene Gendzier, *Notes from a Minefield*, ms, 1993, from which what follows on Lebanon is also drawn.

20. State Department memorandum of conversation.

21. Avi Shlaim, *Collusion across the Jordan* (Columbia, 1988), 388, paraphrasing 1948 JCS records; 491, citing the Israeli state archives. For sources and further discussion, here and below, see *Towards a New Cold War*, chap. 11; *Fateful Triangle*, chap. 2.

22. Ibid., 457f.; Jonathan Marshall, Peter Dale Scott, and Jane Hunter, *The Iran–Contra Connection* (South End, 1987), chap. 8; *Culture of Terrorism*, chap. 8.

23. See Michael Bar-Zohar, *Ben-Gurion: A Biography* (New York, 1978), 261f.; Isaac Alteras, *Eisenhower and Israel* (Florida, 1993), 307ff.

24. *Ha'aretz*, Nov. 11, 1983. Glenn Frankel, *WP*, Nov. 19; Nathan Shaham, *Yediot Ahronot*, Nov. 28, 1986.

25. AP, "McNamara: US near war in '67," *BG*, Sept. 16, 1983; Donald Neff, *Warriors for Jerusalem* (Simon & Schuster, 1984). For detailed examination of the diplomatic background for the war and subsequent diplomacy, and prevailing illusions about these matters, see Norman Finkelstein, "To Live or Perish," ms, 1993.

26. Beilin, *Mehiro shel Ihud* (Revivim, 1985). See "Afterword," *Deterring Democracy*, for excerpts.

27. Neff, op. cit., 340f., and *Middle East International*, 13 Sept., 1991, citing the classified State Department history by Nina Noring and Walter Smith, *The Withdrawal Clause in UN Security Council Resolution 242 of 1967*, Feb. 1978, kept secret "so as not to embarrass Israel," Neff concludes. See also Finkelstein, op. cit.; David Korn, *Stalemate* (Westview, 1992); Quandt, *Peace Process*, 523n26 (the text itself is misleading). See the interchange between Eugene Rostow and David Korn, letters, *New Republic*, Oct. 21, Nov. 18, Nov. 25, 1991; cited in *Deterring Democracy*, "Afterword."

28. *The Rabin Memoirs* (Little, Brown, 1979), 192f. Bar-Lev, *Ot*, March 9, 1972, cited by Amnon Kapeliouk, *Le monde diplomatique*, Oct. 1977; Weizmann, *Ha'aretz*, March 29, 1972, cited by John Cooley, *Green March, Black September* (Frank Cass, 1973), 162. The official documents appear in John Norton Moore, ed., *The Arab–Israeli Conflict* (Princeton, 1974), vol. 3, pp. 1103–11.

29. Korn, op. cit., epilogue; Rabin, op. cit.; Tillman, *The United States in the Middle East* (Indiana, 1982), chap. 6. On Kissinger's geopolitical fantasies while in government, see *Towards a New Cold War*, chap. 6; see 406n16 for some earlier examples, scarcely to be believed.

30. Shlaim, op. cit., 364. On West Bank water and political settlement, there is a substantial literature; see now Miriam Lowi, "Bridging the Divide," *International Security* (Summer 1993) and her *Water and Power* (Cambridge, 1994).

31. Gvirtzman, *Ha'aretz*, May 16, 1993. Gvirtzman, interview, Israel Zamir, *Al Hamishmar*, March 12, 1993, translated by Israel Shahak, "Collection: the settling ideology and its opponents," April 1993. Stauffer, David Francis, *CSM*, Sept. 17, 1993.

32. Draper, *NYT Book Review*, May 17, 1981; Eric Pace, *NYT*, Oct. 7, 1981. For more on the matter, see *Towards a New Cold War*, 460n19, *Fateful Triangle*, 84n88, and texts; *Pirates and Emperors*, chap. 1.

33. On Israeli attitudes during this period, see particularly Amnon Kapeliouk, *Israël: la fin des mythes* (Albin Michel, Paris, 1975). This important study by a leading Israeli journalist was offered to many U.S. publishers, but none was willing to publish it despite the enormous market for material on Israel (not with such factual materials, however). For citations, see *Towards a New Cold War*, *Fateful Triangle*.

34. "Memorandum of Conversation," meeting with Jewish leaders, June 15, 1975; *MERIP Reports*, May 1981. See *Towards a New Cold War*, 457n27.

35. *Dilemmas of Security* (Oxford, 1987), 70.

36. Shipler, interview with Hillel Schenker, *New Outlook* (Tel Aviv), May 1984. Quandt, Saunders, in Quandt, ed., *The Middle East: Ten Years after Camp David* (Brookings Institution, 1988). Quandt, *American–Arab Affairs*, Fall 1985.

37. For discussion and sources, here and below, see *Fateful Triangle*, chap. 5; *Pirates and Emperors*, chap. 2; *Necessary Illusions*, App. I.2, V.2,4.

38. Friedman, *NYT*, Jan. 9, Feb. 20, Feb. 18, 1985; Sciolino, July 27, 1993. Quandt, *Peace Process*, 340.

39. Editorial, *WP*, April 22, 1982; Greenway, *BG*, July 29, 1993.

40. Amnon Levi, *Hadashot*, July 28, 1993. Uri Lubrani, Israel's coordinator of Lebanese policy, and Foreign Minister Shimon Peres, Ethan Bronner, *BG*, July 29, Aug. 1, 1993. See my article in *Z magazine*, September 1993, for a much fuller account.

41. Chris Hedges, *NYT*, July 31, 1993. On the establishment of the "Big Lie," see Abraham, *Lies of Our Times* (October 1993). Fisk, *Independent*, Feb. 27, 1994, reviewing the prevailing double standard on the occasion of the Hebron massacre at the Tomb of the Patriarch, as the familiar record was replayed.

42. O'Brien, *Independent*, Aug. 20, 1993.

43. AP, *BG*, May 22, 1992. AP, *BG*, Sept. 21; *FT*, Nov. 17, 1993. AP, *BG*, March 11; *FT*, March 22, 23, 1994.

44. For ongoing review, see references of note 37. Also "Afterword," *Deterring Democracy*, and my article in Peters, *Collateral Damage*.

45. Between 1973 and 1987, the United States vetoed nineteen Security Council resolutions concerning Israel and Middle East peace, voting alone. Mark Curtis, *Obstacles to Security*. For more detail and later examples, see *Deterring Democracy*, chap. 6, and sources cited.

46. Jules Kagian, *Middle East International*, Dec. 17, 1993; *Middle East Justice Network*, Feb.–March 1994. On the background and status of UN 194, see Thomas and Sally Mallison, *The Palestine Problem in International Law and World Order* (Longman, 1986), chap. 4.

47. Paul Lewis, *NYT*, March 19; Neff, Jules Kagian, *Middle East International*, April 1, 1994.

48. *NYT, BG*, Nov. 8; AP, Dec. 7, 1989. Pp. 131–34, above. See *Culture of Terrorism, Necessary Illusions*, and *Deterring Democracy* for details and general discussion.

49. *Peace Process*, 417f.

50. Painter, op. cit., 208f. Quotes from Charles Lindblom and Benny Temkin.

51. Editorial, *NYT*, Aug. 31, 1993.

52. Rubinstein, *Ha'aretz*, Oct. 23, 24, 1991.

53. Chagai Porshner, *Davar*, Nov. 12, 1992; "Kav La'oved" (Workers' Hotline) Newsletter, March 1993; Panel Debate, "The Social Rights of Palestinian Workers in Israel," May 6, 1993. Press release, Dr. Yael Renan, Kav La'oved Executive Committee, June 27, 1993. On Jan. 12, 1994, Kav La'oved instituted a lawsuit in the Israeli courts calling for restitution of $1 billion taken for insurance deductions without benefits, and full rights for Palestinian workers employed in Israel; *Workers' Hotline*, Feb. 1994. The government was joined in opposing the lawsuit by the PLO, which wants the funds stolen from the workers to be given to the PLO authorities. Rubik Rosenthal, *Ha'retz*, Feb. 25, 1994; Israel Shahak, *From the Hebrew Press*, VI.5, May 1994.

54. Peace Now, *The Real Map: A Demographic and Geographic Analysis of the Population of the West Bank and Gaza Strip*, Report No. 5, Nov. 1992, translated from Hebrew. Schiff, *Ha'aretz*, April 2, 1993; Israel Shahak, "Collection," April 1993 (see note 31).

55. Shragay, *Ha'aretz*, July 9, 13, 1993; translated by Israel Shahak.

56. Michael Jansen, *Middle East International*, 28 August, 1993.

57. For details, see Awad Mansour, *Clever Concealment* (Palestine Human Rights Information Center, Jerusalem, February 1994), based largely on the Israeli press and government records.

58. Coon, *Town Planning Under Military Occupation* (Al-Haq, Ramallah, 1992), 158, 203, 193. Also economist Aisling Byrne, "West Bank road plans leave nothing to negotiate," *Middle East International*, June 25, 1993.

59. For extensive detail, see Yossi Beilin, op. cit.

60. David Hoffman, "Israel's $10 Billion Nevermind," *WP Weekly*, June 21–27; Julian Ozanne, Jerusalem, *FT*, Sept. 23, 1993, paraphrasing Shochat.

61. Friedman, *NYT*, July 28, 1991.

62. Quandt, *Peace Process*, 573–76 (notes). See *Necessary Illusions*, App. IV.4, for a detailed record. Also Nabeel Abraham, "The 'Conversion' of Chairman Arafat," *American–Arab Affairs* 31, Winter 1989–90.

63. See *Necessary Illusions*, chap. 4, p. 85.

64. Aharon Barnea, *Hadashot*, Jan. 31 (Israel Shahak, Jerusalem, Report no. 116, Feb. 9, 1993). Mahanaimi, *Ha'olam Haze*, Aug. 1; Amir Oren, *Davar*, Aug. 13 (Shahak, Report no. 121, Aug. 15; *Middle East International*, 10 Sept., 1993).

65. Nahum Barnea, *Yediot Ahronot*, Feb. 24, 1989.

66. *Hadashot*, Feb. 14; Friedman, *NYT*, March 12, 1989.

67. For an account of the Intifada drawn from the Israeli press and personal experience, see my "Scenes from the Uprising," *Z magazine*, July 1988; *Necessary Illusions*, App. IV.2. There is a substantial literature, among others, Z. Lockman & J. Beinin, eds., *Intifada* (South End, 1989); Joost Hiltermann, *Behind the Intifada* (Princeton, 1991); Patricia Strum, *The Women are Marching* (Lawrence Hill, 1992).

The record in earlier years is sampled from contemporary reports in *Peace in the Middle East?*, *Towards a New Cold War*, and *Fateful Triangle*. See also Geoffrey Aronson, *Creating Facts* (Institute for Palestine Studies, 1987). There is extensive evidence in the Israeli press, the reports of Al-Haq and other human rights groups, and other sources, though little in the U.S. mainstream.

68. Chronology, *Middle East Journal*, Spring 1988; Attorney Avigdor Feldman, *Hadashot*, Jan. 1, 1988; *The Other Front* (Jerusalem), Oct. 3, 1989; Netzer, *Davar*, Jan. 20, 1993. See also "Scenes."

69. Israeli Government Election Plan, Jerusalem, 14 May 1989, official text distributed by the Embassy of Israel in Washington; reprinted in *J. of Palestine Studies*, Autumn 1989. The prime minister had released a four-point plan a month earlier with somewhat different terms. See *Jerusalem Post*, April 14, 1989; for discussion, Norman Finkelstein, *Middle East Report (MERIP)*, #158, May–June 1989. See references of note 44 for further detail.

70. Aaron David Miller, member of the Policy Planning Staff, U.S. State Department, keynote address, Center for Strategic and International Studies, Dec. 7, 1989, the day after the Baker Plan was officially released (see below). *American–Arab Affairs* 31, Winter 1989–90. Other participants also praised "the Shamir initiative of May 14th," mentioning only the elections provision (Helena Cobban).

71. Thomas Friedman, *NYT*, Oct. 19, 1989. Baker's five points, Daniel Williams, *Los Angeles Times*, Oct. 29; U.S. Department of State press release, Dec 6; Friedman, *NYT*, Dec. 7, 1989. Note that the scanty references to Baker's five points were misleading, since the terms of the Shamir–Peres Plan to which they refer were not reported, and still have not been in the mainstream. Quandt writes that "the most important of these points [the five points of the Baker Plan] was the notion that the Palestinians could bring to the negotiations any position related to the peace process" (*Peace Process*, 391). That is incorrect; the Baker Plan was explicit in restricting Palestinians to discussion of implementation of Israel's proposals. Like others, Quandt does not refer to the official Israeli position. On the latter, see also Israeli Arabist Gen. (ret.) Mattityahu Peled, in Bennis and Moushabeck, op. cit.; Peled says that the actual author was Rabin.

72. Lionel Barber and Alan Friedman, *FT*, May 3, 1991. AP, Dec. 20, 1989, Feb. 9, 1990. Official State Department response to an inquiry from Senator Daniel Inouye, Jan. 26, 1990. See *Deterring Democracy*, chaps. 5, 6. Further material appears in Alan Friedman, *Spider's Web* (Bantam, 1993).

73. *NYT*, Oct. 30, Sept. 22, 1991.

74. Atherton, "The Shifting Sands of Middle East Peace," *Foreign Policy*, Spring 1992. It is illuminating to observe the fate of efforts by local actors to pursue their own plans. One important recent case is the initiative of the Central American presidents to pursue a peace plan (the so-called "Arias plan") in August 1987, much to the distress of the Reagan administration. The conventional interpretation is that they succeeded in doing so. That is demonstrably false. The United States at once moved to undermine the plan, and quickly accomplished this result, in large part thanks to the refusal of the U.S. media to report even the basic facts. The plan was quickly shaped into an instrument of U.S. domination. For a detailed record as the exercise proceeded, see *Culture of Terrorism*, *Necessary Illusions*, and *Deterring Democracy*. It will be a long time before this intriguing story enters history.

75. Cobban, *CSM*, March 12; Lewis, *NYT*, March 15, 1991. Khalidi, *J. of Palestine Studies*, Autumn 1991. See my articles in *Z magazine*, October, December, 1991, for a different view, outlined in references of note 44, and reiterated here.

76. Friedman, *NYT*, Nov. 4; Haberman, *NYT*, Nov. 10, 17, 1991. On Friedman's intriguing record, see *Necessary Illusions*, particularly App. V.4 .

77. James Baker's "Letter of Assurance to the Palestinians," Oct. 18, 1991; Quandt, *Peace Process*, App. M.

78. Gazit, *Yediot Ahronot*, April 1992, cited by Israel Shahak, *Middle East International*, March 19, 1993.

79. *Hadashot*, July 12, 1993.

80. *Yediot Ahronot*, June 11, 1993.

81. On Indyk, see Greg Sheridan, "Our Man in the White House," *The Weekend Australian*, Jan. 30–31, 1993.

82. Rubinstein, *New Outlook* (Tel Aviv), Jan./Feb. 1993; also Julian Ozanne, *FT*, Feb. 15, 1993. Middle East Watch (New York), vol. 5, issue 4, *Palestinian Deportees*, Aug. 1993. Akiva Eldar and Eitan Rabin, *Ha'aretz*, Dec. 31, 1992. On the facts and legal background, see Angela Gaff, *An Illusion of Legality*, Occasional Paper No. 9, Al-Haq (Ramallah), 1993 .

83. Yaari, op-ed, *NYT*, Jan. 27, 1993; Chaim Cooper, *Israel Shelanu* (Hebrew language American weekly), Jan. 22, 1993. An accurate account was given by columnist Alexander Cockburn, *Los Angeles Times*, Feb. 7, 1993.

84. Peter Grier, *CSM*, March 18, 1993.

85. On the scale and character of the phenomenon from 1967, see my *Peace in the Middle East?* (Pantheon, 1974), chap. 5; *Fateful Triangle*, chaps. 2.3, 4.7, and later sections; and more recent publications, some cited earlier.

86. *NYT*, Aug. 31, 1993; their Western liberal lovers have now defected, Friedman adds. On further examples of the genre, see *Letters from Lexington*, chap. 18.

87. Quandt, *Peace Process*, 266.

88. For details, see Montague Kern, *Television and Middle East Diplomacy: President Carter's Fall 1977 Peace Initiative* (Center for Contemporary Arab Studies, Georgetown, Occasional Papers Series, 1983). See *Necessary Illusions*, chap. 4, for context and discussion.

89. Joel Brinkley, *NYT*, Sept. 8; Cowell, Dec. 12, 1989.

90. Clyde Haberman, *NYT*, Aug. 30, 1993.

91 . See, among others, *Pirates and Emperors*, chap. 2 (in large part reprinted in Edward Said and Christopher Hitchens, *Blaming the Victims* (Verso, 1988), a book that actually received some reviews—unusual, for material of a critical character— with this chapter singled out for furious diatribes from the mainstream press to the *J. of Palestine Studies*); and *Necessary Illusions*, App. 5.4, including sources for what follows.

92. Szep, *BG*, Sept. 3; editorial, *NYT*, Sept. 5; Friedman, *NYT* Week in Review, Sept. 5; Sciolino, Sept. 12; Lewis, Sept. 13, 1993. References are to the PLO Charter, which has an interesting history, still unrecorded in interesting respects. For some commentary years ago from Israeli sources, see *Fateful Triangle*, 68–69.

93. Personal interviews, West Bank, April 1988; Israel Shahak's regular reports, which have been an unparalleled source of information for many years; personal communications, Israeli and Palestinian sources.

94. Rubinstein, Shalev, and others, *Ha'aretz*, Aug. 24, 25, 27, 1993. Haetzni, *Ma'ariv*, Aug. 29, 1993.

95. Toledano, Andoni, *Middle East International*, Aug. 28, 1993. Toledano reprinted from *Ha'aretz*, Aug. 13.

96. Youssef Ibrahim, *NYT*, Aug. 25, 1993. On the range of reactions of Palestinians in the territories, refugee camps, and elsewhere, see Lamis Andoni, *CSM*, Aug. 30, Sept. 2; Landoni, Julian Ozanne, James Whitthington, *FT*. Sept. 1, 1993. Youssef Ibrahim, *NYT*, Aug. 30, 1993, focusing on Palestinians "living under Syrian tutelage in Damascus." Chris Hedges reported that "in a two-hour walk through the [Becca refugee camp in Jordan] there was not one photo or portrait of the P.L.O. chairman visible"; *NYT*, Sept. 10, 1993.

97. For an extreme example, see the lead story in the *NYT Week in Review* by Youssef Ibrahim, Sept. 12, a poetic evocation of "a people emerging from the wilderness of its own history" as the Palestinians, "now defined by the land they call home," "strode into a new era alongside their old enemy, the Israelis"—even if it is only minds that "have been changed, not maps."

98. Harrison, op-ed, maps, *NYT*, Sept. 10; Greenway, senior associate editor, *BG*, Sept. 9, 1993.

99. *Yediot Ahronot*, Sept. 2; Israel Shahak, "The Real Significance of the Oslo Agreement, " Report No. 125, Sept. 10, 1993. Anthony Flint, *BG*, Sept. 17, 1993.

100. For extensive review, and indications of implications for the future, see references of notes 57, 58.

101. Editorial, Beilin op-ed, Friedman, *NYT*, Aug. 31, 1993. The draft agreement was published in Israel, *Yediot Ahronot*, Aug. 31; English version, AP, *NYT*, Sept. 1, 1993. Friedman, interviews in Israeli press, April 1988; see *Necessary Illusions*, App. V.4. See also *Letters from Lexington*, chap. 18, on media attitudes generally.

102. For immediate and in my view accurate interpretation, see Edward Said, "Arafat's Deal," *Nation*, Sept. 20, 1993; Shahak, "Real Significance." My own views, reiterated here, appear in *Z magazine*, Oct. 1993, written before the disclosures from early September.

103. *NYT*, Sept. 10, 1993.

104. Andoni, see pp. 245–46, above. Rafael Man, *Ma'ariv*, Sept. 9, presenting and discussing the text. A Reuters version of the agreement published in the *Boston Globe* opens: "The Government of Israel *and the PLO* . . . ," the words highlighted here added to the texts that were published in Israel and the United States; *BG*, Sept. 19, 1993.

105. The suggestion was made by Azmi Bishara, professor of philosophy at Bir Zeit University, in an astute analysis of the agreement; radio interview with David Barsamian, Sept. 21, 1993.

106. *Davar*, Sept. 15, 1993.

107. *Report on Israeli Settlement in the Occupied Territories* 3.5, Sept. 1993, Foundation for Middle East Peace. Efraim Davidi, *Davar*, March 9; Schiff, *Ha'aretz*, March 5; Fishman, *Hadashot*, March 5; Rubinstein, *Ha'aretz*, March 5, 1993. These and other sources cited in Israel Shahak, Report No. 118, March 9, 1993.

108. Roy, "Separation or Integration," *Middle East Journal* 48.1, Winter 1994.

109. Alex Fishman et al., *Hadashot*, Nov. 19, 1993. *The Other Front* (Jerusalem), Feb. 23, 1994.

110. Roy, *CSM*, April 4, 1994; Ford, *CSM*, April 1; Clyde Haberman, *NYT*, March 29, 1994.

111. AP, *BG*, Feb. 25, 1994. Usher, *Middle East International*, March 18, 1993. Earlier undercover operations from 1988 are reviewed in human rights reports, including Middle East Watch, *A License to Kill*, Aug. 1993.

112. Benzamin, *Ha'aretz*, Sept. 3, 5; see Shahak, "Real Significance," for extensive discussion.

113. Benzamin, *Ha'aretz*, Dec. 3, 1993.

114. Oded Lifshitz, *Al Hamishmar*, Sept. 14; Gazit, *Ha'aretz*, Sept. 8, 1993.

115. Peres, *Moked* (TV), Sept. 1; quoted in *News from Within* (Jerusalem), Sept. 5. Rabin, interview, *Jerusalem Post International Edition*, week ending Oct. 16; *Yediot Ahronot*, Oct. 3, 1993.

116. Nathan Krystall, *News from Within*, Oct. 1993. Clyde Haberman, *NYT*, Nov. 17; Joel Greenberg, *NYT*, Nov. 26; Aruri, *CSM*, Dec. 29, 1993.

117. Hillel Cohen, "There is smoke, there is fire," *Kol Ha'ir*, Nov. 12; Zvi Gilat, "Burning and crying," *Yediot Ahronot*, Nov. 9; Amit Gurevitz, *Ha'olam Haze*, Nov. 17. Moshe Zigadon, *Yerushalayim*, Oct. 15, 1993. Shahak, *WP*, April 13, 1994.

118. Torpshtein, *Ha'aretz*, Nov. 22, 1993; Denkner, *Ha'aretz*, Jan. 9, 1994, translated by Israel Shahak; Ford, *CSM*, March 16, 1994. On settler atrocities in Hebron from the mid-1970s, see *Fateful Triangle*, 270, and references of note 67 generally.

119. Greenberg, *NYT*, April 3, 1994; also March 11, 22. Horovitz, *FT*, March 24, 1994.

120. Clyde Haberman, *NYT*, March 25; Graham Usher, *Middle East International*, April 1, 1994.

121. Clyde Haberman, *NYT*, April 11; AP, *BG*, April 11, 1994.

122. Peter Ford, *CSM*, March 16, 1994. B'Tselem, *The Interrogation of Palestinians During the Intifada*, March 1992. 1992 Report and ICRC press release (May 24, 1992), cited in Briefing Paper, Lawyers Committee for Human Rights, Middle East, Feb. 23, 1993. On the general situation, see Emma Playfair, ed., *International Law*

and the Administration of Occupied Territories: two decades of Israeli occupation of the West Bank and Gaza Strip (Clarendon press, Oxford, 1992).

123. Baram, *Middle East International*, April 1; Alon Hadar, *Kol Ha'ir*, March 18, 1994.

124. *Report*, Nov. 1993; Bill Hutman, *JP*, Oct. 12, Nov. 11; AP, *BG*, Oct. 21; Esther Goldbersht, *Ma'ariv*, Oct. 21, 1993. Gur, *JP*, Oct. 18, cited by Jan de Jong and John Tyler, *Challenge* (Israel), Nov.–Dec. 1993.

125. Sela, *Davar*, Nov. 30, translated by Israel Shahak; Bill Hutman, *JP*, Dec. 21, 1993.

126. De Jong and Tyler, op. cit.; *Hadashot*, Oct. 8; Yair Fidel, *Hadashot Supplement*, Oct. 29, 1993.

127. Nirit Zach, "New immigrants directed to the settlements," *Hadashot*, Nov. 21, 1993. *Challenge*, Jan.–Feb. 1994, citing Israeli radio, Jan. 11 and *Yediot Ahronot*, Jan. 12. *Report on Israeli Settlements*, Feb. 1994. Gur, ibid. and Peter Ford, *CSM*, March 18, 1994. Rabin, *Ha'aretz*, Dec. 9, 1993. See also *Clever Concealment*.

128. Yerach Tal, et al., *Ha'aretz*, Dec. 24, 1993. *Report on Israeli Settlement*, March 1994, citing *Yediot Ahronot*, Aug. 20, 1993.

129. Lewis, *NYT*, Sept. 16, 1993.

130. *NYT*, Sept. 10, 1993; *Jewish Post*, Dec. 18, 1991.

131. Rubinstein, *Ha'aretz*, Aug. 30; reprinted in *The Other Front* (Jerusalem), Sept. 1, 1993. *FT*, Sept. 4, 1993.

132. Richard Bernstein, "For Jews in America, a Time For New Hope and New Fear"; Rosenthal, former *Times* chief editor, *NYT*, Sept. 3. Safire, *NYT*, Sept. 2, 1993.

133. Lamis Andoni, *CSM*, Sept. 2, 1993. See references of note 96.

134. Israeli Ministry of Defense, *Jerusalem Post*, Feb. 15, 1985; cited by Coon, op. cit., 30.

135. *Davar*, Feb. 17, 1993, translated by Zachary Lockman; *Middle East Report* (MERIP), Sept.–Oct. 1993.

136. Peter Waldman and Robert Greenberger, "Palestinians Stay in Israel's Orbit Under Accord; Arab States Locked Out of Near-Captive Market," *WSJ*, May 2; "Framework for Peace," *NYT*, May 5; Marlise Simons, *NYT*, April 30; Thomas Friedman, *NYT*, May 3; Ozanne, *FT*, May 5; Andoni, *CSM*, May 5; Clyde Haberman, *NYT*, April 26; Ibrahim, *NYT*, May 6; Ozanne, *FT*, May 4, 1994.

137. Steven Greenhouse, *NYT*, Sept. 30, 1993.

138. *News from Within*, Alternative Information Center, Jerusalem, Aug. 5, 1993.

Notes to Epilogue

1. *Israeli-Palestinian Interim Agreement on the West Bank and the Gaza Strip*, signed in Washington, Sept. 28, 1995; State of Israel, Ministry of Foreign Affairs, Jerusalem. Henceforth *IA*. For more on Oslo II and related circumstances, see my article in Z magazine, Jan. 1996.

2. On developments through mid-1995 and further background, see my *Powers and Prospects* (South End, 1996), chap. 6. See now also Naseer Aruri, *The Obstruction of Peace* (Common Courage, 1995), Meron Benvenisti, *Intimate Enemies* (California, 1995), Norman Finkelstein, *Image and Reality in the Israel-Palestine Conflict* (Verso, 1995), Donald Neff, *Fallen Pillars* (Institute for Palestine Studies, 1995), Sara Roy, *The Gaza Strip* (Institute for Palestine Studies, 1995), Edward Said, *Peace and its Discontents* (Vintage, 1995), Graham Usher, *Palestine in Crisis* (Pluto, 1995). For regular reports from the scene, see *From the Hebrew Press: Monthly Translations and Commentaries from Israel*, by Israel Shahak (Middle East Data Center, POB 337, Woodbridge VA 22194).

3. On the usage with reference to Central America, see *Necessary Illusions*, 121f.

4. *NYT*, Nov. 6, 1995.

5. *Yediot Ahronot*, March 14; Steven Erlanger, "Is Peace's 'Honest Broker' Too Close to Peres," *NYT*, May 5, 1996. On Tunis, see *Pirates and Emperors*; *Necessary*

Illusions; my chapter in Alexander George, ed., *Western State Terrorism* (Polity-Blackwell, 1991).

6. *Ha'aretz*, July 6, Oct. 12, 1995 (*The Other Front*, Jerusalem).

7. Shalom Yerushalmi, *Ma'ariv*, Oct. 25; Barak, cited in *News from Within* (Jerusalem), Dec. 1995; Barzilai, *Ha'aretz*, Oct. 24, 1995.

8. Tanya Reinhart, *Ha'aretz*, May 27, 1994. The same point has been made by Benvenisti and others. For comparison of the two programs, see Norman Finkelstein, "Whither the 'Peace Process,'" ms., 1996.

9. See pp. 227f., above. Rabin cited by Tony Banks, *Jane's Defence Weekly*, May 7, 1988. For further detail, see *Necessary Illusions*, chap. 5 and App. 5.4.

10. Cited by John Battersby, *CSM*, Sept. 28, 1995.

11. B'Tselem, *Neither Law nor Justice* (Jerusalem, August, 1995); Human Rights Watch, *World Report 1996* (New York, 1996).

12. On the backgrounds, see Roy, *op cit.*

13. Maps, Interim Agreement. *Yediot Ahronot*, Oct. 6, 1995. Danny Rubinstein, *Palestine-Israel Journal*, Winter 1995. See Map page 273.

14. *IA*, Articles XVII, XVIII; Annex III, Articles 16, 22. Aluf Ben, *Ha'aretz*, Feb. 7, 1995. For further information and background, see Israel Shahak, *Ideology as a Central Factor in Israeli Policies* (Hebrew), May-June 1995.

15. Barnea-Shiffer, *Yediot Ahronot*, March 8, 1996.

16. Nir, *Ha'aretz*, Feb. 15; Gid'on Levy, *Ha'aretz*, May 14, April 23. Yacov Ben Efrat, *Challenge* (Israel), No. 32, 1995. Shahak, *Ideology*. Ran Kislev, *Ha'aretz*, Jan. 17, 1995. See p. 255 above, and for further details, *Powers and Prospects*, pp. 156f.

17. B'Tselem, *Impossible Coexistence*, Sept. 1995.

18. Sarah Helm, *Independent*, Oct. 3; Patrice Claude, *Le Monde*, Oct. 5 (*Guardian Weekly*, Oct. 16), 1994. Benvenisti, cited by Barton Gellman, *Washington Post* (*GW*, Jan. 22, 1995).

19. *IA*, Article XIII; Annex I, Articles V, VIII, XI.

20. *IA*, Article XIX; Annex III.

21. Kav La'Oved *Newsletter*, Oct. 1995.

22. Rubinstein, "Two Banks of the Jordan," *Ha'aretz*, Feb. 13, 1995. See *Powers and Prospects* for more extensive quotes. Military orders, see p. 267, above.

23. Shaked, *Yediot Ahronot*, Oct. 13, 1995.

24. Moshe Semyonov and Noah Lewin-Epstein, *Hewers of Wood and Drawers of Water* (Cornell, 1987). Shlomo Abramovitch, *Sheva Yamim*, March 3; Hanoch Marmari, *Ha'aretz*, March 9, 1995. Gay Ben Porat, *Ma'ariv*, Feb. 9; Yosef Elgazi, *Ha'aretz*, March 22; Hagar Enosh, *Yediot Ahronot*, April 2, 1996.

25. *The Other Front*, Oct. 1995; *News from Within*, Nov. 1995. For further details and sources, see *Powers and Prospects*.

26. Ibid. *Report on Israeli Settlement*, March 1996. Tvi Zinger, *Yediot Ahronot*, March 14, 1996. Gazit, Rubinstein, cited in *Report on Israeli Settlement*, March 1995. 1995 growth rate, *ibid.*, Jan. 1996 (*J. of Palestine Studies*, Spring 1996). Sarah Kaminker, *Town Planning in the Arab Neighborhoods of East Jerusalem: A Policy of Land Use Denial* (Society of St. Yves, Catholic Legal Resources Center for Human Rights, 1996), forthcoming.

27. *Report on Israeli Settlement*, Jan. 1996. Safran, *BG*, June 2, 1996.

28. *Ha'aretz*, Oct. 26, 1995; *News from Within*, Dec. 1995.

29. *IA*, Annex III, Appendix I, Article 40 and Schedule 10.

30. Julian Ozanne and David Gardner, *FT*, Aug. 8; Stephen Langfur, Allegra Pachecho (Society of St. Yves), *Challenge*, Nov.–Dec. (also *Middle East International*, 3 Nov.); Cohen, *Ha'aretz*, Aug. 21, 1995.

31. *Outlook* (Vancouver), Oct./Nov. 1995.

32. Dror Nissan, *Davar Rishon*, Nov. 27, 1995. On the inducements and expansion of settlements after Oslo I, see *Powers and Prospects*.

33. Benvenisti, *Intimate Enemies*, p. 222.

34. Neff, op. cit.

35. P. 224, above. *Report on Israeli Settlement*, Nov. 1995; Rabin, *Ha'aretz*, Oct. 6 and *Kol Ha'ir*, Oct. 13, cited in *Challenge*, Dec. 1995.

36. Et-Tur, Sur Bahar/Umm Tuba, and others. For maps of East Jerusalem, see Kaminker, op. cit. The Israeli map states that "Names and boundary representations are not necessarily authoritative."

37. *Yediot Ahronot*, Oct. 6; *NYT*, Nov. 17, 1995. See Map page 273.

38. *B'Tselem Report*, May 1995, citing Sarah Kaminker; summary and excerpts in *Ha'aretz*, May 15; *News from Within*, June 1995. Also Aaron Back and Eitan Felner, senior staff members of B'Tselem, *Tikkun* 10.4, 1995. Graham Usher, *Middle East International*, May 12, 1995. See also Clyde Haberman, *NYT*, May 14, 15, 1995.

39. Sarah Kaminker and Associates, *Planning and Housing Issues in East Jerusalem*, June 1994. On measures within Israel, see *Towards a New Cold War*, ch. 9; Walter Lehn with Uri Davis, *The Jewish National Fund* (Kegan Paul, 1988). For background see also Ian Lustick, *Arabs in the Jewish State* (U. of Texas, 1980).

40. Kaminker, *Town Planning*.

41. See p. 70, above. Chicago Council on Foreign Relations, *American Public Opinion and US Foreign Policy*, 1995. Said Aburish and Tim Llewellyn, *Independent*, 23 June, 1995.

42. See pp. 265, 226f., above.

43. Amy Dockser Marcus, *WSJ*, May 30, 1996.

44. *Ibid.*, Nov. 2; Julian Ozanne, *FT*, Oct. 24, 1995. On the tacit alliance in earlier years, see *Towards a New Cold War*, chap. 11 (1977). Poverty, *Jerusalem Post*, Nov. 30, 1995. Also *News from Within*, reporting Dec. 1995 study of the National Insurance Institute, Feb. 1996.

45. Rabin, see p. 257, above. Usher, *MEI*, Jan. 6, 1995.

46. See pp. 214–18, above, and sources cited. Arens, *Ha'aretz*, April 21, 1996.

47. Serge Schmemann, Elaine Sciolino, *NYT*, Nov. 14; Schmemann, *NYT*, Nov. 29; Reuters, Oct. 13; *Economist*, July 15; Reuters, *Guardian*, July 10, 1995. Fisk, *Independent*, Oct. 22, 1994. Sneh, Reuters, *Independent*, Feb. 2, 1996, speaking over Israeli radio.

48. HRW, *Civilian Pawns: Laws of War Violations and the Use of Weapons on the Israel-Lebanon Border* (May, 1996). On April 8, a Lebanese boy was killed by a roadside bomb in the village of Bra'ashit (elsewhere, Bradchit) north of the security zone, followed by Hezbollah rocketing and Israeli bombing of a village. Israel disclaimed responsibility for the roadside bomb. UN forces in the vicinity note, however, that 10 days later Israeli forces were placing boobytrapped roadside bombs there. Relying on UN sources, Robert Fisk reports that an Israeli patrol placing these bombs came under Hezbollah fire, leading to the Israeli attack on the UN base in Qana that killed more than 100 refugees. *Independent*, June 1, 1996.

49. Editorial, *NYT*, April 12; Steven Erlanger, *NYT*, April 22; Serge Schmemann, *NYT*, May 13, 1996.

50. Clinton cited by Donald Neff, *MEI*, May 10, 1996. Friedman, *NYT*, April 28, 1996.

51. Reuters, *BG*, June 1, 1996. AP, Reuters, *BG*, May 13; Michael Jansen, *MEI*, May 24, 1996, reporting Tibnit bombing.

52. Eban, *Jerusalem Post*, Aug. 16, 1981. Kimmerling, *Ha'aretz*, April 26, 1996 (*MEI*, 10 May).

53. Developed with the backing of President Kennedy, according to Kennedy's deputy special counsel Myer Feldman, also special counsel to President Johnson, who reports that Kennedy persuaded the International Atomic Energy Commission to allow Israel to develop its atomic arsenal, the only exception to his opposition to

proliferation. Jordana Hart, *BG*, Oct. 24, 1994. That special dispensation has remained, extending also to toleration of Israel's kidnapping of Mordechai Vanunu, who exposed some of the facts, and his sentencing to 18 years in prison, where he has remained in solitary confinement since 1986.

54. *Ha'aretz Supplement*, May 10, 1996. The *Times* "adaptation" (May 27) revises what is "in our hands" to "the White House, the Senate and much of the American media," the remainder of what "we have" omitted.

55. Beirut bombing, Nora Boustany, *WP Weekly*, March 14, 1988; Bob Woodward, *Veil* (Simon & Schuster, 1987, 396f.). See my article in George, op. cit., for further discussion.

56. John Battersby, *CSM*, Dec. 5, 1994; May 17, 1995. Usher, op. cit. AI, *Human Rights and US Security Assistance* 1995, 1996. HRW, *World Report 1996* (covering 1995).

57. Rony Shaked and Yovel Peleg, *Yediot Ahronot* (American edition), Nov. 4, 1995. Mark Dennis, *FT*, March 2/3 1996.

58. Usher, op. cit. AI, *Human Rights and US Security Assistance*, 1996. HRW, *Torture and Ill-Treatment: Israel's Interrogation of Palestinians from the Occupied Territories* (1994). "Israel Proposes to Legalize Torture," *B'Tselem Human Rights Report*, Spring 1996. See also Al Haq, *Torture for Security* (Ramallah, 1995), reporting that 85 percent of Palestinians taken into custody and "at least 94 percent of all those interrogated" are subjected to torture and ill-treatment. It notes further that more than 80,000 Palestinians were detained from December 1987 to May 1992, about a quarter of the population of the territories between the ages of 15 and 54, by far the highest incarceration rate in the world, Human Rights Watch reported. "Security offenses" were defined by military order to include carrying published materials without permit, flag raising, etc. For many years, Israel has also been kidnapping and killing suspects captured in international waters, a practice that sometimes receives casual mention in the press. See references of note 5.

59. David Shribman, *BG*, Sept. 29; Reuters, *BG*, Nov. 5, *FT*, Nov 6; Schmemann, *NYT*, Nov. 5, June 2, 1996; Haberman, *NYT*, Nov. 6; Frankel, *WP* weekly, Nov. 27–Dec. 3; editorial, *WP* weekly, Oct. 2–8; *GW*, Oct. 1, lead story; John Battersby, *CSM*, Sept. 28; Ethan Bronner, *BG*, Sept. 28; Stephen Howe, *NS*, 17 Nov. 1995.

60. *NY Review*, April 4, 1996.

61. Peretz, Interview, *Ha'aretz*, June 4, 1982. On the Palestine-North America comparison, see Finkelstein, *The Rise and Fall of Palestine* (Minnesota, 1996).

62. *Ha'aretz*, Jan. 3, 1996; *News from Within*, Jan. 1996.

INDEX